THE

Reconstructed

1790 CENSUS OF GEORGIA

Substitutes for Georgia's Lost 1790 Census

Compiled by

Marie De Lamar & Elisabeth Rothstein

CLEARFIELD

Reprinted for Clearfield Company by
Genealogical Publishing Company
Baltimore, Maryland
2011

Originally published as *Substitutes for
Georgia's Lost 1790 Census* by Delwyn Associates,
Albany, Georgia, 1976.
Reprinted with an added index by
Genealogical Publishing Co., Inc.
3600 Clipper Mill Rd., Suite 260
Baltimore, Maryland 21211
1985, 1989, 2006
Library of Congress Catalogue Card Number 84-73075
International Standard Book Number 0-8063-1111-8
Made in the United States of America

Publisher's Note
This book is offset from the original mimeographed edition
and thus preserves all the typographical irregularities of the original.

Contents

Burke County 1

Camden County 19

Chatham County 29

Columbia County 56

Effingham County 67

Elbert County 73

Franklin County 90

Glynn County 103

Greene County 108

Liberty County 130

Richmond County 140

Washington County 153

Wilkes County 164

Note to the Reader

It would be impossible to reconstruct a complete 1790 census of Georgia due to the loss of so many records of this period. The statistics of the 1790 census somehow escaped the fire when the British burned Washington. They give *only* the population of each county, as follows:

Burke	9,467	Greene	5,405
Camden	305	Liberty	5,355
Chatham	10,769	Richmond	11,317
Effingham	2,424	Washington	4,552
Franklin	1,041	Wilkes	31,500
Glynn	413		

It has been the endeavor of the compilers of this book to place as many persons as possible in their county of residence in 1790. Wills, deeds, tax digests, court minutes, voters' lists, newspapers, etc. have been searched to complete this listing.

It is possible that duplications occur and this would seem more likely than that there were two persons of the same name in the same county. From the available records it is not possible to determine if there are two persons of the same name or if there is a duplication.

Although Columbia and Elbert counties were not formed until December 10, 1790, and there would not have been a 1790 census for them, they have been included. The total population of Richmond County (above) includes Columbia, just as the total population of Wilkes includes Elbert.

It is hoped that this book will be of help to those doing research in Georgia in the 1790 period.

BURKE COUNTY

Burke County was created from St. George Parish in 1777. A part of Burke County was set off to Jefferson County 1796, a part to Screven County 1798 and a part to Jenkins County 1905. The County seat is Waynesboro, Georgia.

The Burke County Courthouse has suffered three fires resulting in the loss of early records. There are few records prior to 1856.

Headright grants Burke County in the years 1790 through 1795:

Adams, Ephraim
Adkinson, Jos.
Akridge, Eliz.
Akridge, Ezekiel
Albritton, Jno.
Alday, Ann
Allen, Daniel
Allen, Jno.
Allen, Wm.
Anclaux, Nicholas
Arnold, Aaron
Ashbury, Jonathan
Atkinson, Jeremiah
Atkinson, Jos.
Bailey, Jos.
Balch, Eliz.
Bargeron, Elisha
Bass, Dewry
Beasley, Jno.
Beasley, Thos.
Beasley, Thos. Sr.
Beason, Peter
Beckham, Abner
Belcher, McCain
Belcher, Philip
Bell, Allen
Berryhill, Andrew
Betsell, Jno.
Bigham, Jas.
Bird, Jesse
Black, Wm.
Blanchard, Judith
Bonnell, Anthony
Booth, Wm.

Bothwell, David Revd.
Boyd, Archibald
Boyd, Jas.
Boyd, Saml.
Boyett, Eliz.
Boykin, Francis
Boykin, Jesse
Bradshaw, Brice
Brandon, Josiah
Brannon, Thos.
Brannon, Wm.
Braydy, Jas.
Brazeal, Henry
Brinson, Adam
Brinson, Fereby
Brinson, Jno.
Brinson, Moses
Brinson, Susannah
Brown, Benj.
Brown, Jno.
Bruce, Jas.
Brummet, Jno.
Bryant, Jno.
Bryant, Moses
Bryant, Needham
Buckhalter, Jno. Michael
Burke, Thos.
Burleson, Jesse
Burney, Richd.
Burns, Thos.
Burnsides, Jno.
Burson, Jos.
Burton, Rachel
Burton, Thos.

Burton, Wm. Allen	Dukes, Susannah
Byne, Wm.	Duncan, Andrew
Cahoon, Aquilla	Durham, Matthew
Calhoon, Jas.	Dye, Hopkins
Callingham, Jno.	Dyer, Elijah
Cannon, Caleb	Easter, Elisha
Carroll, Jno.	Easter, Ephraim
Carter, Alex	Eastis, Elisha
Carter, Geo.	Eastwood, Elijah
Cassells, Wm.	Eastwood, Israel
Catcham, Nancy	Elliott, Wm.
Cavenah, Chas.	Ellison, Robt.
Chambers, Jonas	Emanuel, Amos
Chance, Philemon	Emanuel, David
Charis, Jos.	Embry, Jesse
Clark, Arthur	Eubank, Daniel
Clark, Thos.	Evans, Daniel
Clark, Wm.	Fair, Saml.
Clarke, Benj.	Farmer, David
Cleland, Mary	Farmer, Wm.
Coleman, Francis	Farrow, Jesse
Collins, Saml.	Fenn, Jno.
Conner, Jos.	Fenn, Travis
Conyers, Jno.	Finley, David
Conyers, Jno. Jr.	Finney, Jno.
Conyers, Jno. Sr.	Finney, Wm.
Crawford, Strauder	Fitzgerald, Mary
Crutchfield, Richd.	Fleetin, Richd.
Curry, Carey	Fleming, Robt.
Daniel, Elias, Jr.	Flemming, Jno.
Daniel, Jno.	Floyd, Eady
Dansmore, Patrick	Ford, Jno.
Darcey, Benj.	Forsyth, Benj.
Darcey, Joel	Forsyth, Robt.
Davenport, Jno.	Forth, Henry
Davidson, Jno.	Forth, Sarah
Davis, Benj.	Foyil, Eliz.
Davis, Gehazi	Foyil, Jno.
Davis, Jas.	Freeman, Jacob
Davis, Jno.	Freeman, Jno.
Davis, Mary	Freeman, Jno. Jr.
Dean, Luke	Freeman, Jno. Sr.
Dean, Seth	Freeman, Noah
Dickey, Patrick	Freeman, Wm.
Dickson, Jno.	French, Robt.
Dillard, Thos.	Fryar, Jno.
Donelson, Jane	Fulgham, Jno.
Donelson, Jean	Fulton, Jno.
Donelson, Robt.	Fussell, Wm.
Douglas, Edw.	Gabard, Thos.
Douglas, Jas.	Gaits, Saml.
Douglas, Nancy	Gardner, Jas.
Douglas, Robt.	Garvin, Robt.
Dubose, Isaac	Gates, Chas.

Gates, Saml.
Gay, Jas.
Gay, Jno.
Gay, Wm.
Gevinn, Jas.
Gibbons, Wm. Jr.
Gilkey, Robt.
Glisson, Abraham
Godbe, Cary
Godbe, Wm.
Godbee, Saml.
Goodall, Pleasant
Goodman, Theodoric
Goodwyn, Jas.
Goodwyn, Theodrick
Gorbett, Geo.
Gorman, Wm.
Graham, Jno.
Grant, Jos.
Gray, Jas.
Gray, Mathias
Gray, Zachariah
Green, Benj.
Green, Jno.
Green, Wm.
Griner, Jacob
Grubar, Jacob
Grubar, Solomon
Grubbs, Jno.
Hadden, Wm.
Haddin, Wm. Jr.
Hadding, Wm.
Hadley, Benj.
Hadley, Wm.
Halwell, Luther
Hammett, Jno.
Hammock, Wm.
Hampton, Lerraney
Handbern, Jno.
Handley, Jesse
Hannah, Thos.
Hannah, Wm.
Hargrove, Howell
Harrell, Mary
Harrill, Geo.
Harrington, Mary
Hart, Wm.
Harthorn, Eliz.
Hartsfield, Jno.
Harvey, Blassingame
Haslip, Terobabel
Hayman, Henry
Hayman, Stephen
Hayman, Stouton

Heath, Richd.
Henderson, Jno.
Henderson, Michael
Henry, Jno.
Herring, Wm.
Herrington, Richd.
Hersley, Tarlton
Hickson, Jno.
High, Jno.
Hilburn, Holiman
Hill, Edw.
Hill, Mary
Hill, Stark
Hines, Sarah
Hines, Wm.
Hodges, Francis
Hodges, Jos.
Hodges, Joshua
Hogg, Jas.
Holladay, Jos.
Holliday, Jos.
Hollinger, Wm.
Holly, Jonathan
Horn, Henry
Horne, Moses
House, Jessee
Howard, Saml.
Howell, Henry
Howell, Jno.
Howell, Lewis
Hudspeth, Chas.
Hull, Sarah
Hurst, Major
Hurst, Wm.
Hydrick, Geo.
Ingram, David
Ingram, Richd.
Irwin, Eliz.
Irwin, Robt.
Jackson, Abraham
James, James
Jeffers, Jno.
Jenkins, Ruth
Johnson, Jas.
Johnson, Jas. Jr.
Johnson, Micajah
Johnson, Stephen
Joiner, Isarel
Jones, Batt
Jones, Eliz.
Jones, Jno.
Jones, Wm.
Jordan, Charity
Jordan, Jno.

Jowedin, Sterling
Kellebrew, Lawrence
Kemp, Danl.
Kengrey, Danl.
Kent, Jno.
Key, Tandy C.
Kezay, Richd.
Kilbee, Christopher
Kilpatrick, Thos.
Kimbrel, Chas.
Kitts, Jno.
Laine, Etheldred
Lambert, Andrew
Lambert, Jas.
Lancaster, Jos.
Lane, Etheldred
Larcey, Wm.
Larice, Wm.
Lary, Jeremiah
Lassater, Jno.
Lassater, Saml.
Lawson, Hugh
Lee, Wm.
Lefever, Abraham
Lefever, Jas.
Lester, Ezekiel
Lester, Jas.
Lester, Jno.
Lester, Wm.
Lewis, Abraham
Lewis, Abraham, Jr.
Lewis, Elazer
Lewis, Jno.
Lewis, Nancy
Lindsey, Eliz.
Little, Archibald
Little, Frederick
Lively, Matthew
Locke, Jesse
Lockhart, Isaac
Lodge, Francis
Lord, Wm.
Low, Aquila
Lowry, Jno.
Lungino, Bartholomew
Mackay, Jas.
Mann, Newby
Mann, Nuby
Manson, Jno.
Marbury, Horatio
Marshall, Jno.
Marshall, Matthew
Martin, Jacob
Martin, Jno.

Martin, Martin
Mason, Jno.
Matthew, Jane
Matthews, Jas.
May, Mark
McAnally, Jno.
McCarrel, Jno.
McClamy, Mark
McConkey, Andw.
McCullen, Bryant
McCullers, Britain
McDade, Chas.
McDonald, Alex
McGee, Shadrack
McGehee, Saml.
McGruder, Jno.
McKegney, Jas.
McKengney, Jas.
McKenzie, Aaron
McKinsee, Jno.
McKonkey, Jas.
McMahan, Jno.
McMullen, Jas.
McNatt, Clary
McNiely, Danl.
McNorrill, Wm.
Medzgar, David
Meloy, Barney
Melton, Jeremiah
Melton, Nath. Sr.
Mercer, Mary
Miller, Philip
Mills, Archibald
Mincy, Philip
Mitchell, Floodde
Monroe, Wm.
Moon, Saml.
Moore, Jno.
Moore, Saml.
Moore, Willis
Moreland, Jno
Morell, Michael
Morgan, Morgan
Morrell, Matthew
Morrison, Agnes
Morrison, Jno.
Murphee, Demsey
Murphee, Mills
Murphy, Willis
Nail, Elisha
Neelson, Christian
Neely, Jno.
Neily, Jas.
Neily, Mary

Keily, Thos.
Nelson, Thos
Newman, Thos.
Nicholson, Jno.
Nobles, Landers
Numan, Wm.
Oar, Wm.
Odam, Isaac
Oliver, Jas.
Osborn, Robt.
Osborne, Robt.
Pace, Jas.
Painter, Jno.
Parker, Amos
Parker, Gabriel
Parker, Jacob
Parker, Jonathan
Parker, Saml.
Parker, Wm.
Parrimore, Wm.
Parris, Francis
Patterson, Robt.
Pearce, Jno.
Peel, Wm.
Perry, Isaac
Phillip, Wm.
Pickeron, Darcus
Pior, Robt.
Pinnion, Jas.
Powell, Benj.
Powell, Cader
Powell, Geo.
Powell, Stephen
Prescott, Willis
Price, Edw.
Price, Job
Proctor, Thos.
Pugh, Whitson
Reaves, Geo.
Red, Jas.
Reddick, Nicholas
Reeves, Jos.
Richardson, Burrill
Roberts, Abram
Roberts, Jno.
Roberts, Thos.
Robinson, Jas.
Robinson, Jno.
Robinson, Wm.
Rogers, Robt.
Royal, Saml.
Sackett, Simon
Sample, Nathl.
Samples, Saml.

Sapp, Caleb
Sapp, Darling
Sapp, Jas.
Sapp, Shadrock
Sasser, Stephen
Sasser, Thos.
Sasser, Wm.
Scarborough, Aaron
Scarborough, Arthur
Scarborough, Moses
Scarborough, Saml.
Scott, Wm.
Sevarr, Jno.
Sharp, Jno.
Sharp, Mary
Shaw, Wm.
Sheffield, Jno.
Sheffield, Mark
Sherod, Simon
Shirley, Martin
Simmons, Willis
Skinner, Nicholas
Skinner, Wm.
Slater, Wm.
Smith, Isam
Smith, Jno.
Smith, Jos.
Smith, Saml.
Smith, Wm.
Sneed, Catherine
Spell, Celah
Spence, Moses
Spencer, Jno.
Spives, Geo.
Spivey, Francis
Spivey, Jas.
Spurlock, Jno.
Stafford, Joshua
Stallings, Jno.
Stallions, Jesse
Stanford, Stephens
Stannaland, Jno.
Stephens, Benj. Sr.
Steptoe, Jno.
Steptoe, Thos.
Sterling, Jno.
Stoeo, Wm.
Stone, Wm.
Stradley, Nimrod
Strawder, Francis
Streetman, Sarah
Stringer, Danl.
Stringer, Jno.
Stringer, Wm.
Wm.

Stubbs, Jas.
Sumner, Jos.
Sunner, Saml.
Sweeny, Barnard Wm.
Sykes, Margarett
Tacker, Wm.
Tallas, Jno.
Tallis, Willoughby
Tanner, Jos.
Tapley, Jno.
Tapley, New
Tarver, Benj.
Taylor, Aaron
Taylor, Ann
Taylor, Caleb
Taylor, Champman
Taylor, Edmond
Taylor, Ward
Taylor, Wm.
Thomas, Gideon
Thomas, Peter
Thompson, Elihu
Thompson, Laban
Thompson, Wm.
Tillman, Wm.
Tilman, Francis
Tilman, Wm.
Tippinn, Phillip
Tippins, Phillip
Tipton, Thos.
Todd, Eliz.
Tomlinson, Ann
Tommerlin, Betty
Tompkins, Christopher
Tonny, Mary
Trant, Jno.
Tucker, Sarah
Turner, Venerius
Vance, Davis
Varner, Geo.
Vaughter, Whorton
Verner, Geo.
Vickers, Jno.
Vining, Shadrack
Wade, Saml.
Walding, Saml.
Walker, Joel
Walker, Jno.
Walker, Landers
Walker, Sanders
Wallis, Absalom
Ward, Elijah
Ward, Eliz.
Ward, Francis

Warlick, Valentine
Warmack, Mary
Warnock, Jesse
Warnock, Mary
Warren, Carless
Warren, Richd.
Wasden, Thos.
Watkins, Jno.
Watson, Joshua
Watson, Nelly
Weathers, Edw.
Weathers, Geo.
Welch, Jacob
Wells, Jno.
Wells, Julius
Welsh, Jno.
Were, Jas.
Wheeler, Ambrose
Whigham, Agnes
Whigham, Alex.
Whigham, Jno.
Shite, Saml.
Whitehall, Lewis
Whitehead, Amos
Whitley, Jno.
Williams, Jas.
Williams, Jno.
Williams, Noah
Williamson, Acquilla
Williamson, Robt.
Wilson, Agnes
Wilson, Mary
Wimberly, Zacharia
Winket, Saml.
Wood, Wm.
Woods, Jno.
Wright, David
Young, Jacob
Young, Jas.
Young, Pearson
Young, Wm. Sr.

Tax-defaulters 1790-
1793. Published in
the Augusta Chronicle
and Gazette.

Officers of Militia
    Districts:

Col. Daniel Evans

Captains:
Bickham, Abner
Buford, Jno.

Edwards, Wm.
Emanuel, Jno.
Evans, Danl.
Fenn, Jno.
Fussell, Wm.
Green, William
Harvey, Blasingame
Harvey, Jas.
Kilbee, Christopher
Lasseter, Jno.
Little, Wm.
Lott, Reubin
McCuller, Bryant
McKenzie, Jno.
Sapp, Dill
Stringer, Noah
Terry, Champness
Watson, Willis
Whitaker, Benj.
Whitaker, Hudson
White, Saml.

Also Captains' Wambles,
Gray, Barnes, Skinner,
Coursey, Bell, Roberts,
and Wynn

Defaulters:

Abbot, Bennett
Adams, Elcy
Adams, Jesse
Adams, Jno.
Ailey, Elijah
Allen, Isabella
Allen, Jno.
Anderson, Thompson
Arline, Jno.
Augur, Isaac
Barry, Jos.
Beckett, Isaac
Beckham, Saml.
Beckham, Wm.
Bedsell, Godfrey
Belden, Wm.
Benton, Eliz.
Blair, Jno.
Blockman, Jas.
Booth, Dred
Boothe, Jno.
Bowen, Jonathan
Boykin, Wm.
Brandon, Jno.
Brannon, Jas.
Brown, Henry

Brown, Jas.
Brown, Jeremiah
Browning, Elis
Bryant, Benj.
Bryant, Jno.
Burnett, Sol.
Burnett, Wm.
Burrows, Robt.
Canady, Wm.
Cannon, Jno.
Cannon (widow)
Carpenter, Thos.
Carr, Patrick
Carter, Chas. Sr.
Catlett, Wm.
Chambers, Jno.
Chance, Vinson
Clashier, Jno. C.
Coleman, Jacob
Coleman, Jno.
Coleman, Moses
Collins, Jos.
Collins, Willis
Copeland, ___?___
Conner, Chas.
Cooper, Frederick
Costy, Jesse
Coward, Jas.
Cowen, Edw.
Cox, Jas.
Crews, Jno.
Crozier, Jno.
Dabney, Christian
Davenport, Joel
Davis, Tho.
Davies, Wm.
Day, Richd.
Dean, Jas.
Dicks, Jno.
Dickson, Jno.
Dickson, Jos.
Dinney, Robt.
Douglas, Alexdr.
Douglas, Eliz.
Douglas, Wright
Downey, Huze
Drawdy, Danl. Jr.
Draughon, Biol
Dukes, Danl.
Dunmphin, Jas.
Dunn, Jno.
Dunn, Tho.
Eastwood, Elisha
Edmonds, Jas.

Ellery, Isham
Elliott, Saml.
Eubanks, Danl.
Eubanks, Thos.
Farniel, Danl.
Ferm, Zachariah
Ferrell, Enoch
Finney, Jno.
Fitzgerald, Mrs. __?__
Floyd, Chas.
Foreman, Wm.
Forth, Thos.
Gainer, Jno.
Gardner, Rudolph
Garrett, Elijah
Gates, Valentine
Glover, Darling
Goodwin, Zachariah
Green, Jno.
Green, McKean
Green, Sollivent
Green, Wm.
Griffin, Jas.
Grimes, Francis
Grubbs, Jno.
Hadley, Thos.
Hall, Mary
Hamilton, David
Hanbury, Jno.
Hancock, Douglas
Hardwick, Wm.
Hargroves, Dr.
Harold, Kerson
Harrell, Elisha
Harvard, Jno.
Hayman, Henry, Sr.
Hayman, Jas.
Heart, Wm.
Hedgepath, Josiah
Hefcoat, Wm.
Henderson, Robt.
Hendry, Geo.
Hewbanks, Daniel, Jr.
Hicks, Saml.
Hickson, Thos.
Higdon, Robt.
Hill, __?__
Hill, Gillon
Hilliard, Henry
Hilliard, Major
Hilliard, Silas
Hillseamore, Richd.
Hinson, Chas.
Hinson, Phillip

Hollerman, Hartman
Hollingsworth, Stephen
Hollingsworth, Zebulon
Holloway, Jeremiah
Holly, Jno.
Holly, Jonathan
Holton, Francis Sr.
Hood, Wm.
Howell, Theophilus
Howell, Wm.
Hudler, Jno.
Hume, Jno.
Hunter, Jno.
Hutcheson, Mrs. __?__
Iverson, Saml.
Jackson, Abraham
James, Wm.
Jamieson, David
Jeffreys, Jas.
Jenkins, Phillip
Johnston, Wm.
Joiner, Jno.
Jones, Benj.
Jones, David
Jones, Jno.
Jordan, Elijah
Jordan, Henry
Jordan, Thos.
Kelly, Wm.
Kertin, Mrs. __?__
Kersey, Elijah
Knight, Jno.
Knight, Robt.
Lamb, Abraham
Lamb, Abraham Jr.
Lamb, Bethal
Lamb, Sol.
Lamb, Thos.
Land, Isaac
Lockhart, Jos.
Long, Geo.
Long, Jas.
Lott, Wm.
Lowrey, Robt.
Lyon, Jas.
McCall, Jos.
McCormack, Saml.
McCoy, Jesse
McCoy, Wm.
McCullers, Jno.
McGee, Henry
McGowen, Jas.
McKay, Jno.
McMillan, Abraham

McMillan, Matthew
McNatt, Jesse
McNeely, Patrick
McQueen, Alexdr.
Mace, Wm.
Mare, Wm.
Martin, Clem
Martin, Murdock
Massey (widow)
Matthews, Wm.
Matthis, Josiah
Melton, Peter
Mercer, Thos.
Merrian, Anthony
Mitchell, Thos.
Montgomery, Jno.
Montgomery, Saml.
Moore, Jas.
Moore, Lewis
Moore, Reubin
Moore, Saml.
Moore, Wm.
Moore, Wm. Sr.
Moore, Wm. Jr.
Mowet, Geo.
Newman, Wm.
Nichols, Shadrack
Nicholson, Jno.
Nixon, Chas.
Norris, Geo.
Norris, Thos. Lamb
Odom, Archibald
Odom, Jas.
Odom, Sybert
Oliver, Chas.
Oliver, Thos.
Oliver, Wm.
Palmer, Saml. J.
Parker, __?__
Parker, Gabriel
Parker, Jas.
Parsons, Jos.
Patterson, Francis
Perkins, Wm.
Pierce, Randall
Pierce, Thos.
Pierse, Wm.
Pitteren, Mary
Pollard, Wm. Sr.
Powell, Alexdr.
Powell, Jas.
Powell, Jos.
Price, Jas.
Price, Richd.

Pritchett, Rodom
Reddick, Shadrick
Rees, Jno.
Reeves, Benj.
Reeves, Geo.
Richards, Jno. Hart
Richardso.., Wm.
Ridley, __?__
Rix, Johanan
Roberts, Jeptha
Rogers, Jno.
Rogers, Jos.
Rogers, Peleg
Rogers, Richd.
Rogers, Thos.
Robertson, Bailey
Robertson, Edw.
Robertson, Jno.
Rowell, Jno.
Russell, Sol.
Sackett, Simon
Salisbury, Wm. Sr.
Salter, Jno.
Sample, Saml.
Sapp, Caleb
Sasser, Britton
Schley, Richd.
Schley, Michael
Scott, Phillip
Seaver, Jno.
Seloy, Benj.
Shaffer, Henry
Sharp, Jno.
Sheffield, Austin
Shelman, Jno., Esq.
Sheppard, Andrew
Sheppard, Jno.
Sheppard, Labon
Sherwood, __?__
Shores, Richd.
Simmons, Caleb
Simmons, Chas.
Simmons, Jno.
Skinner, Jesse Sr.
Skinner, Jesse Jr.
Skinner, Jonas
Skinner, Nathan
Skinner, Nathaniel
Skinner, Wm.
Smith, Frederick
Smith, Jas.
Smith, Jos.
Smith, Thos.
Sneed, Robt.

Spell, Geo.
Spence, Robt.
Spencer, Jno. Butler
Spight, Jos.
Spight, Moses
Spikes, Jonas
Spivey, Jas.
Spooner, Zoar
Stanol (?), Jno.
Stanson, Wm.
Stephens, Chas.
Stephens, Gabriel
Stephens, Jno.
Stephenson, Jno.
Stewart, Archibald
Stewart, Jno.
Stone, David
Strawder, Wm.
Streetman, Martin
Stringer, Francis
Sumner, Richd.
Tabley, Key
Taggert, Jno.
Tapley, Wm.
Tanner, Thos.
Tarver, Thos.
Taylor, Aaron
Taylor, Jordan
Taylor, Joshua
Thomas, Gideon
Thomas, Gilshot
Thompson, Jas. Sr.
Thornton, ___?
Thornton, Saml.
Thorp, Wiley
Thrower, Levi
Tilley, Jno.
Tison, Isaac
Tomlin, Redden
Tommey, Mary
Trammel, Elijah
Tucker, Henry C.
Tucker, Hezekiah
Tucker, Isaac
Tucker, Thos.
Umphrees, Wm.
Ussary, Abner
Waller, Wm.
Ward, Elias
Warren, Carlos
Warren, Gabriel
Welch, Jno.
Welch, Jos.
Welen, Jno.

Wells, Jno. Jr.
Wells, Stephen
Whiddon, Lott
Whigham, Wm.
White, Edw.
White, Wm. B.
Wilkey, Jno.
Wilkey, Jonathan
Williams, Fanny
Williams, Lewis
Williams, Patrick
Williamson, Jno.
Winney, Josiah
Womble (widow)
Wright, Wm.
Wylly, Edw.
Wynn, Jno.
Wynne, Jones
Yeaton, Jno.
Young, Edw.
Young, Jas.
Young, Jno.

Grand Juror list as
published in the Georgia
Gazette, Southern Centi-
nel and Universal Gazette,
and the Augusta Chroni-
cle and Gazette 1790-1795:

Alet, Henry
Allen, Thos.
Atkinson, Jeremiah
Barns, Jesse
Bowling, Robt.
Brack, Benj.
Brinson, Adam
Bryan, Moses
Byne, Edmund
Byne, Wm.
Carter, Isaiah
Clements, Wm.
Colhoon, Aquilla
Coursey, Wm.
Davis, Benj.
Davis, W____
Dillard, Thos.
Douglas, Wm.
Edwards, Wm.
Elliott, Wm.
Fleming, Wm.
Ford, Jno.
Foyer, Zachariah Lewis
Fryer, Zachariah L.

Gray, Basil
Gray, J.
Gray, Jas.
Gray, Mathias
Grey, Matthias
Green, Benj.
Iverson, Robt.
Johnson, Stephen
Johnston, Stephen
Jones, Batte
Jones, Thos.
Kemp, Jonathan
Lamar, Saml.
Lanier, Saml.
Lasseter, Jno.
Lasetter, Saml.
Lewis, Jacob
Little, Wm.
Lott, Reubin
Lowe, Edmund
McCullers, Bryant
Marshall, Matthew
Martin, Wm.
May, Thos.
Moore, Jno.
Murphy, Mills
Parker, Saml.
Parramore, Wm.
Perry, Isaac
Roberts, Gray
Roberts, Jno.
Ronaldson, Robt.
Royal, Wm.
Ryals, Wm.
Sapp, Benj.
Sapp, Elijah
Sapp, Wm.
Scruggs, Gross
Seegar, Geo.
Skinner, Nicholas
Skinner, Wm.
Tapley, Jno.
Tarver, Bird .
Thomas, Phillip
Tomlin, Jno.
Tomlinson, Jno.
Vaughn, Ephriam
Walker, Jno.
Walker, Isaac
Walton, Robt.
Wheeler, Isaac
Whitaker, Hudson
Whitehead, Amos
Whitfield, Lewis

Weimingham, Jas.
Welsch, Jas.
Williams, Arthur
Williams, Chas.
Williamson, Arthur
Winn, Peter, Sr.
Womble, Allen
Wyche, Jno.
Wynn, Peter Sr.

Estate and Miscellaneous
Legal notices as printed
in the Georgia Gazette,
Southern Centinel and
Universal Gazette, and
the Augusta Chronicle
and Gazette. 1790-1795:

Alet, Henry
Babcock, Wm.
Bailey, Jos.
Benton, Wm.
Bickham, Jas. dec'd.
Booth, Wm.
Boozman, Mary
Boozman, Saml.
Bottomly, Michael
Bowling, Robt.
Brack, Eleazer
Brack, Eliz.
Brack, Richd. dec'd.
Bryan, Geo.
Bryan, Moses
Bryant, Henry
Bryant, Mary
Bryant, Wm.
Carter, Alexdr.
Carter, Isaiah
Clarke, Henry
Clarke, Jonathan
Connell, Jno.
Conner, Jno.
Conner, Martha
Corbet, Richd.
Crook, Thos.
Cuyler, Jeremiah
Darcy, Jos.
David, Anne
David, Wm.
Davis, Benj.
Davis, Jno.
Dawson, Eliz.
Dawson, Jno.
Durgan, Wm. Sr. dec'd.

Emanuel, Col. Asa
Emanuel, David
Emanuel, Levi
Fleming, Wm.
Forrester, Steph. dec'd.
Fussell, Thos.
Gay, Mathias
Hackle, Wm.
Hall, Lyman
Hall, Mrs. Mary
Hart, Wm.
Harvey, Jas.
Hawthorn, Robt. dec'd.
Henry, Lyon
Hudson, Martha
Hudson, Wm. dec'd.
Iverson, Robt.
Jackson, Abraham
Johnson, Jesse
Jones, Jno.
Lewis, Jacob
Lewis, Joel
Lewis, Thos. dec'd.
Little, Wm.
Lloyd, Mrs. Patience
Lloyd, Thos.
Lockhart, Saml.
McMullin, Jas.
McMullin, Sarah
Middleton, Hugh
Middleton, Saml.
Miller, Moses
Miller, Nathl.
Miller, Mrs. Sarah
Mims, Judith
Norwood, Geo.
Odom, Eliz.
Odom, Joshua, dec'd.
Ogden, Betty
Ogden, Saml.
Ogelvee, Jas.
Outlaw, Ludowick, dec'd.
Parramore, Matthew dec'd.
Patterson, Robt.
Pollock, Isaac
Price, Wm. dec'd.
Pryor, Anna
Roberts, Eliz.
Roberts, Jas. dec'd.
Ruffin, Jno.
Sapp, Dill
Sapp, Wm.
Selph, Jesse
Sharp, Cade

Sharp, Paschal
Shoemake, Jos.
Storie, Jno.
Storie, Margaret
Sullivan, Wm.
Thomas, Eliz.
Thomas, Turby Phillip
Tillman, Wm.
Tippins, Phillip
Tomkins, Chris.
Tomlin, Jno.
Triplett, Frances
Triplett, Rachel
Wade, Benj.
Wade, Eliz.
Wade, Nehemiah, dec'd.
Walker, Geo.
Walker, Thos. Jr.
Waller, Benj.
Waller, Mary
Waller, Saml.
Washam, Joshua
Watson, Mrs. Caroline
Watts, Edw.
Watts, Jos.
Weathers, Eliz.
Weathers, Geo.
Welch, Jas.
Wells, Absalom
Wells, Mary Jane
White, Jas.
White, Rachel
Williams, Arthur
Willington, Eleanor
Willington, Thos.
Winningham, Jas.
Wyche, Thos.
Yarbrough, Thos.

Burke Co. citizens
signing a character
recommendation concern-
ing John Lasseter, J.P.
Dec. 1794. Appearing
in Augusta Chronicle and
Gazette:

Baduly, Wm.
Barron, Wm.
Bell, Arthur
Bell, Elisha
Bell, Wm.
Boon, Fred
Boykin, Jesse

Boykin, Sol.
Buckley, Butler
Buckley, Jas.
Buckley, Richd.
Carter, Alexdr.
Carter, Isaiah
Coates, Jesse
Cofield, Graham
Davis, Jno.
Dunn, Jno.
Elliott, Amos
Emanuel, Jno.
Fanning, Saml.
Fenn, Jno.
Fenn, Wm.
Gordon, Jno.
Gray, Basil
Hall, Benj.
Hobby, Wm.
Kilbee, C.
Lambert, Jas.
Lambert, Jno.
Lasseter, Jno., J. P.
Lewis, Jacob
Lowe, E.
Lowe, Henry
Mathis, Benj.

Moore, Henry
Odom, Isaac
Ogden, Edw.
Ogden, Wm.
Osborne, Robt.
Perry, Isaac
Poythress, Geo.
Rawls, Jas. Jr.
Russell, Jas.
Skinner, Nicholas
Smith, Thos.
Tarver, Benj.
Thompson, Elihu
Walker, Wm.
Wallas, Absalom
Williams, Chas.
Williams, N.
Wynne, Peter
Wynne, Wm.
Yarbrough, Thos.

Death notices Ga.
Gazette 1790-1793:

Hall, Jno.
Hall, Lyman
Wade, Jno.
Wade, Nehemiah

Telamon Cuyler Collection at University of Ga.--Athens, Ga.

When the State Capital was being moved from Milledge-
ville, Ga. to Atlanta in 1868, the huge amount of old
records in the basement of the Capitol were cleaned out
and not taken to Atlanta. Mr. Telamon Cuyler came into
possession of many of these old records and gave his collection to the University of Georgia.

While they do not contain family data, being princi-
pally petitions to the Governor, jury lists, etc., they do
place people in Burke County at the time covered by this
book.

The collection is available at the University to re-
searchers.

Commissions from Governor
    1790
Burke Co. Militia:

Albritton, Geo.
Alexander, Hugh
Barnes, Jesse
Bealy, Wm.
Bowling, Wm.

Bryant, Henry
Buford, Jno.
Cahoon, Philip
Calhoon, Adam
Clark, Tandy

Clements, Jno.
Darsey, Benj.
Davis, David
Davis, Miles
Dreed, Wm.
Dubose, Isaac
Edwards, Wm.
Evans, Danl.
Farnall, Tho.
Fean, Jno.
Franklin, Tho.
Fussell, Wm.
Gillson, Dennis
Glisson, Frederick
Gray, Basel
Green, Benj.
Green, Wm.
Grey, Zachariah
Harvey, Blassingame Jr.
Harvey, Jas.
Howard, Tho.
Jones, Philip
Lasseter, Jno.
Lawson, Hugh
Little, Wm.
Lott, Reubin
McCarrol, Jno.
McCullers, Bryant
Marshall, Matthew
Martin, Wm.
Mathews, Benj.
Moore, Jno.
Moreland, Wm.
Morrison, Jno.
Murphy, Miles
Neil, Wm.
Nelson, Christian
Parsons, Wm.
Roberts, Jno.
Sapp, Dill
Sharpe, Jno.
Shelmon, Jno.
Smith, Benj.
Stegle, Nicholas
Stringer, Noah
Walden, Henry
Watson, Willis
Whitaker, Benj.
Whitaker, Hudson
White, Saml.
Williams, Noah
Winn, Wm.

Officers of 1st Battalion
Burke Co. Militia 1792:

Bryant, Henry
Buford, Jno.
Coursey, Wm.
Davies, Wills
Dunn, Wm.
Dye, Ralph
Edwards, Wm.
Evans, Danl.
Fryar, Jno.
Gray, Basil
Justice, Aaron
Kilbee, Chas.
Lasiter, Lemuel
Lewis, Thos.
McCarroll, Jno.
McCormick, Michael
McGomery, Jno.
Martin, Martin
Martin, Wm.
Matthews, Benj.
Parrimore, Wm.
Rawles, Jas.
Roberts, Jno.
Robinson, Lark
Salter, Jno.
Sapp, Dill
Stregles (?), Nich.
Thompson, Elihu
Thompson, Laban
Tredwell, Jno.
Watson, Willis
White, Saml.
Williams, Noah
Wright, Jno.

Jurors: 1790-1791:

Allen, Tho.
Atkinson, Jeremiah
Aylet, Henry
Bowling, Robt.
Bowling, Simon
Barnes, Isaac
Barrow, Jas.
Bass, Abraham
Belcher, Allen
Brack, Benj.
Brack, Eli
Brinson, Adam
Byne, Edmund
Calhoun, Martin

Christie, Wm.
Clarke, Tandy
Clements, Wm.
Cock, Caleb
Cock, Zebulon
Dillard, Tho.
Douglas, Wm.
Drew, Wm.
Edwards, Wm.
Elliott, Wm.
Ellison, Robt.
Farmer, Geo.
Fenny, Wm.
Fleming, Wm.
Ford, Jno.
Fryer, Zachariah Lewis
Fussell, Wm.
Gavin, Jas.
Green, Mathew
Hancock, Douglas
Hardin, Wm.
Hooks, Wm.
Johnson, Stephen
Jones, Batt
Jordan, Sterling
Kemp, Jonathan
Lambert, Jas.
Lanear, Saml.
Lasseter, Jno.
Lasseter, Saml.
Lester, Ezekiel
Lodge, Francis
Loftin, Jno.
Lord, Wm.
McCullers, Bryant
McMorel, Wm.
Marshall, Manham
Martin, Wm.
Moore, Jno.
Moses, Bryan
Mulkey, Philip
Murphy, M.
Parramore, Wm.
Perry, Isaac
Redd, Saml.
Rhemy, Wm.
Rine, Wm.
Rivers, Jos.
Roberts, Gray
Ronaldson, Robt.
Royall, Wm.
Sadler, Wm. Allen
Sapp, Benj.
Sapp, Elijah

Schubert, Frederick
Scruggs, Gross
Seegar, Geo.
Skinner, Nicholas
Skinner, Wm.
Snell, Jacob
Stanford, Rich.
Steel, Hugh
Steptoe, Jno.
Tapley, Jno.
Tarver, Bird
Tully, Wm.
Tilmon, Littleberry
Tomlinson, Jno.
Turle, Edw.
Vaughn, Ephriam
Vickers, Jno.
Vining, Jno.
Wade, Jno.
Walker, Tho.
Watson, Joshua
Whitaker, Hudson
Whitehead, Amos
Williamson, Arthur
Winningham, Jas.
Womble, Allen
Yarborough, Tho.

Petitions to the Governor
1789-1793

Adkins, Shadrack
Alberry, Jno.
Allen, Jeames
Allen, Jno.
Allen, Wm.
Anderson, Elisha
Andrew, Saml.
Andrews, Wm.
Attaway, Jos.
Austin, Wm.
Avrit, Alexdr.
Baduly, Wm.
Barnes, Jesse
Barron, Wm.
Barton, Wm. B.
Beal, Nathl.
Bearfield, Wm.
Bell, Green
Bell, Wm.
Blackman, Wm.
Boasman, Saml.
Boatright, David
Boatright, John

Bosman, Jacob
Bosman, Jos.
Bosman, Nathan
Bosman, Saml. Sr.
Bosman, Saml. Jr.
Boykin, Jesse
Boykin, Sol.
Brack, Benj.
Brack, Rich.
Bradley, Wm.
Bragg, Elijah
Brown, Saml.
Brown, Wm.
Bruce, Chas.
Brummutt, Jno.
Bruton, Jas.
Bruton, Jno.
Bryan, Jno.
Buckhalter, Randolph
Burnett, Saml.
Burns, Tho.
Burton, Jno. A.
Burton, Walthall
Byne, Wm.
Cahoon, Aquilla
Caldwell, Hy
Caldwell, Henry G.
Carns, Peter
Carpenter, Baley
Carswell, Mathew
Carter, Alexdr.
Cates, Wm.
Cavanah, Chas.
Cavanah, David
Cent (?), Jas.
Clark, Chris.
Clark, Jno.
Clarke, Tho.
Clarke, Wm.
Clerk (?), Jas.
Coates, Harwill
Cocks, Henry
Coffield, Gresham
Colemon, Wm.
Comer, Chas.
Conner, Chas.
Cook, Geo.
Cook, Joshua
Cooper, Cannon
Copeland, Jas.
Crozier, Alexdr.
Crozier, Jno.
Curry, Nicholas
Cuylers, H.

Dabney, Wm.
Darby, Jno.
Davenport, Jno.
Davies, Francis
Davies, Jno.
Davis, Benj.
Dennis, Abram
Dennis, Jno.
Dixton, Robt.
Douglas, Tho.
Douglas, Wm.
Drake, Tho.
Easter, Augustus
Eastes, Augustus
Ellet, Drury
Ellet, Wm.
Elliot, Henry
Emanuel, Asa
Emanuel, Levi
Eubank, Geo.
Evans, Danl.
Evans, Jno.
Evans, Mordecai
Fairchild, Abraham
Farmer, Geo.
Farmer, Saml.
Fenn, Jno.
Fenny, Wm.
Fenny, Zach.
Flin, Jeremi
Flin, Wm.
Floyd, Jos.
Ford, Jno.
Ford, Tho.
Foster, Jno.
French, Robt.
Fulton, Jno.
Gardner, Simeon
Gibbons, Tho.
Gilstrap, Jno.
Goode, Jno.
Goodwyn, Theo.
Goss, Wm.
Grant, Andrew
Grant, Jno.
Grant, Wm.
Gray, Bazil
Gray, J.
Gray, Mathias
Green, Benj.
Green, Mathew Jr.
Greyham, Jno.
Greyham, Tho.
Grove (?), Wm.

Gwin, Jas.	Jones, Tho.
Haisten, Juhue	Jordon, Baxton
Hale, Jno.	Jordon, Matthew
Halhill (?), Luther	Key, Sandy C.
Hampton, Jos.	Killbee, Christy
Hardwick, Wm.	King, Saml.
Harris, D.	Kirkland, Saml.
Hart, Geo.	Knotts, Nathl.
Hart, Wm.	Kolb, Peter
Harvey, Blass Sr.	Lam, Sol.
Harvey, Blass, Jr.	Lamb, Abram
Harvey, Robt.	Lamb, Barnaby
Harvey, Tho.	Lanier, Lem.
Hatcher, Jno.	Laseter, Lemuel
Hawkins, R. D.	Lawson, H.
Hayman, Henry Sr.	Lawson, Roger
Hayns, Tho.	Lewis, Geo.
Heath, Rich.	Lewis, Jacob
Hemphill, Saml.	Lewis, Jas.
Hendry, Chas.	Lewis, Joel
Hendry, Geo.	Lewis, R. W.
Hendry, Geo. Sr.	Lewis, Tho.
Hendry, Jacob	Lewis, Tho. Jr.
Hendry, Jas.	Little, Wm. Jr.
Henry, Lyon	Logan, Saml.
Hester, Allen	Longan, Saml.
Hester, Jas.	Lott, Abraham
Hinds, David	Lott, Arthur
Hinds, Wm.	Lott, Jas.
Hinson, Wm.	Lott, Jno.
Hitower, Charnel	Lott, Jno. Jr.
Hodges, Jeames	Lott, Mark
Hogan, Wm.	Lott, Nathan
Holton, Saml.	Lott, Reuben
Howell, Deannel	Lott, Wm.
Howell, Wm.	Low, E.
Hudson, Hall	Lyman, Elihu
Ingram, Rich.	McCallum, Jos.
Inmon, Danl.	McCullers, B.
Inman, Jesse	McCullers, Chas.
Iverson, Saml.	McDaniel, Britan
Jeffreys, Jno.	McGehu, Wm.
Jenkins, Starling	McIntosh, Joshua
John, Arley	McMurphy, D.
Johnson, Geo.	McNeil, Danl.
Johnson, Jno.	Mackey, Jas.
Johnston, Jas.	Manson, Jesse
Johnston, Steph.	Martin, Jas.
Jolly, Jno.	Mears, Jno.
Jones, Batt	Miller, Wm.
Jones, Francis	Moor, Arthur
Jones, Frederrick	Moore, Henry
Jones, Jas.	Moore, Jno.
Jones, Jno.	Moore, T. Saml.

Moreland, Jno.
Morgan, Steph.
Moses, Jno.
Murphry, Mills
Murphrey, Morris
Neley, Rich.
Nelson, Tho.
Nelson, Wm.
Newmon, Wm.
Nounlamd (Nowland?), Jno.
Oates, J. P.
Odam, Malachi
Odam, Whitmell
O'Donner, Wm.
Ogden, Wm.
Ounsell, Danl.
Outlaw, Edw.
Owens, Tho.
Palmer, Geo.
Paramon, Wm.
Parris, Francis
Paulett, Jesse
Paulett, Jno.
Peebles, Ephriam
Peoples, Ephriam
Perry, Isaac
Perrymon, Tho.
Pollard, J.
Pollock, Robt. Sr.
Pollard, W.
Pollard, Wm.
Potter, Hughes
Pugh, Francis
Pugh, Wm.
Ratliff, Saml.
Rawls, Jno.
Reece, Jacob
Ritchie, Tho.
Roberts, Wm.
Robinson, Alden
Robinson, D.
Robinson, Philip
Rorial, Steph.
Roughton, Jno.
Rowell, Robt.
Royall, Wm.
Russell, Jas.
Russell, Sol.
Ryall, Winn
Sartam (?), Jas.
Scott, Eliz.
Scruggs, Wm.
Sear, Saml. M.
Seegar, Geo.

Sempel, Nathl.
Sharard, Simon
Sharp, Earl
Sharp, Jacob
Sharp, Jno.
Sharp, Jno. Jr.
Sharp, Joshua
Sharp, Michael
Sharp, Timothy
Shelman, J.
Sikes, Danl.
Skinner, Nicholas
Skinner, Wm.
Smith, Benj.
Smith, Frederick
Sneed, Dudley
Snell, Chris.
Snell, Saml.
Speight, Jno.
Speight, Moses Jr.
Spence, Jno.
Spence, Moses
Spence, Tharp
Spence, Tho.
Spikes, Tho.
Spivey, Jethro B.
Stallings, Jas.
Stataly, Francis
Stewart, Wm.
Stidham, Adam
Stoy, Henry W.
Talor, Chapman
Tanecel, Saml.
Tapley, Jno.
Terry, Champness
Terry, Tho.
Thomas, Gideon
Thomas, Wm.
Thompson, Elihu
Tillmon, L. B.
Tillmon, Wm.
Tindal, Jas.
Tindal, Jno.
Tonnell (?), Fred'k.
Treadwell, Jno.
Triplet, Francis
Vining, Cader
Vining, Jesse
Wade, Hezekiah
Wade, Saml.
Walker, David
Walker, Enoch
Walker, Isaac
Ward, Francis

Warnock, Robt.
Watkins, Jno.
Watson, Willis
Watts, Edw.
Wayne, Wm.
Weathers, Edw.
Welch, Jas.
Wellson, Saml.
Wisleay, Sol.
Whitaker, Amos
Whitaker, Hudson
Whitaker, Jacob
White, Jas.
White, Jno.
Whitehead, Amos
Whitehead, Jacob

Wiggians, Jesse
Willson, Hugh
Womack, Jesse
Womble, Drury
Wood, Joshua
Woods, Wm.
Woods, Willis
Wornock, Jas.
Wornouch, Jno.
Wyche, Tho.
Wyler, U.
Wynne, Peter
Wynne, Wm.
Young, Jas.
Young, Wm.

CAMDEN COUNTY

Camden County was formed in 1777 from Saint Mary and Saint Thomas Parishes. A part of Wayne County was added in 1805. A part of Camden County was set off to Wayne County in 1808 and 1812 and a part to Charlton County in 1854.

Jefferson was the first County seat and Woodbine is now the County seat.

Headrights and
Bounty Grants:
1790-1795

Anderson, Jno.
Atkinson, Jas.
Basket, Thos.
Beasley, Jno.
Bryan, Jos.
Campbell, Jno.
Carnes, Richd.
Clarke, Jacob
Cryer, Morgan
Cryer, Thos.
Eubank, Stephen
Fernando, David
Fort, Drury
Frazier, Stephen
Fulton, Jno.
Garrett, Jno.

Geerman, Christian
Gray, Jno.
Hammond, Abner
Harris, Edwin
Harris, Robt.
Holmes, Jas. M.
How, Robt.
Hudson, Jas.
Hunter, Jno. W.
Jackson, Absalom & Co.
Jackson, Robt.
Jackson, Walter
Jameison, Jno.
Jameson, Jno.
Jamieson, Jno.
Johnson, Walter

Johnson, Wm.
Jones, Jno.
King, Jno.
King, Thos.
Lucenburg, Tabias
March, Geo.
McCall, Thos.
Mears, Saml.
Middleton, Robt.
Mills, Wm.
Mitchell, Abner
Moffett, Danl.
Moore, Jas.
Moubray, Wm.
Moudray, Wm.
Moulfort, Robt.
Norris, Thos.
Oliver, Wm.
Randolph, Isaac
Reddick, Wm. R.
Reddock, Wm. R.
Richardson, Walker
Richey, Jno.
Seagrove, Jas.
Sharp, Saml.
Stafford, Robt.
Stafford, Thos.
Suarvis, Anthony
Swiney, Henry
Taylor, Wm.
Thomas, Allen
Vincent, Jas.
Webster, Saml.
Wood, Jas.
Wood, Matthew
Wright, Jno.
Young, Alex.
Young, Jno.

Camden Co. Land Court
Journal (1787-1790)

Aiken, Tho.
Alexander, Jno.
Allan, Alexdr.
Anderson, Jno.
Armstrong, Jas.
Ashley, Lodewick
Ashley, Nathl.
Ashley, Wm.
Barcley, David
Bartlett, Jonathan
Basket, Tho.
Beazley, Sarah

Bebe, Richd.
Belin, Peter
Bingham, Jno.
Bishop, Elijah
Bolton, Robt.
Boykin, Jno.
Brooks, Peter
Brown, Hugh
Brown, Jno.
Brown, Langley
Bryant, Langley
Bryant, Mary
Cain, Benj.
Carter, Jno.
Cassity, Peter
Clark, Elijah
Clark, Jacob
Clough, Geo.
Cocke, Nathl.
Crozier, Jane
Cryer, Tho.
Cryer, Wm.
Daniell, Chas.
Daniell, Tho.
Davies, Wm. John
Davis, Geo.
Doane, Nemiah
DuBoys, Francis
Dugless, Andrew
Duke, Jno.
Evins, Wm.
Fanshaw, Elijah
Ferrie, Jno.
Finley, Jas.
Fleming, Jno.
Fort, Drury
Fort, Martha
Foster, Richd.
Goodbred, Philip
Goram, Jno.
Gray, Anne
Gray, Jas.
Gray, Jno.
Grove, Jno.
Hadley, Geo.
Hall, Talmage
Hanley, Geo.
Harris, Buckner
Harris, Tho.
Hogan, Danl.
Hopkins, Jno.
Hubbard, Jno.
Hughes, Frederick
Jackson, Susannah

Jenkins, Richd.
Jennings, Patrick
Johnson, Margt.
Johnson, Wm.
Keegan, Allen
Kellogg, Enoch
King, Jno.
King, Wm.
Lamb, Tho.
Longstreet, Wm.
Lyles, Matthew
Mann, Jas.
Marbury, Leonard
Massey, Jas.
McCall, Tho.
McDonal, Hugh
McGirth, Mary
McGirth, Danl.
Merriwether, Jas.
Mickler, Danl.
Moffet, Danl.
Moore, Jas.
Morce, Saml.
Muhlberque, Nicolas
    Victor
Nelson, Jas.
Neblack, Wm.
Neely, Richd.
Norris, Tho.
Osborne, Henry
O'Sullivan, Derby
Palmer, Jno.
Park, Ezekiel Even
Parker, Wm.
Porter, Tho.
Randolph, Geo. (heirs of)
Ransone, Henry
Ready, Wm.
Robinson, Oliver
Seagrove, Jas.
Semple, Alexdr.
Sharp, Saml.
Sherman, Isaac
Sherman, Jno.
Shropshere, Abner
Simmery, Wm.
Simon, Andrew
Simpson, Wm.
Smith, Saml.
Spaldon, Ishem
Stacker, Henry Bodon
Stafford, Robt.
Stafford, Tho.
Stephen, Richd.

Stevens, Richd.
Sweney, Henry
Tate, Jeremiah
Taylor, Robt.
Tetard, Benj.
Thomas, Allen
Thomas, Lucy
Tyner, Jno.
Vanzant, Geo.
Vanzant, Steph.
Vincent, Jas.
Webb, Jno.
Weed, Jacob
Welborne, David
Woreat, Jno.
Wheeler, Isaac
Williams, Abner
William, Wilson
Wingate, Jesse
Woodland, Geo.
Woodland, Jas.
Woodland, Jas. Jr.
Woodland, Susannah
Wright, Tho.
Wright, Henry
Young, Alexdr.
Young, Jno.

Camden Co. Militia
May--Aug. 1793

Anderson, Jas.
Archer, Jos.
Atkins, Wiley
Atkinson, Nathan
Barton, Jas.
Bates, Tho.
Beamis, Ebenezer
Beasley, Jno.
Belvin, Wiley
Bennett, Jas.
Berlingham, Saml.
Bixley, Wm.
Blunt, Steph.
Brown, Jno.
Brown, Robt.
Brown, Robt. Jr.
Bryson, Wm.
Bulkley, Ichabod
Carnes, Robt.
Cartnell, Wm.
Clark, Jos.
Cornelius, Benj.
Courson, Wm.

Crawford, Jno.
Cruse, Jno.
Cryer, Wm.
Dawson, Wm.
Dillingham, Simon
Eason, Jno.
Eason, Robt.
Eason, Wm.
Elliott, Richd.
Ewing, Jos.
Finch, Ichabod
Fowler, Jno. M.
Goodbread, Philip
Gragg, Jas.
Gray, Jno.
Green, Jas.
Hammond, Abner
Hampton, Jno.
Hardee, Jno.
Harrell, Abner
Harris, Sampson
Harris, Tho.
Harris, Walton
Harris, Zach
Hart, Henry
Hatcher, Jno.
Hebbard, Elihu
Howard, Wm.
Hunt, Philip
Jackson, Absalom
Jamison, Ralph
Jenkins, Jno.
Johnson, Benj.
Jordan, Jas.
King, Wm.
Lanier, Lewis
Lawler, Jno.
Lewis, Robt.
Lyons, Danl.
McClane, Tho.
McCrary, Moses
Marshall, Jno.
Mason, Jno.
Mathers, Danl.
Moor, Jas.
Mitchell, Abner
Murphie, Matrick
Nelson, Jas.
Offut, Ezekiel
O'Kelly, Lawrence
Oliver, Francis
Oliver, Wm.
Pitcher, Reubin
Powers, Tim

Rudulph, Tho.
Ryley, Tho.
Seagrove, Robt.
Skrine, Tho.
Smith, Ezekiel
Smith, Saml.
Spalding, Isham
Stephens, Richd.
Stiver, Michael
Stith, Peyton K.
Strawhon, Neal
Suaris, Anthony
Tate, Jeremiah
Taylor, Jno.
Taylor, Robt.
Taylor, Wm.
Thomas, Allen
Thomas, Wm.
Thompson, Isham
Treman, Stephen
Tylor, Wm.
Webster, Saml.
Williams, Wilson
Woodland, Jas.
Wright, Habk.
Wright, Henry
Wright, Jas.
Wright, Tho.
Wright, Wm.

Camden County men
holding County and
State offices
1787-1795

Armstrong, Jas.
Ashley, Nathan
Carnes, Richd.
Crews, Isaac
Fleming, Jno.
Hall, Talmadge
Hammond, Abner
Jordan, Jas.
King, Jno.
King, Thos.
Lindsey, Jas. M.
Moubray, Wm.
Norris, Tho.
Osborne, Henry
Randolph, J. F.
Rudulph, Thos.
Stafford, Thos.
Weed, Jacob
Williams, Abner

Williams, Wm.
Wright, Henry

Camden Co. Grand Jurors
as published in the
Southern Centinel and
Universal Gazette 1794

Burroughs, J.
Fowler, Jno. M.
Gascoigne, Richd.
Goodbread, Phillip
Harris, Robt.
Hebbard, E.
Jackson, Absalom
Johnston, Wm.
King, Jno.
King, Tho.
McGillis, R.
March, Geo.
Mills, Wm.
Moubrey, Wm.
Niblack, Wm.
O'Kelly, Larence
Seagrove, Jas.

Estates and Misc. Legal
Advertising as printed
in the Georgia Gazette,
Southern Centinel and
Universal Gazette, and
Augusta Chronicle and
Gazette   1790-1795

Armstrong, Jas.
Brown, Hugh
Bryan, Langley
Bryant, Langley
Carr, Tho.
Fleming, Jno.
Jackson, Absalom
Jackson, Jas.
Jameson, Jno.
Jones, Noble
King, Tho.
McCredie, Andrew
McGillis, Randolph
McIntosh, Wm.
Moffatt, Danl.
Munro, Saml.
Osborne, Henry
O'Neal, Ferdinand
Randolph, Jno. F.
Seagrove, Jas.

Seagrove, Robt.
Smith, Saml.
Styers, Michael
Vaughn, Jno. Daniel
Wright, Henry
Wright, Mrs. Mary
Wright, Wm.

Camden County Deed
Books "A" and "B".
Deeds made during the
years 1788 through
1795:

Grantor
Ashley, Nathaniel
Ashley, Wm.
Bacon, Danl.
Borel, Claud
Bryant, Langley
Burrows, Jno., Exq.
Cryer, Tho.
Dallas, Wm.
Dilworth, Jno.
Fernandez, David, dec'd.
Fernandez, Rachel
Fort, Drury
Freeman, Diana
Freeman, Stephen
Gallup, Prentiss
Geerman, Christian
Hall, Talmadge
Hammond, Abner
Hammond, Ann
Hibbard, Elihu, Esq.
Hudson, Jas.
Hunter, Jno. W.
Jamieson, Jno.
Jamieson, Ralph
King, Jno.
King, Sarah
Meers, Saml.
Mills, Jeannett
Mills, Wm.
Mills, Wm. Sr.
Norris, Tho.
Norris, Wm.
Pendleton, Sol., dec'd.
Reddick, Wm. R.
Reddy, Mary
Reddy, Wm.
Seagrove, Ann
Seagrove, Jas.
Seagrove, Robt.

Skrine, Thomas
Smith, Samuel
Steel, Thos.
Suaris, Antoine
Tally, Wm.
Taylor, Wm.
Vincent, Jas.
Wagnon, Rebecca
Webster, Saml.
Weed, Jacob
Williams, Abner, dec'd.
Williams, Eliz.
Williams, Hannah
Williams, Wilson
Wheeler, Isaac
Wood, Matthew
Woodland, Eliz.
Woodland, Jas.
Wright, Eve
Wright, Habukkuk
Wright, Jas. Nickles
Wright, Wm.
Young, Alexdr.

Grantee
Alexander, Jno.
Ashley, Ludowick
Ashley, Nathl.
Ashley, Wm.
Bacon, Danl.
Bartlett, Jonathan
Belen, Peter
Blount, Redding
Carnes, Richd.
Cook, Geo.
Cornelius, Benj.
Conyers, Steph.
Cryer, Wm.
Dallas, Wm.
Dawson, Lemuel Gulliver
Dillingham, Simeon
Dilworth, Jas.
Duke, Jno.
Durkee, Nathl.
Elliott, Richd. M.J.
Fernandez, David
Finley, Jas.
Fleming, Jno.
Fort, Jane
Gascoigne, Richd.
Geerman, Christian
Hebbard, Elihu
Higginbotham, Burris
Jackson, Pharabea

Jameson, Jno.
Jameson, Ralph
Jamieson, Jno.
Johnston, Wm.
King, Thos.
Lamb, Charlotte Cryer
Lamb, Tho.
Norris, Tho.
Norris, Wm.
O'Kelly, Lawrence
Oliver, Wm.
Osborne, Henry
Pendleton, Nathl.
Phillips, Danl.
Ready, Wm.
Seagrove, Jas.
Seagrove, Robt.
Skrine, Jno. D.
Skrine, Mary
Skrine, Susannah
Steel, Thos.
Suarez, Antoine
Tally, Jno.
Tally, Mary
Tally, Wm. Jr.
Vincent, Jas.
Weed, Jacob
Wheeler, Isaac
Williams, Wilson
Wright, Habbakkak
Wright, Jas. Nickles
Wright, Thos.

Witnesses and names from items recorded in book other than deeds:

Bryant, Langley
Caskan, Jas.
Christopher, Spencer
Christopher, Spicer
Corker, David, dec'd.
Freeman, Diana
Freeman, Steph. dec'd.
Gascoigne, Richd.
Jackson, Absalom, dec'd.
Johnston, Wm.
Judson, Jos.
Keegan, Allen, dec'd.
McClain, Thos.
Seagrove, Robt.
Stafford, Robt.
Stafford, Thos.
Stanley, Jno., dec'd.

Wright, Henry
Wright, Jas.
Young, Alexdr.

Appointments as Justices
of Peace, Camden Co. as
published in the Augusta
Chronicle and Gazette
1792

Brown, Hugh
Cathan, Jas.
Fleming, Jno.
Johnson, Wm.
Miller, Danl.
Williams, Wilson
Woodland, Jas. Sr.
Young, Alexdr.

1788 Voters as recorded
in Deed Book "A"
(Page unnumbered)
Camden County

Aiken, Jas.
Alexander, Jno.
Bartlett, Jonathan
Beasley, Jas.
Brown, Hugh
Brown, Robt.
Bryant, Langley
Clarke, Jacob
Crawford, Jno.
Cryer, Tho.
Cryer, Wm.
Dillingham, Simeon
Eason, Jno.
Finley, Jas.
Fleming, Jno.
Fort, Drury
Gray, Jas.
Gray, Jno.
Hall, Talmage
Hughes, Frederick
Jenkins, Richd.
Keane, Benj.
Lamb, Tho.
Lutzenburg, Tobias
Lyles, Matthew
McClure, Jos.
Malpas, Jas.
Moffat, Danl.
Moore, Jas.
Niblack, Wm.

Norris, Tho.
Osborne, Henry
O'Sullivan, Derby
Robertson, Oliver
Seagrove, Jas.
Seagrove, Robt.
Semple, Alexdr.
Simpson, Wm.
Smith, Samuel
Smitton, Wm.
Spalding, Isham
Stevens, Richd.
Taylor, Robt.
Tate, Jeremiah
Thomas, Allen
Touchton, Danl.
Tyner, Caleb
Tyner, Jno.
Warren, Joshua
Weed, Jacob
Wheeler, Isaac
Williams, Abner
Williams, Wilson
Woodland, Geo.
Woodland, Jas.
Wright, Henry
Wright, Wm.
Young, Alexdr.

1789 Voters as recorded
in Deed Book "A" (unnum-
bered page) that were
not on the list in 1788

Aiken, Tho.
Bolina, Jas.
Bolton, Robt.
Burkett, Tho.
Carter, Jno.
Doane, Nehamiah
Douglas, Andrew
Fort, Drury
Hall, Talmage
Harris, Tho.
Hughes, Frederick
King, Wm.
Lamb, Tho.
Lyles, Matthew
Mickler, Danl.
Miller, Danl.
Nelson, Jas.
Parker, Wm.
Reddy, Wm.
Scallions, Andrew

Semple, Alexdr.
Sherman, Jno.
Stafford, Robt.
Stafford, Tho.
Taylor, Wm.
Tieagan, Allen
Wright, Tho.

Camden County
1794 Tax List:

Atkinson, Nathan
Bailey, Jno.
Baskett, Rebeka
Belving, Willey J.
Blackmone, Steph.
Brown, Hue
Brown, Robt.
Bryant, Langley
Buckley, Ich.
Burrows, Jno.
Burrows, Jno. Alty
  for Sam Meers
Beesly, Jno.
Carns, Richd.
Castmell, Wm. & Co.
Chatham, Jane Seagrove
Clayton, Isac
Clayton, Jacob
Cornelus, Geo. and
  Hart, Henry
Courson, Wm.
Crews, Jno.
Crawford, Jno.
Cryher, Morgan
Cryer, Tho.
Cryer, Wm.
Cuins, Jacob
Dallis, Wm.
Dawson, Wm.
Dillingham, Simeon
Dilworth, Jno.
Doherty, Jas.
Dorrel, Samuel & Tho.
Duff, Jas.
Dushe, Peter
Elliott, Alex.
Elliott, Richd.
Elliott, Wm.
Eton, Jno.
Fenley, Archibald
Fhilaire, Jacinthe
Fort, Drury
Fort, Drury, Ex. for
  Robert Bolton

Fowler, J. M. for
  Hammond & Fowler
Fowler, John M.
  Atty. for G. Cook
Garvin, David
Gascoigne, Richd.
Gibson, Wm.
Goodbread, Phillip
Gorman, Jno.
Gorman, Wm.
Gray, Jno.
Gray, Lewis
Guillett, Wm.
Hadduck, Zach.
Hall, Jno.
Hamilton, Edw.
Hammond, Jas.
Hampton, Jno.
Hardee, Jno.
Harrel, Abraham
Harris, Robt.
Holmes, Jas.
Howard, Whilliam
Hubbard, Elihu
Hudson, Jas.,
  Guilder, Philip
Hull, Jno.
Hunt, Phillip
Irvine, Tho.
Jameson, Jno.
Jamieson, Jno., Atty.
  for Steph. Freeman
Johnson, Wm.
Johnson, Wm.
Johnstone, Danl.
Jones, Jno.
Judson, Jos.
Keggan, Allen
King, Jno.
King, Wm.
King, Tho.
Lang, Isaac
Lang, Sarah
Langstaff, Jas.
Lee, Hugh
Lindsey, Jas.
Lyons, Danl.
Marck, Geo.
Marreer, Jno.
Mathers, Danl.
Measles, Sen.Charlton Jr.
Measles, Charlton
Measles, Joshua
Mickler, Peter
Miller, Eley

Mills, Wm.
Mitchel, Abner
Moats, Jno.
Moats, Mathew
Moats, Wm. and Spanish
  Joe commonly cald
  their Pole
Moore, Jas.
Moore, Jas.
Moubray, Wm.
Moubray, Wm., Atty.
  for Jas. McCoumb
Mickler, Jacob
McClane, Susanah
McClane, Susannah
McGillis, Randolph
Nelson, Jas.
Niblack, Wm.
Norris, Tho.
O'Kelly, Larance
Oliver, Frances
Palmer, Nathl.
Pitcher, Reuben
Randolph, J. F.
Rawlings, Benj.
Reddock, Jas.
Reddy, Wm.
Rudolph, Thos.
Seagrove, Robt.
Simpson, Wm.
Singletary, Danl.
Smith, Samuell
Smith, Samuell, Atty.
  for J. Flemming
Sterling, Frances
Swares, Antirine
Talley, Wm.
Tanner, Jno.
Tates, Jerimiah
Taylor, Jno.
Taylor, Robt. Sr.
Taylor, Wm.
Thomas, Allen
Thompson, Reuben
Thompson, Reuben &
  Parris, Jno.
Tims, Benj.
Tims, Tho.
Vencent, Geo.
Vincent, Jas.
Vincent, Jas., Atty
  for Henry Conklin
Vincent, Jas., Atty.
  for Eliza Fenshaw

Vincent, Steph.
Walton, Asa
Williams, Wilson
Williams, Wilson Ex
  for Abraham Williams
Williamson, Andrew
Wood, Mathew
Woodland, Jas.
Woodland, Jas. Jr.
Wright, Habakuh
Wright, Henry & Son
Wright, Jas. N.
Wright, Jas., Atty.
  for Mary Mickler
Wright, Tho.
Young, Alex.
Young, Jno.
Young, Jno.
_____ Samuel
____ddock, Wm.

Camden County Jurors
1794

Bacon, Daniel
Balkey (?), Ichabod
Beasley, Jas.
Bennett, Jas.
Blackmar, Steph.
Bryant, Langley
Colemon, Jno.
Craford, Jno.
Eason, Wm.
Elliott, Wm.
Fitch, Andrew
Gascongee, Rich.
Godfrey, Jno.
Goodbread, Philip
Gray, Jno.
Guilder, Philip
Hatcher, Jno.
Jameson, Jno.
Johnson, Wm.
Kennedy, Richd.
King, Wm.
Lee, Hugh
McClean, Tho.
McMillian, Alexdr.
March, Geo.
Mickler, Jacob
Myers, Michael
Niblack, Wm.
Orear, Benj.
Paris, Jno.

Powers, Timothy
Rudolph, Michael
Stafford, Robt.
Waterman, Eleazer
Woodland, Jas.
Wright, Wm.

From Vol. III. Joseph
Habersham Collections.
"Being the whole of the
inhabitants" presum-
ably in the 1790's:

Archer, Jos.
Anderson, Jas.
Bacon, Danl.
Beazely, Jno.
Beazly, Jas.
Belvin, Wiley I.
Bennett, Jas.
Bingham, Jno.
Blackmar, Steph.
Brewston, David
Briggs, Elkanah
Brown, Hugh
Brown, Robt.
Bryant, Langley
Bulkley, Ichabod
Carmill, Wm.
Carnes, Rich.
Carr, Tho.
Clarke, Jacob
Clayton, Isaac
Coleman, Jno.
Cornelion, Geo.
Craford, Jno.
Cryer, Wm.
Cunns, Jacob
Dawson, Wm.
Dillingham, Simeon
Dilworth, Jno.
Dorrel, Saml.
Douglas, Andrew
Eason, Jno.
Eason, Wm.
Elliot, Wm.
Elliott, Alexdr.
Elliott, Rich.
Finch, Ichabod
Fitch, Andrew
Fort, Drury
Fowler, Jno.
Freeman, Steph.
Gascongne, Rich.

German, Christopher
German, Jno.
Gilder, Philip
Godfrey, Jno.
Goodbread, Philip
Gray, Jas.
Gray, Jno.
Hackett, ------
Haddock, Zach.
Hall, Talmage
Hammond, Abner
Hampton, Jno.
Harris, Robt.
Harris, Tho.
Hatcher, Jno.
Holmes, Jas.
Hopkins, C. B.
Howard, Wm.
Hubbard, Elihu
Hudson, Jas.
Hunter, I. W.
Jameson, Jno.
Jinkins, Philip
Johnston, Benj.
Johnston, Wm.
Jones, Jno.
Judson, Jos.
Keggan, Allen
Kennedy, Rich.
King, Jno.
King, Jno.
King, Tho.
King, J. P. Thomas
King, Wm.
Lambe, Tho.
Lee, Hugh
Lewis, Robt. B.
McClean, Tho.
McCleery, Jno.
McGillies, Benedict
McMillion, Alexdr.
March, Geo.
Mason, Jno.
Mathers, Daniel
Meers, Saml.
Mickler, Jacob
Micken, Peter
Miller, Danl.
Mills, Wm. Jr.
Mills, Wm. Sr.
Moore, Jas.
Mowbray, Wm.
Mowbrey, Wm.
Neilson, Jas.

Niblack, Wm.
Norris, Tho.
O'Kelly, Lawrence
Oliver, Francis
Oliver, Wm.
Orear, Benj.
Palmer, Nathl.
Paris, Jno.
Parker, Jno.
Powers, Timothy
Randolph, Jno. F.
Reddick, Wm.
Reddy, Wm.
Rudolph, Michael
Rudolph, Tho.
Seagrove, Jas.
Seagrove, Robt.
Wimpson, Wm.
Smith, Ezekiel
Smith, Saml.
Snares, Anthony
Spalding, Isham
Stafford, Robt.

Stafford, Tho.
Stevens, Rich.
Stillwell, Wm. L.
Styers, Michael
Tate, Jeremiah
Taylor, Jno.
Taylor, Wm.
Thomas, Allen
Tisker, Allening
Tolland, Jno.
Vincent, Jas. S.
Washburn, Jos.
Waterman, Eleazer
Williams, Wilson
Woodland, Jno. Jr.
Woodland, Jas. Sr.
Wright, Henry
Wright, Jas.
Wright, Tho.
Wright, Wm.
Young, Alexdr.
Young, Jno.

CHATHAM COUNTY

Created February 5, 1777, from Creek cession of May

20, 1733, Chatham was an original County previously

organized in 1758 as the Parishes of Christ Church and

(a portion of) St. Phillip. It was here that the colony

of Georgia was established when General James Edward

Oglethorpe founded Savannah on Yamacraw Bluff Feb. 12, 1733.

Chatham Co. Will Book
  A-B-C-D-E
1789 -- 1791

Adams, Samuel
Allen, Robert H.
Arnets, Jonathan
Barber, Penny
Bauchanneau, Nich
Beatty, Dr. John
Bigbee, Francis
Bolton, Robt. Jr.
Bull, Absalom
Bull, Thomas

Butler, Jno.
Cable, Denbo
Campbell, Jno.
Carson, Jno.
Clark, Jas.
Clay, Jos.
Clyatte, Jas
Clyatte, Sarah
Coales, Wm.
Cohen, Philip, Jacob

(29)

Conner, Simon
Course, Daniel
Course, Jno.
Cowling, Slaughter
Crookshanks, Patrick
Davis, Wm.
Dawson, Richd.
Delk, David
Demere, Mary
Demere, Mary Eliz.
Demere, Raymond
Densler, Catherine
    Barbary
Densler, Henry
Densler, Michael
Deveaux, Ann
Deveaux, Jno. Bermers
Deveaux, Wm. Esqr.
Deveaux, Wm. Fairchild
Dillon, Edmund
Dowl, Tho.
Dunn, Geo.
Elbert, Eliz.
Elbert, Saml, dec'd.
Emanuel, Asa
Eppinger, Barbarah
Eppinger, Jno.
Evans, Martha
Forsythe, Mary
Gable, Abraham
Galache, Ann Eliz.
Galache, Jas.
Gale, Dr. Wm.
Geoghegan, Ignatius
Gibbons, Sarah
Gibson, Daniel
Gibson, Robt.
Gibson, Sarah
Gilbert, Jno.
Glass, Jno.
Glen, Jas.
Glen, Jno., Esq.
Goffe, Jane
Greene, Catherine
Habersham, Jno.
Hainer, Nichols, Jr.
Hale, Jno.
Hamilton, Jno.
Hanner, Eliz.
Hanner, Nicholas
Harden, Edw.
Harden, Wm.
Harn, Saml.
Harn, Wm.

Harris, Mary
Harris, Mordica
Harris, Wm.
Helena, Beal
Herb, Fredk. Jr.
Herson, Herman
Houstown, Jas.
Irvine, Wm.
Jackson, Abrah.
Johnston, Andrew
Jones, Geo.
Jones, Noble W.
Jones, Seaborn
Jones, W.
Keith, Alexdr.
Kerr, Eliz.
Kerr, Peter
Lafitte, Peter S.
Leaver, Gabriel
Lebey, Andrew
Lehre, J.
Levett, Francis
Lewden, Wm.
McFarlen, Jno.
Macleod, D.
Mayer, Augustus
Maxwell, Walter
Mayer, Aug.
Milledge, Jno.
Miller, Jacob
Mills, Sarah
Mills, Thos.
Mirrilies, Jas.
Montford, Henry
Moore, Aaron
Moore, Catherine
Morel, Peter Henry
Morgan, Wm.
Myers, Jas.
Netherclift, J.
Netherclift, T.
Netherclift, T. Jr.
Nevill, Jno.
Nixon, Jno.
Norton, Jos.
Nunes, Moses
Nungazer, Geo.
Nungazer, Henry dec'd.
Nungazer, Mary Appolonia
Oates, Jno.
Oatt, Barbara
Palmer, Mary
Palmer, Thos.
Pendleton, Susan

Penman, Jno. dec'd.
Penman, Robina
Pinder, Wm.
Plumer, Ezra
Plumer, Mary
Polock, Isaac
Port, Jas.
Pray, Job
Peaddick, Saloma
Rents, Jno.
Reynolds, Jno. N.
Richards, Jno.
Richardson, Geo.
Richardson, Margt.
Ring, Chris.
Ring, Ann Margaret
Ritton, Michael
Robertson, Jno.
Rogers, Wm.
Ross, David
Ross, Donald
Ross, Hugh
Ross, Jane
Ross, Jno. A. G.
Ross, Sarah
Russell, Ann
Russell, Jane
Russell, S.
Russell, Wm. dec'd.
Salfner, Mathew
Scheuber, Justus H.
Scott, Hugh
Shad, Catherine
Shad, Sol. dec'd.
Sharp, Jas. B.
Shaffer, Balthaser
Sheftall, Levi
Sheftall, Mordecai
Sheftall, Moses
Shick, Jno.
Simpson, Jno.
Smith, Jno.
Smith, Thos.
Solomon, Baker
Spencer, Eliz.
Spencer, Geo. Basil
Spencer, Jos. Wm.
Spencer, Wm. H.
Stiles, Benj. dec'd.
Storie, Jno.
Taylor, J. G.
Thies, Peter
Ties, Jacob
Timmons, Catherine

Timmons, Jno.
Tobler, Ulrich
Tuft, Syniston
Vollotton, David Moses
Vollotton, Francis
Wallace, Wm.
Watlington, Jno. N.
Watt, Alex.
Welscher, Jos.
White, Jas.
White, Jno. Younger
Whitefield, J.
Wiggins, Edmund
Wiggins, Mary
Williams, Stephen
Wilscher, Jos. Esq.
Wilson, Geo.
Winn, Banister
Womack, Jno.
Wood, Jacob
Woodhouse, Geo.
Young, Chas.
Young, Dr. Jas. Box
Young, Sophia
Zubly, Rev.Jno.J.dec'd.

Chatham County Deed
Books G, H, I, K
1789 - 1790 - 1791
(There is no Book J)

Grantors
Abrahams, Jos.
Anderson, Jno.
Anderson, Susanne
Atkinson, Andrew
Baas, Rebecca
Baas, Saml.
Bland, Mary
Bowen, Mary
Bowen, Saml. Flint
Brickell, Jno.
Brown, Ann
Brown, Wm.
Butler, Jos. dec'd.
Butler, Meshack
Carragan, Edw.
Carson, Jno.
Cecil, Harriet
Cecil, Leonard
Cochran, Jas.
Cohen, Judith
Cohen, Moses

(31)

Connor, Simon
Course, Danl.
Course, Eliz.
Course, Mary
Course, Wm.
Courter, Harmon
Courvoisie, Francis
Courvoisie, Mary
Cuthbert, Jos.
Day, Jos.
Dean, Jos.
Dean, Steph. dec'd.
DeCosta, Abraham
Delaroque, Jno.
DeLyon, Isaac
DeLyon, Reina
Demere, Raymond
Deveaux, Peter
Ewing, Mary
Ewing, Wm.
Farrow, Jno.
Fell, Eliz.
Fell, Isaac
Fendin, Susannah
Forster, Jos.
Fox, Benj. dec'd.
Geoghegan, Ignatius
Gibbons, Ann
Gibbons, Jos.
Gibbons, Thos.
Gibbons, Wm. Jr.
Gordon, Catherine
Greer, Grace
Greer, Robert
Guerard, Ann
Guerard, Godin
Habersham, Hester
Habersham, Jas.
Hall, Lyman
Hall, Mary
Hamilton, Jno.
Harrison, Catherine
Inman, Joshua
Jackson, Abraham
Jackson, Ann Agnes
Jackson, Jas.
Jackson, Mary E.
James, Chas.
Jones, Geo.
Jordan, Wm.
Lange, Ann Marie Gertrude
Lange, Jno. Peter
Leaver, Gabriel
Leaves, Eliz.

Leaves, Gabriel
Leaves, Jno.
Leaves, Mary
Lewden, Wm.
Lindsey, Rev. Benj.
Lindsey, Mary
Lloyd, Ed.
Lockerman, Persiana
Lockon, Peter
Lynes, Moses
McConky, Ann
McConky, Jas.
McCullock, Jno.
McFarlane, Jno.
McFarlen, Jno.
McFarlin, Jno.
McIntosh, Jno.
McIntosh, Lachlan
McIver, Alexdr.
McLeod, Jno.
McQueen, Jno.
Mann, Luke
Marbury, Leonard
Mathers, Peggy
Mathers, Wm.
Meers, Saml.
Milledge, Jno.
Milledge, Phillip
Millen, Steph. dec'd.
Miller, Jos.
Miller, Mary
Miller, Nicholas
Miller, Susannah
Mills, Sarah
Mills, Thos.
Mingledorf, Annete
Mingledorf, Geo.
Minis, Abegail
Montfort, Robt.
Morel, Ann
Morel, Henrietta
Morel, Jno.
Morel, Peter Henry
Motts, Matthew
Muire, Sarah
Murrilies, Jas.
Netherclift, Thos.
Newell, Rebecca
Newell, Thos.
Odingsells, Chas
Orrick, Ann
Patterson, Jno.
Peacock, Michael
Pendleton, Nathl.

Penman, Jno.
Pleym ?, Andrew
Polack, Cushman
Polock, Isaac
Polock, Rachel
Pooler, Ann
Pooler, Jno.
Pugh, Willoughby
Putnam, Henry
Ray, Jno.
Ray, Sarah
Ray, Wm.
Readick, Michael
Rees, David
Rees, Eliz.
Reisser, Dorothy
Reisser, Nathl.
Richards, Barbara
Richards, Jno. Hart
Richards, Martha, dec'd.
Ross, Donald
Russell, Jane
Seagrove, Ann
Seagrove, Jas.
Seymour, Richd.
Sheftall, Mordecai
Spencer, Geo. Basil
Spiers, Alex. J.
Stallings, Jas.
Stirk, Saml.
Stewart, Grissell
Stoner, Francis
Stoner, Peter
Storie, Jas., dec'd.
Storie, Jno.
Storie, Margt.
Strahacker, Rudolph
Street, Jane
Street, Jno.
Sullivan, Danl.
Tattnall, Josiah
Thies, Peter
Thorpe, Geo.
Threadcraft, Geo.
Throop, Geo.
Tondee, Chas.
Tondee, Peter, dec'd.
Tuft, Soonickson
Ulmer, Phillip
Wade, Jno.
Wagnon, Jno. Peter
Waldhoeur, Jacob C.
Waters, Tamar
Watt, Alexdr.

Wall, Benj.
Wiggins, Mary
Winekoff, Matthew
Woodhouse, Robt.
Wright, Rebecca
Wright, Saml.
Zubly, Ann
Zubly, Jno.

Grantees
Abrahams, Isaac Jacob
Abrahams, Jos.
Armour, Jno.
Becroft, Saml.
Benedix, Isaac
Berrien, Jno.
Bland, Mary
Bolton, Robt. Jr.
Bolton, Robt.
Bryan, Wm.
Blogg, Wm.
Brooke, Thos.
Brooks, Francis
Brown, Wm.
Butler, Benj.
Butler, Jno.
Butler, Jos.
Butler, Meshack
Butler, Shadrack
Butler, Wm.
Cantor, Jacob Jr.
Catonnet, Mary Alexis
Cecil, Leonard
Clark, Jas.
Cleckley, Jno. Web
Cochran, Jas.
Coddington, Francis
Collins, Cornelius
Connor, Simon
Course, Wm.
Courvoisie, Francis
Coxe, Jno.
Cumming, Jno.
Currie, Jno.
Day, Jos.
deLamotta, Emanuel
Delaroque, Jno.
Delavaver, Frances,
    Marie Loys Dumoussay
De La Villabucker, Nicho-
    las Francis Magon
DeLyon, Isaac
Demere, Mary
Demere, Raymond

Dickson, Jno.
Dillon, Edmond
Dresler, Chas.
Dumoussay, Frances
    Marie Louis
Durr, Geo.
Elon, Elisha
Emanuel, Asa
Ernest, Jno. Balthazer
Ewing, Wm.
Fell, Frederick Shick
Fell, Isaac
Felt, Eliz.
Felt, Isaac
Fox, Benj. Jr.
Fox, Jno.
Fox, Wm.
Galache, Ann
Galache, Jas.
Geoghigan, Ignatius
Gibosn, Danl.
Gibbons, Barack
Gibbons, Thos.
Gibbons, Wm.
Gibbons, Wm. Sr.
Grayson, Jno.
Greer, Robt.
Guerard, Ann
Haist, Geo.
Hall, Jas.
Hall, Jno.
Hamilton, Jno.
Herb, Jno.
Higgins, Ichabod
Hobbs, Jno.
Hogg, Thos.
Holmes, Robert
Houstoun, Geo.
Houstoun, Jno.
Jackson, Ebenezer
Jackson, Jas.
Jackson, Ebenezer
Jackson, Jas.
Johnston, David
Jones, Geo.
Jones, Noble W.
Kaupt, Jno.
Kieffer, David
Kirk, Jas.
Lamb, Wm.
Lange, Wm. Henry
Lawton, Robt.
LeConte, Wm. dec'd.
Leion, David

Lewden, Wm.
Lindsey, Benj.
Lloyd, Benj.
Lynes, Benj.
McAllister, Richd.
McConky, Jas.
McCredie, Andrew
McIver, Jno.
McLean, Josiah
McLeod, Anthony
McLeod, Donald
Maclean, Jos.
Maclean, Sophia Sarah
Mann, Luke
Mann, Luke Jr.
Mann, Thos.
Mayer, Augustus
Merreties, Jas.
Millen, Anna Catherine
Millen, Catherine
Millen, Geo.
Millen, Godlip
Millen, Jno. dec'd.
Millen, Mary Ann
Millen, Sarah
Miller, Morris
Minis, Leah
Mitchell, David Brydie
Mitchell, Thos.
Montfort, Robt.
Moore, Ann
Moore, Wm.
Morel, Peter Henry
Morgan, Richd.
Muire, Eliz.
Murray, Lucia
Murrino, Ann
Netherclift, Thos.
    Gordon
Oakman, Wm.
Odingsells, Chas.
Orrick, Ann
Orrick, Anna
Orrick, Jno.
Orrick, Jno. Hall
Owens, Owen
Patterson, Jno. Jr.
Patterson, Teathover
Polack, Cushman
Possner, Jos.
Pugh, Willoughby
Ray, Jno. Burris
Rives, Jos.
Roberts, Jos.

Scheuber, Justus H.
Scrimminger, Chas.
Seymour, Richd.
Shad, Sol.
Shaw, Jas.
Shick, Frederick
Smith, Jno.
Smith, Mary
Spencer, Ann
Spencer, Mary
Spencer, Wm. Henry
Spencer, Wm. Jos.
Stallings, Jas.
Stephens, Wm.
Stirk, Saml.
Stone, Henry Dassex
Storie, Jane
Sullivan, Danl.
Tattnall, Josiah Jr.
Thompson, Claud
Thompson, Claude
Thompson, Wm.
Tondee, Chas.
Tunno, Adam
Turner, Lewis
Vial, Lawrence
Wall, Benj.
Wallace, Jas.
Watt, Alexdr.
Welscher, Jos.
Williams, Saml.
Williamson, Gernier
Wilson, Jas.
Winekoff, Ann
Wright, Edw.
Yonge, Christiana
Zubly, Jno. Joachim

Witnessess to deeds and
names in records other
than deeds that were
recorded in these books:

Abrahams, Levy
Adams, Ann
Adams, Edmund
Adams, Jane Stutz
Adams, Nathl.
Archer, T.
Ash, Matthias
Barnard, Jas.
Belsell, Jno.
Bennett, Jos.
Berrien, Thos.

Bolton, Jno.
Bolton, Robt.
Bond, Venable
Bourquin, David Francis
Bowen, Jas.
Bowen, Saml.
Box, Richd.
Brailsford, Jno. N.
Brickell, Jno.
Britton, Steph.
Brown, Wm.
Bullock, Archibald
Bullock, Jas.
Burke, J.
Burrows, J.
Burrows, Jno.
Butler, Shem
Campbell, Jno.
Capers, Richd.
Carraway, Jas.
Carson, Jno.
Cecil, Leonard
Champagne, Eliz.
Champagne, Nicholas
Champion, Jno. B.
Clark, Ann Ross
Clark, Jean, dec'd.
Clark, Mark
Clark, Wm.
Clarke, Jas.
Clarke, Jonathan
Clay, Jos.
Clay, Jos. Jr.
Clyatt, Jas.
Clyatt, Sarah
Coddington, F.
Conner, Simon
Cornick, Jos.
Course, Danl.
Course, Jno.
Courvoisie, Francis
Coxe, Jonathan
Crookshanks, Chas.
Crookshanks, Patrick
Cunningham, Jno.
Currie, Jno.
Cuthbert, Jos.
Cuyler, T.
Davies, Edw.
DeLyon, Abraham
Densler, Michael
Deveaux, Peter
Deveaux, Wm.
Dicks, Alexdr.

Dicks, Andrew
Dorsey, Thos.
Dorsey, Thos. E.
Doyle, Francis
Dunlap, Jos.
Eirick, Catherine
Elon, Ann
Elon, Elisha
Fahm, Frederick.
Faming, Chevalier Noel
Faries, Geo.
Farrow, Jno.
Farrow, Rosetta
Fenn, Jno.
Fox, Martha
Frish, Chas.
Gable, Abraham
Galache, Eliz. Ann
Geoghegan, Ignatius
Germain, Michael
Gibbons, Ann
Gibbons, Jno.
Gibbons, Thos.
Gibbs, Eliz.
Glen, Jos.
Godwin, Richd.
Goldwire, Benj.
Gordon, Wm.
Gotier, Josiah
Green, Michael
Griffith, Edw.
Griggs, Jane
Habersham, Jno.
Habersham, Jos.
Hall, Eliza Ann
Hall, Jno.
Hammond, Catherine
Harris, Chas.
Harris, Thos.
Harris, Wm.
Hearn, Philip
Hensler, Jno.
Herb, Frederick
Herb, Jno.
Heros, Jno.
Heros, Lucy
Herson, Herman
Hilbert, Conrad
Hobkirk, Wm.
Hobrirk, Wm.
Hogg, Eunice
Holman, Thos.
Husso ?, Robt.
Ingram, Jas.

Irvine, Jno.
Jackson, A.
Jackson, Abraham
Jackson, Ann Eliza
Jackson, Ebenezer
Johnson, Jas. Jr.
Johnston, David
Johnston, Jas. Jr.
Jones, Benj.
Jones, Mary
Jones, Geo.
Jones, Mary Gibbons
Jones, N. W.
Jordan, Jas.
Karr, Peter
Keebler, Joshua
Kershaw, Isaac
Kettler, Mary
Kirk, Jas.
Krutz, Conrod
Laffitte, Peter S.
Lamb, Wm.
Langley, Saml.
Lawrence, J. T.
Leavenworth, Eli
Leaver, G.
Lee, Sol.
Leion, David
Lewden, Wm.
Lewis, Christiana
Lindsey, Benj.
Lloyd, Ben
Lloyd, Benj.
Loffitte, Peter S.
Long, Frederick
Love, Jno.
Lucas, Jno.
Lyman, Elihu
McAllister, Matthew
McAllister, Richd.
McConky, Jas.
McIntosh, Jno.
McIntosh, Leah
McKinty, Patrick
McLachlan, Mary
McLallas, Danl.
McLaughlin, Isaac
McLean, Andrew Cowper
McLean, Catherine
McLean, Mary
McLean, Wm.
McLeod, Jno.
McQueen, Alexdr.
McQueen, Jno.

Maxey, Jonah
Maxwell, Walter
Maxwell, Wm.
Milledge, Jno.
Miller, Jos.
Miller, Peter
Mills, Eliz.
Mills, Jane
Mills, Wm.
Minis, Abraham
Minis, Esther
Minis, Francis
Minis, Isaac
Minis, Phillipa
Minis, Philip, dec'd.
Mitchell, D. B.
Mitchell, David B.
Mitchell, David Brydie
Montaigut, D.
Montaigut, David
Montfort, R.
Moore, Wm.
Morel, Jno.
Morel, Peter Henry
Mossman, Jas.
Murphree, Wright
Myers, Jas.
Newell, Thos.
Norton, Jonathan
Nunez, Aaron
Oates, Peter
Oakman, Wm.
O'Bryan, Henrietta
Palmer, Thos.
Papot, Peter
Parker, Thos.
Pendleton, D.
Pendleton, Gid D.
Pendleton, Gideon
Pendleton, Nathl.
Penman, Edw.
Phelps, Jas.
Pitt, Thos.
Poullin, Ann Stutz
Poullin, Jno.
Powell, Geo.
Pray, Jno.
Prescott, Ebenezer
Prescott, Eliz. Stutz
Prioleiu, Jno.
Pugh, David
Pyke, Wm.
Robertson, Jas.
Robinson, Peter

Ross, Ann, dec'd.
Ross, Donald
Ross, Hugh Sr., dec'd.
Ross, Hugh, Jr., dec'd.
Ross, Jane
Ross, Jno. Graham
Ross, Miss Sarah
Ross, Wm., dec'd.
Rutherford, Jas.
Scheuber, J. H.
Schuber, Justus H.
Schueber, J. H.
Schueber, Justus H.
Scott, Hugh
Seagrove, Robt.
Seymour, Richd.
Shaeffer, Balthaser
Sheftall, Benj. Jr.
Sheftall, Mordecai
Sheftall, Moses
Shick, Frederick
Shick, Jno.
Simpson, Jno.
Smith, Jas.
Smith, Jos.
Spears, Alexdr. J.
Stallings, Ezekiel
Stallings, Jas.
Stephens, Martha
Stephens, W.
Stephens, Wm.
Stewart, Mrs. Ann
Stewart, Jno.
Stirk, Jos.
Stutz, Jos.
Sullivan, Danl.
Sutherland, Jno.
Tattnall, Josiah, Jr.
Tobler, U.
Tobler, Ulric
Towers, Jno.
Towers, Robt. Jr.
Turner, J. H.
Turner, Jno.
Valleau, Miss Ann
VanYeverson, M.
Waldburger, Bartholomew
Waldburger, J.
Waldburger, J.
Waldburger, Jacob
Wall, Benj.
Wall, Richd.
Wallace, Jno.
Warren, Elias

Waters, Jno.
Watt, Alexdr.
Watt, Wm.
Wilby, Benj.
Welscher, Jos.
White, Jas.
Whitefield, J.
Whitefield, Jas.
Whitefield, Martha
Whittendal, Jno. Thos.
Whittendal, Mary
Wiggins, Mary
Wiggins, Mary
Williamson, Jno.
Williamson, Jno. G.
Wilson, David
Wood, Jacob
Woodhouse, Geo.
Woodhouse, Robt.
Wright, Wm.
Wylly, Richd.
Yorke, Saml.
Young, Jas. Box
Young, Sophia
Young, Thos.

Headrights and Bounty
Grants 1790 - 1795:

Greer, Robt.

Legal Advertising
appearing in the Georgia
Gazette, Augusta Chron-
icle & Gazette, Southern
Centinel & Universal
Gazette 1790 - 1795

Cecil, Leonard, Esq.
Delegall, David Sr.,dec'd.
Forster, Jos.
Gibbons, Thos.
Goode, Jno.
Grier, Robt.
Jones, Noble W.
Leake, Richd.
McCall, Thos.
McCaule, Francis
McCredie, Andrew
McIntosh, Barbara
McIntosh, Lachlan
Maxwell, Wm.
Miller, Jos.
Montaigut, David

Moore, Wm.
Pray, Job
Pray, Jno.
Putnam, Henry
Rentz, Agnes
Rentz, Jno.
Shaw, Jonathan
Sheftall, Mordecai
Spalding, Jas.
Stephens, Wm.
Tattnall, Josiah
Wright, Saml.

Governor & Council
Minutes
May 10, 1790 - Dec. 16, 1790
Militia of Chatham Co.

Barnard, Robt.
Barnett, Wm.
Butler, Benj.
Butler, Meshack
Day, Jos.
Densler, Michael
Elfe, Thos.
Gibbons, Thos.
Gunn, Jas.
Hall, Jno.
Jones, Jas.
Lloyd, Edw.
McQueen, Jno.
Maxwell, Wm.
Montford, Robt.
Moore, Wm.
Roberts, Jos.
Shad, Solomon
Sheftall, Benj.
Shick, Frederic
Tatnall, Josiah
Taylor, Jno.
Thompson, Wm.
Welcher, Jos.
Young, Isaac

Deaths from the
Georgia Gazette
1790 through 1793

Beal, Mrs. Eleanor
Beggs, Alexdr.
Bell, David
Bourquin, Benedict
Bourquin, David
Butler, Jos.

Carragan, Elw.
Cecil, Leonard
Cohen, Moses
Cumming, Lawrence
Day, Maj. Jos.
Delany, Thos.
DeGlaubick, Baron
Demere, Raymond
Dorsey, Col.___?___
Dowies, Hugh
Elbert, Eliz.
Galache, Jas.
Germain, Michael
Gibbons, Mrs. Sarah
Greene, Geo. W.
Hanner, Nicholas
Herb, Frederick
Hendley, Geo.
Herson, Mrs. Herman
Hornby, Phillip
Huntzinger, Michael
Ingerfall, Jno.
Jones, Mrs. Anne
Karr, Peter
Lange, Jno. Peter
Leaver, Gabriel
Lee, Sol.
Lefils, Bernard
McCall, Eliza Henrietta
McCredie, Sarah
Macleod, Jno.
Martin, Wm.
Maxwell, Sally
Miller, Geo.
Miller, Jno. Phillip
Mills, Thos.
Montfort, Capt. Robt.
Montfort, Saml. B. R.
Oakman, Mrs. Mary
Oakman, Wm.
Orrick, Jno.
Owens, Mrs. Hannah
Pauls, Casper
Pechin, Peter
Polack, Abraham
Pray, Clarisa
Randolph, Richd.
Russell, Jane
Sheftall, Benj.
Simpson, Jno.
Stephens, Mrs. Margt.
Stone, Mrs. Susannah
Taylor, Jas.
Tuft, Sinnickson

Vanderlocht, Wm.
Ward, Wm.
Whitefield, Jas.

1790 Tax Digest:
Earliest surviving tax
digest of Chatham Co.

Abendanon, David
Abraham, a free negro
Abrahams, Abrah. &
    Isaac
Abrahams, Levy
Ackhard, Lewis
Adams, Edmund, est.
Adams, Elijah
Adams, Elisha
Adams, Jas.
Adams, Jno.
Adams, Nathan, Jr.
Adams, Nathl.
Addington, Henry
Adinal, Jas.
Ainsley, Benj.
Akins, Terry
Alexander, Chas., est.
Alexander, Jas.
Alger, Jas.
Allard, Lewis Nicholes
Allard, Mary
Allard, Peter
Allen, Geo.
Allen, Joshua
Allen, Wm.
Allen, Wm.
Allen, Wm.
Allison, Wm. B.
Alner, Jas.
Alsop, Geo.
Alter, Mary
Alter, Peter
Anciaux, Nicholas
Anciaux, Miss Eliza
Anciaux, Mrs. Lydia
Anderson, Adam
Anderson, Deb.
Anderson, Clement Wm.
Anderson, Douglas
Anderson, Geo. & Deb.
Anderson, Geo.
Anderson, Henry
Anderson, Jas.
Anderson, Jno.
Anderson, Jno

Anderson, Susannah
Antoine, Andrew
Antonio, Emanuel
Antonio, Jno.
Ariano, Peter
Arinandus, Casper
Armour, Jno.
Arnold & Simkins
Arnold & Tingley
Arnold, Jos.
Asbury, Jno.
Ash, Geo., est.
Ashton, Saml.
Asmus, Jno.
Asper, Michael
Asselin, Anthony
Atkerson, Geo.
Atsat, Jno.
Audebert, Jno.
Audibert, Jno. Baptist
Auga, Madame
Austin, Henry
Austin, Mary Ann, est.
Austin, Jas.
Avery, Frederick
Baas, Saml.
Baas, Saml.
Bache, N.
Bachler, Garton
Bachler, Jno.
Backet, Jno.
Badulet, Madam
Bagley, Israel
Baileu, Abner
Bailey, Dudley
Bailey, Ransford
Baillie, Geo.
Baillie, Harriet.
Baker, Jesse
Baker, Jos.
Baldwin, Ebenezer
Ball, Ezek.
Balthazer, Sarah
Baptist, Jean
Barber, Mrs.
Barnard, Jno. & Timothy
Barnard, Robt.
Barden, Wm.
Barden, Wm. Jr.
Barnard, Wm.
Barnes, ___
Barnet, Richd.
Barnet, Timothy
Barret & Co.

Barry, J. B.
Barry, Jas.
Barry, Jas. J.
Bartholomew, Geo.
Bassit, Abrah.
Baxter, Josiah
Baylor, Jno.
Baylor, Matthew
Beach, Adam
Beach, Nathl.
Beach, Thos.
Beattie, Eleanor
Beck, Jno.
Backford, Benj.
Becu, Abrah.
Beecroft, Saml.
Beggs, Thos.
Behn, Arthur
Belcher, Jas.
Belcher, Phillip
Belcher, Wm.
Bell, David, est.
Bell, Wm.
Ben, free negro
Benedix, Isaac
Bennett, ___
Benois, Lewis
Benson, Ben
Benton, E.
Berneviz, Wm.
Berry, Francis Hubert
Berry, Jos.
Bertrand, Lewis
Besinger, Peter
Bethune, Jas.
Bettison, David
Bexley, Jno.
Bishop, Madame
Bichon, Bernard
Bill, Avery
Bill, Every
Bird, Andrew
Birdsdale, Decker
Birky, Rudolph
Bishop, Seth
Bisset, Alexdr. est.
Blackstock, Jno. est.
Blanc, Jno.
Blasuis, Frederic
Blogg, Wm.
Blount, Hugh
Blount, Steph.
Boardman, Hill & Wms.
Bold, Benj.

Bollinger, Frederic
Bolton, Jno.
Bolton, Robt.
Boorom & Carpenter
Boorom, Isaac
Bostwick
Bostwick, Heyman
Boucher, Adrian
Boudon, ----
Bouquet, Pierre
Bourke, Jane
Bourquin, Benedict
Bourquin, David F.
Bourquin, Henry
Bourquin, Jane Judith
Bourquin, Jno.
Boutinat, Derivaus
Bowen, Ann
Bowen, Jas.
Bowen, Mary D.
Bowen, Oliver
Bowen, Saml. F.
Bowman, Jno.
Bowman, Jno.
Boyd, Chas.
Boyd, Jno.
Boyd, Susannah
Boyington, Joshua Jr.
Box, Eliz.
Box, Phillip
Box, Thos. R.
Box, Wm. G.
Boxwood, Jas.
Bradford, Wm.
Brady, Thos.
Brailsford, Jno. H.
Brickell, Jno.
Brisbane, Adam F.
Britton, Jno.
Britton, Steph.
Britton, Steph. Jr.
Brooks, Francis
Brower, Jno.
Brown, David
Brown, David
Brown, Franklin
Brown, Henry
Brown, Jas.
Brown, Richd.
Brown, Ruth
Brown, Mrs.
Brown, Mrs. Ruth
Brown, Thos.
Brown, Maj. Wm.

Brown, Wm.
Brownell, David
Brownhill, Thos.
Broyce, Jno. C.
Brunie, Thos.
Bryan, Andrew
Bryan, Fanny
Bryan, Jas., est.
Bryan, Jos.
Brydie, David
Bryson, Widow
Buchenau, widow
Buchhalter, Isaac
Buckhalter, Jesse
Buckhalter, Joshua
Buck, Jno.
Buckle, Margareth
Bull, Jno.
Bull, Serina
Bulloch, Jas.
Bulloch, Mary
Bulloch, Mary, est.
Bulloch, Priscilla
Bulloch, Wm. B.
Bunce, Wm.
Bunwitz, Wm.
Butler, Benj.
Butler, Jno.
Butler, Jos, est.
Butler, Jos.
Butler, Wm.
Burchill, Arthur
Burden, Richd. Ash.
Burges, ----
Burgois, Peter
Burke, Mrs.
Burke, Jno. est.
Burke, Dr. Michael
Burke, Thos.
Burkit, Jos.
Burkit, Jos.
Burn, Hugh
Burnett, Anthony
Burney, Andrew
Burney, Jno.
Burns, ----
Burnsides, Wm.
Cadmis, Abraham
Caig & Co.
Cain, Jos.
Caldwell & Ogelby
Caldwell, Jno.
Callaghan, Thos.
Callahan, Wm.

Camp, Wm.
Camp, Wm.
Campbell, Jno.
Campbell, McCartan, est.
Campbell, Peter
Campbell, Peter
Campbell, widow
Canavan, Andrew
Candlish, Alexdr.
Cant, Jno.
Capers, Gabriel
Capers, Morgan
Carlton, Jno.
Carpenter, ?
Carson, Jno.
Carter, Jno.
Carter, Patrick
Carswell, Edw.
Cashan, Jas.
Cattonet, Peter
Chadirac, Mons: Trust
Champaign, Nicholas
Chapman, Israel
Charon, Atmil
Chaurin, Wm.
Chavenet, Policarpe
Chew, Benj.
Childs, Wm.
Chisholm, Angus
Chisler, Danl.
Christie, Robt.
Church, Sylvanus
Clarendon, Mrs.
Clark, Est. of
Clarke, Jas.
Clarke, Jno.
Clarke, Jno.
Clarke, Jos.
Clarke, Lemuel
Clarke, Matthew
Clarke, Wm.
Clarkson, Wm.
Clay, Evans
Clay, Jos.
Clay, Ralph
Cleland, Jas. & Moses
Cleland, Jas. & Wm.
Cline, Abram
Cline, Jonathan
Clyatt, Jas.
Coale, Wm.
Cobbet, Eliz.
Cochran, ----
Coit, Jno.

Coit, Jno.
Cole, Jno.
Coleman, Harry
Coleman, Harry Jr.
Coleman, Levin
Coleman, Peter
Colley, Anderson
Collier, Benj.
Colisseaux, Peter
Columbus, Lewis
Compstock, Jno.
Connor, Bryan
Connor, Geo.
Connor, Simon
Cook, Danl. J.
Cook, Jas.
Cook, Wm.
Coolidge, ---
Cocsan, Peter
Cope, Adam
Cope, Chas.
Cope, Rosannah
Coppat, Aime
Coppe, Madam
Coquilion, Francis B.
Corbert, Jas.
Cornelieson, Jno. Allen
Cornelous, Jno.
Course, Mrs.
Courtenay, Jno.
Courvoisie, Francis
Cowan, Edw.
Cowling, Slaughter
Cox, Casper
Cox, Spence
Cox, Wm.
Cox, Wm.
Craft, D., est.
Crane, Matthew, est.
Crawdie, est. of
Crawford, Wm.
Creighton, E.
Creighton, Edw.
Crookshank, Patrick
Crapps, Jno., est.
Crowell, Ezra
Cruger, Nicholas
Cuddy, Geo.
Cummings, free barber
Cummings, Jno.
Cunes, Jacob
Cuningham, Alexdr.
Cunningham, Harry
Curient, Nicholas

Carnel, Thos.
Curry, Jno.
Cusack, Sarah
Cuthbert, Geo., est.
Cuthbert, Dr. Jas.
Cuthbert, Jas.
Cuthbert, Jos., est.
Cuthbert, Lewis
Cuthbert, Mrs. Penelope
Dacosta, Sarah
Dameron, Saml.
Daniel, Jno.
Daniel, Jno.
Darnel, Henry
Darnel, Wm.
Davidson, Wm.
Davies, Benj.'
Davies, Eliz.
Davies, Jno.
Davies, Jno.
Davies, Jno. M.
Davies, Jos.
Davies, Richd.
Davies, Sarah
Davies, Thos.
Davies, Wm.
Davies, Wm. Jno.
Davis, Francis
Davis, Peter
Davis, Wm.
Davis, Wm., est.
Dawson, Jno.
Dawson, Richd.
Dawson, Thos.
Dean, Steph.
Deane, Jos., est.
Deas, David, est.
deChapedelaine, Hyacinth
Lechenaus, Thos.
DeChesse', Aubert Jas.
DeChessee, the youngar
Delacaze, Jos.
Delacrois, Jean Francois
Lelarocque, Jane
Delarue, D.
Delavel, Jos.
Lelavel, Jos.
Deltose, Jno.
Deleion, David, est.
Delegal, Philip
Delvecque, Jno.
Delyon, Abrah.
Delyon, Abraham & wife
Dement, Absalom

Demere, Mrs. Mary
Demere, Raymond
Dennis, Nicholas Jos.
Dennis, Richd.
Densler, Henry
Densler, Henry
Densler, Michael
Densler, Philip
Deschmettaux, Madame
Devant, Eliz.
Devant, Thos.
Deveaux, Ann
Deveaux, Peter
Deveaux, Wm.
Deville, Jno.
Dews, Jno.
Dial, Saml.
Dick, Jno.
Dickinson, Jeremiah
Dickinson, Jno. D.
Diedrick, Nicholas
Dillon, Ann Mary
Dillon, Jno.
Dillon, Robt.
Divine, Jno.
Dixon, Jas.
Dixon, Wm.
Doddere, Saml.
Dodson, Jno.
Dodson, Wm.
Dollaghan, Thos.
Dolly, London
Dolly, Quash
Donaldson, Wm.
Doniphan, Gerard
Doorman, Hugh
Doors, Jas.
Dopson, Jos. R.
Dorrel, Thos.
Dougharty, Mrs. Warren
Dougharty, Margareth
Doughty, Simon
Dowell, Peter
Dowell, Peter, est.
Dowell, Thos.
Downs, Jeremiah
Doyle, Dennis
Loyle, Francis
Lrouillard, Andrew
D'Scheuber, I. H.
Ducla, Jno. Baptist
Ducla, Maria Louise
duCord, Bouyer
Duger, Hamson

Duke, Green
Dumoussy, Francis
Cuncan, Jas.
Cuncan, Jas.
Dunlap, Jos.
Dunneven, Jas.
Durden, Jesse
Durcis, Marie Magdalene
Durousseaux, Peter
Durr, Geo.
Durrah, Jno.
Easton, Edw.
Ehrhard, David, est.
Ehrhard, Jacob
Eimbeck, Mrs. Ann
Eirick, Cumba
Eirick, Jno.
Elkins, Jonas
Ellerbee, ---
Ellerbee, Edw.
Elliott, Steph.
Elliott, Wm.
Ellis, Edw.
Ellis, Henry
Ellis, Thos.
Ellis, Wm.
Ellis, Zachariah
Elon, Elisha
English, Benj.
English, Thos.
Enoe, Geo.
Eppinger, Geo.
Eppinger, Jas.
Eppinger, Matthew
Eppinger, Jno.
Eppinger, Jno. Jr.
Eppinger, Jno., est.
Ernst, Christina
Evans, Danl.
Evand, David
Evans, Saml.
Evans, Sarah
Evans, Wm. M.
Evarts, Fredrk.
Ewing, Wm.
Ewen, Wm., est.
Exley, Jno.
Fahm, Fredrk., est.
Faham, Jacob
Faries, Geo.
Farley, Jno., est.
Faulkner, Chas.
Fell, Isaac
Fernandez, a Spaniard

Files, Steph.
Fish, Elisha B.
Fisher, David
Fisher, Hendrick
Fisher, Henry
Fisher, Robt.
Fisher, Robt.
Fitzgerald, Edw.
Fitzpatrick, Jno.
Fleming, a negro
Flinn, Jno.
Flint, Tho.
Floyd, Richd.
Flyming, Mrs.
Flyming, Mary
Footman, Richd. S.
Ford, Chas.
Cord, Danl.
Ford, David
Forsyth, Benj.
Foulk, Saml.
Fourrer, Chas.
Fowler, Jno.
Fowler, Robt.
Fox, David
Fox, Richd., est.
Fowler, Saml.
Fowler, Saml.
Fowler, Sarah
Fowler, Thos.
Fox, Eliz.
Fox, Jno. est.
Fox, Josiah
Fox, Martha
Fox, Mary
Fox, Richd., est.
Fox, Wm.
Fox, Wm.
Frand, Steph.
Frannks, Isaac
Fraser, Robt.
Fraser, Dr.
Freeman, Joshua
French, Steph.
Fry, Jno. Newton
Fry, Mary
Fryer, Jno.
Fueller, Jacob
Fulford, Jas., est.
Gable, Jno.
Gaffney, Jas.
Gains, Jesse
Gairdner, Jas.
Galache, Jas.

Galacher, Js., est.
Galphin, Thos.
Gandorich, mulatto
Garbet, Geo.
Gardiner, Isaac
Gardiner, Jno.
Gardner, Danl.
Gardner, Elisha
Gardner, Jno.
Gardner, Thos.
Gardner, Wm.
Gaultier, Genevieve
Gay, Abraham
Gay, Abraham, est.
Gay, Theodore, est.
Gayet, Bertrant
Gerdine, Henry
Gerecken, Wm.
Germain, Michael
Geroud, Danl.
Geroud, Lewis
Gibbons, Ann
Gibbons, Barach
Gibbons, Hannah
Gibbons, Jno.
Gibbons, Jno. B.
Gibbons, Jos.
Gibbons, Thos.
Gibbons, Wm.
Gibbons, Wm. Jr.
Gibbons, est of Wm.
Gibbons, Wm. Jr.
Gibson, Danl.
Gibson, Danl.
Gibson, Sarah
Gibson, Mrs. Sarah
Gilbert, Mary, est.
Gilbert, Wm., est.
Giles, Ebenezer
Giles, Wm.
Gilmer, Peter
Gindrat, Jno.
Gines, Edw.
Givens, Jno., est.
Glass, Jno.
Glen, Jas.
Glen, Jno.
Glass, Jno.
Glover, Jno. G.
Gobert, Benj.
Gobert, Jos.
Godichaw, Jacques
Godwin, Catherine
Gordon, Ambrose
Gordon, Jno.

Gotear, Josiah
Goupy, Jno. Baptist
Graham, Elias
Grant, Mrs. Percival Ward
Grant, Alex'r.
Grant, Harry
Grant, Mrs. Nasan
Gray, Chloe
Gray, Jane, est.
Gray, Jno. T.
Gray, Jurdina
Green, Jno., est.
Greene, General, est.
Greene, Danl. Jno.
Greene, Wm.
Greenhow, Jas., est.
Greenwood, Wm. Jr.
Greer, Jno.
Greer, Mary
Greer, Robt.
Gregory, Ethelred
Gribben, Capt.
Gribben, Patrick
Griffin, Allen
Griffin, Matthew, est.
Griffith, Edw.
Griffith, Edw.
Griggs, Jane
Griner, Sol.
Grommet, Jno.
Guard, Jas.
Guenin, Mons.
Guerard, Robt. G.
Guerard, Wm.
Gugel, Christian
Gugel, Chris.
Gugel, Danl.
Gugel, David
Gugel, Joshua
Guillet, Michael
Guinovily, David Saml.
Gunn, Chris.
Gunn, Jas.
Guy, Geo. W.
Habersham, Alexdr.
Habersham, Jas.
Habersham, Jas. Jr.
Habersham, Jno.
Habersham, Jos.
Hackneys, Henry
Haigs, Geo.
Haist, Geo.
Haist, Harriet
Hale, Bradley
Hall, Mrs. Ann
Hall, Chris.

Hall, Danl.
Hall, Harvey
Hall, Willis
Hamblin, Elhannah
Hamilton, Ann
Hamilton, Arthur
Hamilton, Jno.
Hamilton, Thos.
Hammond, Joshua
Hammond, Elnathan
Hammond, Richd. & Nathl.
Hammond, Saml. & Mrs. Course
Hamson, Sarah
Haner, Nicholas
Harding, Steph. R.
Harding, Wm.
Hardwick, Geo.
Hardy, Thos.
Harn, Jno.
Harper, Thos.
Harper, Wm.
Harral, Geo.
Harris, Cath.
Harris, Chas.
Harris, Francis H.,est.
Harris, Jno. Geo.
Harris, Sarah
Harris, Wm.
Harrison, Mary
Harrison, Jno.
Harrison, Thos.
Harry, free negro
Hartfield, Asa
Hartridge, Jno. E.
Hartstein, Joachim
Harvey, Arnold, est.
Harvey, Robt.
Hasinack, ----
Hathaway, Jno.
Haupt, Jno., est.
Havens, Philetus
Havens, Wm.
Hawthorn, Jos.
Hawthorn, Nathl.
Hawthorn, Nathl,, Jr.
Hayhart, Jacob
Heathcote, Wm.
Heavy, Dennis
Heineman, Jno.
Heisler, Geo.
Heisler, Jno.
Hamphill, Jas.
Henck, Henry
Henderson, widow of Jas.

Henlay, Ann
Henley, Geo.
Henry, Lyon
Herb, Frederic
Herb, Frederic, est
Herb, Jno.
Herb, Ursula
Herback, widow of Casper
Herbach, Henry
Herbach, Jacob
Herbach, Michael
Herbach, widow of Michael
Herbach, Susannah
Heron, Jas.
Herson, Herman
Hickman, Furney
Hicks, Anchelm B.
Higgins, Ichabod
Hilbert, Conrad
Hill, Jos.
Hill, Matthew
Hill, Richd.
Hill, Saml.
Hillary, Geo.
Hill, Thos.
Hirshman, Jno.
Hirshman, Susannah
Hobbs, Jno.
Hobkirk, Wm.
Hodge, ---
Hodgkins, Jno.
Hofman, Martha
Hogg, Eunice
Hogg, Thos.
Holland, Jno.
Holman, ---
Holmes, Jno.
Holtzendorf, Jno. L.
Holzendorf, Wm.
Hood, Jno.
Hopkins, Jason
Hornsby, Chas.
Horsburgh, Jno.
Hoskins, Ceaser (dead)
Hoskins, David
Houghton, Saml.
Houstoun, Lady Ann
Houstoun, Doll
Houstoun, Sir Geo., est.
Houstoun, Hannah
Houstoun, Jas., est.
Houstoun, Jno., est.
Houstoun, Lucy
Houstoun, Sir Patrick, est.

Houstoun, Robt.
Hover, Conrad
Howard, Benj.
Howe, ---
Howell, Jno.
Hoxy, Asa
Hubbard, Jno.
Hughes, Wm.
Hughes, Wm.
Hughes, Wm.
Hughes, Wm.
Huguenet, Louis
Huguenin, David
Hunlook, ----
Hunter, Ephriam
Hunter, Wm.
Idler, Jacob
Ihley, Philip
Ihley, Saml.
Ingersoll, Jno.
Inglis, Wm.
Ingram, Jno. K.
Iting, Frederic
Innes, Danl.
Jack, Archib.
Jackson, Ebenezer
Jackson, Jas.
Jackson, Montague
Jackson, Dr. Robt. D.
Jackson, Roger
Jacobs, Jacob, est.
Jacobs, Jacob, est.
James, E.
Jamison, Jno.
Jamison, Jno.
Janet, free negro
Jaudon, Thos. D.
Jem, free negro
Jervais, Mrs.Anson Ward
Jenkins, Mary
Jenkins, Susannah
John, the wagoner (dead)
Johnson, Alexdr.
Johnson, Isham
Johnson, Jas.
Johnson, Jesse
Johnson, Usual
Johnston, Robertson
Johnston, Alexdr.
Johnston, Andrew
Johnston, Andrew W.
Johnston, Danl.
Johnston, David
Johnston, Eliz.

Johnston, Jas.
Johnston, Jas.
Johnston, Jas. Jr.
Johnston, Jno.
Johnston, Matthew
Johnston, Nicholas
Johnston, Thos.
Joiner, Jno.
Jones, Chas.
Jones, Edw.
Jones, Ceo.
Jones, Henry B.
Jones, Henry C.
Jones, Inigo
Jones, Noble
Jones, Noble W.
Jones, Obadiah
Jones, Wm.
Jordan, Robt.
Joseph, Jno.
Joseph, Jno.
Judah, Mrs.
Kaehler, Jno.
Kain, David
Kane, Mrs.
Kapper, Jacob
Keal, Jno.
Keal, Martha
Kean, Mrs. Susan
Keating, Richd.
Keller, Geo., est.
Kellogg, Jos.
Kelsall, Ann & Jno.
Kenedy, Henry
Ker, Wm.
Ketler, Geo.
Kettles, Jno. L.
Kieffer, Barbara
Kieffer, David
Kieffer, Frederic
Kieffer, Henry
Kinder, Eliz.
King, Wm.
Kingsley, Saml.
Kinsey, Valentine
Kirby, Wm.
Kirk, Jas.
Kirk, Thos.
Klennett, ----
Kollock, Lemuel
Kraft, David, est.
Krafz, Jno. Conrad
Krieger, Jno.
Lecase, Behie

Lachner, Frederic
Laffitte, Mrs.
Laffitte, Peter Saml.
Laffitte, Pierre Thos.
Lagarde, Peter
Lamb, Geo.
Lamb, Wm.
Lambeth, Jas.
Lang, Peter, est.
Lange, Ann Mary Gertrude
Lang, Jno. Peter, est.
Lange, Wm. Henry
Langley, Benj.
Langley, Eliz.
Langley, Nathl.
Langley, Jno.
Langlois, Jacques
Langlois, Jas.
Larmarre, Jacques Lucien
Laroche, Isaac, est.
Lartieque, Gerard
Lavinder, Benj.
Lavender, Benj.
Lavender, Wm.
Laville, Mons'.
Lawrence, Richd. M.
Lawrence, Saml.
Lawrence, Henry
Lawrence, Jas. T.
Lawrence, J. T. &
  Jno. G. Glover
Lawson, Jno.
Lawton, Jos.
Lawton, Jos. J.
Leach, Mrs.
Leach, Eliz.
Lears, Jno.
Leaver, Mary
LeFils, Bernard, est.
Lehalf, Harris
Leion, David
Leion, Hannah
Leqous, ----
Leroy, Francis
Lett, Jno. T.
Leavit, Jos.
Levecque, Pierre Louis
Levett, Francis
Lewden, Wm.
Lewis, Mrs.
Lewis, Nathl.
Lewis, Steph., est.
Lewis, Wm.
Lewis, Wm.

Lewis, Winslow
L'homaca, Antoinette
L'homaca, Eliz.
L'homaca, Lacques
L'homaca, Reine Francois
Lillibridge, Hampton
Lillibridge, Jno.
Limbert, Wm.
Lindsey, Chas.
Lloyd, Benj.
Lloyd, Edw.
Lloyd, Rebecca, est.
Lloyd, Mary's children
Lloyd, Josiah
Lloyd, Thos.
Lloyd, Thos., est.
Long, Frederic
Long, Jno.
Long, Matthew
Longworth, Jas.
Longworth, Jos.
Lord, Geo.
Love, Dr. John
Lowther, Chas.
Lowther, Jno.
Loyer, Abrian
Lousol, Peter
Lucena, Jas.
Lucena, Lucas
Lyle, Robt.
Lyon, Grace
Lyon, Henry
Lyon, Jno.
Lyon, Jno.
Mabry, Parham
McAllister, Matthew
McAllister, Richd.
McCabe, Jas.
McCall, Jno.
McCall, Thos.
McCaskill, Donald
McCaule, Mrs. Eliza
McCollack, Jno.
McConky, Jas.
McCredie, Andrew
McCredie, Mary
McCurdy, Hugh
McDonaldson, Jos.
McFadzen, Jno.
McGarver, Danl.
Machin, Jos.
Machogin, Jno.
McIntosh, Geo
McIntosh, Geo.

McIntosh, Hampden
McIntosh, Henry
McIntosh, Jas.
McIntosh, Lachlin
McKain, Alexdr.
McKeane, Robt.
McKinnon, Jno.
McKinzie, Patrick
McKnight, Mary Ann
McLain, Cath.
McLean, Andrew
McLeod, Donald
McLeod, Norman
McLeod, Roderick &
    Norman
McLeod, Wm.
McMahon, Jno.
McNeily, Danl.
McQueen, Alexdr.
McQueen, Ann
McQueen, Betty
Macray, Jno.
Madden, Peter
Mall, Margareth
Mallory, Francis
Magiapan, Antonio
Manners, David
Manning, Wm.
Mirault, Pierre
Marie, Jos.
Marien, Renault
Martin, Jno.
Martin, Murdoch
Martin, Peter
Mason, Thos.
Mathers, Wm. H.
Mathews, Francis
Matthews, Henry
Matthews, Wm.
Maxwell, Jno.
Mayer, Serenus
Meeck, Edw.
Meeck, Josiah & Edw.
Meers, Richd.
Meigs, Jonathan
Mains, Robt.
Main, Wm.
Melton, Mr.
Melvin, Martha
Merrillis, Jas., est.
Marritt, Mrs.
Middleton, David
Middleton, Wm., est.
Miles, Wm., est.

Milledge, Jno.
Milledge, Phillip
Millen, Geo.
Millen, Godlieb
Millen, Jno.
Miller, Andrew, dec'd.
Miller, Danl.
Miller, David
Miller, Francis
Miller, Jacob
Miller, Jno.
Miller, Jno.
Miller, Jos.
Miller, Michael
Miller, Morris
Miller, Nicholas
Miller, Peter
Miller, Phillip &
    Margaret Young
Miller, Phineas
Miller, Richd.
Miller, Thos.
Miller, Thos.
Milligan, Jno.
Millikin, Thos.
Mills, Thos.
Mills, Wm.
Mills, Wm.
Mills, Wm.
Milton, Thos. S.
Minis, Abigail
Minis, Abraham
Minis, Leah
Minis, Phillip
Minzey, Shadrack
Miraust, Pierre
Mitchell, Alexdr.
Mitchell, David Brydie
Mitchell, Robt.
Mitchell, Thos., est.
Monford, Jas.
Mongin, Jno. D.
Montaigut, David, est.
Montfort, Robt., est.
Montgomery, Bartlet
Montmollin, I. S.
Moor, Jas., est.
Moore, Jno.
Moore, Ann
Moore, Burges
Moore, Jno.
Moore, Susannah
Moore, Susannah
Moore, Wm.

Moore, Wm.
Moore, Wm.
Moore, Wm., Jr.
Mordecai, Saml.
Morecock, Wm.
Morel, Benj.
Morel, Jno.
Morel, Peter Henry
Morgan, Ann
Morgan, Jos.
Morse, Danl. Paisley
Mortimer, Mrs.
Moss, Dr. Geo.
Moseman, Jas.
Mossman, Jas.
Motley, Jno.
Mott, Zephaniah
Motta, Emanuel
Motta, Saunders
Motz, Matthew
Mowat, Danl.
Moxtix, Wm.
Moxham, Jno.
Muckinfas, Jos., est.
Mullady, Robt.
Munns, Chas.
Munn, Chas.
Murdoch, Robt. F.
Murphey, Humphrey
Murphey, Jno.
Murphey, Wm.
Murray, Chas.
Murray, Lucy
Muter, Jas., est.
Myers, Davis
Myers, Geo.
Myers, Jas.
Myers, Jno.
Myers, Thos.
Nelson, Geo.
Nelson, Jas.
Nesler, Adam
Netherclift, Alex.
Netherclift, Ann
Netherclift, Dolly
Netherclift, Mary
Netherclift, Thos.
Nevills, Jacob
Newdigate, Penelope
Newell, Cunningham
Newel, Rebecca
Neewel, Saml.
Newton, Philip
Neye, Thos.

Neyle, Sampson
Neyle, Wm.
Nicholls, Geo. W.
Nickler, Phillip
Nicolson, Jno. Paul
Nightengale, Jno. C.
Niles, Ephriam
Nixon, ---
Nixon, Rev. Wm.
Noel, Jno. Y.
Norden, Lyon
Norment, Wm.
Northrop, Willis
Norton, Jos.
Norton, Thos.
Norvil, Geo.
Nottage, Thos.
Nowlin, Dennis
Nunez, Sue
Nungazer, Geo.
Nungazer, Henry est.
Oakman, Wm., est.
Oates, Jno. Peter
Obar, with Winslow
Odingsells, Chas.
O'duhigg, Francis
Ogies, Madam
Oglivie, Alexdr.
Oliver, Jas.
Olney, Henry
Oronoke, a free negro
Orr, Abraham
Osmond, Lewis
Ostry, Febeau
Overstreet, Jas.
Owens, Owen
Page, Jos.
Paisley, Jno.
Palmer, Mary
Palmer, Thos.
Parler, Ann
Parker, Ann, est.
Parker, Ebenezer
Parker, Timothy
Parker, Wm.
Parseille, Chas.
Parsons, Thos.
Patterson, Chas.
Patterson, widow of Henry
Patterson, Mary T.
Patterson, Wm.
Paulidge, Geo.
Pear, Mrs. Ann
Pedero, Thos.

Pedero, Wm.
Pelot, Francis
Pemberton, Allen
Pendleton, Danl.
Pendleton, Sol., est.
Pendleton, Nathl.
Penman, E.
Penman, Edw.
Penrose, Jno.
Pepper, ---
Peter, Pierre
Phillips, Chas.
Phillip, Jno.
Pierce, Ann
Pierce, Levy
Pierce, Somerset
Pigot, Jno.
Pindar, Wm.
Pindar, Wm., Jr.
Pinson, Valentine
Pitt, Thos.
Plains, Jas.
Planter, Jno.
Plowden, Wm.
Plowright, Robt.
Plumer, Ezra
Porcher, Paul, est.
Port, Jas.
Port, Wm.
Porterfield, Wm.
Posey, Wm.
Postell, Billy
Postell, Jos.
Poullin, Jno.
Powers, Wm.
Prescott, Jos.
Prevost, Madame
Prevost, Wm.
Price, Howell
Price, Peter
Prichard, Jas.
Prichard, Robt.
Primrose, Edw.
Pryce, Chas., est.
Pugh, David Guilford
Pugh, Willoughby
Putnam, Benj.
Putnam, Henry
Puria, Peter
Purnell, ----,
Rabeilliard, Jno. Francis
Radiques, Chas.
Rae, Patrick
Rahn, Jos.

Ralston, Geo.
Rambo, Madame
Randolph, Jno. F.
Randolph, Steph.
Rankin, Mrs.
Rasco, Jas.
Read, Geo., P.
Read, Jacob
Read, Jas. B.
Read, Wm.
Reddick, Catherine
Reddick, Jacob
Reddick, Casper
Reddick, Salome
Reed, Achilles
Reed, Charity
Reed, Jacob
Reese, Enoch Jr.
Reid, Jno.
Beigne, Peter
Remshard, Danl.
Renshaw, Christina
Renshaw, Wm.
Rentz, Jno.
Renzes, Jno.
Repon, Bernard
Revella, Peter
Rhodes, Benj.
Rhodes, Jno.
Rhodes, Jno.
Rhodes, Thos.
Rice, Thos.
Rich, Peter
Richards, Barbara
Richards, Jno.
Richardson, Mrs.
Richards, Jno. Hart
Richardson, Burrell
Richardson, Wm.
Riley, Jno., est.
Ring, Ann Margaret
Ring, Chris., est.
Ritter, Geo.
Ritter, Matthew
Ritter, Michael
Ritter, Peter
Robert, Peter
Roberts, Ezekiel B.
Roberts, Henrietta
Roberts, Jabez.
Roberts, Jas.
Roberts, Jas.
Roberts, Jos.
Roberts, Peter

Roberts, Peter
Roberts, Richeyson, est.
Robertson, Geo.
Robertson, Jas.
Robertson, Jno.
Robertson, Thos.
Robinson, Jno.
Robinson, Thos.
Robinson, Wm.
Rogers, Matthew
Rogers, Moses
Rogerson, Richd.
Roles, Wm.
Roma, Francis
Ross, Cudjo
Ross, Hugh
Ross, Jno.
Ross, Robt.
Ross, Mrs. Susannah
Rountree, Wm.
Rowell, Henry
Rush, Burrows
Russell, Jacob
Ryan, Phillip, Jr.
Sables, Wm.
Sainerie, Francis
St. Hubert, Theresa
St. Marc, Latoison
Salfner, Matthew
Sandidge, David
Sands, Ray
Sargent, Saml. G.
Saucy, Gabriel
Saucy, Joachim
Saunders, Jno.
Saunders, Jno.
Saunders, Mary
Savage, Geo.
Schermerhorn, Peter &
    Cornelius
Scheuber, Justus H.
Schmerber, Jas.
Schweighofer, Thos.
Schweinitz, Jans Christian
Scot, Philip
Scott, ---
Scott, Gavin
Scott, Geo.
Scott, Hugh
Scott, Phillip
Scranton, Jas.
Scranton, Jno. G.
Screven, Chas. O.
Scrimsger, Chas.

Screven, Jno. Sr.
Screven, Jno., Jr.
Scull, Danl.
Seaman, Gideon
Sears, Willard
Searson, Jno. R.
Segar, Claude
Segar, Jos.
Segar, Lewis
Segar, Prosper
Seymour, Gurdon J.
Shad, Sol.
Shaffer, Balthasar
Shaffer, Wm.
Shandley, Thos.
Shaw, Geo.
Shaw, Jas.
Shaw, Jno.
Shaw, Jno.
Shaw, Jno. R.
Shaw, Wm.
Shearman, Zohett
Sheftall, Abr.
Sheftall, Esther
Sheftall, Mrs. Frances
Sheftall, Levi
Sheftall, Mordecai, est.
Sheftall, Moses
Sheftall, Perla
Sheftall, Sarah
Sheftall, Sarah
Sheftall, Sheftall
Sheridan, Owen
Sherman, Danl.
Sherman, Jared
Shick, Geo.
Shick, Frederick
Shick, Jno., Jr.
Shick, Jno. Sr., est.
Shick, Jos., est.
Shick, Peter
Simmons, Jno.
Simons, Moses
Simons, Saul
Simpson, Eliz., est.
Simpson, Green
Simpson, Jas.
Simpson, Jas.
Simpson, Jno.
Sims, ---
Sinclair, Robt.
Sinkins, Arnold
Simkins, Arnold
Skelly, Saml.
Sketo, Jno.

Sleet, Jas.
Smart, Eliz.
Smith, ---
Smith, Archib.
Smith, Benj.
Smith, Chas.
Smith, David
Smith, Danoel
Smith, Eliz.
Smith, Frederic
Smith, Geo.
Smith, Jas.
Smith, Jas.
Smith, Jno.
Smith, Jno. C.
Smith, Sol.
Smith, Steph.
Smith, Thos.
Smith, Thos., Jr.
Smith, Thos.
Smith, Wm.
Smith, Wm.
Smithers, Betty
Snider, Andrew
Snider, Phillip
Snider, Jacob
Sody, Mary & Jane
    Delarrocque
Sommers, Wm.
Speirs, Polly
Spencer, Geo. B.
Spencer, Jabez., dead
Spencer, Jos.
Spencer, Jos. W.
Spencer, Wm. Henry
Squires, David
Stafford, Edw.
Standley, Jno.
Stanley, Michael
Starr, Wm.
Stateham, Robt.
Steadman, Wm.
Stebbins, Clement
Stebbins, Edw. & Clement
Stebbins, Rebecca
Steel, Jos.
Steele, Geo.
Stephen, free negro
Stephens, Wm.
Steward, Wm.
Stewart, Allen
Stewart, Peter
Stewart, Wm.
Stiles, Saml.

Stirk, Saml., est.
Stiles, Richd. M.
S ocks, Saml.
Stokes, Jas.
Stokes, Archibald
Stone, Mrs.
Stone, Ransom
Stone, Richd.
Storie, Jno.
Story, Thos.
Stouff, Isidore
Strange, Owen
Street, Jno.
Stroball, Abrah.
Strohacker, Eliz.
Struthers, Wm.
Stuart, Ann
Stuerman, Henry
Sturivant, Nathl.
Sturtivant, est.
Sturtivant, Nathl.
Sturtivant, Nathl.
Sturtivant, S.
Stutts, Allen
Stutz, Jos.
Stutz, Michael, est.
Suder, Jno.
Suder, Peter
Suder, Peter Jr.
Swarbreck, Edw.
Sykes, Wm.
Taque, Doctor
Tash, Jno.
Tattnall, Josiah
Tauser, Jno.
Taylor, Abraham
Taylor, Charlotte P.
Taylor, Geo.
Taylor, Eliz.
Taylor, Geo.
Taylor, Jno.
Taylor, Wm.
Tebeau, Jno.
Telfair, Edw.
Temple, Jas.
Terrien, Mrs.
Tetard, Benj.
Theis, Jacob
Theis, Jacob, Jr.
Thomas, Jos.
Thomas, Jos.
Thompson, Jas.
Thompson, Jno.
Thompson, Sarah

Thompson, Tabetty
Thompson, Jas.
Thornton, Elam
Throop, Geo.
Tice, Mary
Tichenor, Isaac
Tillinghast, Stukely
Timrod, Susannah
Tingley, Otis
Tiot, Chas.
Tippen, Jos.
Tippin, Benj.
Tippin, Jos.
Tobler, Ulrich
Todd, Jno.
Tondee, Chas.
Toussaint, Jean Baptiste
Trefeten, Benj.
Towers, Asaph, est.
Townshend,---
Townshend, Thos.
Townshend, Thos.
Trammel, Elisha
Tranfield, Mary, est.
Tranfield, Sarah
Treutlin, Frederick
Trevor, Jno.
Tribble, Mrs.
Trinquart, Lewis
Troupe, Geo.
Truchet, Chas.
Trushet, Chas.
Tucker, Ann
Tucker, Jas.
Tunro, A. & Wm.
Turnbull, Andrew
Turnbull, Mrs. Mary
Turnbull, Nicholl
Turner, ----
Turner, Jno.
Turner, Lewis
Turner, Richd.
Ulmer, Phillip
Ulmer, Wm.
Underwood, Wm.
Unselt, Barbara
Usher, Jno.
Usher, Richd.
Vallotton, Benj.
Vallotton, David, est.
Vallotton, Jeremiah
Vallotton, Jeremiah O.
Vallotton, Moses
Vallotton, Paul J.

Vann, Lovey
Vann, Wm.
Vasteen, Jeremiah
Venables, Wm.
Venable, Wm.
Verdery, Peter
Vergnin, Chas.
Verriere, Paul
Vickers, Saml., est.
Walch, Edmund
Waldburger, Mrs. C.
Waldburger, Jno. B.
Waldhouer, Jacob C.
Walker, ---
Walker, Wm.
Wall, Benj.
Wall, Jno.
Wall, Richd.
Wall, Billy
Wall, Saml.
Wall, Saml.
Wallace, Jas.
Wallace, Jno.
Wallace, Wm.
Waller, Saml.
Walters, Wm.
Wambersie, Emanuel
Ward, Jno. Peter
Ward, Richd.
Ward, Riley
Washington, David M.
Waters, Jno.
Waters, Jno.
Waters, Peter
Waters, Saml.
Waters, Wm.
Watlington, Eliz.
Watson, Jas.
Watson, Jas. T.
Watt, Alexdr.
Watts, Robt.
Watts, Robt.
Wayne, Eliz.
Wayne, Richd., Jr.
Wayne, Richd. & Eliz.
Webb, Jno. (a minor)
Webb, Jno.
Webley, Benj.
Welsch, Andrew
Welscher, Jos.
Weston, Job
Weyrich, Jno.
White, ----
White, Edw.

White, Eusebius
White, Jno. Y.
Whitefield, Adam
Whitefield, Eliz.
Whitefield, Jas., est
Whitefield, Jas., est.
Whitefield, Richd.
Whitefield, Saml.
Whiteford, Saml.
Whiteside, ---
Whitley, Jno.
Whitney, Eli
Whittendell, Jno.
Whyche, Geo.
Whyche, Jno., est.
Wilkins, Ann
Wilkins, Camillus
Wilkins, Obadiah
Wilkins, Saml. & Ann
Wilkinson, Jno. B.
Wilkinson, Jos.
Williams, Henry
Williams, Jas.
Williams, Jno.
Williams, Jno.
Williams, Jno.
Williams, Rosannah
Williams, Steph., est.
Williams, Steph. S.
Williams, Thos. F.
Williams, Eliz.
Williamson, Henry C.
Williamson, Jno. G.
Willy, Jas.
Wilson, ---
Wilson, Alexdr.
Wilson, Benj.
Wilson, Delphia
Wilson, Goodwin
Wilson, Jas.
Wilson, Jno., est.
Wilson, Jno.
Wilson, Jno.
Wilson, Jno., est.
Wilson, Wm.
Wilson, Wm.
Wilson, Wm.
Wilson, Wm.
Winn, Bannister
Winn, Thos.
Winslow, Elisha
Winter, Richd.
Wiseman, Jos.
Whitehard, Sarah

Wood, Cath.
Wood, Jas.
Woodbridge, Thos. R.
Woodhouse, Geo.
Woodbridge, Robt. & Geo.
Woodbridge, Robt.
Woodbridhe, Robt.
Woodruff, Geo.
Woods, Jno.
Woods, Margaret
Woodward, Wm.
Woolhopter, Phillip
Woolf, Jacob
Wright, Asabel, est.
Wright, Barbara
Wright, Edw.
Wright, Jno.
Wright, Jno.
Wright, Sarah
Wright, Wm.
Wright, Wm.
Wright, Wm.
Wright, Wm.
Wyld, Cleavers D.
Wyld, Jno.
Wylly, Jas.
Wylly, Jas.
Wylly, Mrs. Mary
Wylly, Richd.
Wylly, Thos.
Wylly, Wm., est.
Yonge, Christiana
Young, Eliz.
Young, Isaac
Young, Jas. B.
Young, Margaret
Young, Phillip
Young, Sophia
Young, Thos., est.
Young, Thos. & Eliz.
Yvonnet, Gabriel
Zane, Jno.

COLUMBIA COUNTY

Established from Richmond County, a part of Columbia County was set off to Warren County, 1793 and a
part to McDuffie County in 1870.

The county seat is Appling, Georgia. Records of
inhabitants of Columbia Co. may be found in Richmond
County prior to 1790.

Georgia's Quaker settlement at Wrightsboro, Ga.
fell into Columbia Co. when the county was taken from
Richmond Co.

The first Baptist Church headed by the famous Dr.
Marshall also came into Columbia Co. from Richmond Co.

Headrights and Bounty Grants: 1790 - 1795

Beckelow, Frederick
Bennett, Ann
Boyd, Saml.
Brown, Frederick
Brownson, Reuben
Bryant, Wm. Sr.
Candler, Henry
Carr, Thos.
Chandler, Henry
Cornelison, Jno.
Cox, Henry
Crawford, Anderson
Darcey, Jno.
Darcey, Jos.
Davis, Clementine
Davis, Kehaze
Eads, Jno.
Ethemton, Wm.
Evans, Jos.
Failey, Thos.
Fee, Jno.
Ferr, Ignatius
Few, Ignatius
Fortune, Wm.
Fuller, Joshua
Gardner, Wm.

Graves, Humphrey
Greer, Robt.
Harrison, Mary
Harville, Jos.
Hillyer, Jas.
Hunter, Jane
Hutchinson, Jos.
Hyler, Jas.
Jenkins, Edmund B.
Johnston, Wm.
Jones, Thos.
Marshall, Jno.
Marshall, Levy
Matthews, Meshack
McDonald, Wm.
McKinley, Jos.
Moore, Jas.
Moore, Mordecai
Nelson, Robt. (heirs of)
Offutt, Lettice
Oliver, Jno.
Pace, Wm.
Parham, Peter
Pearcy, Blake
Pearrie, Jas

Perryman, David
Phelan, Thos.
Powell, Lecretary
Powell, Rachel
Prewitt, Levi
Ray, Jos.
Renolds, Robt.
Rotton, Jno.
Samuel, Edmund
Seay, Wm.
Showers, Jno.
Sidwell, David
Simms, Jas.
Sims, Wm.
Smith, Francis
Smith, Jacob
Smith, Jas.
Southerland, Jno.
Spalding, Henry
Stewart, Ann
Stith, Wm. Jr.
Stone, Jno.
Strength, Jno.
Stubbs, Jos.
Sullivan, Owen
Sullivan, Wm.
Tapley, Arven
Taylor, Henry
Templeton, Thos.
Tindill, Jno.
Todd, Wm.
Travis, Thos.
Vaughan, Alex
Wagoner, Geo.
Wagoner, Henry
Walton, Wm.
Wright, Johnson
Young, Geo.

Columbia County offi-
cers appointed:
  Dec. 10, 1790
Crawford, Anderson
Crawford, Peter
Gardner, Lewis
Jinkins, Edmund B.
Marshall, Danl.
Pearre, Jno.
Walton, Jno.

Justices of Inferior
Court appointed Dec.11,
1790:
Elam, Daniel

Harris, Nathan
Haynes, Thos.
McNeil, Jas. (1791)
Sims, Jas.
Wilson, Perry

Justices of Peace
appointed Dec., 1790:
Andrew, Benj.
Booker, Wm.
Crawford, Peter
Ellis, Sol.
Fleming, Jas.
Forster, Jno.
Hamilton, Jas.
Hamilton, Thos.
Howard, Rhesa
Johnston, Abrah.
Kennon, Wm.
Lawson, Jno.
Moore, Jno.
Robertson, David
Tankersly, Jno.
Travis, Wm.
Wright, Abednigo

Justices of Peace
1791 - 1792
Allen, Robt.
Appling, Jno.
Barnes, Lewis
Bennion, Wm. Sr.
Booker, Eideon
Bugg, Sherwood
Collier, Thos.
Cobb, Howell
Crawford, Anderson
Crawford, Chas.
Crawford, Peter
Drane, Walter
Elam, Danl.
Few, Ignatius
Few, Wm. Jr.
Foster, Jno.
Goodwin, Peter
Hamilton, Jas.
Hamilton, Thos.
Hayes, Andrew
Haynes, Thos.
Hatcher, Jno.
Howard, Rhesa
Hunt, Fitzmorris
Johnston, Abrah.
Jones, Adam

Jones, Saml.
McFarland, Jas.
McNeil, Jas.
Mabrey, Joel
Malone, Peter
Marbury, Horatis
Marshall, Levi
Marshall, Moses
Maxwell, David
Meriwether, Nicholas
Moore, Thos.
Napier, Thos.
Randolph, Robt.
Rees, Ben
Simms, Jas.
Stith, Jno.
Tankersly, Jno.
Thomas, Wm.
Thorn, Merrimon
Walton, Jno.
White, Richd. F.
White, Thos.
Wilson, Peter

Militia officers Jan. 1791 from Southern Centinal & Universal Gazette:

Batley, Jas.
Bledsoe, Peachey
Booker, Jno.
Booker, Wm. F.
Brady, Saml.
Bruce, Jno.
Burnett, Jno.
Cobb, Jno.
Collins, Jno.
Doughety, Neal
Douther, Wm.
Duncan, Matthew
Few, Wm.
Few, Wm. Jr.
Fryer, Hayden
Harrison, Clem King
Harrison, Gad. W.
Hatcher, Jno.
Hays, Andrew
Hunt, Fitz M.
Lamas, Jas.
Lamkin, Jno.
Lawson, Jno.
Jenkins, Edw. B.
Jones, Thos.

Marbury, Horatio
Meriwether, Nicholas
Monk, Jno.
Offutt, Jesse
Pace, Doldzil
Rees, Benj.
Vann, Edw.
Sanders, Jesse
Sanders, Yancey
Shackleford, Jno.
Steel, Sampson
Sturgis, Thos.
Tindall, Booker
Travis, Jno.
White, Richd. P.
Williams, Jno.

Wills 1790 - 1793 from Will Book "A"

Abbott, Joel
Aldridge, Nicholas
Aldridge, Rebbekah
Aldridge, Saml.
Allen, Andrew
Appling, Martha
Armor, Jas.
Bain, Jno.
Beall, Zebedee
Bennett, Jno.
Butler, Benj.
Caldwell, Jas.
Coldwell, Jane
Crawford, Peter
Credille, Thos.
Culbreath, Jane
Culbreath, Peter
Divine, Jas.
Dixon, Jno.
Dorsett, Eleanor
Dorsett, Jno.
Dunn, Waters
Few, Ann
Few, Wm.
Griffin, Jeremiah
Gunby, Wm.
Hay, Andrew
Haynes, Thos.
Hoofe, Wm.
Horne, Jesse
Horne, Persilla
Johns, Eliz.
Johns, Jno.
Kendrick, Jno.

Lacy, Jane
Lacy, Jno.
Lamkin, Jas.
Lamkin, Winifret
Langston, Jno.
Langston, Saml.
Linn, Anne
Linn, Chas.
Linn, Geo.
McNeil, J.
Marshall, Danl.
Marshall, Jos.
Morton, Jos.
Morton, Mary Ann
Ramsey, Hannah
Ramsey, Jas.
Ray, Nancy
Roberts, Nathan
Ross, Ann
Ross, Edw.
Ross, Jas.
Shackleford, Jno.
Smith, Ebenezer
Smith, Jno.
Smith, Rebekah
Smith, Wm.
Stanford, Jonathan
Stanford, Nelle
Stubblefield, Margaret
Stubblefield, Peter
Taylor, Ann
Walker, Elisha
Wright, Albert

Militia, Capt. Foster's
Company, March, 1793:

Austin, Jno.
Beckham, Dempsey
Beckham, Young
Backsted, Israel
Bell, Wm.
Boyd, Jno.
Boyd, Nicodemus
Bradbury, Jas.
Broughs, Jas.
Brown, Edw.
Bugg, Jno.
Burk, Edw.
Burroughs, Bennett
Caldwell, Jas.
Caldwell, Jno.
Caldwell, Paul
Clyatt, Isaac

Collier, Jno.
Cone, Jno.
Cone, Middleton
Cone, Saml.
Cone, Wm.
Cousins, Jas.
Crawford, Jno.
Downs, Ambrose
Downs, Richd.
Evans, Jno.
Ford, David
Foster, Jno.
Gardner, Alexdr.
Garnett, Jas.
Garnett, Jno.
Germany, Jas.
Glover, Jesse
Grantham, David
Griffin, Abel
Griffin, Asa
Griffin, Lewis
Griffin, Rowland
Griffin, Thos.
Hanson, Thos.
Hearill, Reubin
Hines, Robt.
Jones, Jas.
Jones, Joel
Jones, Jno.
Jones, Thos.
Kelley, Morriss
King, Jno.
Leanes, Jacob
Leith, Jno.
McNier, Saml.
Magehee, Wm.
Melson, Saml.
Millar, Jacob
Morriss, Jno.
Nixon, Robt.
Pace, Dreadzil
Raser (Roser?), Isaac
Redman, Benj.
Rich, Jno.
Ricketson, Benj.
Robertson, Allen
Shackleford, Jno.
Shackleford, Mordecai
Skinner, Henry
Snider, Jno.
Stallings, Ezekiel
Swan, Jno.
Whitcumbe, Nolley
Williams, Edw.

Grand Jurors Feb.1793
thru Aug. 1795 from
the Southern Centinal
& Georgia Gazette:

Appling, J.
Appling, Jno.
Brownson, Reubin
Bugg, Sherwood
Burroughs, Jas.
Carroll, Wm.
Cooper, Saml.
Crawford, Chas.
Gardner, Alexdr.
Grinage, J.
Grubbs, Benj.
Hanson, Thos.
Hay, Andrew
Jones, Adam
Jones, Richd.
Loftie, Daniel
Marbury, Joel
Marshall, Levi
Moore, J.
O'Neal, Edw.
Ramsey, Jno.
Ross, Jas.
Shaw, Robt.
Sims, Jas.
Tankersley, Jno.
Walker, David
West, Jas.
Wilson, Perry
Winkfield, J.
Wright, J.

Legal notices 1794-
1795. Southern Centi-
nel & Universal Gazette
& the Augusta Chronicle
& Gazette:

Andrew, Benj.
Andrew, Jas.
Barnett, Claiborne, dec'd.
Belingslea, Francis
Blair, Hugh
Bonner, Robt.
Bowdre, Elisha
Bowdre, Robt.
Boyd, Jno.
Brooker, Jno.
Brown, Frederick
Bugg, Sherwood

Burnett, Clayborn
Burroughs, Jas.
Bynum, Jno.
Caldwell, Paul
Caldwell, Sarah
Carmichael, Jno.
Carmichael, Mary
Clarke, Jesse
Clarke, Wm.
Cornett, Eli
Crawford, Anderson
Crawford, Nelson
Crawford, Wm.
Culbreath, Jas.
Culbreth, Jane
Culbreth, Peter
Davis, Clementine
Dorsett, Jno. Sr.
Drane, Walton
Ford, Jno.
Ford, Wm.
Foster, Jno.
Germany, Jas.
Gibson, Jno.
Gordon, Jno.
Gore, Jacob
Gore, Rachel
Greer, Thos. Jr.
Greer, Thos. Sr.
Hamilton, Concord
Hamilton, Thos.
Hampshire, H.
Haynes, Thos.
Hinton, Micajah
Hinton, Wm.
Hornby, Francis
Howard, Martha
Howard, Rhesa
Howard, Saml.
Johns, Robt.
Johnson, Abraham
Johnstone, Alexdr.
Jones, Thos. S.
Kendall, Henry
Lee, Ambrose
McColeal, Jas.
McNeal, Malcolm
McNeal, Michael
Maberry, Joel
Maddox, Jno.
Maddux, Wm.
Marshall, Danl.
Matthews, Jenny
Matthews, Mary

Matthews, Meshack
Maxwell, David
Meed, Jane
Miller, Nathl.
Mitchell, Wm.
Moseley, Benj.
Moseley, Jane
Newsom, Sol.
Offutt, Sampson
O'Neal, Edw.
Paris, Peter, dec'd.
Pearre, Jno.
Peliott, Jno.
Perry, Thos.
Prier, Jane
Prier, Phillip
Pryor, Phillip
Ramsey, Randolph
Randolph, Mrs. Eliza
Randolph, Robt.
Shields, Wm.
Short, Edw.
Short, Thos.
Sill, Jno.
Spencer, Peter
Standley, Jas.
Steele, S.
Stubblefield, Peter
Sturges, Andrew
Tankersley, Jno.
Tapley, Joel
Tapley, Mary
Tapley, New
Taylor, Wm.
Thorn, Merryman
Wall, Ann
Walton, Jno.
Walton, Wm.
Williams, Benj.
Willingham, Wm.
Wilson, Party
Wilson, Pearre
Wright, A.
Wright, Albert
Wright, Isaiah
Wright, Josiah

Columbia Co. Muster
rolls 1793:

Aldridge, Alsner
Aldridge, Wm.
Alridge, Reuben
Andrews, Benj.

Atkinson, Valentine
Bailey, Jas.
Barbree, Stancil
Barnay (?), Jno.
Batharton, Wm.
Bayne, Jno.
Beaver, Martin
Bell, Francis
Bell, Robt.
Blanton, Jno.
Blitcher, Benj.
Boneman, Jobe
Booker, Jno.
Bowdre, Robt.
Brady, Stancel
Brown, Elisha
Brown, Frederick
Brunson, Reuben
Bullmen, Geo.
Burnett, Jno.
Cammenn, Jno.
Carrol, Jno.
Carrol, Wm.
Castles, Jno.
Chambers, Thos.
Chambers, Wm.
Cliet, Jesse
Cliot, Jonithan
Cobb, Danl.
Coe, Joshua
Collert, Wm.
Corvin, Thos.
Crance, Lewis
Crane, Wm.
Crawford, Jno.
Davis, Blanford
Davis, Joseth
Davis Vachel
Day, Jno.
Delaney, Lewis
Dunn, Benj.
Dunn, Jos.
Durden, Elisha
Durden, Josiah
Eades, Jno.
Finney, Dury
Finni, Benj.
Fleetwood, Jno.
Flinn, Jno.
Flinn, Michel
Folds, Geo. Jr.
Folds, Richd.
Folis, Thos.
Ford, Willis

Fuqua, Moses
Fuqua, Prator
Fuller, Abner
Fuller, Jno.
Fuller, Ryal
Gardner, Asshel (?)
Gartnell, Jno.
Gatter, ----
Gilpin, Ignatius
Gore, Jacob
Grubbs, Joab
Gunby, Wm.
Hand, Henry
Hand, Jno.
Harris, David
Harris, Nathan
Harrison, Benj.
Harvil, Jas.
Hatcher, Jno.
Holder, Wm.
Howard, Jas.
Huff, Wm.
Hughes, Wm.
Hunt, Fitzmorris
Jones, Harrison
Jones, Nimrod
Jones, Thos.
Jones, Wm.
Kelly, Jno.
Kendrick, Jno.
Kendrick, Thos.
Kindill, Henry
Langston, David
Laughton, Saml.
Lawson, Jno.
Linsey, Dennis
Linsey, Wm.
Low, Isaac
McCloud, Robt.
McCord, Jno.
McDonald, Andrew
McDonald, Jas.
McDuffee, Jno.
McNair, Gilbert
McNair, Jno.
McNeal, Turquil
McSwine, Jno.
Maddox, Jos.
Magahee, Jno.
Magee, Routon
Mains, Saml.
Marress, Edw.
Mathews, Jos.
Mathews, Wm.

Matthiss, Jesse
Mayhall, Wm.
Millegan, Wm.
Monk, Jno.
Moor, Obadiah
Nash, Jno.
Nelson, Chas.
Nelson, Jas.
Newberry, Levi
Newbury, Tho.
Newman, Thos.
Nokels, Lavin
Nunn, Wm.
Owen, Spencer
Perry, Eli
Pharies, Wm.
Phillips, Ichabod
Phillips, Wilda
Pierce, ---
Pool, Saml.
Powell, ---
Radsford, Absolam
Radsford, Miles
Ray, Jno.
Rees, Benj.
Rich, Jno.
Runnels, Jno.
Runnels, Reuben
Runnells, Chas.
Russell, Andrew
Sampler, Chas.
Sampler, Jesse
Savidge, Jas.
Savidge, Osel
Shows, Danl.
Shows, Jno.
Sims, Man
Slaten, Saml.
Smith, Ebeneezer
Smith, Francis
Smith, Jas.
Smith, Jno.
Standford, David
Standford, Thos.
Stanford, Robt.
Steel, Sampson
Stith, Jno.
Sturgis, Jno.
Suder, Jno.
Sulivant, Wm.
Terry, Thos.
Tindil, Booker
Tindil, Pleasant
Tindil, Wm. Jr.

Tindill, Jno.
Tinsley, Jas.
Travis, Jno.
Underwood, Wm.
Van, Edw.
Varum, Isum
Vaughn, Joshua
Vinson, David
Walker, Wm.
Ward, Thos.
Watson, Benj.
Watson, Lewis
Watson, Tho.
Whitaker, Saml.
White, Jos.
Whitaker, Joshua
White, Robt.
White, Wm.
Wilkins, Wm.
Willoby, Wm.
Wilson, Perry
Wood, ---
Word, Saul
Wright, Isaiah
Young, David
Youngblood, Jacob
Youngblood, Joshua
Zachary, Burton
Zachary, Wm.

Names from Estate
Records:

Aldridge, Jas.
Bealle, Jonathan
Bealles, J. N.
Bealles, Wm. P.
Blackwell, Geo.
Bletaher, Benj.
Bowdre, Robt.
Bullock, Burel
Collins, Jonathan
Course (?), Saml.
Cousins, Chas.
Crawford, A.
Crawford, Mr.
Culwell, Jno.
Davidson, Jas.
Davis, Blandford
Davis, Tho.
Day, Stephen Jr.
Dent, Geo.
Dougherty, Jno.
Dougherty, Neil

Durkee, Nathl.
Durkee, Wm.
Edmondson, Jos.
Evans, E.
Evans, Eliz.
Evans, Henry
Evans, Susannah
Eades, Tho.
Foster, Hardy
Foster, Jonathan
Gardner, Lewis
Gardner, Mary
Gardner, Sarah
Garnette, Zachariah
Germany, Jas.
Griffin, A.
Griffin, Abel
Hanson, Tho.
Hay, N.
Horn, Ferrybe
Horn, Jesse
Horn, Wm.
Howard, Tho.
Huff, Wm.
Jarvis, F.
Jarvis, Floyd
Jenkins, Benj.
Jenkins, E. B.
Jenkins, P.
Jenkins, Priscilla
Jones, H.
Killingsworth, M.
King, Jonathan
King, Saml.
Liverman, B.
McCoy, Jno.
McDonald, Jno.
McInsey (?), Jesse
Maires, Tho.
Marshall, Sol.
Maxwell, David
Monk, Aninan (?)
Monk, Silas
Odom, Archibald
Pool, Saml.
Rambo, T.
Richeron (?), Marmaduke
Sanders, Lewis
Shackleford, J. W.
Shackleford, Mordecai
Shaw, Robt.
Simons, A.
Sims, Abner
Sims, Jas.

Skinner, Jonathan
Smith, L.
Snider, B.
Snider, Barnett
Snider, Jacob
Spider, E.
Tinsley, Jas.
Tolds (?), Geo.
Tuiss (?), Tho.
Vinson, M.
Walker, Elisha
Ward, Sol.
Ward, Tho.
Warren, A.
Warren, Allen
Whitcomb, N.
White, Benedict
Whitecum, Holley
Wilkins, Wm.
Williams, Jno.
Williams, Jonathan
Winfrey, Jesse
Wood, Jonathan
Yarbrough, Littleton
Zachry, Peter

Names from Deeds
1790 - 1794

Allen, Jas.
Allen, Robt.
Appling, Wm.
Arres (Ayers?), Benj.
Athy, Zephaniah
Ayers, Abrah., dec'd.
Ayers, Jane
Banks, Gerard
Barnett, Joel
Barnett, Nathl.
Batson, Jos.
Bayless, Isham
Bealle, Jas.
Bealle, Jno.
Beck, Jno.
Bellamy, Wm.
Benedict, Isaac
Bennet, Anne
Bennett, Anne
Blair, Hugh
Bledsoe, Benj.
Booker, Gideon
Boyd, Eliz.
Boyd, David
Boyd, Jno.

Boyd, Nicodemus
Bradley, Joshua
Bragg, Elijah
Brantley, Philip
Brown, Frederick
Brown, Wm.
Brownson, Reuben
Bugg, Nicholas Hobson
Bugg, Sherwood
Burke, Rich
Caldwell, Paul
Candler, Henry
Carmichael, Jno.
Carmichael, Mary
Carnes, Tho.
Carr, Catherine
Carter, Kindred
Cartledge, Edmond
Cartledge, Jas.
Chandler, Wm.
Chattin, Jno.
Clarke, Gilbert, dec'd.
Cobbs, Jno.
Cobbs, Frederick
Coleman, Paul
Coleman, Sarah
Coleman, Sussannah
Collage, Margaret
Cone, Wm.
Cousins, Wm.
Crawford, Anderson
Crawford, Chas.
Crawford, Francis
Crawford, Nelson
Creemor, Wm.
Culbreath, Jno.
Culbreath, Peter
Cumming, Tho.
Currie, Jno.
Daniel, Wm.
Darsey, Jos.
Daugherty, Neil
Daugherty, Patrick
Davis, Foster
Davis, Jno.
Davis, Jos.
Day, Stephen
Dean, Jacob
Danelly, Jas.
Dorsett, Jno.
Dorsey, Seakin(?) Larkin(?)
Douglas, Jno.
Downs, Jno.
Downs, Jno.

Dozier, Jas.
Drane, Wm.
Dunn, Nehemiah
Emmett, Jas.
Evans, Wm.
Farrer, Absalom
Few, Benj.
Finney, Benj.
Flournoy, Robt.
Fluker, Jno.
Ford, Wm.
Foster, Jno.
Fuller, Jno.
Fuller, Joshua
Galtney, Jno.
Garnett, Eli
Garnett, Jno.
Germany, Jno.
Germany, Wm.
Glasscock, Tho.
Graves, Wm.
Gray, Tho.
Green, Amos
Greer, Gilbert
Grenage, Joshua
Grubbs, Francis
Hamilton, Jas.
Hamilton, Tho.
Hargroves, Jno.
Harris, David
Harris, Nathan
Harrison, Rich
Hastings, Robt.
Hawkins, Jas.
Haynes, Anthony
Heard, Barnett
Higginbotham, Burroughs
Hitcherson, Jas.
Hodgens, Jno.
Holland, Jno.
Holliday, Ambrose
Holliday, Wm.
Holt, Wm.
Howard, Rhesa
Hudnall, Ezekiel
Hughes, Wm.
Hunt, Henry
Hunter, Dalzeel
Jackson, Benj.
Jackson, Isaac
Jackson, Tho.
Jennings, Wm.
Johnson, Alexdr.
Jones, Basil

Jones, Hezekiah
Jones, Jno.
Jones, Tho.
Kagle, Roger
Kelly, Morris
Lamar, Jno. Sr.
Lamkin, Jeremiah
Lanton, Tho.
Lantorn (?), Tho.
Laughlin, Tho.
Laughlin, Wm.
Lee, Timothy
Leigh, Walter
Linn, Anne
Linn, Chas.
Linn, Jane
Linn, Wm.
Lovell, Jas.
Low, Isaac
Lowe, Isaac
Lowtrip, Abagail
Loyd, Thos.
McCardel, Henry
McCarty, Danl.
McCarty, Jno.
McCorkle, Robt.
McCormick, Jos.
McDonald, Jno. M.
McFarland, Jas.
McGee, Hugh
McMillan, Jas.
McMinn, Jno.
McMurphy, Danl.
McNeil, Jas.
McNeil, Michael
Maddox, Jos.
Maddox, Wm.
Magruder, Ninian offcutt
Mahan, Patrick
Marshall, Jno.
Marshall, Jno.
Matthias, Eliz.
Meriwether, Nicholas
Meriwether, Tho.
Meriwether, Tho. Jr.
Middleton, Robt.
Miles, Wm.
Millbanks, Wm.
Mitchell, Mary
Moncrief, Caleb
Moncrief, Mary
Moore, Rich.
Moore, Mordecai
Moore, Tho.

Morris, Jno.
Morris, Rees
Morton, Jos.
Morton, Saml.
Moses, Philip
Mullen, Jas.
Napier, Richd.
Napier, Tho.
Naylor, Geo.
North, Jno.
Offcutt, Ezekiel
Olive, Jno.
Oliver, Saml.
Overby, Peter
Pace, Dredzill
Parrish, Peter, dec'd.
Payne, Scott
Payne, Wm.
Perkins, Joshua
Phillips, Jas.
Porter, Benj.
Porter, Chas.
Prather, Edw.
Ramsey, Jas.
Ramsey, Randall
Ramsey, Randolph
Randolph, Robt.
Reed, Jas.
Rees, Benj.
Reeves, Jno.
Richardson, Jos.
Ricketson, Benj.
Roseborough, Eliz.
Roseborough, Geo., dec'd.
Sanders, Abraham
Sanders, Jesee
Sanders, Joel
Savage, Loveless
Scott, Jno.
Scruggs, Jas.
Sharpe, Jos. Lewis
Shepherd, Wm.
Shields, Wm.
Short, Tho.
Sims, Benj.
Slater, Jno.
Smalley, Michael
Smith, Ebenezer
Smith, Ezekiel
Smith, Jno.
Smith, Wm.
Sorrah, Jno.
Staples, Tho.
Stewart, Jas.

Stewart, Jno.
Stewart, Wm.
Story, Prudence
Story, Robt.
Story, Robt., dec'd.
Stubbs, Jno. Jr.
Sudthard, Jno.
Tarver, Wm., dec'd.
Tarvin, Geo.
Taylor, Chas.
Taylor, Jno.
Thomas, Camm
Thomas, Jos.
Thomas, Peter
Thomas, Wm.
Timmerman, Godfrey
Tindel, Wm.
Tindell, Booker
Tindell, Wm. Sr.
Tinsley, Jas.
Tomason, Turner
Tudor, Jno.
Upton, Geo.
Upton, Philip
Upton, Sarah
Vernon, Isaac
Vinson, David
Walker, David
Walton, Wm.
Ward, Saul
Ward, Tho.
Ware, Robt.
Waters, Jas.
Watkins, Robt.
Watkins, Tho.
Watson, Jno.
Watson, Tho., dec'd.
Webster, Jacob
Whitcomb, Notley
Wilkes, Jas.·
Williams, Daniel
Willingham, Jno. Jr.
Willingham, Ollie
Willingham, Tho.
Wright, Dyonisius
Wright, Isaiah
Wright, Jno.
Youngblood, Abraham

EFFINGHAM COUNTY

Effingham County was created by the Act of February 5, 1777 from the two Colonial Parishes of St. Matthew and St. Phillip. These two Parishes had been organized in 1758 from land acquired in 1733 from a Creek cession. A part of Effingham was included in Screven County in 1793. It was in this County that the Saltzbergers from the German Palatinate settled after their arrival in Georgia.

Headrights and Bounty Grants: 1790 - 1795

Ammons, Wm.
Anderson, Margt.
Bailey, Chris.
Beall, Jesse
Bealy, Jas.
Bechtly, Geo.
Bell, Jesse
Bennett, Richd.
Bennett, Wm.
Bevill, Paul
Bird, Abraham
Bird, Israel
Bird, Saml.
Bishop, Martha
Bishop, Wm.
Blackenrigg, Jean
Blanton, Jno.
Bonell, Anthony
Bonnell, Danl.
Bonnell, Jno.
Bostick, Saml.
Bostwick, Saml.
Bowen, Martha
Boykin, Jno.
Bray, Thos.
Brazell, Jno.
Brazell, Robt.
Brewer, Jas.
Brewer, Jas. Sr.
Brownson, Nathan

Buckhalter, Jno. Michael
Campbell, Thos.
Caplen, Jas.
Carter, Isaac
Carter, Matthew
Caswell, Jno.
Caughran, Jos.
Cavenah, Nicholas
Clifton, Jno.
Clyatt, Jas.
Cone, Aaron
Cone, Wm.
Cook, Benj.
Cooke, Jas.
Copeland, Jas.
Cox, Jasper
Craddox, Saml.
Crawford, Chas.
Daly, Benj.
Dasher, Benj.
Dasher, Jno. M.
Davis, Jas.
Davis, Jno.
Davis, Wm.
Deloach, Hardy
Deloache, Hardy, Sr.
Denmark, Stephen
Denmark, Wm.
Dickson, Michael
Dickson, Robt.

(67)

Dikes, Geo.
Dill, Phillip
Dougherty, Jos.
Driggers, Jno.
Dunwoody, Robt.
Dupies, Wm.
Durrance, Francis
Durrence, Wm.
Everage, Marmaduke
Everett, Jno.
Everitt, Jno.
Fletcher, Jno.
Gardner, Wm.
Garrett, Jno.
Geiger, Abraham
Geiger, Felix
Geiger, Jno.
Gieger, Felix
Gill, Jas.
Gill, Robt.
Gindrat, Henry
Gnann, Andrew
Goldsmith, Jno.
Goodman, David
Grant, Peter
Groover, Jno.
Grover, David
Grover, Jno.
Grover, Mary
Gruber, Sol.
Hagen, Jno.
Hall, Bradley
Hardzman, Thos.
Harris, Jno.
Harvey, Emanuel
Hawthorn, Jos.
Hawthorn, Nathl.
Heisler, Geo.
Heyton, Wm.
Hilliard, Jesse
Hines, Jas.
Hodges, Elias
Hodges, Jno.
Hodges, Wm.
Hogan, Absalom
Hogan, Jno.
Hollaman, Ann
Hollingsworth, Valentine
Hollingsworth, Vear
Howard, Daniel
Howell, Caleb
Howell, Danl.
Huffman, Jacob
Hunter, Miles

Ivey, Robt.
Johnson, Danl.
Johnston, David
Johnston, Wm.
Joice, Henry
Jones, Drury
Jones, Francis
Jones, Mathew
Journingan, Jas.
Joyce, Henry
King, Wm.
Kirby, Wm.
Kogler, Jno.
Lanair, Clement
Lane, Alex. Jr.
Lane, Thos.
Lanier, Ann Mary
Lanier, Jno.
Lastinger, Hannah
Lastinger, Jno.
Lenair, Clement
Lenair, Jno.
Lenair, Lemuel
Lewis, Wm.
London, Jno.
Loper, Joshua
Lott, Jno.
Lott, Nathan
Lovett, Tho.F.(heirs of)
Lowther, Edw.
Lunday, Nathl.
Malet, Gidson
Malsap, Jeremiah
Marcus, Jno.
Martin, Jas.
Martin, Jno.
Martin, Martin
Matthews, Jno.
McBride, Jno.
McCall, David
McCall, Jesse
McCall, Jno.
McCall, Sherod
McCall, Thos.
McCall, Thos. Jr.
McCall, Wm.
McGehee, Shadrack
McKinsey, Jno.
Mezell, Luke
Mezell, Wm.
Michael, Wm.
Mikell, Barnett
Mikell, Jas.
Mikell, Jno.

Mills, Eliz.
Mincey, Abraham
Mixon, Jess
Mock, Jos.
Moore, Jno.
Moore, Saml.
Morgan, Wm.
Moulfort, Robt.
Needlinger, Jno. G.
Newill, Jno.
Nowtan, Geo.
Obryan, David
Obvey, Henry
Parker, Gabriel
Patterson, Archibald
Perryman, Jas.
Phillips, Royall Budd
Pierce, Joshua, Sr.
Pierce, Stephen
Plunner, Jos.
Porter, Jas.
Porter, Wm.
Powers, Jno.
Pridgen, Luke
Pridgen, Mark
Purvis, Jas.
Ratliff, Eliz.
Rawls, Cotton
Rees, Joel.
Rester, Frederick
Rhae, Jno.
Rahn, Jonathan
Rogers, Jos.
Rollison, Jno.
Royal, Saml.
Rupert, Jno.
Rushing, Wm.
Ryall, Arthur
Ryan, Chas.
Ryan, Jos.
Scheuber, Justice H.
Schweighoffer, Thos.
Scott, Alexdr.
Scott, Robt.
Self, Ezekiel
Sellers, Saml.
Shaffer, Jno.
Sheffield, Austin
Shepperd, Mourning
Shiffield, Wm.
Sloan, Jno.
Smith, Godhielf
Smith, Jas.
Snyder, Jno.

Stewart, Alex.
Swieghoffer, Abel
Tanner, Asa
Taylor, Josiah
Tennill, Thos.
Thomson, Claud
Thornton, Jno.
Thrower, Wm.
Tilman, Gideon
Travis, Simeon
Treutlén, Christian
Truetlen, Christian
Tusing, Paul
Waldon, Jno.
Wells, Henry
Wiggins, Frederick
Wiggins, Jos.
Wilder, Sarah
Wilkins, Wm.
Williams, Saml.
Wilson, Jas.
Wise, Wm.
Wolf, Geo.
Wolf, Jno.
Woodhouse, Robt.
Woods, Thos.
Wylly, Thos.
Zeigler, Emanuel
Zeigler, Geo.
Zittarover, Jno. G.
Zittler, Danl.(heirs of)

Miscellaneous legal
notices appearing in
1790-1795 in Augusta
Chronical and Gazette,
Georgia Gazette and
The Southern Centinal
and Universal Gazette:

Biddenback, Christian
Biddenback, Miss Mary
Board, Abraham
Boston, Jas.
Bowen, Clifton
Bowen, Martha
Boykin, Jno.
Burns, Mary
Bryant, Jas.
Campbell, Sarah
Campbell, Thos.
Cooper, Jos.
Cramer, Ann Catherine
Cramer, Christopher.

Crawford, Alexdr.
Crawford, Mrs. Mary
Crum, Harmon
Cuyler, Jeremiah
Dasher, Jno. Martin
Dasher, Martin
Davis, David
Davis, Jno.
Davis, Jos.
Davis, Wm.
Dickson, Robt.
Doughtery, Jacob
Douglass, Jas.
Dykes, Jesse
Dykes, Levi
Foy, Jno.
Fraser, Dyer
Fraser, Eliz.
Gibbons, Fitz
Gindrat, Henry
Goldwire, Jno.
Goldwire, Jno. Sr.dec'd.
Goldwire, Jno. Jr.
Green, Jno.
Green, Willeway
Greenhow, Jas.
Hare, Jno.
Hatcher, Jno.
Hilyards, Jesse
Hines, David Sr.
Hines, Jas.
Holloway, Jno.
Hudson, Chris. Sr.
Hudson, Chris. Jr.
Jernigan, Elias
Jernigan, Moses
Johnston, Jos.
Jones, Drury
Jones, Jno.
Joyce, Henry
King, Henry
King, Wm.
Kraus, Saml.
Laird, Absalom
Lane, Mrs. Mary
Lane, Thos.
Lanier, Clement
Limeburger, Mrs. Apolina
Limeburger, Christian
     Irael
London, Jno.
Luncy, Nathl.
Lyon, Jos.
McCall, Geo.

McCall, Sarah
McCall, Thos.
McCoy, Wm.
McDonald, Alexdr.
McDonald, Jno.
Mark, Saint
Martin, Hon. Clement
Martin, Wm.
Milker, Jno.
Mills, Mrs. Mary
Mills, Wm.
Mixecn, Jesse
Moore, Jno.
Moore, Wm.
Moss, Jno
Nelson, Malcolm
Nolan, Dennis
Nowlan, Geo.
Oakman, Mrs. Mary
Odom, Jno.
Pearce, Stephen
Polhill, Thos.
Porter, Wm.
Porter, Wm. Jr.
Potter, Jno.
Rahn, Jonathan
Rolberger, Joanna
Ravot, Abraham
Rushen, Jno.
Rushin, Wm.
Sharp, Joshua
Shoars, Wm.
Shorter, Rachel
Sibley, Isaac
Stiner, Christian
Stiner, David
Stiner, Mrs. Margt.
Summerall, Miss C.
Summerall, Jesse
Taylor, Wm.
Thornton, Jno.
Tillman, Gideon
Tuly, Wm.
Webb, Henry
Wells, Henry dec'd.
Wells, Jacob
Whitney, Lott
Williams, Robt.
Williams, Willis
Williamson, Aquilla
Wilson, Jesse
Wylley, Thos.

Effingham County
Deed Book "A-B"
1789 - 1790

Grantors
Bandy, Jno.
Barber, Jno. Sr.
Beddenback, Apolina
Beddenback, Matthew
Belville, Rebecca
Belvill, Robt.
Blackmon, Ann
Blackmon, Wm.
Burgstiner, Danl.
Colson, Wm.
Dell, Dorothy
Dell, Phillip
Gnann, Jacob
Holleman, Ann
Hudson, Robt.
Lane, Thos.
Leimburger, Apolonia
Lowrman, Jno.
Marran, Margt.
Mizell, Luke
Ravot, Abraham
Ravot, Mary
Ray, Wm.

Grantees
Barber, Jno. Jr.
Beddenback, Christian
Beddenback, Matthias
Bilbo, Jas.
Dasher, Jno. Martin
Garnett, Thos.
Jones, Jas.
Lundy, Jane
Lundy, Mary Esther
Lunday, Theophilus
McKinty, Patrick
Moore, Jno.
Peterson, Jno.
Porter, Wm.
Smith, Jas.
Stuart, Alexdr.
Stuart, Jas.
Thorn, Wm.
Weitman, Danl.
Womack, Frederick
Zettrower, Jno. Geo.

Witnessess and miscel-
laneous documents:

Beville, Paul
Blasingame, Harvey
Burgholder, Rudolph
Burgstiner, Danl.
Cleary, Jno. R.
Daly, Benj.
Davis, Ann
Dell, Phillip
Dickson, Michael
Dickson, Robt.
Douglass, Jas.
Emanuel, Asa
Holleman, Nancy
Horton, Moses
Howell, Caleb
Howell, Danl.
Hudson, Isaac
Jackson, Jos.
Jones, Drury
Lowrman, Jas.
Lowrman, Jno. Jr.
Lowrman, Mary
Lundy, Francis
Lundy, Geo.
Luncy, Theophilus
McConky, Henry
Mannen, Wm.
Moore, Jno.
Neidlinger, Hannah
Neidlinger, Jno. G.
O'Bryan, Wm.
Roberts, Elias
Scruggs, Richd. Jr.
Spence, Jno.
Spencer, Jno.
Stiles, S.
Thorn, David
Threadcraft, Geo.
Thrower, Levi
Triebner, Chris.
    Frederick
Truetlin, Chris.
Truetlin, Jno. A.
Waldhaeur, Jno.
Webb, Wm.
Wells, Andrew. Elton
Williams, Robt.
Womack, Allen
Womack, Wm.

Effingham County Militia
Officers published Oct.
1790 in Augusta Chron-
icle and Gazette:

Cone, Aaron
Cope, Jno.
Dasher, Christian
Dasher, Jno. Martin
Durrence, Wm.
Everett, Jno.
Howell, Caleb
Howell, Danl.
Hudson, Nathl.
Joyce, Henry
Knight, Thos. Jones
Kogler, Jno.
Lanier, Benj.
Lanier, Clement
Lanier, Jno.
Lott, Jno. Sr.
Lott, Jno. Jr.
McCall, Geo.
McCall, Jno.
Mikell, Jno.
Miles, Stephen
Mizell, Jno.
O'Neil, Wm.
Rahn, Jonathan
Rahn, Matthew
Rushing, Wm.
Sheppard, Wm.
Spencer, Wm.
Wylly, Thos.
Zettrover, Ernest

Effingham Co. Militia
Feb. 1794. Original
may be found in State
Department of Archives
and History:

Bennett, Richd.
Bennett, Wm.
Carswell, Jno.
Cook, Lewis
Denmark, Stephen
Dukes, Jno.
Geiger, Abraham
Geiger, Cornelius
Geiger, Etheldred
Geiger, Felix
Geiger, Jno.
Gills, Jos.

Goldsmith, Jno.
Gruver, David
Gruver, Sol.
Lane, Alexdr.
Lane, Bryant
Lane, Jno.
Lastinger, David
Martin, Geo.
Owens, Jno.
Porter, Robt.
Rawls, Capt. Jno.
Rester, Frederick
Robison, Jonathan
Sheffield, Austin
Spurlock, Saml.
Thomson, Jno.
Williams, Lewis
Wright, Jno.

Trustees of Ebenezer
Congregation, Sept.
wl. 1793 printed in
Ga. Gazette:

Seckinger, Jonathan
Haughleiter, Jno.
Elzy, Michael
Kegler, Jno.
Neidlinger, Jno. G.
Rahn, Jonathan
Rahn, Matthew
Smith, Godheip
Michter, Jno.
Biddenback, Matthias dec'd.

Grand Jurors Feb.1795,
Published in Southern
Centinel and Universal
Gazette and Augusta
Chronicle and Gazette:
Bell, Jesse
Bishop, Wm.
Dasher, Jno. M.
Grabershine, Jno.
Greenhow, Jas.
King, Wm.
McKinty, Pat.
Porter, Wm.
Rahn, Jonathan
Rahn, Jos.
Schweighoffer, Abell
Seckinger, Jonathan
Smith, Gottlieb
Wilson, Jas.
Wisenbaker, Jacob

(72)

Tax-defaulters, 1791:

Board, Abraham
Bryant, Jas.
Cooper, Jos.
Crum, Harmon
Davis, David
Doughtery, Jacob
Foy, Jno.
Gibbons, Fitz
Hare, Jno.
Hatcher, Jno.
Hilyard, Jesse
Holloway, Jno.
Jernigan, Elias
Jernigan, Moses
Johnston, Jos.
Jones, Jno.
Laird, Absalom
McCoy, Wm.

Mark, Saint
Milker (?), Jno.
Moss, Jno.
Nolan, Dennis
Odom, Jno.
Potter, Jno.
Rahn, Jonathan
Sharp, Joshua
Shoars, Wm.
Sibley, Isaac
Taylor, Wm.
Thornton, Jno.
Tillman, Gideon
Tuly, Wm.
Wells, Jacob
Whitney, Lott
Williams, Robt.
Williams, Willis
Williamson, Aquilla

ELBERT COUNTY

Created by Legislative Act, December 10, 1790, from
Wilkes County. In 1811 a part of this County went into
making up Madison County and in 1853 a part into Hart
County. There was actually no 1790 census of Elbert
as it was created after the 1790 enumeration. These
names are included here however because they represent
a large portion of Wilkes County as it stood prior to
1790.

Headrights and
Bounty Grants:
1790 - 1795
Allen, Nathl.
Armstrong, Jno.
Baker, Jno.
Barnett, Jno.
Bibb, Wm.
Brazeal, Frederick
Cash, Howard
Cloud, Ezekiel
Cochran, Wm.
Collins, Zachariah
Cook, Benj.

Cook, Francis
Creswell, David
Darden, Geo.
Evans, Major
Fain, Chas.
Fleming, Moses
Franklin, David
Gaines, Francis
Ginn, Jesse
Gordon, Alex
Grimes, Wm.

Hannah, Jas.
Higginbotham, Benj.
Higginbotham, Jacob
Higginbotham, Wm.
Higginsbotham, Saml.
Hightower, Wm.
Hill, Jacobs
Hubbard, Jno.
Hunt, Richardson
Johnson, Edmond
Leapour, Jas.
Long, Jos.
Long, Nimrod
Lowry, Jas.
Lowry, Wm.
Lumpkin, Geo.
Martin, Jas.
Maxwell, Thos.
Mayers, Jacob
Means, Wm.
Moore, Jos.
Moore, Saml.
Norris, Wm.
Patton, Jas.
Pitchford, Wm.
Pruitt, Jacob
Pullian, Robt.
Reyley, Jas.
Rogers, Jno.
Rose, Henry
Russell, Christian
Saunders, Ricd.
Seals, Thos.
Sewell, Wm.
Shackleford, Jno.
Shaw, Danl.
Smith, Valentine
Spairs, Jno.
Staples, Jno.
Stubblefield, Wm.
Tait, Jas.
Talbott, Jno.
Turk, Jno.
Tweedle, Jno.
Upshaw, Jno.
Walton, Wm.
Webb, Wm.
Webster, Jno.
Westbrook, Stephen
White, Jesse
Wilkins, Element
Wilmouth, Stephen
Wilson, Jason
Woods, Middleton
Yeasley, Jno.

Returns of Administrators and Guardians 1791 - 1795

Adams, David
Adams, Jas.
Adams, Jas. dec'd.
Alston, Wm.
Appleby, Wm.
Aycock, Wm.
Baker, Absolom
Banks, Wm.
Blake, Wm.
Brazdal, Jno. dec'd.
Brazdal, Mary
Brewer, Elisha
Brewer, Elisha dec'd.
Brewer, Jno.
Brown, Jas.
Burk, Thos.
Burton, Archer
Burton, Thos.
Calvert, Jos.
Cameron, Jas.
Cameron, Jno.
Cameron, Thos.
Carter, Jas.
Chisholm, Wm.
Clarke, Chris.
Coker, Isaac
Colbert, Nicodemus
Collers, Matthew
Cook, Thos.
Cooke, Jas. dec'd.
Cooke, Jas. Watson
Cooke, Reuben
Cosby, Jas.
Coulter, Richd.
Crawford, Arthur
Crenshaw, Maybourn dec'd.
Crocket, Robt.
Crocket, Saml. dec'd.
Davis, Absolom
Davis, Lewis dec'd.
Davis, Wm.
Dudley, Jas.
Dudley, Jno. dec'd.
Easter, Robt.
Easton, Chas. dec'd.
Ferrell, Jno.
Ferrell, Martin
Fortson, Benj.
Fulgham, Matthew dec'd.
Fulgham, Stephen
Furgus, Jno.

Gaar, Abraham
Gaar, Adam Sr. dec'd.
Gaar, Benj.
Gaar, Lewis
Gaar, Michael, dec'd.
Gill, Jno.
Gray, Hezekiah
Green, Burton
Haines, Moses
Haines, Stephen Sr.dec'd.
Hambleton, Francis dec'd.
Haney, Thos.
Hatcher, Wm.
Hawthorne, Jno.
Haynes, Moses
Head, Benj.
Henderson, Jno.
Henderson, Jos. dec'd.
Hudson, Cuthberd
Johnson, Andrew
Johnston, Jno. H.
Keys, Jno.
Kidd, Wm.
King, Jos.
Kinkade, Hugh dec'd.
Lear, Jonathan
McAlpin, Sol.
McClary, Robt. dec'd.
McClusky, Jas.
McConnell, Manuel
McCurdy, David dec'd.
McCurdy, Jno.
McKenzie, Wm.
Morris, Jas. dec'd.
Morris, Isaac
Morris, Sally
Morris, Sherod
Mackey, Jno.
Miller, Jno. dec'd.
Moss, Wm.
Napier, Thos.
Newman, Jno.
Oliver, Caleb
Pollard, Jno.
Pope, Henry
Ragland, Evan
Rogers, Jno. dec'd.
Rogers, Nancy
Rose, Henry
Ross, Jno.
Rucker, Jos.
Satterwhite, Francis
Scales, Thos.
Sheppard, Peter

Sherman, Ann dec'd.
Sigmon, Jno.
Smith, Jno.
Spears, Saml.
Staples, Jno.
Stodgill, Joel dec'd.
Stodgill, Martitia
Stroud, Isham dec'd.
Stubbs, Peter
Sutton, Alsay
Sutton, Wm. dec'd.
Tait, Jas.
Tate, Zimre
Thomas, Joel dec'd.
Thomas, Wm.
Thompson, Jesse
Thompson, Oliver dec'd.
Thompson, Robt.
Thompson, Wm. Sr.
Tuttle, Jas. Sr.
Vodan, Bradock dec'd.
Walthall, Garrard
Walton, Wm.
Watkins, Saml.
Westbrook, Stephen
Wever, Jno. Sr.
Williams, Nat. J.

Will Book "A"
1791 - 1795

Avren, Jno.
Aycock, Wm.
Bibb, Sally S.
Bibb, Wm.
Booker, Wm. Sr.
Brownen, Jesse
Calvert, Jno.
Clark, Johnston
Clark, Sarah
Cleveland, Jacob
Cleveland, Jeremiah
Coil, Jas.
Coker, Isaac
Cook, Thos.
Easter, Jas.
Easter, Sarah
Ellington, Stephen
Elliott, Andrew
Elliott, Jas.
Freeman, Jenny
Gatewood, Richd.
Giles, Jno.
Green, Burton

Grimes, Hildred
Grimes, Wm.
Harvie, Wm.
Harvy, Richd.
Hatcher, Wm.
Head, Eliz. Janet
Heat, Jas.
Henley, Jno.
Higginbotham, Benj.
Higginbotham, Eliz.
Hodge, Wm.
Human, Bazzle
Human, Isabel
Jones, Jesse
Kidd, Webb
Lankester, Wm.
Ledbetter, Drury
MacMillian, Jon
McCurdy, Jas.
McCutchen, Wm.
McNeel, Jno.
Megredy, Robt.
Megredy, Silas
Meredith, Jas.
Meredith, Sarah
Morrison, Jas.
Pearpoint, Larkin
Ragland, Benj.
Scott, Thos. B.
Smith, Jasper
Smith, Rebeckah
Statham, Love
Stokes, Sarah
Stokes, Wm.
Tate, Wm.
Thompson, Jno. Farley
Thompson, Robt. Sr.
Thompson, Saml. M.
Thompson, Wells
Thompson, Wm. Sr.
Tuttle, Isaac
Walker, Jeremiah
Walker, Milly
White, Jno.
White, Reuben
Williams, Jaret
Williams, Jos.
Willy, Thos.
Wray, Phillip

Deed Book "A"
1789 - 1792

Grantors
Adams, David

Almand, Jas.
Baker, Absolom
Baker, Jno.
Baker, Mary
Barnett, Benj. Johnson
Barnett, Lucy
Barnett, Nathan
Barnett, Patsey
Bell, Eliz.
Bell, Jos.
Bond, Nathan
Brown, Sarah
Brown, Thos.
Brown, Wm.
Burton, Jacob
Burton, Nancy
Butler, Jas.
Butler, Salley
Carrell, Mary
Carrell, Peter
Carter, Thos. Sr.
Chambers, Lettice
Chambers, Robt.
Clark, Chris.
Colbert, Susanna
Collins, Zachariah
Coleman, Jno.
Colson, Abraham
Cook, Deborah
Cook, Francis
Cook, Jas.
Cook, Sarah
Cosby, Robt.
Coulter, Francis
Coulter, Sarah
Cowdon, Robt.
Crosby, Jno.
Cunningham, Ann
Cunningham, Jno.
Daniel, Nancy
Daniel, Wm.
Darden, Jno.
Davis, Benj.
Davis, Suckey
Davis, Wm. Hackney
Depriest, Jno.
Dooly, Geo.
Doughty, Jos.
Duncan, Henry
Duncan, Joanna
Duncan, Mark
Duncan, Mary
Edwards, Susannah
Edwards, Wm.

Elliott, Sarah
Elliott, Wm.
Evens, Geo.
Farrow, Perin
Freeman, Jas.
Gilleylen, Agness
Gilleylen, Jacob
Glover, Jno.
Goss, Benj.
Goss, Eliz.
Gregg, Thos.
Guttery, Betsy
Guttery, Robt.
Haley, Mary
Haley, Wm.
Harbour, Catharine
Harbour, Esaias
Head, Benj.
Hendrick, Eliz.
Higginbotham, Frances
Higginbotham, Jos.
Hightower, Jno.
Hightower, Sarah
Hill, Moses
Hillery, Hendrick
Hubbard, Benj.
Hubbard, Catron
Hubbard, Jno.
Hubbard, Sally
Hudson, Cutbird
Hudson, Eliz.
Human, Alex.
Hunt, Richardson
Hutchings, Chas.
Johnson, Andrew
Johnson, Jno. H.
Johnson, Nancy
Jones, Eliz.
Jones, Isaac
Jones, Jno.
Kennedy, Eliz.
Kennedy, Robt.
Little, Isabell
Little, Jas. Sr.
Lovelady, Jane
Lovelady, Thos.
McDonald, Helen
McDonald, Hugh
McDonald, Jas.
Martin, Eliza
Martin, Robt.
Meadows, Isaac
Meadows, Mary
Merritt, Benj.

Merritt, Mary
Middleton, Eliz.
Middleton, Robt.
Morse, Saml.
Nail, Julian
Nail, Mary
Nunnelee, Jas. Franklin
Nunnelee, Keziah
Nunnelee, Wm. Womack
Oliver, Dionysius
Oliver, Frances
Oliver, Jno.
Oliver, Mary Ann
Pace, Agnes
Pace, Barnabas
Peek, Jno. C.
Pettigrew, Geo.
Pollard, Jno.
Pollard, Polly
Porter, Benj.
Ready, Jas.
Reed, Collin
Rice, Leonard
Rice, Sary (Sarah)
Richardson, Walker
Rogers, Jno.
Ross, Jno.
Ross, Marget
Scott, Nancy
Scott, Thos.
Shackleford, Edmond
Smith, Wm.
Streetman, Garrett
Streetman, Mary
Suttles, Isaac
Tait, Jas.
Tait, Rebecca
Tate, Wm.
Teasley, Fanny
Teasley, Silas
Thompson, Isham
Thompson, Jno. Farley
Thompson, Robt.
Thompson, Sally
Thompson, Sarah
Thompson, Wm.
Trentham, Absolom
Trimble, Katharin
Trimble, Moses
Tureman, Eliz.
Tureman, Geo.
Tuttle, Jas. Sr.
Tuttle, Jas. Jr.
Tuttle, Nicholas

Tweedle, Jno.
Tweedle, Sarah
Walker, Eliz.
Walker, Jas.
Walthall, Edw.
Walthall, Nancy
Watkins, Wm.
Wattson, Jno.
White, Jno.
White, Milley
Wilkins, Eliz.
Wilkins, Thos.
Wimbish, Saml.

Grantees

Acheson, Nathan
Adams, David
Alice, Chas.
Alice, Francis
Allen, Nathl.
Allen, Wm.
Almand, Jas.
Alston, Wm.
Arnold, Jonathan
Arnold, Wm.
Baker, Jno. Armstrong
Ballenger, Jno.
Barnett, Wm.
Beverly, Anthony
Blackburn, Saml.
Bond, Eliz.
Bond, Nathan
Bonds, Richd.
Brown, Benj.
Brown, David
Brown, Jas.
Brown, Jno.
Brown, Thos.
Butler, Patrick
Camron, Jas.
Carter, Jas.
Certain, Josiah
Childs, Nathan
Coker, Isaac
Coleman, Jas.
Cook, Jas.
Corethers, Robt.
Cothers, Wm.
Coulter, Richd. Jr.
Crafford, Oliver
Crow, Jas.
Daniel, Allen
Daniel, Wm.

Davis, Rody
Depriest, Jno.
Dickson, Arthur Bridge
Dudlee, Wm.
Duncan, Henry
Eberhart, David
Elliot, Wm.
Farrow, Britton
Farrow, Jno.
Farrow, Micajah
Farrow, Needham
Farrow, Sally
Farrow, Wilie
Flanigin, Wm.
Fortson, Thos.
Gatewood, Richd.
Gilleylen, Jacob
Glover, Benj.
Goode, Wm.
Graham, Wm.
Greenwood, Jno.
Grimes, Wm.
Guy, Wm.
Hailey, Wm.
Halley, Wm.
Hanna, Jas.
Hatcher, Wm.
Harbour, Esaias
Harbour, Talmon
Harmar, Christ.
Harper, Jno. Peterson
Hatcher, Wm.
Head, Thos.
Higginbotham, Wm.
Huddleston, Robt.
Human, Bazzie
Hunt, Jas.
Hunt, Richardson
Johnson, Jno. Hutchins
Key, Wm. Bibb
McCune, Wm.
McDonald, Jas.
McDonald, Jno.
McGuire, Thompson
McKenzie, Wm.
Martin, Barkley
Martin, David
Matkin, Jas.
Meadows, Isaac
Middleton, Robt.
Moore, Wm.
Morse, Jno. Julian
Moseley, Robt.
Nelson, Major

Nunnelee, Eliz.
Oliver, Dionysius Sr.
Oliver, Jas.
Oliver, Jno.
Oliver, Peter
Owens, Elijah
Patterson, Jno.
Patterson, Wm.
Penn, Thos.
Pinnel, Thos.
Porter, Benj.
Posey, Thos.
Ragland, Evan
Reed, Collin
Rice, Leonard
Rogers, Mary
Rogers, Thos.
Rowzy, Jno.
Rucker, Geo.
Ryelye, Jas.
Scales, Jno.
Scales, Thos.
Scott, Jas.
Sewell, Saml.
Shackleford, Edmond
Shackleford, Henry
Shewmaker, Lindsey
Staples, Jno.
Statham, Jno.
Stenchcomb, Absolom
Stinchcomb, Alex.
Suttles, Isaac
Sutton, Jeams
Smith, Eliz.
Smith, Jno.
Smith, Valentine
Tait, Jas.
Tait, Zimry
Tate, Jas.
Terrill, Jos.
Tureman, Martin.
Tuttle, Jas.
Tuttle, Jas. Jr.
Vineyard, David
Walker, Jas.
Walker, Jere
Walker, Jeremiah
Watkins, Robt.
Webb, Austin
Webb, Claban
Webb, Claborn
Webster, Jonathan
Westbrook, Stephen
White, Jno.

Woldridge, Wm.
Woods, Middleton
Wyche, Peter

Witnesses and other
documents in Deed Book:

Aberhart, Geo.
Aberhart, Jacob
Allbritton, Jno.
Allen, Reuben
Almand, Jno.
Arnold, Wm.
Ashley, Wm.
Baker, Absolom
Baker, Saml.
Baker, Saml.
Barren, Thos.
Barnett, Jo.
Barnett, Nyal
Barnett, Wm.
Bass, Jared
Beck, Jno.
Bell, Jas.
Blankenship, Womack
Bond, Jos.
Boyd, Jno.
Bradford, Wm.
Brawner, Basil
Brawner, Jno.
Brewer, Edmund
Brown, Francis
Brown, Meroday
Brown, Rolen
Brown, Wm.
Bryan, Augustine
Buchanan, Jno.
Bugg, Jacob
Burk, Thos. Sr.
Burke, Robt.
Burton, Thos.
Caldwell, Harry
Call, Richd.
Carter, Jas.
Carter, Jno. M.
Carter, Thos.
Chambers, Robt.
Christopher, Wm.
Clark, Agatha
Clark, David
Clark, Judith
Clarkson, Jno.
Cleghorn, Jas.
Cleghorn, Jno.

Cockbun, Geo.
Cockburn, Geo.
Colbert, Thos.
Colbert, Tukedmark
Coleman, Jno.
Cook, Edoshus
Cook, Francis
Cook, Jas.
Cosby, Robt.
Coulter, Chas.
Coulter, Seara
Cowdon, Robt.
Cox, Jesse
Crosby, Jno.
Crossley, Jno.
Crutchfield, Geo.
Cunningham, J.
Cunningham, Jno.
Dailey, Jno.
Daniel, Allen
David, Jno.
Davis, Wiley
Depriest, Jno.
Dunn, Jno.
Easter, Jno.
Easter, Wm.
Eaverhurt, Jacob
Ellington, Stephen
Ellis, Chas.
Ells, Jno.
Farer, Parent
Floyd, Richd.
Furgus, Jno.
Gatewood, Larkin
Gillylen, Jacob
Goin (?) Elisha
Goode, Edwd.
Gorham, J.
Gorham, Jenny
Goss, Chas.
Greenstreet, Jas.
Gresham, J.
Hanna, Jas.
Hansard, Wm.
Harbin, Thos.
Harbin, Wm.
Harbour, Talmon
Harbour, Thos.
Hatcher, Wm.
Haynes, Sarah
Haynes, Moses
Haynie, Bridgor
Head, Jas.
Heard, Stephen

Heatley, Jas.
Henry, Benson
Higginbotham, Saml.
Higginbotham, W.
Hillery, Thos.
Hobby, Wm. J.
Hodge, Alex.
Holbrook, Jesse
Howard, Nehemiah
Hudson, Chris.
Hubbard, Richd.
Hudson, Wm.
Hunt, R.
Hunt, Richardson
Hunter, Saml.
Hutchings, Chas.
Jackson, Robt.
Johnson, Andrew
Johnson, Edmond
Jones, Abraham
Jones, Jesse
Jones, Jno.
Jourdan, Jno.
King, Jno.
Lamar, Z.
Lewis, Philip
Loveman, Robt.
Luckie, Hez.
McCleskey, Jas.
McDonald, Donald
McDonald, Hugh
McEver, Andrew
McEavert, Andrew
McGarry, Edw.
McKenzie, Jno.
Mackie, Saml.
Mackie, Thos.
Madkin, Jas.
Martin, Murdock
Matkin, Daniel
Matthews, Jno.
Maxwell, Jno.
Merrett, Benj.
Middleton, Robt.
Miller, Peter
Moon, Robt.
Moore, Jos.
Morris, Jno.
Moss, Wm.
Mounger, Henry
Mouson, Jean
Nailer, Jas.
Nunnelee, Jas. F.
Nunnelee, Walter

Odom, Jacob
Oliver, Dionysius Jr.
Oliver, Jno.
Oliver, Jno. Jr.
Oliver, Thos.
Oliver, Wm.
Owens, Jno.
Patterson, Jno.
Perry, Thos.
Pollard, Richd.
Pope, Leroy
Pope, W.
Ragland, Evan
Richardson, Walker
Rogers, Benj.
Rogers, Jas.
Rogers, Jno.
Rogers, Thos.
Rogers, Unity
Rosel, Jona.
Russell, Thos.
Sandidge, Clabourn
Setterwhite, Francis
Sayler, Christ.
Scott, Thos. B.
Shackleford, Edmond
Shackleford, Wm.
Shepherd, Jas.
Shields, Jno.
Sigmon, Jno.
Skelton, Jno.
Skelton, Robt.
Skinner, Archer
Sled, Joshua
Smith, Nathl.
Stephen, Alex
Stubbs, Eliz.
Suttle, Isaac
Sutton, Reuben
Tait, Jas.
Tait, Wm.
Tait, Wm. H.
Talbot, Jno.
Taliaferro, Ben
Tate, Jas.
Taylor, Robt. H.
Terrell, Jno.
Thompson, Drewry
Thompson, Jno.
Thompson, Peter
Thompson, Wm.
Thompson, Wm. Jr.
Thornton, Reuben
Trimble, Jno.

Turman, Martha
Turner, Thos.
Tuttle, Nicholas
Tweedle, Jno.
Vann, Martha
Vineyard, Isham
Vinson, Jesse
Voden, Bradock
Walker, Geo.
Walker, J.
Walker, M.
Walker, Milly
Walton, Geo.
Ware, Henry
Webb, Thos.
West, Eli
Whyte, O.
Williams, Nat. J.
Williamson, W.
Wilson, Jason
Wingom, Phillip
Wood, Geo.
Woods, M.
Worsham, R.
Wyter, D.

Deed Book "B"
1790 - 1792

Grantors

Allen, Benj.
Baker, Benj.
Baker, Comfort
Barden, Charlott
Barden, Gilbert
Brown, Amy
Brown, Benj.
Brown, Jno.
Brown, Nancy
Bugg, Jacob
Bugg, Nancy
Butler, Mary
Butler, Zachariah
Carter, Jas.
Carter, Lucy
Clark, Bolign (Bolling)
Clark, Martha
Clemm, Adam
Clemm, Jemmia
Colson, Abraham
Colson, Nancy
Coulter, Richd.
Crow, Hannah

Crow, Jas.
Daniel, Nancy
Daniel, Wm.
Edwards, Susannah
Edwards, Wm.
Freeman, Jas.
Fulgham, Stephen
Gordon, Catharine
Gordon, Wm.
Hill, Moses
Jones, Cartna
Jones, Nathan
Luckie, Jane
Luckie, Jno.
McCluskey, Mary
McCluskey, David
McDonald, Jas.
McDonald, Sarah
Middleton, Robt.
Nelson, Martha
Nelson, Saml.
Pinion, Ann
Pinion, Thos.
Powers, Eliz.
Powers, Frances
Saylors, Eliz.
Steagall, Eliz.
Steagall, Richd.
Stephens, Nancy
Suttle, Margret
Suttle, Wm.
Thompson, Isham
Thompson, Sarah
Thornhill, Leonard
Thornhill, Mary
Wilmoth, Thos.
Wingfield, Jno.
Wingfield, Mary

Grantees
Allen, Benj.
Allen, Wm.
Allston, Wm.
Black, Wm.
Brown, Wm.
Carter, Thos. Sr.
Coulter, Chas.
Dudley, Wm.
Ellis, Robt.
Ewing, Wm. A. D.
Fannin, Jno. Hubberd
Gordon, Wm.
Guttery, Robt.
Harbin, Thos.

Haynie, Bridger
Hill, Jno.
Kennedy, Chas.
Lowry, Edmond
Lowery, Jno.
Mecune, Wm.
Oliver, Wm.
Patton, Wm.
Pickings, Wm.
Prewett, Jacob
Ragland, Benj.
Rodgers, Thos.
Rogers, Wm.
Scales, Thos.
Skelton, Robt.
Smith, Eliz.
Tait, Jas.
Turman, Martin
Tuttle, Jas. Sr.
Vanhook, Aron
Vinson, Jesse
Walker, Andrew
Wilkins, Thos.
Williams, Wm.

Witnesses of others
mentioned:

Allen, Nathl.
Bell, Jas.
Bobo, Lewis
Brasel, Jno.
Brown, Peter
Carter, Wm.
Chandler, Jos.
Clark, Edw.
Coleman, Jno.
Cosby, R.
Crosby, Jno.
Ferguson, John
Fulgham, Matthew, dec'd.
Gill, Jno.
Goode, Wm.
Hairon (?), Hugh
Hancock, Thos.
Hansard, Wm.
Hodge, Wm.
Hollinshed, Saml.
Howard, Julius
Hudson, Chas.
Hunter, Saml.
Johnston, Elisha
Johnston, Jno. H.
Jones, Isaac

Jones, James
Lowery, Jas. Jr.
Lowery, Mashack
McAlhenan, Jno.
McDonald, Donald
McElhanen, Jno.
Menefee, Geo.
Mosely, Henry
Moss, Wm.
Neal, Robt.
Nelson, Matthew
Nelson, Saml.
Newman, Jno.
Owens, Elijah
Phips, Caleb
Potter, Sol.
Rogers, Jno.
Rowel, Jesse
Russell, Thos. C.
Stephens, Stephen
Tollett, Jno.
Walker, Archelaus
Walker, H. Graves
Walraven, Jno.
Watkins, Wm.
Wilmoth, Ezekiel
Wilmoth, Nancy
Wilmoth, Wm.
Woods, Middleton
Woods, Wm.

Land Warrants
1785 - 1795

Allen, Nathl.
Aderhold, Conrad
Allen, Reuben
Brady, Jno.
Brazel, Frederick
Bray, Jno.
Bates, Francis
Brawner, Bazel
Cain, Rosannah
Cain, Ruth
Coleman, Jno.
Collins, Jno.
Collins, Zachariah
Davis, Gideon
Davis, Wiley
Davis, Absolom
Elliott, Wm.
Forbes, Atkins
Fleming, Robt.
Franklin, David

Green, Jesse
Greenwood, Fleming
Gurthie, Robt.
Gilmer, Thos.
Gill, Jno.
Grover, Stephen
Gregg, Henry
Harper, Jno. P.
Hall, Wm.
Howington, Wm.
Hightower, Thos.
Hilley, Thos.
Hunter, Saml.
Hodge, Jno.
Henderson, Jno.
Hendricks, Hillary
Hendricks, Sarah
Hunt, Richardson
Higginbotham, Jacob
Hambleton, Isiah
Ishaw, Edw.
Johnson, Wm.
Kain, Richd.
Karr, Walter
King, Thos.
Lamb, Jno.
Long, Nicholas
Long, Jos.
McDonald, Hugh
McDonald, Jno. W.
McKinsey, Jno.
McRight, Matthew
Maxwell, Jas.
Maxwell, Thos.
Norris, Wm.
Pickens, Joshua
Pollard, Jno.
Pope, Leroy
Robartson, Jno.
Ross, Drury
Ryal, Jno.
Selman, Thos.
Smith, Wm.
Spurlock, Jas.
Stinchcomb, Absolom
Thornton, Thos.
Whitney, Jno. M.
Wyche, Geo.
Wyche, Peter

Sworn in as Justices
of Peace, Jan. 1791.

Allen, Reuben

(83)

Banks, Jno.
Barnett, W.
Caldwell, Harry
Cook, Francis
Cunningham, Jno.
Fergus, Jno.
Higginbotham, Wm.
Hunt, R.
Ragland, Evan
Scott, Thos. B.
Tait, Jas.
Walker, J.

Appointed as Commissioners over roads, Jan. 1791

Allen, Wm.
Bailey, Hezekiah
Blackwell, Jos.
Fergus, Jno.
Nunnelee, Walter
Oliver, Jno.
Pettigrew, Jno.
Tait, Jas.
Thompson, Wm.

Some early settlers whose names appeared on records 1790 - 1795

Alexander, Isaac
Brawner, Jno.
Campbell, Duncan
Chislom, Wm.
Cochran, Wm.
Conway, Phillip
Easton, Richd.
Fleming, Robt.
Ford, Isaac
Gantt, Benj.
Gibbs, Herod
Gillelan, Jacob
Grimes, Wm.
Harris, Chris.
Hawthrone, Jno. Sr.
Jordan, Jno.
Jordan, River
King, Jno.
McDougle, Alexdr.
McKee, Thos.
Park, Jas.
Park, Robt.
Prior, Jos.

Ross, Drury
Sheperd, Peter
Shoemaker, Lindsey
Strong, Wm.
Thomas, Wm.
Thurmond, Phillip
Van Hook, Saml.
Wallace, Jno.

Tax defaulters 1793

Abbott, Wm.
Akin, Saml.
Allen, Drury
Almond, Jas.
 Baughman, Jno.
Beard, Jno.
Bullard, Thos.
Calvert, Jno.
Casey, R.
Children, Jas.
Chrisa ?, Elijah
Coil, Jno.
Cook, Smith
Cothron, Jno.
Currey, Larkin
Davis, Larkin
Dobbs, Silas
Falkner, Wm.
George, Wm.
Gorman, Jno.
Ham, Jno.
Hendrick, Whitehead
Hill, Moses
Homer, Joshua
House, Quilton
Howard, Benj.
Huddleson, Robt.
Hughbanks, Richd.
Johnson, Jno.
Johnson, Andrew
Jones, Jas.
Jones, Robt.
Linsey, Reubin
Little, Absalom
McCurrda, Jno.
Martin, Claborn
Martin, Jas.
Martin, Jno.
Mirat (?), Abraham
Mobley, Allen
Orr, Daniel
Paxton, Jas.

Perfel ?, Jno.
Phips, Lewis
Pool, Wm.
Post, Jno.
Reed, Robt.
Reyley, Jno.
Rush, Jeptha
Russ, Wm.
Shiers, Wm.
Simmons, Jas.
Simmons, Jesse
Sitton, Reubin
Smith, Archer
Stiles, Wm.
Stone, Uriah
Stricklin, Jacob
Taylor, Benj.
Thomason, Geo.
Waters, Matthew
Wilmoth, Wm.

Voters for delegates
to Constitutional
Convention, 1795:

Abbit, Wm.
Abbot, Wm.
Aiken, Tho.
Aiken, Wm.
Allen, Beverly
Allen, Wm.
Almond, J. P.
Almond, J. L.
Aycock, Wm.
Bailey, Ezekiel
Bailey, Moses
Baker, Jno.
Baker, Jno. A.
Barnett, Nathl.
Barnett, Nelson
Barnett, Wm.
Bell, J. L.
Beverly, Anthony
Blackburn, Saml.
Blacke, Jno.
Blackwell, Jeremiah
Blackwell, Jos.
Blake, Wm. Jr.
Blake, Wm. Sr.
Blankenship, Womack
Bond, Richd.
Border, Gilbert
Brawner, Benj.
Brawner, Henry

Brawner, Jesse
Brawner, Jno.
Brawner, Wm.
Brady, D.
Brady, Jas.
Brown, Benj.
Brown, Jas.
Brown, Jno.
Burch, Wm.
Burdin, Archibald
Burton, Tho.
Carter, Thos.
Cameron, Jas.
Carter, Tho. Jr.
Casey, Jno.
Certain (?), Jas.
Chandler, Hezekiah
Chiles, Jno.
Clark, Chris.
Clark, David
Clark, Edw.
Cleveland, Jacob
Cleveland, Jno.
Clark, Joshua
Clark, Saml.
Clark, Zack.
Coker, Isaac
Colbert, Jas.
Collins, Zach.
Collins, Wm.
Colson, Abram
Cook, Benj.
Cook, Benj. Jr.
Cook, Dudley
Cook, Endosine (?)
Cook, Geo.
Cook, Jno.
Cook, Josiah
Cook, Reuben
Cook, Smith
Cook, Fra
Cook, Tho.
Cook, Wm.
Cook, Wm.
Cosby, Chas.
Cosby, D.
Cosby, Richmond
Cosby, Robt.
Cotter, Jno.
Curry, L. W.
Crow, Jos.
Dailey, Saml.
Daniel, Wm.
Davis, Isaac

Deadwyler, Jos.
DePriest, Jno.
Dudley, Jas.
Dudley, Wm.
Eavenson, Eli
Ellot, Andrew
Fannin, Benj.
Fannin, Laughlin
Ford, Isaac
Forson, Beal
Forson, Wm.
Foster, Tho.
Forkner, Wm.
Freeman, Jas.
Gar, Adam
Gatewood, Henry
Gatewood, Jno.
Gatewood, Larkin
Gill, Jno.
Glover, Beal
Glover, Jas.
Goss, Benj.
Goss, Chas.
Green, Burket
Greenwood, Jno.
Gray, Hezekiah
Hall, Wm.
Ham, Ambrose
Hansford, Wm.
Harper, Charter
Harper, J. P.
Hathcock, Jno.
Hathorn, Robt.
Heard, Jno.
Henderson, Geo.
Hendrick, Chas.
Hendrick, Jesse
Hendrick, Whitehead
Higginbotham, Benj.
Higginbotham, Caleb
Higginbotham, Francis
Higginbotham, Jacob
Higginbotham, Jno.
Higginbotham, Jos.
Hickerson, Larkin
Higginbotham, San'd.
Higginbotham, Saml.
Higginbotham, Wm.
Hightower, Wm.
Hightower, Charnel
Howell, Abel
Hubbard, Jno.
Hubbard, Richmond
Huddleston, Jos.

Huddleston, Robt.
Hudson, _____
Hudson, Nat.
Huff, J. L.
Hunt, Henry
Hunt, Richards
Hutson, C.
Irins, Geo.
Jones, Allen
Jones, Thos.
Kidd, J.
Kidd, Webb
King, Ezekiel
King, Lombard
Lindsey, Reuben
Lovelady, Thos.
Lowrey, Elisha
Lowery, J. L.
Lowery, Jas.
Lowery, Jno.
McClusky, Jas.
McDowell, Tho.
McKay, Jno.
McKee, Jno.
McKee, Wm.
McKiver, Jno.
Martin, David
Martin, Jno.
Means, Wm.
Merit ____
Melver (Melvin?), Andrew
Miller, Jacob
Millican, Jno.
Mogin (?), Saml.
Moore, Lewis
Morrison ____
Morrison, J. H.
Morris, Wm.
Morris, Wm.
Moseley, Henry
Mosely, Lewis
Moseley, Robt.
Moseley, Robt.
Napper (Napier?), Tho.
Odom, Jacob
Oliver, Wm.
Pace, Barnabas
Paxton, Robt.
Penn, Thos.
Porterfield, David
Prewit, Jacob
Prewit, Wm.
Rice, Leonard
Ross, Jesse

Rousey, Jno.
Rousy, Edmund
Rucker, Jno.
Satterwhite, Frank
Satterwhite, Jno.
Scott, Tho. B.
Sewell, Joshua
Sewell, M.
Shackleford, Edmund
Shackleford, Henry
Shackleford, Jno.
Smith, Nat.
Smith, Val.
Sewell, Wm.
Spears, Jno.
Spears, Wm.
Statom, Jas.
Statom, Jno. Sr.
Stinchcomb, Absalom
Stubs, Peter
Suttles, Isaac
Suttles, Wm.
Sutton, Jas.
Tait, Jas.
Tate, Arthur
Tate, Wm. H.
Terry, Jos.
Thornton, Danl.
Thornton, Reuben
Tolbert, Saml.
Turman, Jos.
Turman, Leonard
Tuttle, Jos.
Vineyard, David
Ware, Edw.
Ware, Wm.
Webb, Pleasant
Webb, Chas.
White, Danl.
White, Jesse
White, Luke
Wilcox, Moses
Wilkins, Jno.
Williams, Jos.
Williams, Tho.
Wilson, Jas.
Wingfield, Jno.
Wood, Middleton
Wood, Saml.
Wood, Saml.
Wych, Geo.
Wyche, Peter

Officers, Elbert Co.
Militia 6/21/1791

Allen, Wm.
Bailey, Hezekiah
Blackwell, Jno.
Brawner, Jas.
Burton, Archibald
Burton, Thos.
Colbert, Rich.
Colbert, Thos.
Coleman, Jas.
Collins, Jno.
Cook, Jas.
Cunningham, Jno.
Depriest, Jno.
Dudley, Jas.
Grinnell, Jno.
Hansford, Wm.
Hatcher, Wm.
Higginbotham, Benj.
Hightower, Wm.
Hodge, Jno.
McDonald, Hugh
Means, Robt.
Means, Wm.
McClusky, David
McClusky, Jas.
Neilson, Saml.
Patton, Wm.
Penn, Thos.
Ragland, Evan
Rucker, Jno.
Scott, Thos.
Sewell, Joshua
Stokes, Montford
Stricklin, Henry
Thomas, Joel
Thompson, Wm.
Vainyard, Jno.
Walker, Archibald
Wildred, Jos. Dred

Legal Notices 1794-1795
from Augusta Chronicle
and Gazette, and the
Southern Centinel and
Universal Gazette;

Adams, David
Adams, Jane
Alexander, Geo.
Barnett, Wm.
Bonds, Richd.

Brinton, Andrew
Calvert, Jas.
Clark, Chris.
Cook, Reubin
Cooke, Jas.
Cooke, Jas. Watson
Darden, Geo.
Davis, Wm.
Easton, Chas.
Easton, Jno.
Easton, Reubin
Easton, Sally
Garr, Adam
Garr, Lewis
Garr, Michael
Gragg, Jas.
Greenwood, Jno.
Grimes, Mildred
Grimes, Wm.
Harvie, Wm.
Heard, Stephen
Henderson, Jos.
Higginbotham, Saml.
Meredeth, Jas.
Miller, Jno.
Mosely, Lucas
Patten, Saml.
Satterwhite, Francis
Scott, Thos. B.
Wills, Jno.

Some Elbert Co. Jury
Lists 1791 - 1793:

Adams, David
Aikens, Tho.
Alexander, Geo.
Allen, Benj.
Allen, Wm.
Baker, Saml.
Banks, Ralph
Barker, Wm.
Barnett, Jno.
Barnett, Leonard
Barnett, Nathan
Boyd, Jno.
Brawner, Jno.
Brown, Benj.
Brown, Francis
Brown, Jno.
Bugg, Jacob
Burton, Robt.
Burton, Thos.
Caldwell, Henry

Chapman, Wm.
Cladus, Geo.
Cloud, Noah
Collins, Zachariah
Cook, Benj.
Cook, Jas.
Cosby, Chas.
Cosby, Henry
Cosby, Jno.
Cosby, Robt.
Crouder, Robt.
Crowder, Jno.
Cullen, David
Davis, Moses
Deadwiler, Chris.
Dudley, Wm.
Easter, Jas.
Easter, Rich
Evins, Nathan
Fannin, Laughlin
Fleming, Moses
George, Wm.
Greenwood, Jno.
Gregg, Tho.
Griffith, Robt.
Hammon, Jacob
Harper, Jno. P.
Hart, Benj.
Haynes, Moses
Henderson, Jno.
Higginbotham, Benj.
Higginbotham, Caleb
Higginbotham, Wm.
Hightower, Wm.
Hinton, Hardy
Hodge, Wm.
Hogg, Jno.
Holly, Thos.
Howard, Julius
Hudson, Chas.
Hudson, David
Hudson, Jno. Sr.
Hunt, Richardson
Hunter, Saml.
Hutchins, Jno.
Johnston, Jno.
Key, Jno. M.
Keyes, Jno.
Kilgore, Jno.
Lamb, Jno. Sr.
Litch, Wm.
Lovelady, Thos.
McCluskey, Jas.

McDaniel, Jno.
McGardy, Edw.
Mandline, Francis
Milroy, Avington
Martin, Thos.
Montgomery, Saml.
Moon, Wm.
Moore, Jno.
Morris, Jno.
Morse, Wm.
Muckleroy, Avington
Murdock, Patrick
Nail, Jos.
Napier, Tho.
Neil, Jos.
Nelson, Saml.
Nunnelle, Jas. F.
Nunnelee, Walter
Oliver, Jno.
Pace, Barnabas
Palmer, Jno.
Patton, Jas.
Patton, Wm.
Pulliom, Robt.
Ragland, Evan
Ready, Jas.
Richardson, Walker
Ross, Robt.
Rucker, Jos.
Russell, Jos. R.
Russell, Nathan
Satterwhite, Francis
Smith, Nathl.
Statham, Jno.
Strong, Wm.
Tait, Jas.
Tate, Wm.
Teasley, Jno.
Templeton, Jno.
Thomas, Wm.
Thompson, Alexdr.
Thompson, Drury
Thompson, Isham
Thompson, Jno. F.
Turman, Geo.
Turman, Martin
Turman, Robt.
Turman, Tho.
Tuttle, Jas. Jr.
Tyner, Richd.
Underwood, Jos.
Vineyard, Jas.
Vineyard, Jno.
Walker, Jeremiah

Walthall, Edw.
Walthall, Jas.
Watts, Geo.
Webb, Austin
Westbrook, Jno.
White, Danl.
Wilkins, Jno.
Wilkins, Tho.
Willen, Wm.
William, Danl.
Wolridge, Wm.

Elbert Co. Muster Roll
1793

Alexander, Adlay
Alexander, Elias
Alexander, Isaac
Alexander, Jno. B.
Alexander, Nathl.
Alexander, Jas.
Arnold, Jonath.
Bennett, Benj.
Black, Robt.
Bond, Richd.
Broner (?), Rolling
Bush, Jeptha
Casey, Abraham
Chesser, Benj.
Chesser, Tho.
Chesser, Wm.
Cleveland, Wiat
Cook, Wm.
Depriest, Randolph
Dobbs, Elias
Dobbs, Jno.
Dobbs, Josiah
Dobbs, Silas
Floman, Jno.
Fowler, Jno.
Greenstreet, Jas.
Harbor, Talmon
Hayns, Stephen
Homes, Joshua
Howard, Benj.
Hunt, Jas.
Johnson, Donald
Johnson, Peter
Jones, Robt.
King, Jno.
McAlplin, Sol.
McDonald, Donald
McDugle, Daniel
McDugle, Jno.

McKinsey, Wm.
Marsh, Gilbert
Michel, Jno.
Montgomerh, Jno.
Montgomery, Saml.
Mooney, Chris.
Murrah, Jno.
Numan, Jno.
Owen, Elijah
Nail, Jos.
Parks, Jno.
Richardson, Amos
Ronvel (?), Jno.
Ross, Jno.
Ryle, Jno.
Seals, Tho.

Shiers, Wm.
Skelton, Jacob
Skelton, Jno.
Skelton, Sol.
Smith, Gabrel
Smith, Ralph
Thomas, Ezekiel
Thomas, Wm.
Tottman, Benj.
Vales, Saml.
Vinson, Liab ?
Watts, Edw.
Watts, Geo.
Wellmott, Wm.
Wheeler, Wm.
Williams, Wm.

FRANKLIN COUNTY

An original County created by Legislative Act February 23, 1784, from land ceded by the Cherokees May 31, 1783, and the Creeks Nov. 1, 1783. Land in Franklin County was given as Bounty Grants to Revolutionary War Veterans. The County seat is Carnesville.

Headrights and Bounty Grants 1790 - 1795

Alexander, Isaac
Alexander, Jno. Brown
Allen, Benj.
Allen, Nathl.
Allen, Wm.
Anderson, Jas.
Anderson, Jno.
Anderson, Wm.
Anthony, Micajah
Armstrong, Jas. Col.
Arnold, Jas.
Arrington, Jno.
Aycock, Richd.
Aycock, Wm.
Ayers, Abrham
Ayres, Abrham
Bailey, Wm.
Bartan, Ruth

Beall, Daniel
Bickerstaff, Jno.
Black, Saml.
Blanton, Jno.
Bobo, Lewis
Bowen, Joel
Bowen, Jos.
Bowie, Jas.
Boyd, Jno.
Bradford, Oseah
Brewer, Geo.
Brewer, Wm.
Brewton, Jas.
Briers, Lawrence
Briggs, Isaac
Brooks, Jno.
Brown, Jno.
Bryan, Saml.
Bryant, Jno.
Bryant, Wm.

Burney, David
Burns, Andrew
Burns, Andrew, Jr.
Burns, Eliz.
Burns, Felix
Burns, Jean
Burns, Jno.
Burns, Martha
Burns, Mary
Burns, Robt.
Caldwell, Alex
Calwell, Henry
Campbell, Duncan
Campbell, Jno.
Carter, Josiah
Carter, Thos.
Chandler, Jos.
Churchill, Nathl. H.
Clark, Jno.
Clark, Jno. Sr.
Clarke, Jno.
Clarke, Jno. Sr.
Cleveland, Jeremiah
Cleveland, Neal
Cleveland, Wm.
Cole, Josiah
Cole, Wm.
Coleman, Eden
Coleman, Jno.
Collier, Jno.
Colton, Richd.
Comer, Jno. Jr.
Cothan, Thos.
Crawford, Peter
Creswell, Saml.
Culbertson, David
Culpepper, Malachiah
Cunningham, Jno.
Cup, Michael
Dabbs, Jos.
Daniel, Wm.
Daniell, Chas.
Daniell, Thos.
Daniell, Wm.
Dawson, Richmond
Day, Ambrose
Diamond, Jno.
Diamond, Wm.
Dobbs, Jos.
Doolen, Danl.
Doolen, Jno.
Downs, Ambrose
Dunkon, Henry
Durkee, Nathl.

Durkie, Nathl.
Easley, Danl.
Easly, R.
Echols, Benj.
Edmonds, Jas.
Elam, Danl.
Elese, Robt.
Ellerson, Jas.
Elliott, Wm.
Embry, Jonathan
Emmett, Jas.
Evans, Harwood
Evans, Henry
Fanning, Jno.
Farmer, Wm.
Few, Wm. Jr.
Finney, Jas.
Flemming, Elijah
Flimming, Jno.
Flemming, Wm.
Flewellin, Alex
Freeman, Jas.
Gammage, Thos.
Gardner, Jno. T.
Gardner, Saml.
Garren, Moses
Gartrell, Francis
Gaugh, Wm.
Gideon, Francis
Gilbert, Thos.
Gilliam, Richd.
Gilliam, Wm.
Gorham, Jenny
Gorham, Jno.
Goreham, Jno.
Gorham, Sanford
Gorham, Wm.
Graham, Jno.
Graves, Geo.
Graves, Humphrey
Graves, Joshua
Graves, Perry
Graves, Thos. Jr.
Graves, Thos. Sr.
Graves, Wm.
Gresham, Thos.
Griffith, Jno.
Grimes, Jno.
Gunnells, Jos.
Guy, Wm.
Hall, Jno.
Hamilton, Archibald
Hampton, Jno.
Haney, Geo.

Haney, Thos.
Harns, Bucker
Harrington, Jno.
Harris, Buckner
Harris, Sampson
Harrison, Benj.
Hawkins, Benj.
Hay, Gilbert
Hay, Hugh
Hay, Jas.
Hay, Wm.
Hays, Henry
Heard, Jno.
Henning, Geo.
Hewett, Wm.
Hightower, Wm.
Hill, Jas.
Hillhouse, David
Hinton, Harvey
Hobbs, Joel
Hooper, Jesse
Hooper, Jno.
Houston, Wm.
Howard, Geo.
Howard, Hermon
Howard, Julius
Howard, Nehemiah
Hubbard, Benj.
Hudson, Cuthbert
Hudson, Joachim
Humphrey, Jos.
Hunter, Dalziel
Hunter, Evan T.
Jackson, Robt.
Jackson, Walter
Jamerson, Wm. C. & Co.
Jarratt, Howell
Jennings, Jonathan
Jennings, Wm.
Johnson, Jas.
Johnson, Wm.
Jones, Ambrose
Jones, Malachia
Jones, Thos.
Jones, Wm.
Jordan, Fleming
Jordan, Jno.
Keating, Edw.
Kennerly, Thos.
King, Edw. Edmond
King, Edw.
King, Jno.
Knox, Saml.
Lamar, Zachariah

Lambkin, Saml.
Legett, Jno.
Lewis, Freeman
Lipham, Frederick
Little, Jas.
Lockhart, Richd.
Long, Evans
Long, Nimrod
Longstreet, Danl.
Luckey, Alex.
Luckey, David
Luckey, Wm.
Lyner, Chris.
Mackie, Jno.
Mackie, Saml.
Marbury, Horatia
Martin, Wm.
Matthews, Danl. Jr.
McBee, Jas.
McCannon, Jas.
McClair, Lewis
McCutchin, Jas.
McDonald, Chas.
McDonald, Hugh
McDougal, Alex
McFall, Geo.
McGarey, Edw.
McGarrey, Edw.
McGary, Edw.
McGowan, Robt.
McIntosh, Lochlin
McWeir, Alegany
McWeir, Thompson
Melone, Peter
Meriwether, Thos.
Milligan, Jas.
Milligan, Moses
Milton, Jno.
Montgomery, Jno.
Moore, Richd.
Morgan, Danl.
Morris, Jas.
Morrell, I.
Muling, Henry
Mullen, Jno.
Myrick, Jno.
Neilson, Saml.
Nelson, Saml.
Ogletree, Jno.
Oliver, Jas.
Parks, Jas.
Patton, Wm.
Payne, Thos.
Pennington, Jacob

Phillip, Saml.
Phillips, Jno.
Phillips, Jos.
Pool, Baxter
Pope, Leroy
Porter, Benj.
Porter, Thos.
Powell, Anthony
Pulliam, Robt.
Randle, Thos.
Randolph, Isaac
Roberts, Jno.
Robertson, David
Robertson, Jno.
Robinson, David
Rogers, Jno.
Rose, Henry
Russell, Jos. M.
Rutherford, Claborn
Sandidge, Jno.
Sexon, Davis
Shareman, Robt.
Sharp, Jas. B.
Sheilds, Thos.
Shelly, Phillip
Shields, Thos.
Shipley, Robt.
Singleton, Robt.
Skelton, Robt.
Slatter, Sol.
Slatter, Wm.
Sled, Jos.
Sled, Joshua
Smellers, Jos.
Smith, Benj.
Smith, Jno.
Smith, Ralph
Smith, Thos.
Smyth, Thos.
Smyth, Thos. Jr.
Spain, Jno.
Sparks, Matthew Jr.
Sparks, Wm.
Spencer, Wm.
Spruce, Wm.
Starr, Jno.
Stead, Wm.
Stephens, Jos.
Stewart, Isaac
Stith, Paton R.
Stith, Wm.
Stokes, Jno.
Stokes, Wm.
Stonecyffer, Jno.

Stripling, Francis
Strong, Wm.
Sturgess, Danl.
Summerlin, Henry
Talbot, Patsy
Talbot, Thos.
Tatem, Abner
Taylor, Grant
Taylor, Jos.
Taylor, Robt.
Templeton, Jno.
Terendate, Danl.
Terrell, David
Terrell, Jos.
Thetford, Wm.
Thomas, Benj.
Thomas, Gills
Ghomas, Massa
Thomas, Wm.
Thompson, Abraham
Thompson, Peter
Thornton, Stephen
Thrasher, Robt.
Towns, Jno.
Trailer, Wm.
Trewitt, Riley
Trimble, Moses
Walker, Phillip
Wallis, Carnill
Wallis, Micajah
Walton, Jess
Walton, Simon
Walton, Walker
Waters, Jno.
Weatherby, Geo.
Webster, Jno.
White, Jno.
White, Richd.
Whitney, Jas. R.
Whitney, Jno. M.
Whitsill, Geo.
Whitworth, Jno.
Wilbourn, Wm.
Wiley, Peter
Wilkinson, Wm.
Williams, Jas.
Williams, Jno.
Williams, Jos.
Williams, Joshua
Williams, Wm.
Williams, Wm. C.
Williamson, Chas.
Williamson, Jas.
Williamson, Micajah

Williamson, Micajah, Jr.
Williamson, Peter
Williamson, Robt.
Wilson, Benj.
Wilson, Jos.
Wilson, Milley
Wilson, Perry
Wood, Josiah
Woods, Josiah
Woods, Middleton
Woods, Saml.
Woods, Wm.
Wright, Obediah
Wyatt, Peyton
Young, Danl.

Legal Ads in Augusta
Chronicle & Gazette &
the Southern Centinal
& Universal Gazette:
1795

Clark, Jno. Jr.
Cleveland, Jno.
Cleveland, Larkin
Coffee, Nathan
Dobbs, Jos.
Franklin, Abner
Gilbert, Thos.
Harden, Wm.
Hardin, Mark
Hooper, Obediah
Humphries, Jos.
Lane, Jno.
Millens, Jno.
Payne, Jno.
Stoneycypher, Jno.
Terrell, Jos.
White, Benedict
Woods, Middleton

Muster Roll, Nov.
20, 1793, Capt.
Thos. Crews' Co.

Baker, Thos.
Banks, Elijah
Bankston, Jno.
Barnet, Jno.
Bulard, Jno.
Cockburn, Archable
Conkburn, Geo.
Demey, Jno.
Demey, Josiah

Deprest, Jas.
Dunagain, Joshua
Eds, Isaac
Ganner, Geo.
Glenn, Wm.
Gullet, Andrew
Hearn, Hen.
Henan, Wm.
Holcom, Jno.
Holcom, Jos.
Holcom, Thos.
Holcom, Moses
Holcom, Sherard
Hollongsworth, Saml.
Hughet, Sol.
Jones, Milachi
Little, Jas. H.
Martain, Elijah
Penace, Hugh
Pennington, Jacob
Rabourn, Jell (?)
Rabourn, Jno.
Reed, Saml.
Savage, Elia
Stringer, Geo.
Stuard, Jno.
Terril, Jos.
Terril, Moses
Turner, Jno.
V n, Jos.
Vann, Geo.
Varniel, Wm.
Wiley, Jas.
Witherspoon, Wm.
Wafford, Benj.
Wofford, Jas.
Young, Jno.
Young, Robt.

Muster Roll
Oct. 1, 1793
Capt. Saml. Walters Co.

Anderson, Robt.
Barrett, Benj.
Barrett, Wm.
Barron, Jno.
Barrot, Joel
Barton, Benj.
Been, Robt.
Beeson, Jonathan
Bobo, Sampson
Bond, Chas.
Brogdon, Merideth

Burges, Elias
Burges, Josiah
Casey, Abraham
Cawthon, Chas.
Cawthon, Claborn
Cawthorn, David
Cleveland, Wm.
Cleveland, Wm. Jr.
Connor, Jno.
Connor, McMillion M.
Crane, Joel
Crane, Wm.
Denmon, Jas.
Dobbs, Lodday
Gates, Wm.
Gilbert, Chas.
Handon, Sevan
Haney, Geo.
Harden, Mark
Henderson, Robt. L.
Hudson, Burrel
Humphres, Geo.
Humphres, Shadrack
Jackson, Wm.
Leech, Wm.
McDougla, Jno.
Mason, Jno.
Matthews, Jas.
Maybe, Mattethias
Nale, Jno.
Niel, Jno. M.
Oaldom, Jno.
Payne, Jno.
Payne, Rewbin
Payne, Wm.
Pullom, Benj.
Raylah, Jno.
Read, Jas.
Shewmaker, Jesse
Sneed, Wm.
Sparks, Jas.
Thomas, Jesse
Wagnon, Jno.
Walker, Chas.
Walker, Elijah
Walker, Jacob
Walker, Randal
Wall, Henry
Walters, Jno.
Walters, Moses
Walters, Peter
Walters, Robt.
Warren, Chas.
Warren, Valentine
Wright, Jno.

Muster Roll
Oct. 10, 1793
Capt. Jno. Stoneycffer's
Company:

Able, Jno.
Benden, Jno.
Bond, Chas.
Bond, Wm.
Briges, Walton
Bryan, Edw.
Bryan, Elijah
Bryan, Jno.
Burket, Geo.
Carter, Jno.
Clark, Jno.
Cleveland, Absolom
Cleveland, Jeremiah
Cleveland, Wm.
Cox, Thos.
Daughtrey, Chris.
Edds, Joel
Edwards, Jos.
Franklin, Abnon
Gibson, Jas.
Gough, Jesse
Gough, Thos.
Gough, Wm.
Gurdain, Thos.
Hancock, Isham
Harrington, Cunnil
Hill, Jesse
Holcom, Henry
Hooper, Jno.
Hooper, Obadiah
Hunt, Jas.
Hunt, Jno.
Jackson, Benj.
James, Jackson
Johnston, Nelson
Jones, Jno.
Jones, Jos.
Killey, Thos.
Lankford, Wiet
Legrand, Jesse
Martain, Merritt
Morgain, Danl.
Mullin, Jno.
Oxsin, Geo.
Payn, Saml.
Philpott, Norman
Ray, Jno.
Readin, Saml.
Rice, Edw.
Shanke, Elijah

Sharp, Robt.
Shelley, Absolom
Shelley, Amous
Shelley, Rubin
Sherril, Geo.
Smith, Henry
Smith, Jesse
Smith, Wm.
Smith, Wm. Jr.
Sparkes, Jenk
Sparks, Jeremiah
Stewart, Jno.
Stonesipher, Jno. H.
Swift, Jno.
Swift, Wm.
Taylor, Jeremiah
Thrasher, Robt.
Todhunter, Evin
Walters, Clement
Walton, Walker
Ward, Jno.
Ward, Saml.
White, Abe
White, Jepthah
White, Wm.

Muster Roll, Oct. 25, 1793
Capt. Ben Easleys' Co.

Barber, Matthew
Barber, Will
Barton, Robt.
Bickerstaff, Johnson.
Branham, Jno.
Bridges, Berry
Bridges, Haynes
Bridges, Henry
Bridges, J.
Bridges, Wiseman
Cameron, Ambrose
Clark, Saml.
Clask, Zack
Cloud, Ziak
Coil, Jno.
Cuningham, Jos.
Dawson, Jno.
Doggett, Geo.
Doggitt, Will
Doughton, Wm.
Easley, Benj.
Easly, Jno.
Epperson, Saml.
Eubanks, Richd.
Fleming, Wm.

Garrison, Shadrack
Gates, Jas.
Gates, Josiah
Goodlet, Jas.
Goolsby, Aaron
Gordon, Thos.
Gordon, Will
Grady, Jno.
Green, Sutton
Gruas (Guess?), David
Gunnels, Jno.
Harden, Jno.
Hart, Jno.
Henderson, Jno.
Henderson, Jones
Hepkins, Saml.
House, Jas.
Jennings, David
Jinnings, Johnathan
Jones, Thos.
Killough, Allen
Kinna, Danl.
Kirkpatrick, Thos.
Lane, Jonathan
Lively, Jno.
Lyner, Christee
Mackey, Gallant
Manifee, Geo.
Manifee, Richd.
Morton, Joel
Nailon, Dixon
Nelson, Thos.
Parmely, Saml.
Pattern, Saml.
Petergrow, Geo.
Ramsay, Jno.
Robertson, Benj.
Rodgers, Ben
Rodgers, Dimpsey
Scott, Jas.
Scott, Wm.
Scroggins, Geo.
Silmon, Ely
Simmons, Jesse
Spurlock, Allen
Stewart, Robt.
Stewart, Wm.
Stubblefield, Will
Sumerlain, Jacob
Summerlin, Lazarus
Swringe (?), Peter
Tanner, Jos.
Tillery, Henry
Vasdimon, Will

(96)

Vint, Wm.
Waddell, Alexdr.
Wakefield, Chas.
Weterson, Jno.
Willson, Arkeclair
Young, Robt.

Deed Book C
1786 - 1792
Deed Book H
1792 - 1793

Grantors
Anderson, Henry
Ayres, Danl.
Ayres, Nancy (Anna)
Barnett, Caroline
Barnett, Jno.
Benton, Mordecai
Black, Henry
Black, Wm.
Britt, Chas.
Bryan, Jno.
Bryan, Nancy
Burns, Aquilla
Caldwell, Alexdr.
Caldwell, Ruthy
Carter, Ann (Nancy)
Carter, Jno.
Carter, Mary
Carter, Thos.
Clarke, Geo.
Clarke, Jno.
Clarke, Moses
Cleveland, Fanny
Cleveland, Larkin
Coffey, Mary
Coffey, Nathan
Cothum, Eliz.
Cothum, Thos.
Cox, Mary
Cox, Thos.
Downs, Ambrose
Downs, Sabra
Echols, Benj.
Echols, Sabra
Fairchilds, Abihud (?)
Gilbert, Chas.
Gilbert, Hannah
Gilbert, Sarah
Goodwin, Jno.
Gorham, Jinny
Gorham, Jno.
Harrington, Sarah

Harrington, Thos.
Harris, Buckner
Hay, Wm.
Hening, Geo.
Humphries, Jos.
Humphries, Rebekah
Hunter, Saml.
Hunter, Sarah
Isaacs, Elisha
Langford, Sarah
Langford, Wyatt
Lindsey, Jno.
Lindsey, Mary
McGowan, Robt.
Middleton, Robt.
Morgan, Betsy
Morgan, Danl.
Morgan, Deborah
Morgan, Jno.
Mosely, David
Mullin, Eliz.
Mullin, Jno.
Neale, Joanna
Neale, Jno.
Payne, Jno.
Payne, Nancy
Payne, Poyndexter
Payne, Yamkey (?)
Philpott, Martha
Philpott, Warren
Poague, Marg.
Poague, Robt.
Powell, Richd.
Rice, Edw.
Riggs, Bethuil
Savage, Wm.
Sledd, Joshua
Sledd, Winifred
Smith, Jno.
Spratlin, Jas.
Spratlin, Winifred
Stone, Uriah
Stoneycyffer, Ann
Stoneycyffer, Jno.
Stoneycyffer, Nancy
Strother, Jno.
Talbott, Mathew
Talbott, Thos.
Thomas, Jesse
Thompson, Clare (Claus?)
Thrasher, Benj.
Thrasher, Eliz.
Thrasher, Robt.
Thrasher, Sarah

Vance, Patrick
Vance, Sarah
Walters, Jno.
Walters, Mary
Walton, Mary
Ward, Bryan
Ward, Bryant
Ward, Saml.
Whealer, Jos.
Whiteaire, Thos.
Williamson, Micajah
Williamson, Peter
Williamson, Sally

Grantee

Arthur, Matthew
Ashworth, Benj.
Ayres, Danl.
Baker, Wm.
Barber, Geo.
Bean, Robt.
Benton, Mordecai
Benton, Nathan
Black, Wm.
Bobo, Sampson
Brown, David
Brown, Jno.
Bryan, Jno.
Bryan, Thos.
Bryan, Zach.
Burgess, Josias
Burns, Aquilla
Bush, Danl.
Caldwell, Alexdr.
Calhoun, Jas.
Canter, Thos.
Carnes, Thos. Peter
Cawthon, Wm.
Clarke, Jesse
Clarke, Wm.
Cleveland, Absalom
Cleveland, Jno.
Cleveland, Wiat
Cobbs, Jno.
Cockburn, Geo.
Coffee, Nathan
Cook, Jos.
Cox, Thos.
Crain, Joel
Darden, Jno.
Eads, Mary
Early, Jeffery
Early, Jno.
East, Jos.

Echols, Benj.
Ellison, David
Estes, Asa
Fleming, Robt.
Franklin, Abner
Fulton, Saml.
Gambol, Saml.
Gamble, Jno.
Gates, Benj.
Gates, Jas.
Gates, Wm.
Gilbert, Chas.
Goodwin, Jno. Jr.
Goolsby, Isaiah
Gorham, Jno.
Gough, Wm.
Hambleton, Rachel
Harbour, Isaiah
Harris, Buckner
Harrison, Benj.
Hay, Wm.
Helms, Jno.
Hennan, Wm.
Henning, Geo.
Herrington, Jno.
Houghton, Joshua
Isaacs, Elijah
Isbell, Pendleton
Isaacs, Saml.
Jones, Russell
Lafferty, Jno.
Lane, Jno.
Langford, Wyett
Lee, Joshua
Liner, Henry
Luckie, Jno.
McCann, Jas.
Martin, Jos.
Mathews, Geo.
Mathews, Jas.
Molton, Jos.
Mosely, David
Morgan, Danl.
Morgan, Jno.
Mullins, Jno.
Mullins, Jno. Sr.
Murray, Thos.
Naile, Jno.
Newberry, Jas.
Nicholas, Williams
Norrington, David
Owen, Wm.
Oxshire, Geo.
Pace, Barnabas

Palmer, Sol.
Parmer, Jonathan
Payne, Jno.
Payne, Poindexter
Payne, Thos.
Philpott, Warren
Sanders, Joshua
Sherrill, Geo.
Sherrill, Saml.
Shipley, Robt.
Sinclair, Jos.
Simons, Jas.
Smith, Jno.
Smith, Mary
Snow, Edmind
Sparks, Elijah
Stoneycypher, Jno.
Strong, Elijah
Strong, Wm.
Swift, Wm.
Talbott, Thos.
Taliaferro, Jno. Boutwell
Terrill, Hezekiah
Thomas, Jesse
Trentham, David
Turner, Jno.
Walker, Chas.
Walker, Jesse
Walters, Clement
Walters, Peter
Walton, Walker
Warren, Thos.
Webb, Pleasant
Whealler, Wm.
Wheeler, Jos.
White, Jno.
Whitney, Jno. M.
Wilkins, Clement
Williamson, Elijah
Williman, Chris.
Wofford, Wm.
Wright, Obadiah
Wyley, Jas.

Witnesses & those own-
ing adjoining land:

Able, Jno.
Adams, Robt.
Adams, Thos.
Alexander, Isaac
Allen, Jas.
Anderson, Robt.
Armstrong, Jno.

Ashley, Wm.
Bailey, Wm.
Baker, Saml.
Barnett, Jno.
Beall, Danl.
Bean, Robt.
Bell, Hannah
Bell, Jas.
Renton, Mordecai
Black, Henry
Blackwell, Dunstan
Bragdon, Meredith
Branham, Spencer
Brewer, Benj.
Brogdon, Robt.
Brown, Alexdr.
Brown, David
Bryan, Wm.
Bugg, N. H.
Burgess, Elias
Bush, Danl.
Butler, Patrick
Cabbin, Jno.
Cain, Jno.
Call, Richd.
Call, Wm. Jr.
Cambridge, Jno. M.
Camp, Edw.
Campbell, Aaron
Campbell, Duncan
Cannon, Russell
Cargo, Saml.
Carnes, Peter
Carns, T. P.
Carr, Thomas
Caursey, Peter
Cawthon, Wm.
Christmas, R.
Clark, Barnes
Clarke, Eliz.
Clarke, Geo.
Cleveland, Benj.
Cleveland, Jeremiah
Cleveland, Jno. C.
Cleveland, Larkin
Cleveland, Wm.
Cloud, Jno.
Cobb, Jno.
Cobbs, Howell
Cobbs, Jno.
Coffee, Nathan
Colbert, Nicodemus
Coleman, Thompson
Collins, Jas.

Cosby, S.
Creswell, David
Cunningham, Jno.
Dabbs, Jos.
Daniell, Wm.
David, Wiley
Davis, Wm.
Demsey, Jno.
Depriest, Jno.
Dobbs, Loddy
Doolen, Daniel
Doss, Joel
Durham, Nathan
Eads, Sol.
Early, Betsy
Early, Jacob
Echols, Benj.
Echols, Betse
Edwards, Jos.
Elder, Joshua
Elliott, Wm.
Embry, Jno.
Embry, Nancy
Espy, Thos.
Estes, Jno.
Estes, Richd.
Fergus, Jno.
Floro, Peter
Flournoy, R.
Flournoy, Robt.
Fountain, Jas.
Franklin, Abner
Frazier, Andrew
Frazier, Jno.
Freeman, Holman
Freeman, Jas.
Freeman, Jno.
Fryar, Feilding
Fryar, Zach. Lewis
Fuller, Isaac
Gaines, Gerome
Gardener, Jno. F.
Gibson, Jas.
Gilbert, Chas.
Gilbert, Thos.
Gilen, Jas.
Giles, Jas.
Gillaspy, David
Glascock, Thos.
Goode, Edw.
Gorham, J.
Gorham, Jno.
Gough, Wm.
Gregg, Thos.

Grigg, Thos.
Guillam, Richd.
Guillam, Susanna
Guillam, Wm.
Halcom, Henry
Halcom, Thos.
Hammett, W. M.
Hammitt, Wm.
Haney, Geo.
Hardin, Mark
Hardy, Jno. Francis
Harrington, Jno.
Harris, Buckner
Harrison, Thos.
Harrison, Thos. Sr.
Hay, Wm.
Hays, Wm.
Head, Richd.
Head, Wm.
Henderson, Robt.
Hollingsworth, Jacob
Houston, Jno.
Howard, Julius
Hudson, Cutbird
Hudson, Jos.
Hughy, Peter
Humphries, Jos.
Hunt, Jas.
Hunt, Nathl.
Isaacs, Saml.
Jackson, Absalom
Jackson, Robt.
Jones, Edw.
Jones, Richd.
Jones, Wm.
Joyce, Alexdr.
Kelly, Thos.
Kirkpatrick, Jas.
Lane, Chas.
Lane, Jno.
Lawrence, Wm.
Lee, Wm.
Leech, Henry B.
Lindsey, Jacob
Lindsey, Jno.
Linn, Jno.
Little, Jas. H.
McCall, T.
McConnell, Wm.
McCree, Wm.
McDonald, Hugh
McGowan, Robt.
McLane, Jas.
McMillan, Alexdr.

Mackie, Jno.
Madison, Jas.
Mains, Robt.
Marbury, Leonard
Marbury, Wm.
Marcus, Jno.
Marks, Jas.
Mathews, Geo.
Mathews, Jas.
Middleton, Robt.
Miller, Willis
Moore, Jno.
Morgan, Danl.
Moss, Wm.
Mounger, H.
Mullins, Jno.
Ogg, Geo.
Owen, Wm.
Pannill, J.
Parr, Benj.
Partin, Josiah
Patrick, Paul
Patterick, Wm.
Patton, Arthur
Patton, Saml.
Payne, Jno.
Payne, Moses
Payne, Nathl.
Phillips, Saml.
Philpott, Warren
Phinnizg, Ferdinand
Pope, Jno.
Pulliam, Jos.
Quillen, Chas.
Reiley, Wm.
Reveir, Wiat,
Robison, Jno.
Routon, Jno.
Rush, Jesse
Russell, Ailsey Martin
Russell, J. M.
Ryan, Jos.
Sapp, Wm.
Scott, Thos. B.
Seale, Anthony Sr.
Selfridge, Robt.
Shackleford, Jas.
Shaw, Mary
Shelby, Jno.
Sloan, Wm.
Smith, Jno.
Smith, Wm.
Stevenson, E.
Stith, Will

Stoneycyffer, Jno.
Strickland, Jos. Sr.
Strickland, Jos. Jr.
Strickland, Sol.
Sutten, Ralph
Tait, Jas.
Talbot, Mathew
Taylor, Edmund
Taylor, Grant
Taylor, Rowland
Terrell, Wm.
Terrill, Jas.
Thrasher, Robt.
Thomas, Ezekiel
Thompson, Wells
Thompson, Wm.
Thorne, Merryman
Tony, Littleberry
Towns, Jno.
Turner, Jno.
Wagnon, Jno. P.
Walker, Geo.
Walker, Phillip
Walker, Wyatt
Wall, J.
Walters, Robt.
Walton, Jesse
Walton, Thos.
Walton, W.
Ward, Saml.
Ware, Jno.
Watkins, Jno.
Watkins, Robt.
Webb, Claiborn
Webb, Jesse
Webster, Jno.
Westbrook, Stephen
Whitmire, Thos.
Williams, Jno.
Williamson, Peter
Williamson, Robt.
Willis, Britton
Wilson, Jno.
Wilson, Mildred
Winter, Nelly
Woffard, Nathl.
Wooten, Thos.
Wright, Nancy
Wyche, Peter

Jury List. 1790:

Ayers, Baker, Sr.
Ayers, Baker, Jr.

Ayers, Danl.
Bobo, Lewis
Bridges, Wm.
Bryant, Jno.
Campbell, Aaron
Carter, Thos.
Cawthon, Cleyborn
Clark, Geo.
Cleveland, Jno.
Cox, Thos.
Crain, Joel
Crews, Thos.
Fleming, Geo.
Gilbert, Chas.
Harden, Wm.
Harper, Wm.
Herrington, Jno.
Hunt, Jas.
Jones, Peter
Jones, Wm.
Lain, Jno.
Langford, Wyatt
Lewis, Wm.
McCann, James
Mullin, Jno. Sr.
Payne, Jno. Sr.
Payne, Jno. Jr.
Payne, Wm.
Philpot, Warren
Porter, Saml.
Redding, Jno.
Sinclair, Jos.
Sparks, Jere
Sparks, Thos.
Stoneycypher, Jno.
Swift, Wm.
Vanse, Patrick
Watters, Moses
Wilburn, Wm.
Williams, Martin
Williamson, Robt.
Wright, Obadiah

Gates, Benj.
Gough, Jesse
Guest, Moses
Gunnolds, Jos.
Harrington, Jno.
Jones, Wm.
Lain, Jno.
LeGrand, Jesse
Naylor, Dickson
Payne, Jno. Jr.
Payne, Jos.
Pennington, Jacob
Quillian, Wm.
Sinclair, Jos.
Terrell, Jos.
Trammell, Wm.
Tuggle, Wm.
Walters, Jno.
Walters, Peter
Watson, Benj.
White, Benedick
Williamson, Robt.
Wright, Obadiah

Jury List 1791:

Asher, Wm.
Ayers, Danl.
Black, Wm.
Box, Jos.
Clarke, Jno.
Cleveland, Jno.
Crews, Thos.
Edwards, Jos.
Franklin, Abner

GLYNN COUNTY

Created in 1777 from two of the former Colonial Parishes, St. Patrick and St. David. Brunswick is the County seat.

In 1791, Glynn County is said to have had a population of only 413 of which 215 were slaves and 70 were free white males 16 years and upwards.

Headrights and Bounty Grants   1790 - 1795

Adkins, Arthur
Batting, Jas.
Bunkley, Britain
Bunkley, Britton
Burnett, Jno.
Burnett, Moses
Cannon, Jos.
Carr, Thos.
Clubb, Geo.
Club, Jas.
Club, Wm.
Cobb, Jas.
Cole, Jas. A.
Cole, Jno.
Cree, Moses
Crumb, Sol.
Demere, Raymond Jr.
Demere, Raymond Sr.
Gary, Saml.
Goode, Jno.
Graham, Jas.
Grant, Andrew
Grant, Wm.
Harris, Saml.
Helvestin, Jacob
Helvestin, Jas.
Hopkins, Elisha B.
Howell, Jno.
Johnson, Jno.
King, Roswell
Leake, Richd.
Lewis, Freeman
Manor, Henry
McCormack, Jos.
McIntosh, Wm.Jr.
McQueen, Jno.
Miller, Joshua
Moore, Jas.
Morgan, Jno. F.
Obryant, Jno.
Oneal, Ferdinand

Osgood, Josiah
Ostend, Obediah
Payne, Jno.
Pearce, Jno.
Piles, Jno.
Spalding, Jas.
Spalding, Thos.
Stone, Henry
Terry, David
Toutchston, Danl.
Touceston, Chris.
Waters, Thos.
Wright, Mary
Wright, Saml.

Glynn Co. Tax Digest 1790
Lt. Bradley's Dist.

Adkins, Arthur
Arskins, Jno. Sr.
Arskins, Jas.
Archibald, Jos.
Bessett, Alexdr.
Bradley, Reehard
Bruce, Rebecca
Braddock, Jno.
Burnett, Moses
Brinkley, Brittain
Best, Jno.
Burnett, Est. of Jno.
Clubb, Thos. (est.)
Clubb, Geo.
Clubb, Jas.
Collee, Micader
Clubb, Wm.
Crum, Sol.
Dilworth, Jno.
Demere, Raymond, Jr.
Dudley, Edw.
Edwards, Jno.

Eubanks, Stephens
Eubanks, Richd.
Goode, Jno.
Geary, Saml.
Grant, Andrew
Hall, Jas. M.
Harrison, Jas.
Hillery, Chris.
Hendricks, Wm.
Helveston, Jacob
Hopkins, Elisha B.
Harris, Wm.
Harris, Wm. Jr.
Helveston, Jas.
Haughton, Jno.
Harris, Lewis
Jackson, Wm.
Jones, Jas.
Jones, Jno.
Jenkins, Geo.
Leake, Richd.
Manson, Duncan
Moore, Jas.
Myrover, Henry (est.)
Miller, Jno.
Mazo, Wm.
McLeod, Jas.
O'Cannon, Jos.
Peal, Wm.
Piles, Jno.
Palmer, Martin
Piles, Miss Ebe?
Spalding, Jas.
Somerford, Richd.
Stevens, Wm.
Touchston, Richd.
Touchston, Chris.

Stock Marks & Brands 1787 - 1795

Arskins, Jno.
Atkinson, Jas.
Baisden, Jas.
Bissett, Alexdr.
Braddock, Jno.
Bunkley, Britain
Burnett, Jno. Jr.
Burnett, Moses
Clubb, Wm.
Crum, Sol.
Demere, Raymond Sr.
Demere, Raymond Jr.
Grant, Wm.

Graves, Jno. W.
Grant, Andrew
Harris, Lewellyn
Harris, Wm.
McIntosh, Sarah Simons
McIntosh, Wm.
Moore, Jas.
Morgan, Jno. T.
Palmer, Jno.
Palmer, Martin
Payne, Wm.
Stevens, Wm.
Peacock, Jno.
Terry, David
Tompkins, Wm.
Wright, Saml.

Inhabitants who sustained losses in the Indian War----1788:

Brantley, Jeremiah
Burnet, Jno.
Cole, Jno.
Corker, Edw.
Corker, Steph.
Cree, Moses
Dampior, Stephen
Demere, Raymond
Goff, Charity
Halviston, Jaccob
Harper, Lenard
Harris, Eliz.
Harris, Saml.
Hillary, Chris.
Jenkins, Geo.
Johnston, Jno.
McCormack, Mrs.
McFee, _____
Palmer, Martin
Pilchar, Edw.
Scart, Jno.
Spalding, Jas.
Steven, Wm.
Sumerland, Wm.
Tompkins, Jno.
Williams, Wm.

Deed Books 1787 - 1795

Grantor
Arskins, Dorcas
Arskins, Jas.

Arskins, Jno., dec'd.
Arskins, Jno. Jr.
Arskins, Wm.
Barnaby, Rebecca
Barnaby, Wm.
Bruce, Rebecca
Bunkley, Briatin
Bunkley, Mary
Clubb, Eliz.
Clubb, Geo.
Clubb, Selah
Clubb, Wm.
Fabian, Jno.
Hall, Jas. H.
Harris, Marg.
Leake, Richd.
McIntosh, Donald
Miller, Jno.
Miller, Joshua
Miller, Mary
Moore, Eliz.
Parsons, Hillery
Pilcher, Stephen
Powell, Abraham
Spalding, Jas.
Spalding, Margery
Spalding, Thos.

Grantee
Alexander, Adam
Bourneman, Benj. W.
Club, Wm.
Clubb, Geo.
Clubb, Jas.
Cook, Robt.
Copeland, Jas.
Demere, Raymond
Donny, Wm.
Graves, Jno.
Harrison, Gilbery
Harrison, Jas.
Harrison, Jno.
Hillery, Chris.
Leake, Richd.
Limbert, Jno. Wm.
Moore, Jas.
Palmer, Martin
Peacock, Wm. Jr.
Spalding, Thos.
Wright, Saml.

Witnesses and other
entries in Deed Book:

Bissett, Alexdr. dec'd.
Bruce, Jas., dec'd.
Bruce, Rebecca
Goode, Jno.
Hall, Jas. H.
Hodges, Jno.
Leake, Jean
Moore, Jas.
O'Neal, Ferdinand
Tompkins, Jno.
Tucker, Thos.

Administrations
and Wills.
1792 - 1795

Aikens, Arther
Harris, Wm.
Harris, Wm. Sr.
Helveston, Jacob
McIntosh, Jno. Jun.
Payne, Wm. Sr.
Spalding, Jas.
Sullavant, Danl.

Administrators and
Executors--1792-1795

Batting, Jas.
Cooper, Jno.
Grant, Sarah
Grant, Wm.
Harris, Marg.
Harris, Wm. Jun.
Helveston, Jas.
Helveston, Sarah
McIntosh, Lachlon
Manson, Dennison
Payne, Mary
Spalding, Margery
Sullevant, Danl.

Security & Appraisers
of estates--1792-1795

Bradley, Richd.
Burnett, Jno.
Dudley, Jno.
Fablan, Jno.
Gaines, Danl.
Garey, Saml.

Goode, Jno.
Harrison, Jas.
Hillary, Chris.
Jones, Edw.
McIntosh, Jno.
Mackinstosh, Wm.
McLeod, Jas.
Miller, Jno.
Mitchell, Abner
Moore, Jas.
Parsons, Hillery
Piles, Jno.
Purvis, Geo.

Legal ads and Miscel-
laneous items in South-
ern Centinel & Universal
Gazette, Georgia Gazette,
Augusta Chronical &
Gazette----1790 - 1795:

Batting, Jas.
Biffett, Alexdr.
Boon, Garrett
Braddock, Jno.
Bruce, Jas.
Burnett, Jno.
Clubb, Eliz.
Clubb, Thos. dec'd.
Clubb, Wm.
Cole, Jno.
Demere, Raymond
Fabin, Jno.
Graves, Jno. W.
Gray, Jas. Sr.
Hall, Jas. H.
Harris, Wm. Sr.
Harris, Wm. Jr.
Harrison, Jas.
Hart, Benj.
Hillery, Chris.
Lambert, Jno.
Lambert, Wm.
Limbert, Jno. Wm.
Leake, Richd.
McIntosh, Jno. Jr.
McLeod, Jas.
Manson, Duncan
Marbury, Leonard
Millen, Jno.
Miller, Jno.
Moore, Eliz.
Moore, Jas.
Palmer, Martin

Payne, Mary
Payne, Wm.
Piles, Jno.
Pitchard, Richd.
Spalding, Jas.
Spalding, Marg.
Stevens, Wm.
Touchton, Christopher
Towers, Robt.
Wright, Saml.
Williams, Wm.

Glynn Co. Militia
Aug. 1793-Jan. 1794

Armstrong, Jno.
Atkerson, Jas.
Atkins, Wm.
Best, Jno.
Black, Steph.
Braddock, Jno.
Brantley, Jeremiah
Brucus, Wm.
Bryant, Jno. B.
Bryant, Jno. C.
Bunkley, Brittain
Burnett, Jno.
Calder, Jas.
Carnal, Wm.
Carnes, Robt.
Clubb, Wm.
Cockburn, Ezek.
Connerway, Jeremiah
Copeland, Jas.
Cree, Moses
Cumming, Thos.
Demere, Raymond
Divine, Jas.
Eason, Jno.
Gayrie, Saml.
Grant, Andrew
Grant, Jas.
Hagwood, Jno.
Harris, Wm.
Hart, Abraham
Harris, Saml.
Hart, Thos.
Hartzog, Henry
Hodges, Jno.
Hogan, Jno.
Huston, Wm.
Jones, Jos.
McDonald, Robert.
McDonald, Wm.

McLeod, Iurdock
Maynor, Henry
Miller, Joshua
Moore, Jas.
Nicholson, Alexdr.
Oceannon (?), Jos.
Ogden, Isaac
O'Steen, Obediah
Palmer, Martin
Parramore, Thos.
Payne, Jno.
Pearson, Jas.
Phillips, Wm.
Pilcher, Stephen
Porter, Jno.
Powell, Abraham
Powell, Alexdr.
Powell, Jas.
Rottenbury, Richd.
Simmons, Richd.
Stewart, Jno.
Sutton, Abraham
Terry, Stephen
Trawick, Joel
Trawick, Richd.
Tucker, Andrew
Tucker, Hezekiah
Tucker, Thos.
Tucker, Willoughby
Walker, Elisha
Walker, Joel
Walker, Tandy
Walker, Wm.
Ward, Albritton
Wheeler, Jno.
Wheeler, Richd.
Williams, Richd.
Young, Moses

Tax returns.1794

Baisden, Jas.
Best, Jno.
Bithelheimer, Jno.
Bolling, Jas.
Braddock, Jno. (est.of)
Bradley, Richd.
Brantly, Jeremiah
Bunkley, Brittain
Burnett, Jno. (est.of)
Burnett, Moses
Cason, Ransom
Clubb, Geo.
Clubb, Jas.

Clubb, Thos. (est.of)
Clubb, Wm.
Coleman, Peter
Copeland, Jas.
Cree, Moses
Crum, Sol.
Cummins, Thos.
Demere, Raymond
Devine, Jas.
duBignon, Poulain
Edwards, Jno.
Eubanks, Stephen
Fabain, Jno.
Farr, Wm.
Gary, Saml.
Goode, Jno.
Grant, Andrew
Grant, Jas.
Grant, Wm.
Graves, Jno. W.
Gray, Jas. Sr.
Gray, Jas. Jr.
Harper, Leonard
Harrison, Jas.
Harris, Wm.
Hart, Benj. Sr.
Helveston, Est. of Jacob
Helveston, Jeremiah
Helveston, Jno.
Hendricks, Jno.
Hillary, Chris.
Huston, Wm.
Keaton, Kadish
King, Roswell
Lee, Mason
Lesley, Jas.
Limbert, Jno. W.
Lyon, Jno.
McLeod, Jas.
Manor, Henry
Mazo, Jno.
Miller, Jno.
Moore, Jas.
Munden, Jno.
Myrover, Est. of Jno.
O'Bryan, Jno.
O'Cannon, Jos.
Ogan, Jno.
Palmer, Martin
Parsons, Hillary
Payne, Jno.
Payne, Wm. (est. of)
Perry, Doctor
Pilcher, Stephen

Piles, Jno.
Powell, Jas.
Pritchard, Richd.
Purvis, Geo.
Smith, est. of Jas.
Swain, Wm.
Terry, David
Touchston, Chris.
Touchston, Richd.
Tucker, Andrew

Tucker, Thos.
Valley, Geo.
Vaughn, Jno.
Walker, Elisha
Walker, Joel
Walker, Tandy
Walker, Wm.
Waters, Thos.
Williams, Farr.
Wright, Saml.

GREENE COUNTY

Formed in 1786 from the original county of Washington. County seat is Greensboro. Parts of Greene County went into Hancock, Oconee, Oglethorpe, Taliaferro, and Clarke Counties.

Headrights and
Bounty Grants
1790 - 1795:

Abercrombie, Chas.
Adams, Jas.
Adams, Jno.
Anderson, Benj.
Bankston, Jacob
Barnett, Nathan
Barnhard, Geo.
Barnhart, Philip
Barran, Saml.
Baxter, Andrew
Booker, Wm. F.
Borland, Andrew
Brantley, Thos.
Buckhalter, Wm.
Cane, Jno.
Cartwright, Jno.
Cartwright, Peter
Cato, Stearling
Christmas, Nathl.
Clower, Jno.
Coffee, Peter
Comer, Jas.
Conner, Danl.
Cooper, Jos.
Cooper, Thos.
Couplen, Coulston
Curry, Alexdr.
Daniel, Edw.
Daniel, Thos.
Daniel, Wm.
Dawson, Jas.
Ellace, Walter

Fisher, Wm.
Fitzpatrick, Wm.
Flourman, Robt.
Flournoy, Robt.
Flournoy, Thos.
Freeman, Jno.
Gathright, Miles
Gearlin, Jas.
Gearlin, Wm.
Gilbert, Benj.
Graham, Jas.
Graves, Humphrey
Gray, Geo.
Greer, Wm.
Hagerty, Sarah
Harris, Thos.
Harrison, Davis
Harvey, Jas.
Haynes, Thos.
Hill, Robt.
Hill, Wm.
Hogg, Jas.
Housley, Nerred
Jackson, Jos.
Jackson, Peter
Jarrell, Jas.
Lancaster, Wm.
McClelland, Wm.
McClendon, Joel
McGough, Wm.
Mercer, Silas
Middleton, Robt.

Miller, Jno.
Moore, Jeremiah
Moreland, Robt.
Newton, Richd.
Nisbet, Jas.
Pamour, Jos.
Parker, Richd.
Patrick, David
Phillip, Geo.
Phillip, Wm.
Phillips, Jos.
Rabun, Matthew
Ragan, Jno.
Raines, Thos.
Ratchford, Jos.
Reddick, Abraham
Rees, Joel
Robinet, Ezekiel
Robirds, Thos.
Smith, Archibald
Smith, Jno.
Smith, Saml.
Spradling, Joshua
Spratt, Hugh
Stewart, Thos.
Stocks, Isaac
Stone, Matthew
Stringer, Jno.
Swinney, Jno.
Taylor, Jos. G.
Thompson, Benj. Jr.
Thompson, Robt.
Thompson, Zach.
Thornton, Rober
Thweat, Jas.
Veazy, Ezekiel
Wade, Thos.
Wall, Francis
Warerton, Thos.
Washington, Wm.
Whatley, Danl.
White, Jos.
Wilborn, Joshua
Wilborne, Elijah
Wilkinson, Jno.
Williams, Jonathan
Wilson, Jno.
Wilson, Wm.
Wood, Etheldred
Wood, Jane
Zachary, Bartholomew

Will Book "A"
1787 - 1796

Wills & Administra-
tions Deceased:
Allen, Saml.
Anderson, Braza C.
Carmichael, Jno.
Carmichael, Jos.
Culbertson, David
Davis, Jas.
Dobbins, Wm.
Dunn, Jno.
Fitzsimmons, E. L. W.
Gardner, Hezekiah
George, Wm.
Griffin, Andrew
Hall, Jas.
Harris, Wm.
Hodge, Wm.
Holland, Henry
Horkins, Thos.
Kennedy, Wm. (W)
King, Jno.
Love, Col. David
Lowry, Benj.
Maddox, Jacob
Martin, Peter
Meroney, Philip
Miller, Jno.
Moreland, Jno.
Newton, Levi
O'Neal, Axiom
Peeples, Burwell
Price, Jos.
Sansom, Jas. (W)
Stephenson, Jno. (W)
Stocks, Isaac
Toombs, Wm.
Warnock, Matthew
West, Wm.
Woods, Austarcus

Other names mentioned
in Wills & Administrations:
Baxter, Andrew
Carlton, Thos.
Carson, Jno.
Dobbins, Jane
Findley, Jacob
Gray, Jas.
Gray, Thos.
Griffin, Jinney
Griffin, Nancy

Griffin, Peggy
Griffin, Polly
Griffin, Thos.
Harris, Patrick Cunningham
Harrison, Wm.
Kennedy, Fields
King, Curtis
King, Nancy
Lamar, Jno.
Lamar, Thos.
Lowry, Jno.
Lowry, Mary
McAllister, Jno.
Martin, Eliz.
Melton, Wm.
Miller, Agnes
Moore, Jos.
Newton, Jas.
Nisbett, Dr. Jas.
O'Neal, Ruth
Peters, Edmond
Sansom, Francis
Sansom, Jackie
Sansom, Jas.
Sansom, Nancy
Sansom, Pattey
Sansom, Polly
Sansom, Thos.
Sansom, Wm.
Stephenson, Hannah
Stephenson, Thos.
Stephenson, Wm.
Waddell, Jno.
Ware, Jas.
Woods, Hannah
Woods, Jas.

Mixed Records of Wills,
Appraisements & Adminis-
trator Bonds-1787-1796:

Deceased
Alexander, Jas. (W)
Alexander, Nathl.
Allen, Wm. (W)
Ashfield, Dorothy
Barnes, Saml.
Barnet, Abraham
Boman, Wm.
Brasfield, Caleb
Breedlove, Benj.
Burford, Wm.
Burney, Simon (W)
Carter, Thos.

Celsna, Saml.
Chaney, Moses
Felnniken, Jas. (W)
Garret, Jas. (W)
Gilbert, Benj. (W)
Glen, Duke (W)
Greer, Aquilla (W)
Grimmet, Robt.
Hagan, Jas.
Hall, Hugh
Hall, Jas.
Hambrick, Jos. (W)
Hambrick, Thos.
Harris, Joshua
Harris, Saml. (W)
Harris, Thos.
Harrison, Gideon
Harvey, Thos.
Heard, Jno.
Hogg, Wm. (W)
Holliday, Wm.
Houghton, Joshua (W)
Jackson, Edw.
Jackson, Jno.
Jones, Hugh
Jones, Jacob
Jones, Nathan
Jones, Wm.
King, Jos.
Knap, Justice
Laird, Jno.
Lloyd, Jno.
Lyman, Elihu
Maddox, Jacob
Maxwell, Jas.
Miller, Alexdr.
Moon, Jacob
Moore, Frederick
Moreland, Francis
Moreland, Jno.
Morrow, Jno.
Morrow, Marg. (W)
Moseley, Alexdr.
Owen, Thos.
Parker, Jacob
Parker, Moses
Parker, Stephen
Peeples, David
Peeples, Nathan
Reid, Andrew
Rion, Nathan
Sanders, Chris
Sansom, Jno.
Simmons, Joshua

Slaughter, Ezekiel (W)
Slaughter, Jno.
Smith, Jos. (W)
Spikes, Josiah
Thompson, Jno.
Trippe, Henry (W)
Vaughn, Ephraim
Veasey, Jas. (W)
Wade, Edw. (W)
Wade, Edw.
Waggamon, Jno. Michael
Walker, Jno.
Warnock, Matthew
Watts, Thos.
West, Wm.
Whaley, Wm. (W)
Wheaty, Wm.
Wiley, Alexdr.
Willingham, Thos.
Woodall, Jacob

Others named in
these documents:
Abercromby, Chas.
Acee, Dr. L.
Adams, Betsey
Adams, Wm.
Aikens, Jno.
Akin, Jno.
Alexander, Bethiah
Alexander, Mary
Alexander, Jno. Lister
Alexander, Saml.
Alexander, Tabitha
Albord, Jas.
Alford, Julean
Alford, Julius
Allen, Marget
Ashfield, Frederic
Bailey, Jno.
Baird, Jonathan
Baldwin, Mordecai
Bannen, Ellinor
Bannen, Jno.
Barksdale, Jos.
Barnett, Mary
Battle, Jesse
Bennett, Grissel
Bennett, Lucy
Bennett, Stephen
Bilbo, Jas.
Bilbo, Mathew
Blanks, Jas.
Bostick, Littleberry

Boudin, Agnes
Boudin, Wm.
Brantley, Thos.
Brasfield, Lucey
Brewer, Geo.
Brown, Alexdr.
Browning, Jno. Jr.
Buchanan, Jno.
Burford, Mary
Burford, Mitchell
Burger, Jacob
Burke, Chas.
Burney, Hardy
Burney, Jemimah
Burney, Jno.
Burney, Polly
Burney, Shadrack
Bush, Jno.
Butler, Edmund Sr.
Cain, Jno.
Caldwell, Will
Caldwell, Wm.
Cameron, Duncan
Camp, Andr. W.
Carmichael, Jos.
Carson, Adam
Carson, Jean
Carson, Jos.
Carson, Marg.
Carson, Thos.
Cartwright, Hezk.
Casey, Wm.
Cason, David
Cathell, Jas.
Celsna, Jno.
Celsna, Mary
Cimbro, Wm.
Clements, Tyre
Clough, Geo.
Cochran, Wm.
Coffee, Peter
Comer, Anderson
Conner, Jeremiah
Cook, Benj.
Cooper, Elisha
Cook, Jos.
Cooper, Elijah
Copeland, Richd.
Corry, Alexdr.
Corry, Robt.
Cowart, Elias
Credille, Thos.
Creel, Thos.
Cureton, Wm.

Dalton, Christian, dec'd.
Daniell, Chas.
Daniell, Sarah
Daniell, Thos.
Daniell, Wm.
Dawson, Geo.
Deusht, Geo.
Devin, Alexdr.
Devin, Eliz.
Devin, Jos.
Devin, Lucy
Diamond, Jno.
Doddson, Isaac
Dowdle, Jas.
Dunn, Jno.
Easley, Chloe
Easley, D. W.
Easley, Thos.
Espey, Thos.
Evans, Wm.
Ferrel, Byrd
Findley, Eliz.
Findley, Thos.
Fitzpatrick, Wm.
Foster, Arthur
Gann, Saml.
Garner, Saml.
Garrett, Mourning
Gaston, Mathew
Gatland, Shadrack
Gazer, Jno.
Gibson, Humphrey
Gilbert, Benj.
Gilbert, Betsey
Gilbert, Martin
Gilbert, Nancy
Gilbert, Robt.
Gilbert, Sally
Gilbert, Wm.
Gill, Bettey
Gill, Ezekiel
Gill, Judea
Gillam, Ezekiel
Glass, Zachariah
Glenn, Ann
Glenn, David
Glenn, Jno.
Glenn, Wm.
Gordon, Alexr.
Grall, Thos.
Grayhill, Henry
Greer, Aquila
Greer, Eliz.
Greer, Jas.

Greer, Vinson
Greer, Wm.
Greer, Yel
Gresham, Davis
Gresham, L. B.
Grier, Uriah
Hagan, Ann
Hagan, Edw.
Hall, Thos.
Hambrick, Jos.
Hambrick, Larg.
Hambrick, Robt.
Hambrick, Susannah
Hambrick, Thos.
Hamlin, Richd.
Hammond, Martin
Hammonds, Anthony
Harris, Baker
Harris, Jane
Harris, Jeremiah
Harris, Mary
Harris, S. B.
Harris, Thos.
Harrison, Davis
Harvy, Evan
Harvey, Jas.
Harvey, Michael
Harvey, Thos.
Hawkins, Ezek.
Hawkins, Susannah
Haynes, Delia
Haynes, Sary
Haythorne, Martha
Heard, Jas.
Hemphill, Saml.
Henry, Jos.
Hill, Geo.
Hill, Wm.
Hogg, Jno.
Hogg, Martha
Hogg, Mary
Hogg, Saml.
Hoggans, Edw.
Holliday, Elisabeth
Holloway, Barnes
Holmes, Richd.
Houghton, Joshua
Houghton, Sarah
Houghton, Thos.
Houghton, Wm.
Howlin, Peyton
Huck, Wm.
Hunter, Edwd.
Hunter, Phillip

Hutchinson, Wm.
Jackson, David
Jackson, Isaac
Jackson, Jos.
Jackson, Mary
Janiken, Needham
Johnson, Thos.
Johnson, Wm.
Johnston, Jno.
Jones, Betty
Jones, Rachel
Jones, Sarah
Kerr, Jno.
Kilbey, Jno.
Kimbrough, Jno.
King, Alexdr.
King, Eliz.
King, Jas.
Knap, Charely
Knoles, Jas.
Laird, Margery
Lamar, Jno.
Lamb, Robt.
Lanier, Wm.
Leavin, Jno.
Lister, Jno.
Livingston, Aaron
Lloyd, Chas.
Lloyd, Jno.
Lockett, David
Lord, Richd.
Lord, Wm.
Love, David
Low, Danl.
Lowery, Jno.
Lowry, Jno.
Luckey, Jno.
Lumsden, Jerh.
McAlhattan, Abraham
McAlpin, Robt.
McClelland, Francina
McCombs, Andrew
McConel, Jince
McKoy, ___
McKinny, Lemuel
Maddox, Clayborn
Maddox, Jacob
Maddox, Sally
Madock, Wm.
Mills, Geo.
Mitchel, Wm.
Moore, Joshua
Moore, Risdon
Morgan, Jno.

Morrow, Ewing
Morrow, Jos.
Millins, Edmond
Nellams, Nial
Newell, Jas.
Nowlin, Bryan Waid
Nowlin, David
Nowlin, Jas.
Nolin, Lucey
Nowlin, Mary
Nowlin, Peyton
Offing, Jno.
Olfin (?), J.
Orr, Jas.
Owen, Dr. Thos.
Park, Ezekiel
Park, Jas.
Part, Jno.
Park, Robt.
Parker, Danl.
Parker, Jacob
Parker, Jane
Parker, Mary
Park, Saml.
Parker, Stephen
Parker, Wm.
Patrick, Jos.
Payne, Ledford
Pearce, Geo.
Peck, Henry
Peeples, Burwell
Peeples, David
Peeples, Eliz.
Peeples, Francis
Peeples, Nathan
Perkins, Archibald
Phillos, Jos.
Phillips, Wm.
Pickhard, Tho.
Pierce, Jno.
Polk, Andrew
Porter, Oliver
Porter, Robt.
Poythers, Francis
Prichard, Jas.
Reid, Alexdr.
Reid, Eliz.
Reid, Geo.
Reid, Jonadab
Reid, Robt.
Richardson, Danl.
Richardson, Obd.
Right, Wm.
Robbarts, Sallah

Robinette, Ezekl.
Robinett, Jno.
Rogers, Jno.
Ross, Nathl.
Ryan, Eliz.
Ryan, Richd.
Samson, Patsey
Sansom, Wm.
Scurlock, Joshua
Shaw, Saml.
Shelby, Moses
Shelby, Wm.
Simonton, Adam
Slaughter, Ezekiel
Slaughter, Jno.
Slaughter, Lucy
Slaughter, Reuben
Slaughter, Saml.
Smith, Agnes
Smith, Gilbert
Smith, Jos.
Smith, Mary
Smith, Robt.
Smith, Wm.
Spikes, Mary
Stamp, Jno.
Starkey, Eliz.
Stevens, Mathew
Stewart, Henry
Stillwell, Ann
Stokes, Saml.
Stokes, Tabitha
Swanson, Wm.
Tanner, Jno.
Tapperly, Mary
Tarver, Benj.
Taylor, Jas.
Tease, Chas.
Thatcher, Rev. Daniel
Thompson, Agnes
Thompson, Geo.
Thompson, Jos.
Thompson, Robt.
Thornton, Roger
Thornton, Saml.
Thrasher, Jos. C.
Trippe, Jno.
Trippe, Sarah
Turner, Jas. Jr.
Veazey, Eliz.
Veazey, Ezekiel
Veazey, Jesse
Veazey, Jno.
Veazey, Wm.

Veazey, Zebulon
Wade, David
Wade, Edw.
Wade, Mary
Walker, Wm.
Wade, Peyton
Wade, Thos.
Walker, Silvanus
Warnock, Jno.
Warnock, Robt.
Watkins, Jno.
Watts, Benj.
Watts, Thos.
Welch, Benj.
West, Dr. A.
Whaley, Danl.
Whaley, Eli
Whaley, Hannah
Whealy, Eliz.
White, G____
White, Jno.
Williams, Anna
Wilson, Robt.
Winn, Jno.
Woodall, Jno.
Woodall, Jos.
Woodham, Edwd.
Worsham, Mary
Worsham, Richd.

Deed Book #1
(Old Books A & B)
1786 - 1790

Grantors
Adams, Jas.
Adams, Mary
Alexander, Esau
Alexander, Faitha
Alexander, Jas.
Alexander, Tabitha
Alford, Jas.
Anderson, Jean
Anderson, Jno. Jr.
Armour, Andrew
Armour, Eliz.
Atkins, Nathan
Autrey, Jno.
Bachellor, Cornelious
Bachellor, Jean
Bagby, Geo.
Baldwin, Benj.
Baldwin, Sarah
Baxter, Andrew

Booth, Jno.
Browning, Jno.
Burford, Daniell
Burford, Judith
Burford, Wm.
Butts, Karan
Carter, Josiah
Cessna, Jno.
Christmas, Robt.
Clements, Eliz.
Clements, Tyre
Cochran, Abner
Cochran, Nancy
Comer, Anderson
Cribbs, Thos.
Cup, Barbara
Cup, Michael
Daniell, Jas.
Daniell, Mary
Daniell, Wm.
Davis, Absalom
Davis, Nancy
Dunn, Alexdr.
Dunn, Tabitha
Fitzpatrick, Tabitha
Fitzpatrick, Wm.
Frazer, Andrew
Frazer, Jno.
Gay, Allen
Gilbert, Benj. Jr.
Gilbert, Michael
Gilbert, Milly
Gilbert, Sally
Grace, Thos.
Graybill, Mary
Greer, Jean
Greer, Jno.
Greer, Sarah
Greer, Wm.
Greer, Wm.
Grice, Thos.
Hannah, Mary
Hannah, Thos.
Hays, Hugh
Heard, Eliz.
Heard, Thos.
Hoag, Jas.
Jackson, Lucy
Jackson, Peter
Jernigan, Needham
Johnston, Agnes
Johnston, Thos.
Jones, Eliz.
Jones, Nathan

Kilgore, Jno.
Lamar, Frances
Lamar, Jno.
Lancaster, Levi
Landers, Abraham
Landers, Jacob
Lawson, Wm.
Levingston, Robt.
McCall, Thos.
Middleton, Eliz.
Middleton, Robt.
Moore, Wm.
Newton, Levy
Patrick, Wm.
Peters, Richmond
Phillips, Geo.
Phillips, Isaac
Phillips, Wm.
Porter, Nathl.
Porter, Oliver
Price, Meredith
Ray, Wm.
Rayle, Thos.
Reddick, Abraham
Reddick, Hannah
Rice, Jno.
Shelby, Sarah
Shelby, Wm.
Smith, Cornelius
Stuart, Clements
Thompson, Jesse
Wall, Jno.
Wall, Mary
West, Elias
Whatley, Jno.
White, Reubin
Whitton, Auston
Wood, Ethelred
Wood, Jas.
Wood, Mrs. Mary
Wootson, Eliz.
Wootson, Jas.

Grantees
Abercrombie, Robt.
Achin, Jas.
Adams, Jas.
Adams, Jonathan
Adkerson, Nathan
Alford, Wm.
Ashfield, Hannah
Bagby, Geo.
Bailey, Thos.
Barnett, Nathan

Bohannon, Jno.
Boram, David
Brown, Wm.
Burch, Garard
Burch, Jared
Burford, Wm. Jr.
Burns, Andrew
Bush, Thos.
Butts, Azariah
Cain, Jno.
Carmichael, Jos.
Castleberry, Henry
Cato, Starling
Cessna, Chas.
Chappell, Jno. Sr.
Clements, Phillip
Clements, Tyre
Comer, Anderson
Cowart, Elias
Credille, Thos.
Daniell, Thos.
Dunn, Jos.
Ellis, Walter
Evans, Benj.
Findley, Geo.
Finley, Jas.
Fitzpatrick, Dyer
Fitzpatrick, Wm.
Flournoy, Robt.
Frazer, Andrew
Geer, Jno.
Giltart, Michael
Grace, Thos.
Greer, Asel
Hall, Geo.
Harris, Walton
Harvey, Jas.
Hawkins, Saml.
Heard, Thos.
Hill, Robt.
Hoof, Saml.
Houghton, Thos.
Howard, Jos.
Hunter, Phillip
Jenkins, Lewis
Jernigan, Henry
Johnston, Jno.
Jones, Nathan
Jones, Reubin
Knowles, Edmund
Lawrence, Abraham
Levingston, Saml.
Lowe, David
Mainer, Jno.

Matthis, Jno.
Melton, Wm.
Middleton, Holland
Miller, Jno.
Miller, Jno. Adams
Miller, Jno. Allen
Moore, Jas.
Moore, Joshua
Morrow, Jno
Oliver, Thos.
Patrick, Robt.
Phillip, Jos.
Pope, Saml.
Porter, Nathl.
Porter, Oliver
Rabun, Jno.
Rains, Thos.
Reed, Alexdr.
Reed, Saml. Sr.
Richards, Geo.
Roan, Tunstall
Robinett, Jno.
Rogers, Berry
Rogers, Jno.
Rogers, Michael
Ross, Francis
Rutledge, Jas.
Shelby, Moses
Shelby, Wm.
Ship, Richd.
Simonton, Adam
Smith, Robt.
Stanley, Thos.
Stocks, Isaac
Talbot, Jno.
Taylor, Jas.
Thatcher, Danl.
Thomas, Sarah
Thompson, Jas.
Thompson, Zachariah
Tigner, Phillip
Tripp, Jno.
Veazy, Ezekiel
Wade, Edw.
Wade, Peyton
Wade, Thos.
Wardlaw, Wm.
Weeks, Jno.
Whaly, Nathl.
White, Jos.
White, Reubin
Wiggins, Lewis
Wilson, Jno.
Young, Jos.

Witnesses & owners
of adjoining land:

Adams, David
Adams, Jas.
Adams, Jno.
Adams, Jonathan
Akins, Jas.
Alleson, Wm.
Anderson, Jno. Sr.
Andrews, Jas.
Andrews, Jno.
Armor, Jno.
Armor, Martha
Autrey, Alexdr.
Bagby, Geo.
Bailey, Matthew
Baldwin, A.
Baldwin, Marg.
Ball, Richd.
Bankston, David
Baxter, Andrew
Baxter, Jas.
Beard, Edmond
Bedell, A.
Bibb, Thos.
Bishop, Edw.
Bishop, Jas.
Blankenship, Reubin
Booth, Zachrh.
Boram, Jas.
Borland, Andrew
Bowdre, Edmond
Bowdre, Richd.
Boyd, Jno.
Bradley, E.
Brady, Wm.
Braswell, Saml.
Brown, Andrew
Bruce, Townley
Bruster, Hugh
Buckhannon, Jno.
Bucks, Jacob
Bunkley, Jesse
Burch, Richd.
Burford, Leonard
Burk, Chas.
Bush, Thos.
Butler, Edmund
Cain, Wm.
Carr, Thos.
Cartright, Peter
Castleberry, Jeremiah
Cato, Starling

Chambers, Saml.
Christopher, Wm.
Clark, Robt.
Clark, Sampson
Clarke, Barnes
Clay, Nathan
Coats, Lesley
Cobb, Jno.
Cobbs, Jno.
Cobbs, Thos.
Cockran, Jno.
Cochran, Wm.
Conner, Danl.
Cox, Jesse
Curry, Robt.
Danale, Wm.
Daniell, Edmund
Daniell, Levi
Daniell, Wm.
Dawson, Geo.
Dean, Jno.
Dickson, David
Dixon, J. L.
Cuncan, Wm.
Dunn, Simon
Eiland, Jno.
English, Henry
Finney, Jas.
Finney, Jno.
Flournoy, Robt.
Fort, Arthur
Fort, Rhoda
Fowler, David
Fowler, Simmons
Frazer, Jno.
George, W.
Gilbert, Benj.
Gilbert, Michael
Gilmore, Jno.
Graves, Wm.
Gray, Thos.
Graybill, Henry
Green, Wm.
Green, Wm. Jr.
Greene, Wm.
Greer, Jno.
Greer, Robt.
Greer, Wm.
Gresham, Archibald
Gresham, Davis
Hammett, Wm.
Hammock, Jos.
Hardwick, Geo.
Hardwick, Wm.

Harper, Geo.
Harper, Robt. Jr.
Harris, Baker
Harris, Geo.
Harris, Thos.
Harris, Wm.
Harrison, Gideon.
Harvey, Jas.
Haynes, Geo.
Haynes, Henry
Haynes, Isaac
Hays, Robt.
Heard, Jos.
Heard, Wm.
Heath, Mark
Henry, Jos.
Herndon, Reubin.
Hicks, Saml.
Hill, Jno.
Hill, Thos.
Hogan, Edw.
Hornsby, Weldon
Houghton, Thos.
Jackson, Henry
Jackson, Isaac
Jackson, Jas.
Jackson, Jos.
Jenkins, Benj.
Jernigan, Hardy
Jernigan, Needham Jr.
Johnson, Jesse
Johnson, Wm.
Johnston, Malcolm
Jordan, Demcy
Karr, H.
King, Jno.
Lamar, Thos.
Lancaster, Thos.
Lancaster, Wm.
Lawson, Francis
Ledson, Thos.
Livingston, Aaron
Lockhart, Richd
Love, David
Luckey, Thos.
McCall, Thos.
McMurray, David
McNeil, Jas.
MackAllen, Wm.
Maddux, Wm.
Marcus, Jno.
Martin, Jos.
Melton, Wm.
Middleton, Robt.

Mitchell, David
Mitchell, Jno.
Mitchell, Richd.
Mitchell, Thos.
Morrow, Jos.
Mounger (?), Sampson
Murray, Jas.
Napier, Thos.
Nelms, Jno.
Newton, Richd.
Noble, Wm.
Oliver, Jno.
Oliver, Wm.
Ousley, Wm. H.
Parks, Ezekiel
Parr, Jno.
Partin, Morris
Patrick, Rene'
Peek, Henry
Phillips, Hillery
Phillips, Wm.
Phillips, Zachrh.
Pickens, Jno.
Porter, B.
Porter, Oliver
Powell, Moses
Rabun, Jno.
Rabun, Matthew
Ragan, Jno.
Ray, Jno.
Ray, Sarah
Reddick, Abraham
Reed, Alexdr.
Reed, Andrew
Reed, Geo.
Rees, Sally
Richardsin, Jos.
Richardson, Obediah
Robinett, Ezekiel
Robinett, Jno.
Rogers, Josiah
Rogers, Michael
Ross, Geo.
Royston, R. C.
Royston, Richd. C.
Runnell, Thos.
Sampson, Jno.
Sanders, Jesse
Shelby, Moses
Shelby, Wm.
Simonton, Danl.
Simonton, Thos.
Slaughter, Saml.
Smith, Geo.

Smith, Peter
Smith, Robt.
Stewart, Jas.
Stewart, Jno.
Stocks, Isaacs
Stokes, Hartwell
Stringfellow, Enoch
Sweney, Jno.
Swepson, Jno.
Swinney, Jno.
Tait, Jas.
Taylor, Joannah
Taylor, Wright
Thomas, Jno.
Thomas, Jno. Jr.
Thomas, Jno. Sr.
Thomas, Josiah
Thomas, Robt.
Thomas, Theophilus
Thomas, Wm.
Thompson, Benj.
Thompson, Zachrh.
Tigner, Phillip
Tison, Aaron
Tolbert, Jno.
Tolbert, Thos.
Toombs, Robt.
Rowns, Jno.
Trayler, Thos.
Trice, Jas.
Turk, Theodocius
Tyler, Wm.
Veazy, Jas.
Walker, Wm.
Wallace, Jno.
Warnock, Hansell
Watson, Douglas
Watts, Thos.
West, Ellis
White, Jas.
Whitefield, Benj.
Wiggins, Lewis
Williams, Curtis
Williamson, Peter
Willson, Perry
Wilson, Jno.
Wilson, Robt.
Wingfield, Jno.
Wootten, Thos.
Wright, Robt.

1789 Tax List:

Abercromby, Chas.

Adams, David
Adams, Jas.
Adams, Jonathan
Adams, John
Adkinson, Abner
Afssy, Jas.
Afssy, Thos. Sr.
Afssy, Thos. Jr.
Akins, Jas.
Akins, Jno.
Alexander, Asa
Alexander, Jas.
Alford, Jas.
Alford, Jno.
Alford, Jul.
Alford, Wm.
Allen, West
Allison, Robt.
Anderson, Benj.
Anderson, Brazier
Andrews, Jas.
Andrews, Jno.
Armer, Andrew
Armor, Jas.
Armor, Jno.
Autrey, Absalom
Autrey, Alexdr.
Bachelor, Cornelius
Bagby, Geo.
Bailey, Jno.
Bailey, Robt.
Bailey, Thos.
Baldwin, Robt.
Baldwin, Saml.
Baldwin, Thos.
Bankston, Thos.
Barker, Ephram
Barker, Jno.
Barnes, Benj.
Barnett, Abraham
Barnett, Saml.
Barnheart, Geo.
Basdale, Abner
Battle, T.
Battle, Wm.
Baxter, Andrew
Bazar, Caleb
Bazar, Jno.
Beard, Edmund
Beard, Jonathan
Beaser (?), Wm.
Beavers, Daniel
Bell, Nathl.
Billups, Wm.

Bishop, Joshua
Bishop, Wm.
Blakey, Ch.
Clankenship, Danl.
Blankenship, Reuben
Bonner, Thos.
Bonner, Zadok
Booth, Jno. Jr.
Borland, Andrew
Boroum, Wm.
Bradford, Thos.
Bradley, Edwd.
Bradley, Richd.
Brantley, Thos.
Breedlove, Mary
Brewer, Chas.
Brewer, Geo.
Brewer, Jno.
Brown, Wm.
Brown, Wm.
Browning, Jno.
Browning, Jno.
Browning, Robt.
Bryan, B.
Buckhannan, Jno.
Burch, Jared
Burden, Humphrey
Burford, Danl.
Burford, Leonard
Burford, Mitchel
Burford, Sol.
Burford, Wm.
Burford, Wm.
Burford, Wm.
Bush, Jno.
Bush, Thos.
Butlar, Edmond
Cain, Jno.
Cain, Richd.
Caldwell, Wm.
Carlton, Wm.
Carmichael, Jos.
Carregan, Wm.
Carson, Adam
Carson, Jno.
Cartwright, Peter
Cato, Sterling
Cessna, Chas.
Cessna, Jno.
Cessna, Saml.
Christopher, Jas.
Cimbro, Jno.
Cimbro, Shadrick
Cimbro, Wm.

Clements, Jesse
Clements, Tyre
Clendinnon, Mathew
Cochran, Abner
Cochran, Jno.
Cochran, Pickens
Cochran, Wm.
Coffee, P.
Comer, Anderson
Comer, Jas.
Connell, Jesse
Corley, Edmond
Cossey, Wm.
Coulter, Jesse
Cowen, Geo.
Cranford, Saml.
Credille, _____
Cribbs, Gilbert
Cribbs, Thos.
Crocker, Thos.
Cupp, Michael
Curiton, Wm. Jr.
Curry, Alexdr.
Curry, Robt.
Curry, Wm.
Curry, Wm.
Cuzart, Elias
Dale, Robt.
Daniell, Chas.
Daniell, Eustace
Daniell, Jas.
Daniell, Thos.
Daniell, Wm.
Dent, Peter
Dickerson, Wimbowin
Dickison, Joel
Dickson, Robt.
Dismuke, Reuben
Dixon, David
Dixon, Wm.
Dobbins, Wm.
Doddson, Isaac
Doddson, Joshua
Doddson, Joshua
Dodreel, Noe
Dowdle, Jas.
Earls, Will
Edmondson, Richd.
Ellis, ____ese
Ellis, Joshua
Ellis, Walter
Fawner (?), Benj.
Ferrel, Hubbard
Fidler, Jas.

Fidler, Jno.
Findley, Geo.
Findley, Jas.
Findley, Jno.
Findley, Jno.
Findley, Morris
Finney, Alexdr.
Finney, Jas.
Finney, Jno.
Finney, Robt.
Flenniken, Jas.
Foster, Arthur
Frazer, Jno.
Furlow, Jas.
Furlow, Jno.
Furlow, Wm.
Gaither, Brice
Galbreath, Wm.
Gan, Jas.
Gan, Nathl.
Garrett, Jas.
Gaston, Isaac
Gaston, Mathew
George, Jno.
George, Traves
George, Wm.
George, Wm. Jr.
Gilbert, Benj.
Gilbert, Benj. Sr.
Gilbert, Benj. Jr.
Gilbert, Marten
Gilbert, Michael
Gill, Jno.
Gillaspie, Alexdr.
Glass, Wm.
Glass, Zachrh.
Glenn, Ann
Glenn, Wm.
Graham, Jno.
Graybill, Henry
Green, Jas.
Greer, Asel
Greer, Aquilla
Greer, Wm.
Greir, Jno.
Greir, Robt.
Greir, Wm.
Gresham, Ferdinand
Gresham, Javis
Griggs, Jno.
Grimes, Thos.
Gritman, Jno.
Hall, Geo.
Hall, Henry

Hall, Hugh
Halliday, Wm.
Hambilton, Wm.
Hamblen, Richd.
Hambrick, Thos.
Hammond, Anthony
Haralson, Jonathan
Harper, Robt.
Harris, Baker
Harris, Elisha
Harris, Geo.
Harris, Joshua
Harris, Mathew
Harris, Saml.
Harris, Thos.
Harris, Thos.
Harris, Watson
Harris, Wm.
Harrison, Davis
Harrison, Edwd.
Harrison, Geo.
Harvey, Evan
Harvey, Jas.
Harvey, Michael
Harvey, Thos.
Harvey, Wm.
Hawkins, Mathew
Hawkins, Saml.
Hay, Jno. Booker
Hay, Wm.
Hayes, Wm.
Hays, Adam
Hays, Hugh
Hays, Patrick
Heard, Thos.
Heard, Wm.
Heart, Saml.
Henderson, Zach.
Herndon, Reuben
Higgins, Jos.
Hill, Geo.
Hill, Jno.
Hill, Robt.
Hill, Wm.
Hodges, Wm.
Hogar, Isham
Hogg, Jas.
Hogg, Jas.
Hogg, Saml.
Hogg, Wm.
Holmes, Richd.
Hopkins, Lambert
Hopkins, Wm.
Hood, Jno.

Houghston, Henry
Houghton, Hugh
Houghton, Joshua
Houghton, Joshua Jr.
Houghton, Josiah
Houghton, Thos.
Houghton, Wm.
Houghton, Wm.
Howard, Jos.
Howsley, W.
Huff, Saml.
Hughes, Nicholas
Hunter, Philip
Jackson, Henry
Jackson, Isaac
Jackson, Peter
Jackson, Randolph
Jackson, Reubin
Jackson, Thos.
Jackson, Wm.
Jackson, Wm.
Jenkins, Elijah
Jenkins, Jas.
Jenkins, Jno.
Jenkins, Lewis, Sr.
Jernigan, Needham
Johnston, Leroy
Johnston, Thos.
Johnston, Thos.
Jones, Hugh
Jones, N.
Jones, Reuben
Jones, Wm.
Jourdan, Danl.
Justice, Demsey
Justice, Jno.
Karr, Henry
Kee, Jas.
Kelley, Jno.
Kelley, Peter
King, Alexdr.
King, Jno.
King, Jno.
King, Thos.
Kinney, Joshua
Lamar, Jno.
Lamare, Thos.
Lancaster, Levi
Lancaster, Wm.
Lang, Jno.
Lankeston, Jese
Lawed, Sarah
Lawrence, Abm.
Lawson, Francis

Lawson, Will Sr.
Lawson, Will Jr.
Leamonts, Jos.
Leaughton, (torn)
Leonard, Benj.
Littleton, Wm.
Livingston, Robt.
Lockhart, Richd.
Long, Henry
Lord, Wm.
Love, David
Low, Danl.
Loyd, Jas.
Lunsden, Jesse
McAlpin, Robt.
McClellan, Wm.
McClendon, Isaac
McCombs, Andrew
McCoy, Henry
McCoy, Jno.
McCullough, Alex.
McCullough, Wm.
McCutchin, Jos.
McDowell, Robt.
McGahey, Jas.
McGahey, Jno.
McGee, Patrick
McMichael, David
McMichael, Jno.
McNichell, Jno.
McNichell, Wm.
Maddox, Jos.
Maddox, W.
Maddux, Alexdr.
Maddux, Zach.
Mainer, Jno.
Marcus, Jno.
Martin, Godfrey
Martin, Wm.
Meador, Jno.
Meadowns, Jno.
Neagree, David
Melton, Wm.
Merret, Wm.
Metcalf, Isaac
Michael, Wm.
Middleton, Holland
Middleton, Holland, Sr.
Middelton, Robt.
Middleton, Robt. Sr.
Miller, Ellenor
Miller, Jno.
Miller, Jno.
Mitchell, Danl.

Mitchell, Jno.
Mitchell, Thos.
Mobler, Elisha
Mobler, Stephen
Moore, David
Moore, Jacob
Moore, Jas.
Moore, Jeramiah
Moore, Wm.
Morgan, Griffin
Morrow, Jno.
Morrow, Jos.
Morton, Joshua
Mullins, Clem
Mullins, Melone
Nesbit, Jno.
Noles, Edmond
Nowlin, Peyton
ONeal, Axion
O'Neal, Edmond
Orr, Jas.
Orr, W.
Orriak, Jas.
Ousley, Newday
Ousley, Welding
Parker, Benj.
Parker, Danl.
Parker, Js.
Parker, Moses
Parker, R.
Parker, R. Jr.
Parsons, Sam.
Patrick, Jas.
patrick, Jno.
Patrick, Joshua
Patrick, Robt.
Patrick, Wm.
Peak, H.
Phillips, Isaac
Phillips, Jos.
Phillips, Wm.
Phillips, Wm.
Phillips, Wm.
Phillips, Zechemiah
Pickhard, Henry
Pierce, Jno.
Polk, Andrew
Polk, Chas.
Pope, Jesse
Pool, Middleton
Porter, Ab_____
Pound, Newman
Poythes, Th.
Prewet, Jno.

Price, Jos.
Price, Jos.
Price, Merideth
Prickhard, Thos.
Pritchett, Chas.
Purtelar (?), David
Rabun, Mathew
Ransom, Henry
Ray, Jno.
Rean, Tanstall
Reid, Alexdr.
Reid, Alexdr.
Reid, Andrew
Reid, Jno.
Reid, Jno.
Reid, R.
Reid, Saml.
Reid, Saml. Jr.
Reid, Thos.
Reid, Yonadal
Reid, Z.
Reddick, Abraham
Reddock, Wm.
Rice, Jno.
Richardson, Danl.
Richardson, Obadiah
Richee, Wm.
Roberts, Joshua
Robinett, Ezek.
Robinett, Jno.
Rogers, Britain
Rogers, Jas.
Rogers, Jno.
Rogers, M.
Rogers, Wm.
Ross, Adam
Ryan, Richd.
Sanders, Lark
Sanford, Jesse
Sanford, Robt.
Sansom, Jas.
Sansom, Richd.
Scarlet, Jas.
Scot, Swidney
Scot, Wm.
Seawright, Jas.
Shackleford, Jno.
Sharp, Saml.
Shaw, Mathew
Shaw, Saml.
Shelby, Wm.
Shfield, To.
Ship, Benj.
Ship, Richd.

Simmons, Jno.
Simonton, Adams
Sipham, Abram
Slaughter, (torn)
Slaughter, Saml.
Smith, Archibald Sr.
Smith, Archibald Jr.
Smith, Jas.
Smith, Jas.
Smith, Jno.
Smith, Peyton
Smith, Robt.
Smith, Saml.
Smith, Wm.
Spears, Wm.
Spikes, Josiah
Spillers, Danl.
Spradling, Joshua
Stamps, Thos.
Stanley, Thos.
Steedman, Thos.
Stevenson, Thos.
Stewart, Chas.
Stewart, Henry
Stewart, Jas.
Stewart, Jas.
Stewart, Wm.
Stocks, Isaac
Stokes, Geo.
Stone, Wm.
Stringfellow, Enoch
Stroud, Jno.
Sturdivant, Jno.
Sumsder (?), Elijah
Swanson, Wm.
Swepson, Jno.
Swinney, Jno.
Tankersley, Jno.
Tatum, Nathan
Tatum, Seth
Taylor, Jas.
Teas (Taas), Chas.
Thacker, ____
Thomas, Jno. Sr.
Thomas, Robt.
Thompson, Jas.
Thompson, Jno.
Thompson, Jos.
Thomson, Benj.
Thomson, Jas.
Thornton, Rodgers
Thweat, Jas.
Tigner, Phillip
Townsen, Saml.

Trammel, Thos.
Trippe, Henry
Turk, Theodosus
Turner, Jas. Sr.
Turner, Jas. Jr.
Turner, Jesse
Turner, Joshua
Turner, Saml.
Turner, Will
Veazey, Ezekiel
Veazey, Jas.
Veazey, Jas.
Veazey, Jesse
Waddel, Wm.
Wade, Edw.
Wade, Peyton
Wade, Thos.
Walker, Jas.
Walker, Jno. Sr.
Walker, Jno. Jr.
Walker, Mel
Walker, Silvanus
Wall, Francis
Wall, Jno.
Waller, Saml.
Wamack, Wm.
Wamack, Wm.
Ward, Richd.
Warnick, Jno.
Warren, Thos.
Washington, Wm.
Waters, Jos.
Watts, Benj.
Weekes, Wm.
Weeks, Jno.
Whaley, Jno.
Wheeler, Isham
White, Jno.
White, Jno.
White, Jos.
Whitehurst, Jno.
Wiggens, Lewis
Wiggens, M.
Wiley, Wm.
Wilkinson, Jno.
Williams, Edwd.
Williams, Jno.
Williamson, Zorobabl
Willson, Jas.
Willson, Jno.
Wilson, Wm.
Windslette, Saml.
Womack, Wm.
Wood, Aristarcus

Wood, Jas.
Wooten, Ja..
Yarborough, Jas.
Young, Jos.

Muster Roll 1st Batl.
   Aug. 1793
Original in Ga. Dept.
Archives and History

Armstrong, Thos.
Bows, Thos.
Brown, Wm.
Campble, Wm.
Caregon, Wm.
Carlise, Robt.
Coleman, Chas.
Cunningham, Jno.
Dougherty, Chas.
Easley, Danl.
Eliott, Archabel
Eliott, Robt.
Eliott, Wm.
Espey, Jas.
Espey, Jos.
Espey, Thos.
Findly, Jos.
Foster, Arthur
Freeman, Jas.
Galton, Joel
George, Bailey
George, Traves
George, Wm.
Griffin, Edmond
Holmes, Jno.
Holmes, Robt.
Holt, Harmon
Hudson, Hines
Kanedy, Chas.
Lindsy, Jacob
McCutchen, Jos.
McMullin, Jas.
Mooney, Briant
Patton, Arthur
Patten, Jas.
Pope, Burrell
Price, Jos.
Price, Thos.
Ransan, Jno.
Ray, Wm.
Reed, Alexdr.
Reed, Hugh
Reed, Isaiah
Robertson, Andrew

Robertson, Wm.
Ross, Jno.
Rousru, Wm.
Shields, Patrick
Shields, Thos.
Shields, Wm.
Simonton, Thophelis
Smith, David
Smith, Jas.
Smith, Jno.
Smith, Saml.
Stroud, Sherod
Swanson, Andrew
Tanner, Jno.
Tears, Jos.
Tease, Wm.
Thomas, Jas.
Thompson, Jos.
Toan, Geo.
Walters, Jos.
Ward, Richd.
Warnock, Jno.
Watt, Wm.

Muster Roll of
Militia 1st Regt.
   1793

Akin, Jas.
Allen, Josiah
Anderson, Brazar
Bacon, Isaac
Baird, Jonathan
Batchelor, Cornls
Beasley, Robt. C.
Belcher, Obediah
Bevers, Jas.
Boles, Wm.
Buchanan, Jos.
Burford, Danl.
Burford, Wm.
Corry, Robt.
Davis, Thos.
English, Henry
Fain, Wm.
Findly, Jno.
Findly, Robt.
Gibbs, Miles
Hall, Geo.
Hall, Jas.
Hall, Saml.
Hall, Wm.
Haralson, Bradley
Haralson, Jonathan

Harvill, Jas.
Heard, Stephen
Heard, Wm.
Hobbs, Robt.
Hogg, Jno.
Hogg, Saml.
Houghton, Alexdr.
Houghton, Joe
Houghton, Josiah
Houghton, Wm.
Howell, Henry
Hunter, Phil
Meador, Jno.
Meadors, Jonas
Merriwether, David
Ray, Jno.
Shuffield, Geo.
Smedly, Thos.
Standifer, Scotton
Sunter, Stephen
Thomson, Jas.
Thomson, Jno.
Thomson, Robt.
West, Ellis
West, Wm.
Weston, Jno.
White, Jno.
Wilks, Benj.
Woocock, Thos.

1793
Muster Roll of Rifle-
men: 2nd. Batl.: 2nd
Regt. Original in
Ga. Dept. Archives &
History:

Aires, Thos.
Baley, Francis
Batey, David
Brown, Wm.
Butler, Jno/
Carter, Ezekiah
Carter, Isaac
Culver, Celethiel
Culver, Joshua
Dodril, Noel
Gann, Jno.
Gann, Saml.
Gann, Wm.
Greer, Jas.
Harriss, Elisha
Horton, Jas.
Kennelly, Joshua

Lamar, Jas.
Low, Danel
Low, Jas.
Low, Ralph
Low, Thos.
Loyed, Jno.
Loyed, Wm.
Loyd, Chas.
McGlomry, Elijah
Maddux, Leaven
Maddux, Saml.
Maddux, Wm.
Middlebrooks, Micajah
Noles, Richd.
Richardson, Obediah
Shaw, Wm.
Smith, Jno.
Waller, Elisha
Waller, Jas.
Waller, Steph.
Watts, Saml.

Muster roll of Militia
Troop of Dragoons.
Feb. 25. 1794

Browning, Wm.
Byron, Terrance
Capps, Jno.
Curry, Wm.
Dale, Saml.
Devereaux, Saml. M.
Farmer, Abner
Finley, Robt.
Foster, Arthur
Fouche, Jonas
George, Wm.
Gibson, Humphrey
Grinatt, Robt.
Harris, Chas.
Harris, Saml. B.
Harrison, Jno.
Heard, Jos.
Heard, Wm.
Jenkins, Jesse
Jenkins, Little B.
Lynch, Dennis
McDonald, Josiah
McGuire, Jas.
Moer, Jas.
Owen, Geo.
Patrick, Robt.
Phillips, Geo.
Pinkerd, Jno.

Potts, Henry
Reid, Geo.
Scott, Theodore
Scott, Wm.
Shaw, Jos.
Smith, Peyton
Standifer, Skelton
Standifer, Jesse
Stocks, Isaac
Wall, Micajah
Watson, Douglas
Watson, Robt.
Watts, Chas.
Watts, Presly
White, Jos.
Young, Jno.

Legal Ads from
Augusta Chronical &
Gazette, Southern
Centinel & Universal
Gazette, 1794-1795

Armour, Jno.
Barnett, Abraham
Barnett, Mary
Barnett, Saml.
Brewer, Jno.
Carleton, Thos.
Cartwright, Peter
Cathell, Jas.
Cheney, Greenberry
Cochran, Wm.
Fitzpatrick, Wm.
Flanigan, Saml.
Fouer, Geo.
George, Wm.
Gilbert, Michael
Greer, Wm.
Gresham, Davis
Harris, Walton
Houghton, Joshua
Houghton, Thos.
Houghton, Wm.
Hunter, Phillip
Kennedy, Wm.
Kerr, Henry
Lanier, Lewis
Leak, Jas.
Lloyd, Chas.
Lloyd, Jno.
Lowry, Benj.
Lowry, Mary
Lyman, Elihu Esq.

McAlpin, Robt.
Melton, Robt.
Melton, Wm.
Moore, Jacob
Moore, Jos.
Park, Ezekiel
Patrick, Rheny F.
Phillips, Josiah
Phillips, Sylvanus
Phillips, Wm.
Price, Jos.
Price, Rosanna
Simonton, Adam
Stewart, Allen
Thompson, Jas.
Vaughn, Ephriam
Wade, Thos.
Warnock, Robt.
Woods, Aristarcus
Woods, Hannah
Woods, Jas.

Those who sustained
damages from Indians
Jan.1787 to July 1788:

'Abercrombie, Chas.
Adams, Jas.
Akins, Jas.
Akins, Jno.
Alexander, Saml.
Anderson, Jno.
Anderson, Wm.
Armour, Jas.
Armour, (torn)
Armour, Jno.
Aspay, Thos.
Awtrey, Jno.
Baldwin, M.
Baley, Thos.
Barnett, Abraham
Barnett, Saml.
Boyzer, Wm.
Bearden, Humphrey
Bearden, Richd.
Booth, Jno.
Browning, Isaac
Browning, Jesse
Browning, Jno.
Bryant, Simon
Burford, Sol.
Burford, Wm.
Campbell, (torn)
Campbell, (torn) es

Carmichall, Jos.
Carr, Richd.
Catoe, Sterling
Clemons, Jesse
Clemons, Philip
Cochran, Reubin
Combs, Jas.
Coulter, Jesse
Curry, (torn)
Curry, (torn) h
Curry, Alexdr.
Curry, Wm.
Cuzart, Elias
Dale, Robt.
Daniell, Estace
Daniell, Thos.
Daniell, Wm.
Dunn, Jno.
Fielder, Jas.
Fielder, Jno.
Finley, Chas.
Findley, Jno.
Finney, Alexdr.
Fitzpatrick, Wm.
Fuller, Elijah
Furlow, Jno.
Furlow, Wm.
Glenn, Duke
Gresham, Davis
Gresham, Harris
Hall, Hugh
Harrison, Davis
Hart, Saml.
Hayes, Patrick
Heard, Abraham
Heard, Thos.
Hearing, Moses
Henbrick, Thos.
Henderson, Jos.
Hill, Jno.
Horton, Hugh
Hunter, Philip
Jones, Hugh
Jones, Jacob
Jones, Wm.
Lang, Jno.
Lansum, Jas.
Lansum, Richd.
Lard, Jno.
McCormack, Jno.
McMichall, Ezekiel
McMichall, Jno.
Martin, Godfrey
Miller, Alexdr.

Miller, J.A.
Parker, Eliz.
Parker, Moses
Parker, Moses Jr.
Patrick, Jas.
Patrick, Jno.
Phillips, Jos.
Phillips, Sarah
Phillips, Zachrh.
Porter, Nathl.
Porter, Oliver
Pruet, Jno.
Pruet, Michael
Pruet, Saml.
Ramsey, Wm.
Ray, David
Richards, Wm.
Richey, (torn)
Ried, Alexdr.
Russel, David
Sanders, Abraham
Sanders, Jacob
Scarlet, Jas.
Scurlock, Josh.
Sherrill (torn)d
Smith, (torn) lius
Spradling, Zachrh.
Stocks, Isaac
Stuart, (torn)
Thompson, Zachrh.
Tombs, Gabriel
Tombs, Wm.
Trice, Jno.
Veazey, Wm.
Waggonnar, Michael
Warrant, Abraham
Waters, Jas.
Watson, Jas.
White, Jno.
Williams, Edwd.
Wilson, Jno.
Wilson, Wm.
Winslett, Saml.
Wood, Aristarchus
Wood, Jas.
Wormack, Wm.

Marks & Brands
registered in the
Office of Clerk:
Superior Court.
1789 - 1795

Armor, Andrew

Baldwin, Robt.
Bradley, Edwd.
Browning, Jno. Sr.
Browning, Jno. Jr.
Burford, Daniel
Carleton, Thos. Sr.
Carmichael, Jos.
Cartright, Peter
Clayton, Jas.
Clements, Tyre
Clough, Geo.
Cochran, Jno.
Cozart, Elias
Daniell, Chas.
Daniell, Eustus
Daniell, Thos.
Daniells, Wm.
Fielder, Jas.
Fielder, Jno.
Gaston, Matthew
Grimmett, Robt.
Harris, Augustin
Harris, Geo.
Harris, Joshua
Harris, Sampson
Harris, Thos.
Harris, Walton
Harris, Wm.
Heard, Wm.
Hemphill, Saml.
Hoof, Saml.
Hopkins, Lambeth
Livingston, Robt.
Love, David
McMikle, Jno.
Melton, Wm.
Parker, Moses Sr.
Parkerson, Jacob
Patrick, Jas.
Pelley, Jno.
Sampson, Jas.
Stocks, Isaac
Stroud, Jno. Jr.
Walker, Nathl.
Walker, Syl.
Warnock, Jno.
Warnock, Robt.
Warnock, Wm.
Watson, Benj.
Watson, Jas.
White, Jos.
Wiggins, Lewis
Williams, Jno.

Green County Citizens
signing letter to
Gov. Geo. Mathews
    March 16,1795

Armor, Jno.
Beavoir, Jno.
Bird, Capt.
Bird, Jas.
Blair, Jno.
Burns, Terrenu (?)
Cartwright, Jno.
Casson, Adam
Casson, Jos.
Cluff, Geo.
Daves, Thos.
Edwards, Reubin
Findly, Harris
Findly, Jno.
Findly, Leven
Findly, Uz
Findly, Wm.
Fitzpatrick, Benj.
Foster, G. W.
George, Wm.
Gough, Wm. W.
Heard, Geo.
Heard, Stephen Jr.
Hewitt, Jno.
Hewitt, Wm.
Houghton, Thos.
Leak, Jno.
McAlpin, Robt.
McKinsey, Wm.
Meador, Joel
Meador, Jonas
Muss, Jas.
Phillips, Jos.
Right, Mical
Rucker, Presly
Shaw, Jos.
Smith, Peyton Jr.
Stroud, Jno.
Toombs, Wm.
Wall, Micajah
Watkins, Jno.
White, Jos.
Young, Daniel
Young, Jno.

Grand Jurors
July, 1795:

Carmichael, Jos.
Cartwright, Peter
Ce-------, Chas.
Cooper, Elijah
Dubbin, Wm.
Hays, Adam
Hays, Patrick
Hunter, Phillip

Jackson, Jas.
McComb, Andrew
Melton, Robt.
Patrick, Rene
Patrick, Robt.
Watts, Jos.
Watts, Thos.

LIBERTY COUNTY

Created in 1777 as an original county from the three Parishes of St. John, St. James and St. Andrew from land ceded by the Creeks in 1733. County seat is Hinesville. McIntosh County was formed from part of Liberty in 1793.

Headrights and
Bounty Grants
1790 - 1795

Addington, Henry
Anderson, Elijah
Bennett, Hugh (heirs of)
Bennett, Matthew
Bird, Saml.
Blackstock, Jno.
Brownson, Galen
Bryan, Matthew
Burford, Emelia
Burnet, Matthew
Campbell, Wm.
Corker, Edwd.
Denison, Gideon
Dickson, Jno.
Dix, Andrew
Everitt, Jno.
Flourney, Robt.
Golding, Palmer
Gough, Jno.
Gough, Roger S.
Graham, Jas.
Grant, Jno.
Gross, Mund.
Hext, Eliza
Hext, Marid
Hunter, Jesse
Hunter, Miles
Jones, Jas.

Kemp, Jno.
Knight, Zachrh.
Lawson, Jno.
McCrea, Gustavus
McCrea, Jno.
McIntosh, Locklin
McIntosh, Wm. Jr.
McKean, Jno.
Mitchell, Jno. Jr.
Mitchell, Stephen
Montfort, Jas.
Moody, Benj.
Moore, Jno.
Morrison, Jno. (heirs of)
Munson, Robt.
Neal, Thos.
Ogdon, Sol.
Oneal, Ferdinand
Osgood, Josiah
Oswald, Robt.
Perkins, Lewis
Piggot, Jno.
Quarteman, Wm.
Robertson, Christian
Saunders, Roger P.
Shuman, Henry
Stafford, Joshua
Stevens, Jno.

Stewart, Jno.
Thomson, Cloud
Valley, Geo.
Warren, Elias
Warren, Jno.
Warren, Jos.
Watts, Jos.
Way, Jos.
Wetherspoon, Jas.
Whitehead, Jno.
Wilson, Jas.
Winn, Jos.
Witherspoon, Jas.
Woodruff, Jos.
Wooters, Phillip
Wrae, Wm.

Wills--1790 - 1795

Alexander, Adam
Baker, Ann
Baker, Artemas
Baker, Jno.
Baker, Jonathan
Baker, Mary
Baker, N.
Baker, Rebecca
Baker, Sarah
Baker, Stephen
Baker, Thos.
Bacon, Eliz.
Bacon, Jno.
Bacon, Josiah
Bacon, Saml.
Bennett, Hugh
Bennett, Rebecca
Bowen, Mathew
Box, Richd.
Burnley, Saml.
Burnley, Thos.
Carr, Mary
Carter, Hepworth
Carter, Jas.
Christie, Archibald
Collins, Catherine
Dowse, Gideon
Foster, Jno.
Girardeau, Jas.
Girardeau, Richd.
Goulding, Thos.
Goff, Barnett
Graves, Jno.
Hardy, J.
Hastings, Archibald

Hinson, Clayborn
Hinson, Sarah
Hitchcock, Rebecca
Holmes, Lathrop
Hudson, Isaac
Irvine, Chas.
Iverson, Robt.
James, Jas.
Jeffries, Nancy
King, Sarah
King, Thos.
Ladson, Jane
Lambright, Jno.
Lambright, Marg.
Law, Geo.
Lawson, Eliz.
Lawson, Jno.
Lawson, Jno. Sr.
Lawson, Jno. Jr.
Lawson, Wm. C.
Lewis, Elijah
Lines, Dorcas
Lines, Saml.
McCrea, Jno.
McCullough, Marg.
McDonald, Norman
Mann, Jno. P.
Maxwell, Jas.
Maxwell, Jno.
Maxwell, Mary
Maybank, Andrew Jr.
Mell, Thos.
Mulryne, Jas.
Myers, Jno.
Nelms, Jno.
Osgood, Rebecca
Powell, Eliz.
Powell, Jas.
Powell, Josiah, dec'd.
Quarterman, Rebecca
Quarterman, Sarah
Quarterman, Thos.
Quarterman, Wm.
Rees, David
Rees, Eliz.
Sallett, Robt.
Saltus, Saml.
Schmidt, Christina Dorothy
Schmidt, Egidius Henry
Senior, Mary
Shepard, Thos.
Spencer, Wm.
Stephen, Alexdr.
Stevens, Saml.

Stevens, Sarah
Stevens, Thos.
Stacy, Mary
Sumner, Edwd.
Taylor, Nathl.
Taylor, Susannah
Walker, Joel
Way, Ann
Way, Jno.
Way, Wm.
Wilkinson, Jas.
Wilson, Mary
Winn, Peter
Witherspoon, Jas.
Wood, Catherine
Wood, Jas.
Wood, Jos.
Woodward, Wm.

Administrations of
Estates 1790-1794:

Abernathy, Chas.
Alexander, Adam
Bacon, Jno., dec'd.
Bacon, Nathl.
Balckstock, Jno.
Carter, Hepworth
Carter, Thos.,dec'd.
Cashen, Jas.
Cecil, Leonard
Clark, Mathew
Coddington, C.B.
Coddington, Francis
Delegal, David
DeMiklasruveitz, Felix
Dennison, Gideon
Duncan, David, dec'd.
Foster, Geo.
Goulding, Ann
Goulding, Jno.
Goulding, Marg.
Goulding, Palmer
Goulding, Peter,dec'd.
Goulding, Thos., dec'd
Graves, Jno.
Graves, Jno., dec'd.
Graves, Rebecca
Graves, Thos., dec'd.
Graves, Wm.
Green, Mary
Green, Uriah, dec'd.
Hamilton, R.C.
Harris, Chas.

Hext, Jno., dec'd.
Hill, Ebenezer
Howley, Sarah
Irvine, Jno.
Jeffries, Jas., dec'd.
Jeffries, Nancy
Kelsall, Amelia, dec'd.
Kirkland, Wm.
Law, Jos. Sr.
Lawson, Jno. Jr.
McKeen, Jno.
McKnight, Mary Ann
Mann, Jno. Preston
Montaigut, David
Mosse, Geo.
Munro, Eliz.
Myhoney, Dennis, dec'd.
Norman, Wm.
O'Neal, Frederick
Oswald, Thos. H., dec'd.
Plowden, Wm.
Plummer, Jos.
Quarterman, Jos.
Robarts, Jno.
Rolfes, Frederick, dec'd.
Spalding, Jas.
Spencer, Saml.
Stevens, Wm.
Stone, Ann
Stone, Henry D.
Sumner, Job
Swan, Mathew
Tillingast, Danl. Jr.
Timmons, Richd.
Troup, Geo., dec'd.
Watt, Chas.
Winn, Peter
Woodbridge, Thos. M.
Woodruff, Jos.
Woodward, Wm.

Deeds--1790-1795

Grantors
Baker, Whitmarsh
Carter, Jas.
Carter, Martha
Carter, Thos.
Elliott, Thos., dec'd.
Farley, Saml.
Farrar, Field
Files, Stephen
Foster, Geo.
Gilbert, Jno.

McIntosh, Lachlan
McWhirr, Mary
McWhirr, W..
Oswald, Ann
Oswald, Robt.
Ponsheire, Jno.
Ponsheire, Mary
Sandiford, Audley
Smith, Jas.
Spalding, Jas.
Stewart, Danl.
Way, Parmenas, dec'd.
Wilson, Wm.
Winn, Peter
Wood, Eliz.
Wood, Henry
Wood, Jas.

Grantees
Alexander, Adam
Bacon, Josiah
Baker, Martha
Baker, Wm. J.
Bolton, Robert
Cashen, Jas.
Cashin, Jas.
Chesher, Jno.
Farrar, Eliz.
Foster, Geo.
Griffith, Edwd.
Law, Mary Esther
Plowden, Wm.
Saxon, Saml.
Schmidt, Philip Jacob
Shepard, Mary
Smith, Mary Ann Eliz.
Stewart, Col.
Stewart, Danl.
Stone, Henry Dessex
Stone, Thos.
Walker, Joel
Whitehead, Jno.
Wilson, Jas.
Wilson, Wm.

Witnesses and names
in other documents:

Andrews, Benj.
Andrews, Sanders
Ashmore, Jno.
Bacon, Jno.
Bacon, Susannah
Baillie, Robt. Carnaby,
    dec'd.

Barnet, Chas.
Bennett, Reuben
Bolton, Robt.
Bourke, Thos.
Bradwell, Thos.
Brownson, Galen
Bryan, Lathew
Burgess, Jno.
Burke, M.
Catter, Geo., dec'd.
Catler, Mary
Cecil, Leonard
Cecil, Mary
Cecil, Philip
Clayton, Philip
Demere, Raymond
Dennison, Gideon
Dickson, Jno.
Elliott, Amos
Flournoy, R.
Flynn, Jas.
Forester, Alexdr.
Foster, Geo.
Frazer, Simon
Gale, Wm. W.
Goulding, Palmer
Graves, Jno.
Graves, Rebec.
Hardy, Jno.
Hardy, Jno. dec'd.
Hardy, Jos. T. dec'd.
Hardy, Mary
Harrel, Moses
Harrison, Gilbert
Hollstead, Wm.
Hughes, Jno.
Irvine, Jno.
Jones, Wm.
Kelsall, Roger
Leake, Richd.
Lesly, Jas.
Levin, David
Lewis, Jos.
Lines, Saml.
Long, Nicholas
McClennan, Jno. Jr.
McIntosh, Jno.
Mallard, Lazarus
Maner, Wm.
Mather, Jas.
Maxwell, Eliz.
Maxwell, Thos., dec'd.
Maxwell, Wm.
Morel, Henry

Morel, Peter
Newman, Saml.
Oswald, Jos., dec'd.
Flowden, Wm.
Price, Edwd., dec'd.
Price, Sarah
Quarterman, Jos.
Robarts, Wm.
Robinson, Jno.
Sallens, Peter
Sallet, Robt.
Saltus, Saml.
Sandiford, Jas.
Sawyer, Jno. Martin
Shepard, Francis
Shepard, Thos., dec'd.
Smith, Sarah
Smith, T.
Stacey, Wm., dec'd.
Steuart, Josiah
Stirk, Saml.
Sumner, Ann
Sumner, Cynthia
Sumner, Eliz.
Sumner, Mary Osgood
Tatnall, Josiah
Troup, Cath.
Van Dyke, Peter, dec'd.
Walker, Chas.
Wilkinson, Jas.
Winn, Peter
Wood, Dr. Francis
Wood, Henry
Woods, Jacob
Yonge, Thos.

Constables' Bonds
1790

Baker, Nathl.
Baker, Steph.
Baker, Wm. B.
Blackstock, Jno.
Brownson, Galen
Cashen, Jas.
Cassels, Wm. Henry dec'd.
Clancy, Jas.
Couper, Jno.
Dennison, Gideon
Donworth, Mary dec'd.
Foster, Geo.
Girardeau, Jas.
Girardeau, Wm.
Goulding, Jno., dec'd.

Goulding, Palmer
Iverson, Rebecca
Iverson, Robt.
James, Jas.
Jurdine, Leonard, dec'd.
Jurdine, Leonard, 2nd.
Leake, Richd.
McLeod, Jno.
Melvin, Geo., dec'd.
Melvin, Martha
Miller, Jos.
Rudolph, Michael
Smallwood, Benj.
Spencer, Saml.
Spencer, Sarah, dec'd.
Apiers, Alex. Jonhstone
Stacy, Jas.
Stacy, Jno.
Stewart, Jno.
Thorp, Chas.
Tillinghast, Danl., dec'd.
Winn, Peter

Land Warrants--1791

Addington, Henry
Bennett, Hugh
Bennett, Mathew
Bird, Abraham
Graham, Jas.
Knight, Zach.
Piggot, Jno.
Mathes, Francis
Osteen, Thos.
Stafford, Thos. P.
Warren, Elias

1787 Tax List
Sunbury District

Alexander, Adam
Armstead, Jno.
Austin, Davis
Bailie, Robt. C. est.
Baker, Artemas
Baker, Jno.
Belcher, Jas.
Bishop, Peter
Blackstock, Jno.
Cobb, Japheth
Coddington, F.
Cole, Allice
Cole, Jas.
Cole, Mark

Danworth, Peter
Darling, Eliz.
Darling, Euphenie
Dickinson, Jere.
Elliott, Amos
Files, Steph.
Girardeau, Jno. B., est.
Goff, Chas. Barnett
Graves, Jno.
Hardy, Jno.
Harrison, Gilbert
Hastings, Arch., est.
Hoffmire, Peter
Holden, Jonathan
Hunter, Sol.
Kell, Jno., est.
Kelsall, Amelia, est.
Lankford, Jno.
Lawson, Jno. Sr.
Lawson, Jno. Jr.
Legget, Abrah.
Low, Jane, est.
Lynn, Dr., est.
Maxwell, Thos.
Maybank, Andrew
Miller, Elisha
Morris, Thos., est.
Myers, Henry
Powell, Josiah
Price, Edw.
Putnam, Benj.
Putnam, Henry
Rudulph, Michael
Rudulph, Thos.
Saxton, Nathl.
Smith, Levy
Somersall, Stafford
Talbot, Edwd.
Tushet, Chas.
Watson, Jas.
White, Chas.
Woodward, Wm.

Returned as defaulters
but names stricken off:

Baker, Jno.
Bacon, Nathl.
Baker, Artemas
Blackstock, Jo--?-
Dollar, Jno. Sr.
Dollar, Jno. Jr.
Foster, Geo.
Gamble, Wm.

McIver, Alexdr.
Mulpar (?), Thos.
Peacock, Wm. Sr.

Defaulters

Austin, Jos.
Burgess, Richd.
Corker, David
Dunn, Jno.
Elliott, Thos.
Green, Benj.
Hoof (?), Benj.
Howell, Miller
Hunt, Thos.
Iverson, Robt.
Mathe (?), Jas.
Mell, Jas.
Millen, Jno.
Moore, Burges
Murphy, Thos.
Myers, Danl.
Myers, Jno. Sr.
Myers, Jno. Jr.
Myers, Wm.
Neil, Jno.
Paine, Wm.
Pomeroy, Jas.
Shaw, Jonathan
Smith, Jeremiah
Vandyke, Peter
Weeks, Jno.
White, Thos.
Wood, Isaac
Taylor, Wm.

Roster of Jurymen
1787 - 1790

Alexander, Adam
Austin, Davis
Bacon, Josiah
Baker, Artemas
Baker, Jno.
Bacon, Nathl.
Baker, Steph.
Baker, Whitmarsh
Baker, Wm.
Baker, Wm. I.
Baker, Wm. R.
Barber, Robt.
Blackstock, Jno.
Bradford, Jno.
Bradwell, Thos.
Carter, Hepworth

Carter, Jas.
Coddington, Francis
Dollar, Jno.
Donworth, Peter
Dowse, Gideon
Duncan, David
Dunwody, Jas.
Elliott, Jno.
Files, Steph.
Gignilliat, Jas.
Girardeau, Richd.
Goulding, Peter, dec'd.
Grant, Peter
Hardy, Jno.
Hinson, Clayborn
Irvine, Jno.
Jeffries, Jas.
Jurdine, Wm.
Lambright, Jno.
Lawson, Jno. Sr.
Lawson, Jno. Jr.
LeConte, Jno.
McIver, Alexdr.
Maxwell, Jas.
Maybank, Andrew
Nephew, Jas.
O'Neal, Ferdinand
Osgood, Jno.
Osgood, Josiah
Peacock, Wm. Sr.
Peacock, Wm. Jr.
Powell, Jas.
Powell, Josiah
Quarterman, Jos.
Quarterman, Thos.
Rudulph, Michael
Sallett, Robt.
Shaw, Jonathan
Smallwood, Isaac
Somerall, Stafford
Stacy, Jno.
Stevens, Thos.
Thorp, Jno.
Timmons, Richd.
Walthour, Andrew
Watson, Jas.
Way, Jos.
Way, Jos.. Sr.
Way, Thos.
Weed, Henry
Weed, Jno. N.
Winn, Jos.
Winn, Peter
Wood, Henry
Woodward, Wm.

Liberty County Militia Officers Aut. 1790

Alexander, Adam
Baker, Jno. Jr.
Batier, Wm. J.
Brownson, Gillon
Burnley, Saml., Esq.
Carter, Hepworth
Clark, Jos., Esq.
Cooper, Jno.
Croft, Jno.
Dollar, Jno., Esq.
Frazier, Simon, Esq.
Graves, Jno.
Harris, Wm. Thos., Esq.
Houston, Thos.
King, Thos.
McCoy, Wm.
McIntosh, Wm. Jr.
McLean, Andrew
McLeod, Jas.
Mallard, Lazarus
Maxwell, Audley
Oswell, Thos.
Rees, David, Esq.
Stewart, Danl.
Way, Jos.

Militia Payroll 1793 3rd. Co. Liberty County Battalion:

Abbet, Bennett
Adams, Wm.
Blont, Jas.
Blount, Hugh
Dassey, Jas.
Gainery, Bartholomew
Goodson, Josiah
Kemp, Jno.
Lankford, Edmond
Newman, Danl.
Osteen, Obadiah
Osteen, Wm.
Parrot, Nathl.
Payne, Archelus
Pigot, Jno.
Sandford, Joshua
Sargent, Jno.
Smith, Chas.
Stogner, Jno.
Terrill, Pierce
Tippens, Philip
Underwood, Jno.

Walker, Ansiel
Walker, Isham
Walker, Little
Walker, Richd.
Warnal, Wm.
Warren, Elias
Warren, Jno.
Warren, Saml.

Militia Scouts 1792-1796
Baggs, Archibald
Corker, Jesse
Graham, Jas.
Johnson, Jno.
Joyner, Jos.
Pigott, Jno.
Price, Wm.
Stafford, Joshua
Warren, Elias
Warren, Jesse
Warren, Jno.
Way, Moses
Winn, Jos.

Names from Midway
Church records
1789 - 1790 1791

Bacon, Saml.
Baker, Artemas
Baker, Eliz.
Baker, Mary
Baker, Whitmarsh
Baker, Wm.
Baker, Wm. J.
Bird, Saml.
Bradwell, Thos.
Cassels, Elias
Cassels, Sarah
Dunnom, Chas.
Elliott, Jno.
Elliott, Renchie
Girardeau, Richd.
Goulding, Thos.
Iverson, Robt.
Jurdine, Leonard
Lambright, Jno.
McCullough, Jas.
McCullough, Mary
McCollough, Wm.
Norman, Jno.
Norman, Rebecca
Oswald, Ann
Osgood, Jno.

Osgood, Rebecca
Oswald, Thos.
Peacock, Jno.
Plummer, Jos.
Quarterman, Jos.
Quarterman, Rebecca
Quarterman, Sarah
Quarterman, Wm.
Shepard, Thos.
Spencer, Saml.
Stacy, Jno.
Stewart, Danl.
Stewart, Susannah
Sumner, Thos.
Walker, Joel
Walker, Mary
Way, Hannah
Way, Jno.
Way, Jos. Jr.
Way, Sarah
Way, Wm.
West, Wm.
Wilson, Jas.
Winn, Jno.
Winn, Martha
Winn, Peter
Wood, Eliz.
Wood, Jas.

From old newspapers--
Augusta Chronical &
Gazette, Southern Centi-
nel & Universal Gazette,
Georgia Gazette.
1790 - 1795

Anderson, Jno., dec'd.
Andrews, Jos.
Andrews, Micajah
Bacon, Jno. Jr.
Bacon, Jonathan
Bacon, Jonathan Sr.
Bacon, Nathl.
Baillee, Geo. Jr.
Baillee, Robt., Esq.
Baker, Jno.
Baker, Jno. B. dec'd.
Baker, Mrs. Mary
Baker, Thos.
Baker, Wm.
Baker, Wm. Sr.
Baker, Wm. B.
Baker, Wm. J.
Bell, Robt.

Bell, Wm.
Bennett, Eliz.
Bennett, Wm.
Bishop, Jane
Bishop, Peter
Bowen, Matthew
Box, Richd.
Bradwell, Thos.
Brown, Jas.
Burford, Mrs. Amelia
Caldwell, Geo.
Caldwell, Jno.
Campbell, Jno.
Cantey, Joshua
Cassels, Elias
Cassels, Rebecca
Cassels, Wm. Henry dec'd.
Cobb, Harriet
Cobb, Japhet
Coddington, Francis
Collins, Cornelius
Colter, Uriah
Cooper, Jno.
Cooper, Mary
Cooper, Richd.
Corker, David R.
Corker, Jas.
Corker, Nathan
Corker, Stephen
Couper, Jno.
Crawford, Robt.
Delegall, David
Dollar, Jno.
Donworth, Mary
Donworth, Patrick
Donworth, Peter, dec'd.
Dowse, Gideon
Drisdale, Alexdr.
Duncan, David, dec'd.
Dunham, Chas.
Dunham, Jas.
Dunham, Mary
Dunwoody, Jas.
Elliott, Jno., Esq.
Elliott, Jno. Jr.
Elliott, Mrs. R.
Elliott, Thos.
Fabian, Jonathan
Fitzpatrick, Mary
Flynn, Jas.
Foster, Geo.
Frazer, Simon
Fulton, Saml.
Gireadeau, Jas.

Gireaudeau, Wm.
Gordeaux, Peter
Goulding, Ann Mrs.
Goulding, Jno.
Goulding, Jno. dec'd.
Goulding, Palmer
Goulding, Peter dec'd.
Goulding, Peter
Goulding, Peter Jno.(infant)
Goulding, Thos.
Graves, Jno.
Green, Ann
Green, Mary
Green, Thos., dec'd.
Green, Uriah, dec'd.
Guinn, Eliz.
Guinn, Richd.
Hardy, Jno. Esq.
Hardy, Jos. T.
Hardy, Mrs. Mary
Hawthorne, Nathaniel
Hawthorn, Stephen
Henry, Hugh
Hinson, Clayborn
Hinson, Sarah
Hinton, Clayborn
Hudson, Chris., dec'd.
Hudson, Isaac
Humphreys, Spencer
Irvine, Jno.
Islands, Abner
Jackson, Jno.
James, Jas.
Janson, Jno.
Janson, Wm.
Jeffries, Ann
Jeffries, Jas.
Jones, Jno.
Jones, Mary
Jurdine, Jno.
Jurdine, Macy
Kelsall, Miss Amelia
Kirkland, Christiana
Kirkland, Wm.
Kirkland, Wm., dec'd.
Lambright, Jno. J.
Lambright, Marg.
Law, Jos., Jr.
Law, Thos. E.
Leake, Richd.
Lee, Jane C.
Leonard, Henry
Leonard, Dr. Saml.
Lines, Dorcas

Low, Mrs. Mary
Low, Maj. Phillip
McDonald, Ronald
McIntosh, Augus
McIntosh, Geo.
McIntosh, Georgiana
McIntosh, Lachlan
McIntosh, Wm.
McIntosh, Wm. Jr.
McWhann, Wm.
Mallard, Lazarus
Mann, Jno. P.
Martin, Clement
Massey, Jos.
Mathews, Francis
Mathews, Jno.
Maxwell, Audley
Maxwell, Eliz.
Maxwell, Jas. Esq.
Maybank, Andrew
Morris, Thos.
Morris, Thos., dec'd.
Munro, Harry
Munro, Simon
Murphree, Wright
Norman, Jno.
Norman, Mrs. Rebecca
O'Neal, Ferdinand
Osgood, Josiah, Sr.
Oswald, Ann
Oswald, Thos.
Oswald, Thos. H.
Peacock, Jas.
Peacock, Jno.
Peacock, Wm.
Peacock, Wm. B.
Peacock, Wm. Jr.
Pontheere, Jno.
Pontheere, Mary
Powell, Jas.
Powell, Josiah
Powell, Miss K. H.
Quarterman, Jno.
Quarterman, Thos.
Quarterman, Wm.
Quilling, Jno.
Rees, David
Sallens, Peter
Sallens, Peter Sr.
Sallins, Robt.
Sanders, Roger Parker
Schmid, Christina D.
Schmid, Mary Screven
Schmid, Phillip Jacob

Schmidt, E. Henry
Schmidt, Geo. Henry
Shepherd, Mary
Shepherd, Wm., dec'd.
Sheppard, Mary
Sheppard, Wm. dec'd.
Smallwood, Benj.
Smallwood, Francis
Smallwood, Isaac
Smith, Jas.
Spalding, Jas.
Spencer, Saml.
Spencer, Wm.
Stacy, Jas.
Stacy, Wm.
Staley, Jas.
Staley, Jno.
Staley, Jno. Sr. dec'd.
Stevens, Saml. dec'd,
Stevens, Thos.
Stevens, Wm.
Stewart, Danl.
Stewart, Jas. M.
Stewart, Josiah
Stone, Thos.
Stuart, Jas. M.
Sullevant, Danl.
Sumner, Miss Eliz.
Sumner, Thos.
Taylor, Susanna A.
Tillinghast, Danl.
Timmons, Richd.
Vandyke, Miss Ann
Vandyke, Peter.
Walker, Joel
Walthour, Andrew
Way, Ann
Way, Hannah
Way, Jno.
Way, Jos. Sr.
Way, Jos. Jr.
Way, Mary
Way, Moses dec'd.
Way, Wm.
Way, Wm. Jr.
Wells, Mrs. Mary
Whitehead, Jno.
Williams, Stephen
Wilson, Eliz.
Wilson, Jas.
Wilson, Robt. Wm.
Winn, Jno.
Winn, Mrs. Martha
Winn, Peter
Wood, Henry
Wood, Jacob
Wood, Jas.
Wood, Thos.

RICHMOND COUNTY

An original County created in 1777 from the Parish of St. Paul which was previously organized in 1758 from the Creek cession of 1733. Augusta is the County Seat.
Richmond originally included part of four other counties: Columbia, Jefferson, McDuffie and Warren.

Headrights and
Bounty Grants
1790 - 1795

Archer, Jas.
Bailey, Jas.
Barrow, Reuben
Barton, Willoughby
Beal, Jas.
Beale, Jas.
Beall, Hezekiah
Bennett, Jno. B.
Berryhill, Alex
Berryhill, Saml.
Blackstone, Winfred
Bonner, Richd.
Bostick, Wm.
Brassfield, Geo.
Brown, Wm.
Bryant, Archibald
Bryant, Jno.
Bulloch, Richd.
Burch, Chas.
Burch, Edwd.
Burch, Jos.
Burke, Edwd.
Burks, Edwd.
Burnsides, Nathan
Calwell, Paul
Candler, Henry
Carr, Thos.
Carroll, Wm.
Carswell, Alex.
Carson, Jno.
Carter, Giles
Champion, Henry
Clayton, Thos.
Cobbison, Jno.
Collins, Levin
Conner, Wm.
Cowles, Wm.
Crittendon, Thos.
Crook, Jonathan
Crosby, Thos.

Crowley, Pleney
Culpepper, Sampson
Culpepper, Wm.
Daniel, Jno.
Davis, Abiatha
Davis, Jno.
Dawson, David
Deem, Jno.
Donnelly, Jas.
Doss, Jno.
Drane, Walker
Drennen, Danl.
Evans, Danl.
Fail, Arthur
Fee, Jno.
Ferguson, Jos.
Few, Ignatius
Flournoy, Robt.
Folds, Geo.
Foster, Jno.
Fulcher, Jas.
Fuller, Jno.
Fuller, Isaac
Furey, Jno.
Gibson, Jno.
Gill, Days
Glascock, Thos.
Gordon, Ambrose
Graves, Perry
Graves, Robt.
Green, Amce
Green, Moses
Grinage, Joshua
Groathouse, Jacob
Grubbs, Benj.
Hamilton, Jas.
Hammond, Saml.
Harragall, Sarah
Harris, Nathan
Harrison, Reuben

Harvill, Jas.
Haynes, Thos.
Hickson, Jno.
Hill, Joel
Hill, Thos.
Hood, Benj.
Hughs, Wm.
Hunts, Fitz Maurice
Irby, Jos.
Jenkins, Benj.
Johnson, Saml.
Jones, Henry
Jones, Mark
Jones, Robt. (heirs of)
Jones, Robt.
Jones, Thos.
Kelly, Jno.
Kennedy, Jno.
Knight, Nehemiah
Lamar, Basil
Leath, Jno.
Leatherlin, Wm.
Lee, Wm.
Lofton, Ezekiel
Low, Danl.
Maddocks, Jos.
Marbury, Leonard
Marshall, Sol.
Mathis, Meshick
McCenley, Jos.
McCullough, Jacob
McCullough, Jos.
McCullough, Saml.
McDade, Chas.
McDonald, Jno.
McDonald, Mary
McDuffee, Jno.
McGruder, Offett
McLemore, Matthew
McNair, Danl.
McNair, Gilbert
Mead, Wm.
Milligan, Hugh
Milton, Jno.
Mock, Andrew
Mock, Jos.
Montgomery, Jno. H.
Moore, Jas.
Moore, Thos.
Morris, Jno.
Moss, Alex
Mott, Zephaniah
Moxly, Sarah
Murphy, Edwd.

Napier, Thos.
North, Jno.
Patterson, David
Patterson, Jno.
Pool, Saml.
Pool, Wm.
Porter, Chas.
Porter, Thos.
Prater, Sarah
Primrose, Edw.
Rhodes, Jno.
Richardson, Danl.
Richardson, Jno.
Roberts, Jno.
Roberts, Thos.
Satterwhite, Danl.
Shirley, Wm.
Sims, Jas.
Sims, Wm.
Smith, Leonard
Smith, Thos.
Smith, Wm.
Stallings, Ezekiel
Standford, Robt.
Stanford, Jonathan
Steed, Phillip
Stewart, Jno.
Sullivan, Jno.
Sullivan, Wm.
Tabor, Jno.
Tapley, Joel
Thompson, Wm.
Tilley, Cunningham C.
Tindall, Jno.
Tindill, Jno.
Tinsley, Jas.
Travis, Wm.
Tuder, Jno.
Vernon, Nathl.
Walker, David
Walker, Jno.
Wall, David
Walton, Jno.
Walton, Wm.
Waters, Jas.
Watts, Edw.
Weaver, Stephen
Whiteacon, Saml.
Whitten, Robt.
Whittington, C.
Whittington, Wm.
Wilkins, Thos.
Winfree, Jess
Winfrey, Jess

Winter, Frederick
Wright, Abednego
Wright, Jas.
Wright, Jno.
Yarborough, Littleton
Young, David
Youngblood, Peter

Land Court Held
1786 and 1787
Richmond County:

Allen, Gideon
Allen, Saml.
Allison, Henry
Arnett, Geo.
Arnold, Jno.
Atwood, Isaac
Avary, Jno.
Averitt, Arthur
Ayres, Thos.
Ayres, Wm.
Bailey, Briton
Barnett, Joel
Barnett, Wm. Sr.
Barnett, Wm. Esq.
Bassett, Geo.
Berryhill, Alexdr.
Berryhill, Saml.
Binn, Ann
Birch, Chas.
Boothe, Wm.
Boyd, Jno.
Brady, Pat
Bragg, Elijah
Briscoe, Jno.
Brown, Frederick
Brown, Saml.
Bryan, Jane
Bryant, Jane
Bugg, Wm.
Bullock, Burwell
Bullock, Richd.
Burkes, Edwd.
Burnett, Wm.
Burnwell, Cradock
Call, Jno.
Call, Richd.
Carmichael, Jno.
Carr, Thos.
Carroll, Wm.
Carrell, Wm.
Carswell, Edwd.
Chambers, Jno.

Chambers, Wm.
Cox, Calib
Champion, Henry
Clay, Abraham
Clark, Barnes
Clerk, Arthur
Cocke, Nathl.
Collier, Jno.
Collins, Jno.
Collins, Stephen
Conner, Wm.
Cornelison, Jno.
Cox, Martin
Crabb, Asa
Crawford, Anderson
Crawford, Chas.
Crawford, Robt.
Crook, Jonathan
Culbreath, Jas.
Culbreath, Jno.
Culbreath, Thos.
Danelly, Frances
Danelly, Jas.
Davis, Jno.
Davis, Abiathar
Davis, Clementius
Davis, Jno.
Dean, Jno.
Denton, Wm.
Downs, Geo.
Drummond, Walter
Dunn, Nehemiah
Durden, Elisha
Edwards, Catherine
Egan, Wm.
Elbert, Saml.
Elliott, Jno.
Elliott, Wm.
Eubanks, Richd.
Evans, Danl.
Evans, Henry
Evans, Jno.
Faily, Thos.
Farmer, Benj.
Farmer, Wm.
Fears, Absolom
Ferguson, Jos.
Flournoy, Robt.
Forsyth, Benj.
Forsyth, Robt.
Foster, Jno.
Foule, Alexdr.
Franklin, Geo.
Franklin, Wm.

Freeman, Wm.
Fuller, Isaac
Fuller, Joshua
Galphin, Thos.
Gardner, Lewis
Gardner, Wm.
Gilpin, Ignatius
Glascock, Thos.
Gloster, Robt.
Gore, Jno.
Graham, Richd.
Graves, Humphrey
Graves, Joshua
Graves, Thos.
Gray, Robt.
Greene, Isaac
Grinage, Joshua
Grubbs, Benj.
Grubbs, Isaac
Gutrey, Jno.
Hamilton, Jas.
Harris, Jas.
Harris, Nathan
Harrison, Mary
Hatcher, Jno.
Hatcher, Priscilla
Haynes, Anthony
Haynes, Thos.
Hemphill, Saml.
Hicks, Edwd.
Higginbotham, Burris
Hobbs, Jno.
Hodgins, Jno.
Hogan, Thos.
Hogg, Wm.
Holiday, Ambrose
Hollingsworth, Jos.
Holzenback, Jno.
Howard, Thos.
Howell, Jno.
Hughes, Wm.
Hunt, Fitz Maurice
Hunt, Thos.
Hunter, Dalziel
Hylar (?), Jas.
Irby, Henry
Irby, Jos.
Jack, Saml.
Jackson, J.
Jackson, Reuben
James, Jno.
Jameson, Jno.
Jenkins, Benj.
Jernigan, Hardy

Johnson, Alexdr.
Joiner, Benj.
Jones, Henry
Jones, Jas.
Jones, Mark
Jones, Seaborn
Jones, Thos.
Jones, Wm.
Kail, Jno.
Keanor, Wm.
Kelly, Jno.
Kepherson, Jno.
Kennedy, Jno.
Knight, Nehemiah
Lamar, Basil
Lamar, Sarah
Lampkin, Jeremiah
Lee, Wm.
Leonard, Elijah
Leonard, Wm.
Lindsey, Moses
Linville, Wm.
Longstreet, David
Longstreet, Danl.
Loveless, Wm.
Lowe, Danl.
McCullough, Jacob
McDaniel, Wm.
McDonald, Absolom
McDonald, Jno.
McDuffie, Jno.
McGar, Owen
McGee, Wm.
McNair, Gilbert
McKinley, Jos.
McNeil, Jas.
McManes, Jas.
McMurphy, Danl.
McSwine, Patrick
Maddox, Jno.
Maddock, Jos.
Magruder, Ninian Offutt
Maloan, Martin
Mark, Eli
Markham, Arthur
Marshall, Sol.
Mathews, Mary
Matthews, Meshack
Maxwell, David
May, Jos.
Millican, Hugh
Milligan, Hugh
Mock, Andrew
Mock, Jos.

Mooney, Jno.
Moore, Henry
Moore, Jas.
Moore, Martin
Moore, Mordecai
Moore, Thos.
Morgan, Mary
Moseley, Wm.
Mott, Nathan
Murphy, Edwd.
Napier, Jas.
Napier, Thos.
Napper, Absolom
Newberry, Thos.
Newman, Thos.
Offutt, Lettice
Offutt, Nathaniel
Ogg, Geo.
Owens, Benj.
Owens, Ephraim
Pace, Thos.
Pace, Wm.
Parsley, Sarah
Payne, Saml. Sr.
Peak, Jno.
Pearce, Jas.
Pearce, Thos.
Perryman, Richd.
Phillps, Stephen
Pindath, Wm.
Pinson, Vinnie
Polk, Micajah
Poole, Saml.
Porter, Thos.
Price, Rees
Prior, Hadon
Proctor, Jordan
Pursley, Jno.
Pursley, Wm.
Rae, Jas.
Ramsey, Isaac
Ramsey, Randall
Rees, Hardy
Reeves, Sarah
Reeve, Spencer
Ricketson, Marmaduke
Robertson, Mark
Rousseau, Jno.
Rowells, Edwd.
Rowland, Jas.
Russell, Hugh
Salyer, Benj.
Sampler, Thos.
Satterwhite, David

Savage, Loveless
Scavesley (?), Thos.
Sell, Jonathan
Shaw, Robt.
Shields, Wm.
Shoemaker, Josiah
Showes, Jno.
Sikes, Wm.
Sims, Mann
Sims, Wm.
Smith, Frances
Smith, T.
Smith, Thos.
Sorrells, Jno.
Stanford, Elijah
Stanford, Robt.
Stapler, Jno.
Steed, Philip
Stevens, Jno.
Stewert, Ann
Stith, Jno.
Stith, Peyton Randolph
Stith, Wm.
Stokes, Hartwell
Story, Richd.
Sullivan, Owen
Sullivan, Wm.
Sutherland, Jno.
Swint, Jno.
Tabor, Jno.
Tapley, Aaron
Tapley, Joel
Taylor, Henry
Temple, Jas.
Templeton, Wm.
Tindall, Booker
Tindall, Jno.
Tindall, Wm.
Tindell, Jno.
Tinnall, Jno.
Tinsley, David
Tinsley, Jas.
Todd, Wm.
Tolbott, Nathl.
Touchstone, David
Towns, Jno.
Twiggs, Jno.
Upton, Geo.
Vann, Jesse
Vaughn, Alexdr.
Vaughn, Evans
Vernon, Nathl.
Wade, Jno.
Waggoner, Thos.

Wagoner, Jno.
Walker, David
Walker, Robt.
Wall, David
Walton, Robt.
Walton, Wm.
Ward, Chas.
Waters, Jas.
Watkins, Robt.
Watson, Jno.
Watson, Nathl.
Webb, Jeremiah
Wells, Saml.
Whitaker, Saml.
White, Nicholas
Whittington, Cornelius
Whittington, Wm.
Wilkins, Jonathan
Wilkins, Wm.
Williams, Jas.
Williams, Jno.
Willingham, Jno.
Willingham, Wm.
Willshire, Jeremiah
Willshire, Wm.
Windingham, Jno.
Winfrey, Jesse
Winningham, Thos.
Woodruff, Wilson
Wright, Abednego
Wright, Habakkuk
Wright, Isaiah
Wright, Jas.
Wright, Saml.
Wyche, Geo.
Yonge, Geo.
Young, Chas.
Youngblood, Peter
Zachry, Jno.
Zachry, Peter

Wills:1790 - 1793

Adams, Pelithal
Armstrong, Sally
Bacon, Lyddall, dec'd.
Bacon, Mary
Barnes, Jas., dec'd.
Barnes, Jemmina
Barnett, Nathl.
Barnett, Wm.
Barron, Wm., dec'd.
Blackstone, Jas.
Blackstone, Jno.

Blackstone, Winefred
Booker, Jno.
Boyed, Eliz.
Brown, Jas.
Brown, S.
Bryan, Thos.
Buckanan, Jas.
Bugg, Edmd.
Bugg, Eliza
Burnette, Crad.
Burton, Richd.
Campbell, Edwd.
Campbell, McCarton, dec'd.
Campbell, Sarah
Carnes, Thos. P.
Clay, Abia-- dec'd.
Clem, Catherine
Clem, David
Clem, Henry
Clay, Saml.
Clem, Valentine, dec'd.
Coleman, Reuben
Connell, Danl.
Connell, Thos., dec'd.
Crawford, Anderson
Crawford, Frances
Crawford, Joe
Crawford, Nathan
Dikes, Geo.
Dikes, Georges Sr.
Dikes, Jesse
Dikes, Levi
Dikes, Martha
Dikes, Mary
Dikes, Noah
Dikes, Rebecca
Dikes, Unity
Dixon, Ann
Dixon, Caroline McD.
Dixon, Henry
Dixon, Jno. Lydell
Dixon, Maria Felishia
Dixon, Robt., dec'd.
Dixon, Sarah Parks
Dixon, Tillman
Elam, Danl.
Farish, Robt.
Fenwick, Jno.
Forsyth, Fanny
Forsyth, Jno.
Forsyth, Robt.
Forsyth, Robt. Moriah
Freeman, Wm.
Furey, Jno.

Gadsden, Philip G.	Newton, Jesse
Gardner, Jas.	Norwood, Sarah
Girdine, Lewis	Perry, Nathl.
Glascock, Eliz.	Poe, Wm.
Glascock, Thos.	Poston, Jno.
Glascock, Wm.	Powell, Jno.
Gray, Christian	Reardon, Yelverton
Hall, Bolling	Redlick, Wm.
Harris, Lewis	Rice, Jesse
Hart, Esther	Ricketson, Marmaduke
Hay, And.	Rowell, Edwd.
Hayes, Patrick	Rutledge, Edwd., Sr.
Herrin, Ann Madelin	Savidge, Loveless
Herrin, Betsy	Sherwood, Charity
Herrin, Nancy	Sherwood, Mary
Hickenbotom, Burer	Sherwood, Moses
Hicks, Ansell	Sherwood, Wm.
Hicks, Edmond	Slade, Jos.
Hicks, Mary	Smelt, Dennis
Hicks, Nathl.	Statham, Chas.
Hunt, Geo.	Stiles, Jno.
Hunt, Ruth	Stiles, Jos.
Hunter, J. P.	Swain, Jas.
Innes, Andrew	Tatnall, Josiah Jr.
Jack, Saml.	Telfair, Edwd.
Jack, Wm. H.	Thomas, Feaby
Johnston, Abraham	Tighlman, Aaron, dec'd.
Jones, Abraham	Tindill, Betty Ann
Jones, Hez.	Tinsley, Mary
Jones, Seaborn	Townsend, Ruth, dec'd.
Jones, Wm.	Travis, Asa
Kearnes, Thos.	Upton, Jas.
Lamar, Basil	Vaughn, Jas., dec'd.
Lamar, Catherine	Vaugh, Jane
Lamar, Jno.	Vaughn, Jno.
Low, Ann	Vaughn, Robt.
Low, Geo.	Vaughn, Wm.
Low, Isaac, Sr., dec'd.	Walker, David
Low, Isaac Jr.	Wallace, Wm.
Low, Wm.	Walton, Blanche
McDonald, Henry	Walton, Robt.
McDonough	Watkins, Thos.
McDowel, Wm.	Watson, Thos.
McManes, Jno.	Webster, Frances
McTaser, Jno.	Webster, Honner, dec'd.
Meals, Jno., dec'd.	West, Martin
Meals, Joshua	Willcox, Jno.
Milton, Jno.	Williamson, W.
Minor, Wm.	Yarbrough, Jas.
Minor, Wm. Jr.	Yarbrough, Littleton
Mott, Jean	Yarbrough, Martha
Mott, Sarah	Yarbrough, Wm.
Mott, Uriah	Zachry, Betty
Mott, Zephamiah	Zachry, Jas., dec'd.

Zachry, Jno.
Zachry, Mary
Zackry, Peter
Zachry, Wm.
Zimmerman, Godfrey

Administrators and
Guardians Bonds
 1789 - 1790

Arinton, Henry
Barnes, Geo.
Barnes, Jas.
Barnett, Elenor
Barnette, Jesse, dec'd.
Beale, Wm.
Bedingfield, Chas., dec'd.
Bedingfield, Jno.
Bedingfield, Martha
Bedingfield, Mary
Bellamy, Wm.
Bennett, Jno. Baker
Blackwell, Chas.
Blair, Hugh
Blanchard, Reuben, dec'd.
Blanchard, Sarah
Bonner, Richd.
Bostick, Nathan
Boswell, Benj.
Brantley, Benj.
Braswell, Benj.
Britt, Jno.
Bugg, Anselm
Bugg, Jeremiah
Bugg, Nicholas
Bugg, Wm.
Burke, Michael
Butler, Noble
Candelr, Henry
Candler, Wm. Jr. dec'd.
Cargile, Clement
Carson, Jno., dec'd.
Carson, Rachel
Cartlidge, Edmond
Cartlidge, Jas.
Cartlidge, Saml.
Catlett, Jno.
Christopher, Jas.
Clayton, Philip
Coan, Wm.
Cocke, Nathl.
Cobbison, Ann
Cobbison, Jno.
Cockraham, David

Coleman, Anna
Coleman, Caleb, dec'd.
Coleman, Reuben
Conn, Geo.
Covington, Jno.
Covington, Jos.
Crane, Lewis
Cumming, Thos.
Davis, Abiathar
Davis, Theophilus, dec'd.
Dawson, Britton
Dixon, Robt.
Drane,. Walter
Ennis, Andrew
Epsie, Jas.
Epsie, Wm., dec'd.
Evans, Stephen
Everingham, Hannah
Everingham, Jno., dec'd.
Farrar, Fields, dec'd.
Few, Ignatius
Fontain, Mary
Fontain, Peter, dec'd.
Foster, Jno.
Fox, Jas., dec'd.
Fox, Sarah
Gardner, Ashel
Gardner, Jason
Gardner, Jno.
Gardner, Lewis
Gardner, Sarah
Gardner, Wm.
Gartrel, Jno.
Gilphin, Wm., dec'd.
Graves, Geo.
Graves, Thos.
Green, Isaac, dec'd.
Grier, Thos.
Harrison, Benj., dec'd.
Harrison, Mary
Higginbotham, Jacob
Hinton, Allen
Hodgens, Jno.
Hobby, Wm. J.
Howard, Rhesa
Ingram, Jas.
Jackson, Amasa
Jenkins, Arthur
Johnson, Abram
Johnston, Abraham
Johnston, Wm.
Jones, Adam
Lamar, Jno.
Lamar, Zachariah

Lander, Jas., dec'd.
Langston, Saml.
Leith, Jno.
Longstreet, David
Longstreet, Wm.
Lowe, Beverly
McCredie, Andrew
McNeill, Michael
Magee, Hugh
Magruder, Saml.
Matthews, Jesse
Matthews, Mesheck
Morris, Jno.
Morris, Rhesa
Morrison, Francis
Morrison, Jas.
Morrison, Thos., dec'd.
Noel, Jno. Y.
Pace, Mary
Pace, Wm., dec'd.
Parks, Laban
Parks, Mary
Paulk, Micajah
Payne, Saml.
Pearre, Jno.
Pool, Baxter
Rae, Ann
Rae, Jas., dec'd.
Ramsey, Jno.
Ramsey, Randolph
Robeson, David Sr.
Robeson, David Jr.
Rowell, Edwd.
Sanders, Ephraim
Savidge, Amey
Savidge, Robt., dec'd.
Scott, Saml.
Shearer, Alex., dec'd.
Simmons, Chas.
Smith, Edwd.
Smith, Jno.
Smith, Jno. E.
Smith, Thos.
Stith, Wm.
Sutherland, Alex., dec'd.
Thompson, Catharine
Thompson, Wm., dec'd.
Towena, Jno.
Tinsley, David
Townsend, Thos.
Trapnell, Archibald
Twiggs, Jno.
Wagnon, Thos.
Wallace, Wm.

Wallecon, Danl.
Whittington, Cornelius
Whittington, Wm.
Williams, Lud
Wilson, Jno.
Wilson, Perry
Wood, Isaac, dec'd.
Wyche, Geo.

Minutes of Inferior
Court: 1790:

Adams, Eliz.
Adcock, Jas.
Bacon, Agnes
Barnes, Geo.
Barnett, Jesse, dec'd.
Barnett, Wm.
Beckham, Sol.
Bedingfield, Jno.
Bedingfield, Mary
Bennett, Chas.
Blache, S.
Bledsoe, Benj.
Brown, Jas.
Carr, Thos.
Carroll, Wm.
Cone, Wm.
Crawford, David
Crawford, Joel
Davis, Susannah
Dick, Robt.
Ennis, Andrews
Gardner, Jas.
Gaylord, Giles
Gilpin, Ignatius
Goolsby, Wm.
Grenage, Joshua
Harris, Giles
Harrison, Richd.
Hayes, Patrick
Hills, Marg.
Johnston, Wm.
Jones, Abram
Jones, Lewellen
Lampkin, Jas.
Lampkin, Jeremiah
Lampkin, Jno.
Langston, David
Larrie, Jno.
McCarty, Jno.
McFarlin, Edwd.
Maher, Matthias
Middleton, Saml.

Mosely, Benj.
Pearre, Jno.
Pryor, Haden
Rhodes, Jno.
Roden, Zadoc
Spencer, Wm.
Spurlock, Eliz.
Spurlock, Jno.
Spurlock, Robt.
Stith, Wm.
Thompson, Wm.
Tindall, Wm.
Turmerson, Turner
Vedheidingem, Jno.Peter
Williams, Henry
Wilson, Jno.
Wyche, Geo.
Youngblood, Isaac
Zimmerman, Godfrey

Militia Roll: 1782

Barfield, Richd.
Barnett, Jesse
Barnett, Joel
Barnett, Wm.
Beall, Thos.
Beall, Zepha.
Bloodworth, Saml.
Bowie, Jas.
Bowie, Reson
Castleberry, Henry
Catledge, Edwd.
Courton, Richd.
Cowin, Wm.
Criswell, David
Davis, Benj.
Davis, Jas.
Dowdy, Richd.
Duck, Jeremiah
Emmerson, Robt.
Evans, Jno.
Frazer, Alexdr.
Fuller, Isaac
Fuller, Jno.
Fuller, Joshua
Garnett, Ely
Garnette, Jno.
Greef, Joshua
Green, Jno.
Green, Wm.
Hatcher, Jno.
Hill, Edwd.
Hill, Jno.

Hill, Joshua
Hogg, Jas.
Hogg, Jno.
Holladay, Thos.
Holliman, David
Holliman, Mark
Holliman, Richd.
Howard, Benj.
Ilands, Jno.
Irvin, Jno.
Johnson, Jno.
Jones, Robt.
Larvin, Jno.
Lucous, Wm.
McKineah, Jno.
McNeal, Mikel
Maddox, Jno.
Marbury, Leonard
Megee, Hugh
Megee, Luis
Miller, Ezekiel
ONeal, Jno.
Peak, Jno.
Philips, Demey
Philips, Hilley
Powell, Luis
Ramsey, Jno.
Ramsey, Randol
Ramsey, Wm.
Salter, Simon
Shurley, Wm.
Simons, Malbery
Tindol, Jno.
Watley, Owen
Watley, Sherod
Watley, Walton
Watley, Willis Sr.
Watley, Willis Jr.
Whatley, Jno.
Whatley, Richd.
Whitley, Thos.
Wilder, Malichi
Wilsher, Jurdin
Wilson, Jno.
Woard, Benj.
Ward, Elijah
Wright, Bednego
Wright, Thos.

Deed Books "A-1," "A-2" & "B": 1789-1790

Grantors:
Baldwin, Abraham
Bishop, Jas.

(149)

Bishop, Phebe
Britt, Ester
Britt, Jno.
Bugg, Charlotte
Bugg, Nicholas H.
Burch, Edwd.
Burch, Martha
Burnett, Jno.
Burt, Fanny
Burt, Moody
Carr, Fanny
Carr, Thos.
Cobbs, Jno.
Cole, Thos.
Connell, Eliz.
Crawford, Anderson
Crawford, Peter
Dorsey, Leakin
Duncan, Matthew
Dysart, Charity
Dysart, Cornelius
Ege, Jacob
Evans, Sarah
Evans, Stephen
Few, Wm.
Flemming, David
Forsyth, Robt.
Foster, Eliz.
Foster, Jno.
Galt, Gabriel, dec'd.
Garnet, Eli
Garrett, Catharine
Garrett, Jno.
Germany, Saml.
Glascock, Wm.
Graves, Thos.
Handley, Geo.
Howell, Jno.
Hunter, Dalziel
Jack, Kitty
Jack, Saml.
Jackson, Amasa
Jones, Henry
Jones, Jemmimah
Jones, Keziah
Jones, Robt.
Jones, Seaborn
Jones, Wm.
Kelcey, Noah
Lambert, David
McLane, Danl.
McMurphy, Danl.
McMurphy, Susannah
Marbury, Horatio

Marbury, Leonard
Medors, Richd.
Miller, David
Miller, Mary
Milton, Jno.
Moody, Burt
Offutt, Ezekiel
Offutt, Jemima
Payne, Walter
Perry, Jas.
Powell, Jno.
Powell, Marg.
Poynter, Argulus
Poynter, Mary
Rae, Ann
Rae, Jas.
Shoemake, Josiah
Sims, Wm.
Spencer, Mildred
Spencer, Wm.
Stephens, Reb.
Stephens, Wm. Jos.
Sutherland, Eliz.
Sutherland, Jno.
Thompson, Catharine
Thompson, Wm.
Telfair, Edwd.
Tinsley, David
Wagnon, Jno. Peter
Wagnon, Rebecca
Wallace, Wm.
Walton, Geo.
Walton, Wm.
Wambersie, Emanuel
Watkins, Wm., Sr.
Watts, Jos.
Weakley, Eliz.
Weakley, Lewis
Whitten, Robt.
Wright, H.

Grantee
Barksdale, Jeffrey
Barnes, Geo.
Baylis, Isham
Beal, Jno.
Beall, Archibald
Brown, Jas.
Bryan, Jos.
Bugg, Sherwood
Candler, Wm.
Carnes, Thos. P.
Cocke, Nathl.
Cumming, Thos.

Dick, Robt.
Dougherty, Jno.
Dougherty, Jno. Sr.
Duncan, Matthew
Evans, Lucy Williamson
Evans, Mordecai
Few, Ignatius
Gardner, Jas.
Gardner, Lewis
Garnett, Jno.
Glascock, Thos.
Graves, Geo.
Grinage, Joshua
Harris, Nathan
Hays, Wm.
Hunter, Ellinor
Ingram, Jas.
Innes, Andrew
Jack, Saml.
Jackson, Amasa
Jennings, Wm.
Jones, Henry Jr.
Jones, Jas.
Kelcey, Noah
Lee, Wm.
McDonald, Henry M.
McManus, Jno.
Magee, Hugh
Medors, Enoch
Medors, Jno.
Medors, Micajah
Medors, Thos.
Mitchell, Wm.
Murray, David Jr.
Pearre, Nathl.
Pinson, Winny
Rich, Jno.
Rowell, Edwd.
Sanders, Jesse
Shields, Marg.
Spencer, Wm.
Wagnon, Jno. Peter
Wallace, Wm.
Wambersie, Emanuel
Watkins, Jno.
Watkins, Thos.
Watkins, Wm. Jr.
Watts, Jos.
Weakly, Lewis
Wilson, Jno.
Wray, Jno.
Zimmerman, Godfrey

Witnessess and other
names appearing:

Alger, Jas.
Anderson, Geo.
Anderson, Mary
Appling, Jno.
Ashbury, Reb.
Austin, Richd.
Baldwin, David
Barnard, Timothy
Barnes, Geo.
Beal, Wm.
Beall, Jas. E.
Beall, Mitchell Z.
Bell, Richd.
Bettis, Jno.
Bonner, Robt.
Bourquin, Jno. L.
Brown, Jno.
Buffington, Jos.
Burch, Chas.
Carnes, Thos. P.
Carter, Elisha
Catlett, Jno.
Chandler, Henry
Chandler, Wm., dec'd.
Clayton, Philip
Coleman, Susannah
Cone, Wm.
Crawford, Chas.
Culbreath, Peter
Daily, Jno.
Davidson, Robt.
Davidson, Wm.
Depart, Eliz.
Dougherty, Alex.
Dougherty, Jno.
Dougherty, Neill
Dougherty, Patrick
Elam, Danl.
Elam, Wm.
Eubank, Major
Evans, Richd., dec'd.
Evans, Stephen
Fears, Absolom
Few, Benj.
Freeman, W.
Fulcher, Jas.
Gardner, Thos.
Germany, Herd
Germany, Jno.

Gilpin, Ignatius
Glascock, Wm.
Graves, Robt.
Grierson, Jas.
Hamilton, Jas.
Hamilton, Richd.
Handly, Geo.
Harding, Wm.
Hargrove, Emanuel
Hawkins, A.
Hightower, Richd.
Hobby, Wm.
Hubert, Latthew
Hunter, D.
Hunter, Dalziel
Hunter, Eleanor
Jackson, Jno.
Jones, Ambrose
Jones, Jno.
Jones, Lew
Jones, Robt.
Kennedy, Jno.
Kindrick, Nathl. O.
Lamar, Jas.
Lee, Wm.
Leigh, Benj.
Lipsey, Ricketson
Longstreet, Danl.
McFarland, Jas.
McFarland, Wm., dec'd.
McIntosh, Donald
McIntosh, Wm. Jr.
McNeil, Jas.
McNiever, Danl.
Macon, H.
Marbury, Ann
Mead, Stith
Meriwether, Nicholas
Miller, Danl.
Mossman, Eliz.
Munro, Simon
Napier, Thos.
Osborne, Henry
Owens, Ephraim
Pannill, J.
Parett, Elijah
Parker, Jno.
Poage, Jno.
Pool, B.
Porter, Thos.
Ramsey, Jno.
Randolph, Mary
Richardson, Danl.
Roe, Isaac

Romisa, Dirick
Ross, Jas.
Rowell, Jno.
Sanders, Joshua
Savage, Loveless
Shackleford, Jno.
Sheftall, Moses
Simmons, Chas.
Simmons, J. M.
Snebly, E.
Stallings, Jas.
Steurman, Henry
Stith, Wm.
Sullivan, Florence
Talbot, Matthew
Talley, Henry
Tankersley, Jno.
Tate, Robt.
Tharp, Eleazer
Thomas, Robt.
Urquhart, Wm.
Voicle, Louis
Wade, J.
Waid, Chas.
Walker, Geo.
Watts, Edwd.
Whiting, Jno. A.
Willis, Francis
Wood, Ann
Woods, Nathl.
Woodroof, Wilson
Wright, Chas.
Young, Goo.
Youngblood, Peter

Names from old Georgia
Newspapers: 1790-1795

Deaths
1790 -- 1795
Allen, Sherwood
Andrews, Benj.
Arrington, Henry
Bonner, Geo.
Bugg, Thos.
Campbell, McCartan
Catlett, Geo.
Clay, Abia
Cocke, Richd.
Course, Wm.
Dallas, Angus
Dallas, Maria
Dawson, Britton
Dearmond, Ann

Draper, Jno.
Fox, Jas.
Glascock, Wm.
Hallinger, Titus
Handley, Geo.
Harrison, Jno.
Haworth, Edmond
Hills, Nathan
Hobby, Sally
Ingram, Mrs. Mary
Jackson, Mrs. Ann
Jones, Hugh
Leigh, Edmund
Liverman, Miss Livia
McKennie, Jno.
McKinne, Garret
Marshall, Albert
Milton, Augustus Caesar
Montfort, Mary
Naylor, Arista
Nixon, Robt.
Pardue, Morris
Pollock, Allen
Richards, Catharine
Rogers, Wm.
Simmons, Chas.
Spann, Jas.
Spencer, Mrs. Mildred
Stallings, Mrs. Bethia
Stearman, Henry
Sullivan, Florence
VanHeddeghem, Mrs. (?)

White, Pollie
Williams, Col. Jno.
Young, Mrs. Martha

Legal Notices and
Other Newspaper Items:
Berryhill, Alexdr.
Burch, Chas.
Clayton, Phillip
Cone, Wm.
Cowles, Wm.
Fox, Jas.
Glascock, Thos.
Gordon, Ambrose
Hamilton, Thos.
Harris, Jas.
Howell, Jno.
Leigh, Anselm
Longstreet, Wm.
Lowe, Geo.
McLean, Danl.
Milton, Jno.
Pearre, Jas.
Robinson, Jno.
Spurlock, Wm.
Stallings, Jas.
Walker, Geo.
Walton, Jno. C.
Wambersie, Emaniel
Ward, Chas.
Watkins, Robt.
Watkins, Thos.

WASHINGTON COUNTY

An original County formed Feb. 25, 1784, from lands of the Creek cession of 1783. Sandersville is the County seat. From Washington were formed the counties of Greene, Hancock, Johnson and Montgomery.
Fire destroyed all records in County in 1855.

Headrights and
Bounty Grants:
1789 - 1793

Abercrombie, Chas.
Arline, Jno.
Armstrong, Alexdr.
Autry, Absalom
Bacon, Nicholas
Baggs, Jos.

Baker, Joshua
Ballard, Chris.
Banks, Gerard
Bankston, Laurence
Barber, Jos.
Barnap, ?

Bass, Esaw
Beavin, Wm.
Beckcom, Allen
Beckcom, Saml.
Beckcom, Sherod
Beckcom, Simon
Beckcom, Sol.
Bedingfield, Jos.
Beezly, Jos.
Bennett, Arthur
Bennis, Jno. (heirs of)
Bentley, Balam
Bentley, Wm.
Benson, Jno.
Bird, Michael
Black, Jno.
Blunt, Jas.
Borland, Andrew
Boyd, Thos.
Bracken, Isaac
Bracken, Wm.
Braswell, Kindred
Bremer, Jno.
Burge, Jno.
Burnet, Danl.
Burney, David
Carnes, Thos. P.
Carr, Isham
Catchings, Jos.
Catchings, Benj.
Cates, Thos.
Cawthon, Wm.
Chance, Isaac
Chance, Simpson
Chance, Vincent
Chandler, Abednego
Chandler, Mordecai
Chany, Emanuel
Clayton, Jno.
Coats, Lasley
Cobb, Jas.
Cocke, Zebulon
Cockerham, Jas.
Coleman, Jonathan
Colson, Sanders
Comins, David
Comins, Eleazer
Connell, Jesse
Connelly, Jno. Wm.
Cowens, Eleazer
Cowen, Wm.
Cox, Henry
Cox, Jno.
Cox, Wm.

Criddle, Thos.
Crittenton, Jno.
Crosby, Geo.
Culpepper, Sampson
Curry, David
Dameron, Jno.
Daniell, Benj.
Danielly, Jno.
Dannard, Jacob
Dawson, Richmond
Dearizeaux, Stephen
Deas, DeWitt
Deas, Jas.
Deason, Rachael
Dickson, Michel
Dillard, Nicholas
Dixon, Robt.
Douglas, Edwd.
Dowdey, Richd.
Earnest, Geo.
Eiland, Absalom
Elands, Absalom
English, Thos.
Espey, Jas.
Evans, David
Fail, Thos.
Faulconer, Jacob
Featherstone, Howell
Field, Jas.
Franklin, Philimon
Fulton, Saml. Jr.
Fuqua, Prater
Fusils, Thos.
Ganer, Wm.
Gardiner, Jno.
Gibson, Adam
Gidden, Richd.
Glenn, David
Grant, Thos.
Green, Thos.
Greene, Jas.
Griffin, Farnafol.
Griffin, Lenn
Griffin, Major
Hamlin, Richd.
Hammett, Wm.
Handley, Jas.
Harrell, Edwd.
Harris, Geo.
Harrison, Edwd.
Harvey, Blassingame
Hatcher, Henry
Hawkins, Francis
Hawkins, Saml.

Hawthon, Thos.
Hayman, Staunton
Hearton, Thos.
Hemphill, Wm.
Herring, Wm.
Hickman, Theophilus
Hill, Geo.
Hill, Joshua
Hines, Jas.
Hinson, Wm.
Holdness, Jas.
Hollingsworth, Stephen
Holly, Jonathan
Holton, Saml.
Hood, Nathl.
Hooks, Wm.
Hooper, Absalom
Hopkins, Wm.
Horn, Jacob
Horsley, Tarleton
Hoskins, Mariam
Houstoun, Henry
Hubert, Mathew
Hudson, Isaac
Hughes, Jas.
Hunt, Jno.
Hunts, Fitz Maurice
Ingram, Richd.
Jackson, Abraham
Jackson, Absalom
Jackson, Robt.
Jackson, Walter
Jenkins, Francis
Jennings, Sarah
Jiles, Thos.
Johnson, Benj.
Johnson, Jas. Sr.
Johnson, Jno.
Johnson, Wilson
Jordan, Wm.
Keath, Saml. Jr.
Keaton, Jno.
Kelly, Jno.
Kemp, Wm.
Kendrick, Burrell
Kindrick, Nathl.
King, Parks
Kitchen, Benj.
Lamar, Luke
Lamb, Jesse
Lamkins, Saml.
Land, Henry
Langford, Jas.
Lasseter, Hansil

Leapham, Aaron
Lightfoot, Jno.
Lindsay, Jno.
Lingo, Patrick
Lingo, Moses
Linton, Jno.
Little, Wm. Sr.
Lofton, Marg.
Lofton, Van
Long, Nicholas
Long, Nicholas Jr.
Lott, Jno. Jr.
Lott, Mark
Lowry, Simeon
Lynch, Jno.
Mackay, Thos.
Martin, Jos.
Martin, Wm.
Maxwell, Robt.
May, Jas.
McCarcal, Jas.
McClendon, Wilson
McClendon, Joel
McCullen, Bryant
McCullers, Bryant
McDowell, Thos.
McDowell, Wm.
McGehee, Saml.
McGowan, David
McGowan, Robt.
McLane, Danl.
McMillan, Mathers
McMurray, Wm.
McNeely, Danl.
McWilliams, Jno.
Meddow, Jno.
Messer, Thos.
Miles, Jno.
Miller, Alexdr.
Miller, Elisha
Miller, Jonathan
Miller, Jos.
Monger, Sampson
Morgan, Jas.
Motte, Jos.
Motte, Nathan
Nail, Elisha
Neiley, Jno.
Nelson, Wm.
Newnham, Jno.
Nicholson, Benj.
Night, Nehemiah
Norgan, Jas.
Numan, Wm.

Outlaw, Edwd.
Palls, Jas.
Partain, Robt.
Perison, Jno.
Perkins, Adam
Perrett, Wm.
Phillips, Jno.
Phillips, Lochariah
Phillips, Saml.
Pinkston, Danl.
Pinkston, Jno.
Pothree, Francis
Powell, Wm.
Price, Cabor (Cader?)
Price, Wm.
Pullen, Thos.
Rachel, Miles
Raiford, Morris
Ratcliff, Benj.
Ratcliff, Jos.
Rausaw, Wm.
Rayley, Sarah
Reaves, Jos.
Reiley, Jos.
Rentfrow, Wm.
Reyley, Jos.
Reynolds, Absalom
Roan, Tudsdale
Roberts, Alvan
Roberts, Joshua
Robertson, Jno. Sr.
Robertson, Wm.
Robinson, Edwd.
Robinson, Israel
Rochell, Miles
Roe, Jas.
Rogers, Dread
Ross, Moses
Roundtree, Wm.
Row, Hezekiah
Rowton, Jno.
Runnells, Hannan
Runnells, Herman
Ryan, Jos.
Sallis, Jno.
Sallisbury, Jos.
Salter, Jas.
Sampson, Howell
Sanford, Saml.
Scarborough, Miles
Sessions, Jos.
Sharp, Wiley
Sheffield, Robt.
Sheffield, Wm.

Shelby, Jno.
Shelman, I.
Shelman, Jno.
Sheppard, Thos.
Sheppard, Wm.
Shield, Robt.
Shields, Wm.
Shipley, Robt.
Shuffle, Wm.
Sikes, Danl.
Simpkins, Chas.
Sled, Joshua
Snell, Chris.
Spann, Francis
Sparks, Josiah
Spekes, Thos.
Stamper, Howell
Starnes, Ebeneezer
Stinson, Nathan
Stokes, Saml.
Sutton, Jeremiah
Swain, Stephen
Tannyhill, Jno.
Taylor, Joshua
Taylor, Wright
Thomas, Gideon
Thornton, Elam
Thrasher, Geo.
Tillmon, Littleberry
Tillmon, Stephen
Tillmon, Stephenson
Tomlinson, David
Tray, Mary
Trice, Jas.
Underwood, Benj.
Vickers, Benj.
Vickers, Jno.
Vickers, Robt.
Vivan, Thacker
Wadsworth, Jas.
Wadsworth, Jas. Jr.
Walker, Elisha
Walker, Jeremiah
Walker, Silvanus
Walker, Thos.
Wall, Francis
Wallace, Channal
Wallis, Chas.
Ward, Moses
Watson, David
Watts, Jacob
West, Sion
Westley, Lemon
Whatley, Jesse

Whitehead, Amos
Whitehead, Jane
Whitehead, Thos.
Wicker, Robt.
Wicker, Wm.
Wilbourn, Curtis
Williams, Wm.
Winne, Jno.
Wise, Sheridy
Wood, Abraham
Wood, David
Wood, Dempsey
Wood, Sol.
Wood, Wm.

Tax-defaulters, 1791

Airs, Thos.
Averitt, Albright
Averitt, Archibald
Aylett, Archibald
Barbery, David
Bedford, Thos.
Beek, Jos.
Brown, Isaac
Buntery, Zach.
Carpter, Edwd.
Carragin, Edwd.
Carson, Jos.
Chalmers, Geo.
Chaplin, Jos.
Chivers, Joel
Cocks, Wm.
Crother, Jno.
Dennard, Wm.
Dickson, Reubin
Die, Thos.
Ford, Jno.
Frasher, Andrew
Griffin, Jones
Gay, Josiah
Hall, Bradley
Hall, Wm.
Hambleton, Edwd.
Hampton, Mr.
Hampton, Wm.
Harden, Voll
Harris, Jas.
Harvey, Wm.
Hemphill, Robt.
Irwin, Alexdr.
Irwin, Wm.
Jackson, Robt.
Johnson, Benj.

Johnston, Abel
Lafearse, Isaac
Leghorn, Wm.
Longdon, Saml.
McMullen, Jas.
Mikell, Thos.
Miller, Lewis
Mims, Jno.
Newsom, Frederick
Newsom, Jno.
Numan, Jno.
Oates, Jeremiah
Pair, Zach.
Penson, Enoch
Peres (?), Jno.
Pitman, Phillip
Pollet, Jesse
Quails, Jno.
Roberson, Jas.
Sartin, Jas.
Simmons, Jno.
Sims, Jas.
Smith, Israel
Smith, Jno.
Smith, Wm.
Spears, Sol.
Swoaringen, Josiah
Swilley, Jno.
Swilley, Saml.
Taber, Jno.
Taunt, Wm.
Thompson, Gideon
Tompkins, Jno.
Vessells, Jas.
Wauls, Wm.
Welch, Nicholas
Wesley, Lemmons
Wood, Benj.
Young, Edwd.

Muster Rolls, 1793
Capt. Irwins Company

Adear, Jacob
Barron, Absalam
Bassett, Richd.
Benningfield, Jos.
Boars, Joal
Burney, Jas.
Cahoon, Jos.
Curry, Jno.
Dongar, Philip
Fail, Jepthey
Farmer, Thos.

Fluker, Baldwin
Fluker, David
Graham, Saml.
Hagans, Jas.
Hart, Saml.
Irwin, Hugh
Lynum, Wm.
Lyon, Richd.
Marton, Jas.
Melton, Taegle
Morgain, Garland
Niland, Jno.
Nunn, Jas.
Nusom, Frederick
Pitman, Jesse
Prince, Silvenes
Purkins, Jno.
Raney, Jos.
Raney, Wm.
Raskee, Jas.
Robison, Jas.
Robison, Saml.
Rogers, Burrel
Tolar, Lewis
Wall, Henry
Wall, Jos.
Wall, Wm.
Walter, Thos.
Watson, David
Watson, Elisha
Whitehead, Rezin
Wilson, Robt.

Capt. McCavy's Co.
Acney, Wm.
Armstrong, Edwd.
Athorn, Anthony
Briant, Benj.
Burd, Shadrick
Burgamy, Wm. L.
Cain, Jas.
Chavis, Wm.
Clay, Pearee
Clunt, Jas.
Cobb, Liout
Cobb, Benj.
Coldmon, Curtis
Culver, Nathl.
Cumble, Antony
Daniel, Bengamin
Dun, Thos.
Ellis, Ephram
English, Jno.
Garmeny, Wm.

Garner, Richd.
Garner, Urias
Hall, David
Hathorn, Thos.
Hearn, Wm.
Hollon, Suel
Howel, Gabriel
Jackson, Isaac
Jackson, Stephen
Jackson, Tobe
Jiner, Jno.
Jiner, Nathl.
Jinkins, Wm.
Jones, Jonathan
Ledbetter, Isaac
Lilly, Ens.
Linch, Jno.
Lucke, Moses
Morssie, Cashford
Neel, Antony
Niall, Haris
Obannon, Elijah
Pall, Jas.
Parker, Abdl
Powel, Stephan
Pray, Wm.
Purkins, Jno.
Sarsit, Wm.
Standly, Shade
Taylor, Right
Tomson, Jno.
Wicker, Bol.
Wicker, Jula

Capt. Parrott's Co.
Allum, Edmond
Allum, Jno.
Armstrong, Jno.
Burk, Nimrod
Childers, Richd.
Clark, Lewis
Colter, Wm.
Daniel, Chas.
Daniel, Ezekiel
Delk, Jos.
Dennard, Shadrack
Dickson, Reuben
Ekels, Joel
Farr, Peter
Ford, Wm.
Glenn, David
Glenn, Jno.
Glenn, Robt.
Glenn, Wm.

Grice, Richd.
Hampton, Wm.
Hanner, Thos.
Harrel, Bailey
Hart, Saml.
Haviel, Sol.
Herndon, Jos.
Hickmon, Jos.
Higgs, Abraham
Higgs, Jno.
Johnston, Wilson
Kemp, Benj.
Kemp, Jos.
Kemp, Reuben
Kemp, Stephen
Kemp, Wm.
McCagney, Batey
Mims, Jno. Sr.
Mims, Jno. Jr.
Otes, Jeremiah
Parrott, Benj.
Roberts, Richd.
Robertson, David
Rouce, Bartlett
Saffold, Jno.
Smith, Robt.
Spivey, Joshua
Thomas, Wm.
Trapnell, Archibald
Vickers, Drury
Vickers, Joshua
Wallace, Wm.
Wats, Jacob
Wilford, Lewis
Wood, Abraham

Indian Depredations
1788

Aven, Nancy
Burk, Edmon
Carthon, Usley
Cook, Reuben
Culpepper, Chas.
Drake, Wm.
Ellis, Jas.
Franklin, Wm.
Harris, Jas.
Hogen, Griffin
Hudspeth, Robt.
Jackson, Jas.
Martin, Oliver
Pinkerton, Jno.
Powers, Wm.

Scarbrough, David
Shepherd, David
Sikes, Danl.
Sikes, Elesabeth
Soslder (?), Scantling
Spurlock, Allen
Vann, Jno.
Warlick, ___?___
Wood, Jas.

Justices of Inferior
Court: 1792 -- 1793

'Blackshear, David
Brazoal, Henry
Hampton, Jno.
Kendrick, Jno.
Lawson, Hugh
Lott, Nathan
Low, Frances
McKensie, Jno.
Robertson, Jas.
Robertson, Saml.
Rutherford, Thos. B.
Saffold, Wm.
Shephard, Jno.
Stokes, Jno.

Legal ads and notices
in Southern Centinel
& Universal Gazette--
Augusta Chronicle &
Gazette: 1794-1795

Alston, Phillip
Armstrong, Jno.
Bailey, Lewis
Bell, Hugh
Blake, Jno.
Braswell, Wm.
Brinton, Jno.
Britt, Jonathan
Britt, Malachi
Broughton, Jno.
Bugg, Jno.
Cain, Wm.
Carlise, Wm.
Cox, Wm.
Cummings, Robt.
Daniel, Conner
Daniel, Ezekiel
Dennard, Wm.
Dennis, Jno.
Dunn, Jno.

Emanuel, David
Franklin, Geo.
Gallman, Harmon
Golden, Matthew
Haden, Allen
Hagans, Edwd.
Hamill, Sol.
Hampton, Edwd.
Harvey, Jno.
Harvey, Thos.
Harris, Jas.
Harris, Wm.
Herndon, Jos.
Herndon, Lewis
Higgs, Abraham
Hinton, Caleb
Holland, Sewel
Hunter, Wm.
Jackson, David
Johnson, Alexdr.
Johnston, Wm.
Kitchens, Benj.
Levily, Jesse
Lewis, Jacob
Lewis, Joel
Lewis, Thos.
McDonald, Thos.
McLendon, Mark
McLendon, Thos.
Martin, Jno.
Mims, Jno. Jr.
Nelons, Jno. Sr.
Nelms, Jno. Jr.
Parrott, Benj. Sr.
Perkins, Jno.
Raiford, Morris
Raney, Jos.
Riley, Wm.
Ross, Moses
Russell, Jeremiah Sr.
Rutherford, Jno.
Safesbury, Thos.
Sheffield, Jno.
Sheffield, Wm.
Sheppard, Jno.
Smith, Saml.
Smith, Thos.
Spikes, Matthew
Statham, Chas.
Taylor, Jas.
Taylor, Shadrack
Underwood, Josiah
Underwood, Thos.
Vessells, Jas.

Walker, Barbara
Walker, Geo.
Walker, Joel
Walker, Wm.
Ward, Jno.
Ward, Saml.
Watts, Jno.
Welton, Jas.
Wheelon, Amos
Wilkinson, Reubin
Wood, Sol.

Surveyor's Records
Books D-E 1789-1793

Abercrombie, Chas.
Anderson, Jno.
Arline, Jno.
Armstrong, Jno.
Atwood, Isaac
Baker, Jos.
Ballard, Xpher
Banks, Elisha Fowler
Banks, Gerrard
Bankstone, Lawrence
Barron, Jos.
Barron, Wm.
Bass, Esaw
Beacher, David
Beckcom, Allen
Beckcom, Sherwood
Beckcom, Simon
Beckcu, Saml.
Beckcum, Sol.
Beddingfield, Jos.
Bennett, Arthur
Bennet, Capt. Jno.
Bentley, Wm.
Bentley, Balaam
Benion, Jno.
Benion, Wm.
Berryhill, Andrew
Bird, Michel
Black, Jno.
Blackshear, David
Blanchard, Benj.
Blunt, Jas.
Bobb, Thos.
Bonds, Chas.
Borland, Andrew
Bowie, ___?___
Bowin, Jas.
Bowin, Joel
Boyd, David

Bozman, Luke
Brack, Benj.
Brack, Eleazar
Bracken, Isaac
Bracken, Wm.
Brantley, Thos.
Braswell, Kendred
Braswell, Robt.
Braswell, Saml.
Briggs, Jno.
Brinton, Jno.
Brinton, Wm.
Brooks, Jas.
Brown, Henry
Brown, Jos.
Bruner, Jno.
Bruton, Jno.
Bryan, David
Bryant, Jno.
Bullard, Wily
Burge, Jno.
Burk, Nimrod
Burnet, Danl.
Burnet, Sol.
Burney, David
Burney, Jas.
Burney, Jno.
Burney, Randal
Burney, Richd.
Buttery, Zachary
Camp, Saml.
Campbell, Wm.
Carnes, Thos. P.
Carter, Jno.
Caswell, Jno.
Cates, Richd. W.
Cates, Thos.
Catching, Jos.
Cave, Wm.
Cawthon, Wm.
Chance, Henry
Chance, Sampson
Chance, Vincent
Chandler, Mordecia
Chandler, Obednya
Chivers, Joel
Christmas, Nathl.
Clerk, Lewis
Clough, Geo.
Cobb, Jno.
Cock, Zebulon
Cole, Wm.
Coleman, Jonathan
Collins, Jno.

Collins, Wm.
Colson, Sanders
Conner, Danl.
Cooper, Jno.
Cooxy, Wm.
Cox, Henry
Cox, Josiah
Cox, Wm.
Criswell, David
Croome, Elijah
Crosby, Geo.
Culpepper, Jno.
Cummings, Eleazer
Curry, David
Dameson, Jno.
Daniell, Benj.
Daniel, Jno.
Donnelly, Francis
Dardins, Jno.
Davis, Thos.
Dawson, Jas.
Deason, Jno.
Debosk, Capt. Peter
Delk, Jos.
Dees, Duett
Dennis, Jno.
Dixon, Michel
Dickson, Reuben
Dixon, Thos.
Domini, Frederick
Donnaly, Jno.
Douglass, Edwd.
Dowder (?), Richd.
Drew, Josiah
Dukes, Henry (heirs of)
Derdains, Jno.
Eammis, Jonathan
English, Corneluis
Eskridges, Hetor R.
Evans, Robt.
Fagan, Geo.
Fauche, Jonas
Favors, Wm.
Few, Ignatius
Fields, Jas.
Flannakin, Saml.
Flournoy, Robt.
Flournoy, Thos.
Fort, Owen
Forsyth, Robt.
Franklin, Geo.
Gardener, Jno.
Gainor, Wm.
Gilman, Harmon

Glascock, Thos.
Glenn, David
Goode, Edwd.
Grantham, Jno.
Grantham, Wm.
Green, Benj.
Greene, Jas.
Green, Peleg
Greer, Josiah
Greyham, Jas.
Griffen, Leonard
Griffin, Majer
Hadon, Wm.
Hargrove, Josiah
Harris, Jesse
Harrison, Benj.
Hart, Robt.
Hart, Saml.
Hartsfield, Geo.
Heaton, Robt.
Hemphill, Wm.
Herring, Jas.
Higdon, Chas.
Highland, Nicholas
Hickman, Wm.
Hill, Thos.
Hillard, Majer
Hogg, Jacob
Holderness, Jas.
Hallenworth, Stephen
Holly, Jonathan
Holley, Thos.
Holton, Saml.
Hood, Nathl.
Hooks, Wm.
Hopson, Briggs
Horn, Joab
House, Jos.
Howell, Jos.
Hubert, Mathew
Huckeby, Jno.
Hudson, Wm.
Huff, Saml.
Hughs, Jas.
Hutchinson, Jas.
Irwin, Jared
Jackson, Absalom
Jackson, Chas.
Jackson, David
Jackson, Jos.
Jackson, Robt.
Jackson, Walter
Jamison, Wm.
Jenkins, Francis

Jenkins, Zachariah
Johnson, Benj.
Johnson, Danl.
Johnson, David
Johnson, Jno.
Johnson, Jas. Jr.
Johnson, Wm.
Joins, Edmond
Jones, Jesse (heirs of)
Jones, Jno.
Jones, Phillip
Kelly, Jno.
Kelly, Lloyd
Kelly, Wm.
Kemp, Wm.
Kendall, David
Kendall, Jeremiah
Kendall, Wm.
Kettle, Mary
Kimbrough, Jno.
Kindrick, Barrie
Kindrick, Jonas
Kitchens, Benj.
Lamb, Jesse
Lancaster, Wm.
Lawson, Jno.
Leapham, Aaron
Ledbetter, Isaac
Lightfoot, Jno.
Lingo, Moses
Long, Nicholas
Longstreet, Saml.
Lord, Laudwick
Lott, Jno.
Lott, Mark
Lucas, Moses
Madox, Wm.
Marshall, Sol.
Martin, Thos.
Mayo, Mark
McCeymore, Emily
McCall, Thos.
McClendon, Lewis
McCorcle, Jas.
McCullars, Bryant
McDowell, Thos.
McGee, Shadrack
McLane, Danl.
McMillion, Matthew
McMurry, Wm.
Mercer, Peter
Middleton, Robt.
McMillon, Matthew
Millar, Jonathan

Miles, Jno.
Moore, Arthur
Moore, Richd.
Moore, Thos.
Moore, Wm.
Motts, Wm.
Murchant, Isaac
Murchant, Jno.
Murphy, Bartholomew
Nail, Elisha
Nall, Martin
Neal, Thos.
Nelly, Jno.
Nelson, Wm.
Newton, Moses
Nutt, Jno.
Odum, Isual
Outlaw, Edwd.
Paul, Jas.
Parker, Aaron
Parker, Danl.
Parker, Williams
Perry, Isaac
Phillips, Jno.
Pollard, Wm.
Powell, Geo.
Powell, Stephen
Price, Cader
Pugh, Theophilus
Pullen, Thos.
Rachel, Miles
Raney, Jno.
Raley, Sarah
Randolph, Isaac
Ray, Jas.
Rayford, Mauris
Reaves, Jos.
Renfro, Wm.
Robertson, David
Robertson, Edwd.
Roberson, Jno.
Robertson, Jos.
Robinson, Israel
Robinson, Jno.
Robinson, Robt.
Roe, Hezekiah
Rollin, Thos.
Ross, Moses
Roundtree, Wm.
Runnels, Hermon
Ryan, Jos.
Salter, Jas.
Sanderlin, Robt.
Sartain, Jas.

Scarborough, Aaron
Scarborough, Miles
Scarborough, Moses
Seale, Wm.
Sessions, Jos.
Shelman, Jno.
Shelman, Michael
Shaw, Wm.
Smith, Geo.
Smith, Jno.
Smith, Wm.
Sneed, Chas.
Snell, Chris.
Spann, Geo.
Stanley, Sam
Stephen, Benj.
Stewart, Chas.
Stinson, Nathan
Stokes, Jno.
Sturgis, Andrew
Swella, Saml.
Tanner, Noah
Tapley, Jno.
Taylor, Joshua
Taylor, Wm.
Tennille, Benj.
Tennille, Frances
Tharp, Wiley
Thiner (?), Michael
Thomas, Gideon
Thomas, Jas.
Thompkins, Eliz.
Thompson, Benj.
Thornton, Elam
Tilman, Littleberry
Tomlinson, Aaron
Tompkins, Eliz.
Underwood, Benj.
Upton, Benj.
Vickers, Thos.
Vivion, Thacker
Wadsworth, Jas.
Walker, Jas.
Walker, Thos.
Wamock, Jno.
Wallace, Jno.
Ward, Moses
Warthen, Richd.
Watson, Benj.
Watson, David
Watts, Jacob
Watt, Jesse
Watts, Jno.
Welsh, Benj.

Whiggens, Wm.
Whitehead, Jane
Whitehead, Thos.
Wicker, Robt.
Wiggins, Wm.
Wilborn, Curtis

Williams, Chas.
Wilkinson, Reuben
Wood, Abraham
Wood, David
Wood, Sol.
Woodard, Warwick

WILKES COUNTY

Created in 1777 from lands ceded by the Cherokee and Creek Indians in 1773, this is an original county. Washington is the county seat. Wilkes was the parent county of Elbert, Lincoln and Oglethorpe and part of Warren, Green and Taliaferro Counties.

The lengthy remnants of the 1785 and 1792 tax lists are not included in this volume as they have been published several times.

Headrights and
Bounty Grants
1790 - 1795

Abbott, Jos.
Adams, David
Adkins, Asa
Akin, Saml.
Alexander, Edmund
Alexander, Ezekiel
Allen, Benj.
Allen, Jos.
Allen, Nathl.
Armer, Jas.
Armstrong, Alex
Arthur, Mathew
Ashley, Jas.
Atkinson, Nathan
Autry, Alex
Aycock, Richd.
Bailey, Hezekiah
Baldwin, Francis
Baldwin, Mordecai
Ball, Isaac
Ball, Jno.
Ballard, Benj.
Ballard, Reuben
Banks, Jno.
Banks, Richd.
Bankston, Peter
Barnett, Jno.
Barnett, Nial I.
Barnett, Robt.
Barren, Prudence

Bartlett, Robt.
Barton, Robt.
Beasley, Jos.
Beaseley, Richd.
Beasley, Richd.
Bell, Andrew
Bentley, Balam
Benson, Martin
Best, Wm.
Bibb, Jas.
Bird, Philemon
Blacke, Sessums
Blackwell, Jos.
Black, Benj.
Blake, Wm.
Blanchard, Robt.
  (heirs of)
Boggus, Jeremiah
Bolton, Jno.
Bonner, Henry Jr.
Bostwick, Littleberry
Bradford, Nathl.
Bradshaw, Jas.
Brannon, Thos.
Braswell, Saml.
Brazell, Jno.
Brazwell, Bird
Bridges, David
Bridges, Nathl.
Brooks, Jean

Brooks, Jas.
Brown, Alex
Brown, Bedford
Brown, Benj.
Brown, Jno.
Brown, Meredith
Brown, Wm.
Bryan, David
Bullock, Nathl.
Burdett, Humphry
Burk, Chas.
Burke, Robt.
Burke, Thos.
Burke, Thos. Jr.
Burnet, Jno.
Burton, Thos.
Busson, Jonathan
Butler, Jas.
Butler, Patrick
Butler, Zach.
Cade, Drury
Camp, Saml.
Canada, Jos.
Cargmile, Jno.
Carter, Josiah
Cartledge, Martha
Cassells, Wm.
Castleberry, Peter
Castlebury, Richd.
Catching, Benj.
Catchings, Meredith
Catchings, Seymour
Cazey, Danl.
Chambers, Robt.
Clack, Wm.
Clarke, Jno.
Clay, Jesse
Clay, Perceble
Cleghorn, Lettice
Clements, Henry
Cloud, Ezekiel
Cloud, Jno.
Cobb, Ezekiel
Cobb, Rachel
Cochran, Jno.
Cockburn, Geo.
Cocks, Wm.
Coleman, Thos.
Colley, Jas.
Collier, Edw.
Collins, Peter (heirs of)
Collins, Zach.
Combs, Philip
Copeland, Jno.

Course, Jno.
Cowden, Robt.
Cowen, Wm.
Cunningham, Wm.
Cureton, Boland
Dadd, Jesse
Daniel, Wm.
Daniell, Wm.
Davenport, Richd.
Davis, Absalom
Davis, Augustin
 (heirs of)
Davis, Jno.
Davis, Jno. Jr.
Dawson, Martin
Dean, Chas.
Dell, Phillip
Dick, Robt.
Dickens, Jno.
Dismukes, Wm.
Doss, Stephen
Doughty, Jos.
Dozier, Jno.
Dukes, Buckner
Dunn, Wm.
Dysart, Jno.
Eads, Jesse
Eads, Jno.
Eady, Jno.
Early, Jeffry
East, Jos.
Ector, Hugh
Edmonds, Jno.
Edmonson, Jno.
Edwards, Reuben
Elrod, Hannah
Elrod, Jas.
Elsberry, Joes
Elsberry, Jeremiah
Embrey, Wm.
Ervin, David
Eubank, Richd.
Evans, Danl.
Felps, David
Fergus, Jno.
Few, Ignatius
Finch, Wm.
Findley, Thos.
Flemming, Jno.
Fletcher, Wm.
Flint, Tarpley
Flournoy, Robt.
Fort, Arthur
Franklin, Wm.

Fulgham, Matthew	Harper, Edmond
Fulgham, Stephen	Harper, Robt.
Fuller, Jno.	Harper, Saml.
Fulton, David	Harrington, Jno.
Gamage, Wm.	Harris, Geo.
Gammage, Wm.	Harton, Thos.
Garrott, Jno.	Hartsfield, Godfrey
Gathright, Miles	Hartsfield, Jas.
Gest, Adam	Hartsfield, Richd.
Gibbs, Philip	Hawkins, Francis
Gideon, Francis	Hawthorn, Thos.
Gilbert, Saml.	Hawthorn, Wm.
Giles, Thos.	Hay, Wm.
Gilispey, Alex.	Heard, Jesse
Gilmore, Humphrey	Heard, Stephen
Gilmore, Saml.	Heard, Thos.
Golding, Richd.	Heath, Abraham
Goldsbey, Peter	Helton, Abraham
Goldsbey, Richd.	Hicks, Edmond B.
Gordon, Alex	Highsmith, Thos.
Goss, Benj.	Hill, Jno.
Graham, Thos.	Hill, Moses
Graves, Wm.	Hill, Theophilus
Gray, Jas.	Hill, Thos.
Gray, Jos.	Hilton, Abraham
Green, Amos	Hilton, Jas.
Greene, Jas.	Hines, Jas.
Greene, Henry Jr.	Hinton, Micajah
Greenstreet, Jas.	Hodge, Jacob
Greer, Aaron	Hodo, Peter
Greer, Moses	Holliday, Wm.
Griffey, Jno.	Holliman, David
Griffith, Jno.	Hollingshead, Jno.
Griffith, Robt.	Homes, Benj.
Grimes, Jno.	Hopkins, Lambeth
Guise, Jno.	House, Jas.
Guise, Nicholas	Howell, Jno.
Guise, Philip	Hubbard, Benj.
Gunnell, Jos.	Hutchinson, Jas.
Hale, Jesse	Jackson, Benj.
Hale, Joshua	Jackson, Jos.
Hall, Geo.	Jackson, Robt.
Hambricks, Benj.	Jenkins, Sterling
Hamilton, Geo.	Jennings, Priscilla
Hammock, Jno.	Johnson, Andrew
Hammonds, Jno.	Johnson, Cobb
Hammons, Abraham	Johnson, Wm.
Hampton, Benj.	Jones, Edw.
Hannah, Jno.	Jones, Henry
Harben, Thos.	Jones, Wm.
Harber, Esaias	Jordan, Jacob
Hardman, Wm.	Jordan, Josiah
Hardy, Isaac	Jordan, Sol.
Harling, Ezekiel (heirs of)	Josey, Henry

Kain, Richd.
Keen, Gilbert
Keen, Massey
Kellough, David
Kellough, Isaac
Kelly, Barnard
Kelly, Jas.
Kelly, Jno.
Kidd, Jas.
Kilgore, Jno.
Kilgore, Peter
King, Jno.
Kinman, Jas.
Knox, Jno.
Lamar, Basil
Lamar, Zachariah
Lane, Chas.
Lankford, Jno.
Lauderdale, Jno.
Lawrence, Zachariah
Lea, Wm.
Ledbetter, Jno.
Lee, Giles
Lee, Jas.
Leftridge, Jno.
Lindsey, Jno.
Linn, Wm.
Linton, Wm. T.
Lipham, Frederick
Littleton, Wm.
Lockhart, Richd.
Long, Nicholas
Love, Wm.
Lowry, Henry
Loyd, Danl.
Lucky, Wm.
Lyle, Rhoda
Lyman, Elihu
Mackleroy, Reuben
Mackleroy, Wm.
Magee, Wm.
Mann, Milley
Marcon, Jas.
Marks, Jas.
Martin, Robt.
Matthews, Jas.
Matthews, Jeremiah
Matthews, Moses
Matthews, Ralph
May, Balam
May, Jas.
McBurnett, Daniel
McCannon, Jas.
McClendon, Thos.

McClendon, Travis
McClusky, Jas.
McCollum, Jas.
McCormick, Jas.
McCormick, Jos.
McCown, Jas.
McCoy, Danl.
McCree, Wm.
McCuller, Brittain
McCullers, Brittain
McCutchin, Jos.
McDonald, Patrick
McDowell, Thos.
McFall, Geo.
McGehee, Micajah
McKay, Henry
McLeroy, Jno.
Medlock, Jas.
Merony, Jas.
Merrell, Jno.
Middleton, Robt.
Miller, Jonathan
Miller, Wm.
Milligan, Ann
Mills, Alex (hdrs of)
Mills, Alice
Mimms, Wm.
Mims, Jno.
Monk, Silas
Moore, Abednego
Moore, Eliz.
Moore, Jno.
Morgan, Jeremiah
Morgan, Joshua
Norris, Jno.
Morris, Thos.
Moses, Robt.
Mounger, Henry
Mulkey, Jno. (heirs of)
Mulligan, Isaac
Murray, Thos.
Neal, Thos.
Neel, Thos.
Neilson, Saml.
Nelson, David
Nichols, Wm.
Nipper, Jas.
Norris, Josiah
Nugeon, Edmond
Ogletree, Thos.
Olive, Anthony
Oliver, Damiscus
Oliver, Peter
Osborn, Saml.

Pace, Barnabas
Palmer, Edwd.
Palmour, Jno.
Parker, Aaron
Parker, Danl.
Partain, Jno.
Partain, Wm.
Paschall, Wm.
Patrick, Wm.
Patterson, Jas.
Patterson, Jno.
Payne, Thos. Sr.
Pearson, Jones
Peebles, Henry
Pennington, Abel
Perkins, Abington
Perkins, Jesse
Perkins, Jno.
Pettigrew, Geo.
Pharr, Saml.
Phillip, Joel
Phillip, Levi
Pickens, Gabriel
Pollard, Wm.
Ponder, Amos
Pope, Burrell
Pope, Jno.
Pope, Willis
Priest, Jos.
Pulliam, Jno.(heirs of)
Pulliam, Robt.
Quere, Wm.
Radford, Reuben
Ragan, Mark
Ragland, Benj.
Railey, Wm.
Rains, Ignatus
Ralston, Jas.
Ratliff, Wm.
Ready, Jas.
Rice, Jno.
Richards, Wm.
Richardson, Isam
Richardson, Jos.
Richardson, Jno.
Rivers, Danl.
Roberts, Jno.
Robertson, Saml.
Robinet, Jno.
Rogers, Wm.
Roquemore, Jas.
Ross, Jas.
Ruff, Susannah
Runnells, Geo.

Russell, Thos.
Ruston, Jno. B.
Rutledge, Geo.
Ryley, Jos.
Satterwhite, Francis
Saunders, Robt.
Scrivner, Thos.
Scudden, Wm.
Selfridge, Robt.
Sewell, Joshua
Shares, Simon
Sheffield, Zach.
Shelton, Henry
Sheppherd, Peter
Sims, Jenning
Sims, Joel
Sims, Robt.
Simson, Jas.
Skinner, Archer
Slade, Nicholas
Sled, Joshua
Smith, Abraham
Smith, Benj.
Smith, Burnard
Smith, Burrill
Smith, Ebenezer
Smith, Gabriel
Smith, Gay
Smith, Jas.
Smith, Jno.
Smith, Nathl.
Smith, Nathl. A.
Smith, Robt.
Smith, Wm.
Sneed, Chas.
Sorell, Geo.
Sorrell, Jno.
Spikes, Nathan
Spowser, Priscilla
Starnes, Ebenezer
Starr, Henry
Statham, Jno.
Steal, Culbreath
Stewart, Gravener
Stewart, Jas.
Stewart, Thos.
Stocks, Isaac
Stone, Nicajah
Strickland, Sol.
Stringer, Jas.
Stripling, Francis
Stroder, Ezbell
Stubblefield, Peter
Stubblefield, Seth

Stubblefield, Wm.
Sturges, Robt.
Summerlin, Henry
Taber, Jno.
Talbot, Thos.
Talliaferro, Benj.
Tanner, Jno.
Tarver, Jno.
Tatom, Jno.
Tatum, Abel
Tatum, Jno.
Taylor, Edmund
Teasley, Silas
Teaver, Jacob
Thomas, Benj.
Thomas, Etheldred
Thomas, Jno.
Thomas, Saml.
Thornton, Dread
Thornton, Herod
Thornton, Noel
Thornton, Sol.
Thornton, Thos. H.
Thornton, Wm.
Thurman, David
Thurman, Jno.
Tinch, Wm.
Todd, Jno.
Toler, Demsey
Tomlinson, David
Tompson, Saml.
Torrence, Jno.
Trailer, Wm.
Traywick, Francis
Trent, Henry
Tucker, Geo.
Tulley, Moses
Tullis, Moses
Turner, Shadrack
Tuttle, Jas. Jr.
Tuttle, Jas. Sr.
Upshaw, Jno.
Vickery, Wm.
Vineyard, Ishmael
Vineyard, Jas.
Waggner, Jas.
Walker, Henry
Walker, Moses
Walker, Sanders
Walker, Sarah
Walker, Wm.
Wallace, Jas.
Walton, Newell
Walton, Wm.

Ware, Jas.
Warren, Lot
Watkins, Benj.
Watkins, Jno.
Watson, Jno.
Webb, Thos.
Webster, Abner
Webster, Archa
Westbrook, Jno.
Wetherby, Stephen
Whalis, Isham
Whatley, Michael
Whatley, Richd.
Wheat, Jno.
Wheat, Jno. (heirs of)
Wheeler, Emperor
Wheeler, Wm.
Wheelright, Jos.
Whittington, Cornelius
Wilbourn, Thos.
Wilcher, Benj.
Wilder, Dread
Wilder, Eliz.
Wilkins, Clement
Williams, Chris.
Williamson, Jno.
Wilson, Jno.
Wilson, Jos.
Wingfield, Jno.
Wise, Jos.
Wood, Jas.
Woods, Middleton
Woods, Richd.
Wooten, Jeremiah
Wooten, Thos.
Wright, Richd.
Wright, Wm.
York, Jas.
York, Jno.

Jurors 1790
Anderson, Jordan
Angling, Henry
Aspy, Jno.
Banks, Richd.
Blake, Sessoms
Blakey, Jno.
Bohannon, Dunkin
Booth, Abraham
Bridges, Nathl.
Bussey, Thos.
Cammell, Robt.
Carter, Jacob
Cooper, Thos.

Culpepper, Jno.
Dimond, Jno.
Embree, Jno.
Embry, Jos.
Embry, Wm.
Fletcher, Wm.
Gentry, Elijah
Golsby, Richd.
Hill, Jno.
Hitchcock, Wm.
Hitche, Thos.
Hodge, Archibald
Hooper, Thos.
Huddleston, Jno.
Hurley, Henry
Jennings, Moody
Johnson, Thos.
Johnson, Wm.
Jones, Hugh
Lane, Jas.
Lawrence, Jno.
Leverett, Thos.
Lockhart, Jno.
McLean, Jno.
Moore, Richd.
Norton, Thos.
Palmer, Edwd.
Patterson, Wm.
Phillips, Mark
Porter, Nathl.
Potts, Moses
Robertson, Jno.
Robertson, Thos.
Smith, Jno.
Smith, Sherod
Stubblefield, Seth
Tanner, Jno.
Thomas, Saml.
Thompson, Archibald
Tucker, Geo.
Wade, Jas.
Wallace, Wm.
Williamson, Jas.
Wilson, Jas.
Winston, Jno.
Woodall, Chas.
Young, Geo. Jr.

Wills: 1790 - 1791

Testators
Bentley, Wm.
Burney, Simon
Elsberry, Benj.

Hill, Abraham, Sr.
Johnson, Jno.
Loyalless, Jas.
McClendon, Jacob, Sr.
Moore, Jos.
Petit, Benj.
Stewart, Martha
Wilborne, Wm.
Williamson, Micajah Sr.
Wilshire, Benj.
Wingfield, Jno.
Wynn, Thos.
Young, Wm.

Other names in Wills
Abernethie, J.
Armstrong, Jesse
Bailey, Jos.
Ballard, Benj.
Bankston, Nancy
Beazley, Wm.
Bentley, Catherine
Bentley, Jas.
Bentley, Jane
Bentley, Jno.
Bentley, Lewis
Bentley, Susannah
Best, Wm.
Bird, Philemon
Bird, Robt.
Bird, Thompson
Black, Jno.
Blake, Benj.
Blake, Henry
Blake, Mary
Brooks, Martha
Brown, Allen
Burney, Jno.
Cash, Preshus
Clark, Jno.
Clark, Nancy
Cocke, Whitman
Cosby, Hickerson
Crabtree, Jno.
Crawford, Sarah
Darracott, Rebecca
Davis, Saml.
Denman, Jas.
Dupoys, Jos.
Elliott, Benj.
Elsberry, Benj. Jr.
Foster, Pattey
Freeman, Saml.
Gillam, Wm.

(170)

Griffin, Sally
Hammock, Wm. Sr.
Harkens, Jno.
Harvie, Richd.
Hill, Abraham, Jr.
Hill, Christian
Hill, Henry
Hill, Mary
Hill, Mountain
Hill, Myles
Hill, Noah
Hill, Theophilus
Hill, Thos.
Hill, Wylie
Holmes, Jno.
Jains, Wm.
Johnson, Isaiah
Johnson, Jos.
Johnson, Sarah
Johnson, Upton
Johnson, Walter
Johnston, Joshua
Jordan, Josiah
Jordan, Palsy
Kerr, Alle
Kerr, David
Loyalless, Jas.
Loyalless, Sarah
McGinty, Jno.
McKie, Henry
McKie, Sarah
McIlath, Jos.
McClendon, Amos
McClendon, Bethaney
McClendon, Dennis
McClendon, Isaac
McClendon, Jemima
McClendon, Laney
McClendon, Martha
McClendon, Nancy
McClendon, Penelope
McClendon, Saml.
McClendon, Travis
Matthews, Jas.
Meriwether, Frances
Moore, Abednego
Moore, Anass
Moore, Benj.
Moore, Eliz.
Moore, Jesse
Moore, Jno.
Moore, Mary
Moore, Sararener
Moore, Wm.

Ogletree, Wm.
Petit, Jane
Pope, Henry
Pope, Sarah
Pruitt, Elisha
Pugh, Jesse
Richardson, Morgan
Scott, Jas.
Scurlock, Jas.
Smith, Peter
Spratlin, Jas.
Terondet, Danl.
Terrell, Will
Thornton, Sarah
Tyson, Abraham
Walker, Sanders
Wilbourne, Abner
Wilborne, Aephzeleat
Wilborne, Isaac
Wilbourne, Johnston
Wilborne, Nancy
Wilborne, Shapely
Wilbourne, Wilkes
Williams, Danl.
Williamson, Bird
Williamson, Eliz.
Williamson, Jefferson
Williamson, Macajah Jr.
Williamson, Patsy
Williamson, Peter
Wilshire, Ann
Wilshire, Eliz.
Wilshire, Mary
Wilshire, Sarah
Wilshire, Wm.
Wingfield, Ann
Wingfield, Garland
Wingfield, Jno.
Wingfield, Thos.
Wynn, Lucy
Wynn, Mary
Wynn, Obediah
Wynn, Rhodea
Wynn, Thos.
Young, Betsy
Young, Fanney
Young, Jno.
Young, Lucy
Young, Sherwood
Young, Thos.

Deceased
Bowen, Jno.
Cochran, Saml.
Gibson, Walter
Goodin, Wilkinson
Gray, Jas.
Leverett, Robt.
Marks, Jno.
Milner, Willis
Montgomary, David
Rasbury, Wm.
Reynolds, Richd.
Solomon, Ellis
Tatum, Peter
Whatley, Curby

Other names in
these documents:
Baird, Benj.
Baird, Mickey
Ballard, Jno.
Bowen, Horatio
Bowen, Rachel
Bowen, Wm.
Burden, Richd.
Chandler, Jno.
Clement, Stephen
Cochran, Jno.
Cochran, Marah
Cunningham, Jane
Cunningham, Pat
Daves, Patsy
Ellis, Chas.
Ellis, Jno.
Ellis, Jos.
Ely, Wm.
Felts, Jno.
Fennell, Jno.
Gibson, Judah
Gilmer, Jno.
Gibson, Sylvanus
Goodin, Jonathan
Goodwin, Wyche
Gray, Ann
Gray, Flower
Gray, Geo.
Gray, Jno.
Gray, Jos.
Hogan, Eliz.
Hogan, Griffin

Hogan, Mary
Holmes, Jno.
Inloe, Mary
James, Abner
Johnson, Nicholas
Johnson, Richd.
Johnson, Wm.
Jones, Edwd.
Lowery, Judge
McClendon, Saml.
Marks, Jno. Haistens
Marks, Lucy
Marks, Polly Garland
Matthews, Geo.
Matthews, Jno.
Meriwether, Frans.
Meriwether, Thos.
Milner, Benj.
Milner, Jno.
Milner, Pitt
Milner, Salley
Montgomery, Eliz.
Montgomery, Jas.
Montgomery, Matthew
Montgomery, Robt.
Morrow, Robt.
Mosely, Wm.
Penn, Thos.
Rasbury, Eliz.
Rasbury, Jas.
Rasbury, Phillip
Reaves, Jeremiah
Reynolds, Benj.
Reynolds, Jos.
Reynolds, Sarah Ann
Reynolds, Thos.
Roberson, Jas.
Satterwhite, Francis
Soloman, Frances
Stephen, Thos.
Tatum, Epps
Tatum, Howell
Tatum, Nancy
Tatum, Polly
Tatum, Rebeccah
Tatum, Sally
Tatum, Thos.
Terry, Jno.
Thornton, Saml.
Tyler, Henry
Veazy, Wm.

Deeds 1789-1790 from
Book "BB"

Grantor
Barksdale, Stith
Barnett, Mary
Barnett, Wm.
Bowls, Salley
Bowls, Wm.
Brown, Betty
Brown, Thos.
Cloud, Eliz.
Cloud, Jeremiah
Cloud, Jno.
Cloud, Sarah
Cole, Jno. Jr.
Freeman, Holman
Grimes, Jno.
Hanna, Jno.
Hanna, Mary
Harris, Anne (Nancy)
Harris, Buckner
Heard, Eliz.
Heard, Stephen
Hunt, Richardson
Lamar, Sarah
Lamar, Zach.
Lipham, Aaron
Jossey, Henry
Jossey, Mary
McKinney, Littleberry
Sailors, Eliz.

Grantee
Bennett, Reuben
Bonds, Nathan
Davis, Wm.
Freeman, Jno.
Gilmer, Thos.
Gresham, Jas.
Grimes, Jno. Jr.
Grimes, Lucy
Grimes, Sterling
Grimes, Thos. Wingfield
Grimes, Wm. Garland
Hood, Jno.
Hulling, Jas.
Jarrett, Howell
Patten, Wm.
Phillips, Lenyard
Pope, Jno.
Richardson, Jno.
Smith, Jno.
Smith, Wm.

Others
Anthony, Micajah
Banks, R.
Banton, Benj.
Barnett, Nathl.
Blakey, Jos.
Churchill, N. H.
Cowden, Jas.
DeJernett, R.
Elliott, Wm.
Gresham, Edwd.
Gresham, Thos.
Hatcher, Josiah
Leftwich, Jno.
Meriwether, Thos.
Millir, Jacob
Milner, Wm.
Moore, Ebednego
Nelson, Jas.
Reeves, Malachi
Russell, Thos. C.
Sims, Frederick
Sparks, Matthew
Stibblefield, Theodrick
Thornton, Dread
Whatley, Michael
Williams, Drury
Williams, Jos.
Wootten, Thos.
Worsham, Richd.
Wyatt, Jno.

Wilkes County Militia
Oct. 9, 1789

Allen, Wm.
Armstrong, Jas.
Babb, Will
Beason, Robt.
Bridges, Ben
Buckhanan, Jos.
Callahan, Edwd.
Callahan, Wm.
Casey, Wm.
Clay, Jesse
Clay, Royal
Cole, Jno.
Combs, Jno.
Dedgings, Jere
Ealy, Wm.
Edmonson, Humphry
Edwards, Reuben
English, Henry

English, Menas
Garret, Henry
Green, Wm.
Hatcher, Josiah
Haynes, Phelps
Hurt, Joel
Lowry, Ben
McClane, Thos.
McLane, Wm.
Martin, Joshua
Mason, Jno.
Mason, Wm.
Moon, Jos.
Moor, Wm.
Murphy, Jas.
Pierce, Lewis
Prior, Jno.
Prior, Obediah
Ray, Andrew
Ray, David
Ray, Jno.
Richards, Wm.
Robertson, Thos.
Russell, Robt.
Ryan, Nathan
Shropshire, Jno.
Simmons, Richd.
Smart, Thos.
Sorril, Green
Sorril, Jno.
Starky, Aquilla
Starky, Jno.
Stropper, Will
Swanson, Nathan
Taff, Wm.
Tatum, Apps
Tatum, Howel
Tatum, Peter
Vessey, Wm.
Wester, Jno.
Whatley, Archibald
Whatley, Kirby
Whatley, Walton
Whatley, Willis
Whiteside, Jas.
Williams, Archibald
Williams, Sugar (?)

Wilkes Co. Militia
1793

Abercrumbie, Chapman
Alexander, Isaac
Altmon, Thos.

Alvera, Isaac
Anderson, Aaron
Anderson, Martin
Anderson, Thos.
Anderson, Wm.
Andrews, Warren
Anglin, David
Anthony, Jas.
Anthony, Mark
Armstrong, Jonathan
Arnett, Edwd.
Arnett, Saml.
Arnold, Jas.
Arnold, Jno.
Arnold, Wm.
Ash, Wm.
Ashmore, Jno.
Ashmore, Peter
Ashmore, Wm.
Atkins, Wm.
Avera, Arthur
Bags, Jas.
Bailey, Green
Bailey, Simon
Baker, Chas.
Baldwin, Wm.
Ballard, Jno.
Ballard, Lovin
Ballard, Nathan
Ballard, Wm.
Barnes, Benj.
Barnhart, Geo.
Barron, Wm.
Barrons, Jno.
Bearfield, Richd.
Bentley, Jeremiah
Berry, Anderson
Berry, Jelson
Berry, Presley
Binion, Wm.
Blackburn, Nathan
Blanton, Chas.
Bolls, Wm.
Bolton, Jno.
Boother, Andrew
Bovis, Geo.
Bowman, Leonard
Bowram, Benj.
Brady, Jas.
Brewer, Barrot
Brooks, Job
Brooks, Joel
Brown, Edwd.
Brown, Jno.

Brown, Jos.
Buckels, Wm.
Buckner, Ricy
Burd, Phillip
Burd, Price
Burdet, Jas.
Burlong, Henry
Bussey, Benj.
Bussey, David
Bussey, Thos.
Carter, Elisha
Castle, Wm.
Castlebery, Asa
Castleberry, Thos.
Cavgur, Jno.
Chambless, Littleton
Chivers, Larkin
Cole, Wm.
Coleman, Thompson
Combs, Jas.
Combs, Jno.
Combs, Philip
Combs, Sterling
Cooper, Henry
Cooper, Jos.
Cooper, Thos.
Cosby, Hickerson
Cothral, Josiah
Covington, Jno.
Crabtree, Jas.
Creaff, Wm.
Cunningham, Wm.
Daniel, Hopkins
Danily, Andrew
Daricott, Wm.
Davis, Joshua
Davis, Moses
Deale, Peter
Depee, Wm.
Dimond, Jno.
Dix, Tandy
Doss, Crisler
Downs, Henry
Downs, Jonathan
Duke, Buckner
Duke, Taylor
Duty, Littleton
Duty, Richd.
Edmonds, Jno.
Edwards, Jno.
Edwards, Wm.
Eidson, Jno.
Elliott, Benj.
Elliott, Thos.

Fain, Peter
Faver, Jacob
Fellsday, Thos.
Fish, Jno.
Flournoy, Jacob
Floyd, Saml.
Fowler, Hillery
Fowler, Zepheniah
Frazier, Moses
Friend, Thos.
Garley, Abraham
Garrott, Jacob
Garrott, Robt.
Gatril, Francis
Gatrell, Jos.
George, Jas.
Gibson, Jno.
Gordon, Moses
Gosley, Jno.
Grant, Thos.
Graves, Francis
Graves, Jno.
Graves, Jonas
Graves, Richd.
Graves, Thos.
Graves, Wm.
Gray, Danl.
Gray, Jno.
Green, Ephram
Green, Jas.
Grey, Geo.
Grisham, Benj.
Grisham, Geo.
Grisham, Jno.
Grisham, Thos.
Hairege, Jno. J.
Hairrass, Peter
Hamilton, Andrew
Hamilton, Geo.
Hamilton, Robt.
Hammock, Jno.
Hammock, Robt.
Hammock, Saml.
Hammons, Abraham
Hammock, Wm.
Hargrove, Emnl.
Harris, Robt.
Kaverd, Geo.
Hearndon, Lewis
Hearndon, Jos.
Hendley, Derby
Hendrake, Anderson
Hendrake, Thos.
Hendrake, Wm.

Henly, Philip
Henson, Caleb
Hickom, Jos.
Holderness, Wm.
Holliday, Ares
Holliday, Owen
Holliday, Wm.
Holms, Benj.
Horne, Absolom
Horton, Proser
Howard, Jos.
Huckabey, Phillip
Hudgens, Josiah
Hudgens, Wm.
Huett, Wm.
Hughs, Simon
Hurd, Jno.
Hurd, Jno. Jr.
Jackson, Jno.
Jackson, Moses
Jacobs, Mordica
Jard, Cornelius
Jarrot, Howel
Jernegan, Neden
Johnson, Adkerson
Johnston, Alexdr.
Johnston, Elijah
Johnston, Jacob
Johnston, Wm.
Jolly, Michael
Jones, Adam
Jones, Benj.
Jones, Gabriel
Julin, Benj.
Keeth, Jno.
Kelly, Jno.
Kelly, Wm.
Kilgore, Robt.
Kirkwood, Hugh
Kirkwood, Nathan
Lane, Jas.
Ledbetter, Isaac
Ledbetter, Jno.
Lee, Jessee
Lemar, Jesse
Levens, Jas.
Leverett, Absolom
Leverett, Henry
Leverett, Thos.
Lipham, Moses
Long, Evans
Lovin, Adam
Lunsford, Enoch
McCorkle, Jas.

McCorkle, Jno.
McCrary, Matthew
McFarlen, Peter
McFarlin, Wm.
McKenney, Wm.
McKinney, Jno.
McMillan, Jas.
McMurry, Fredrick
McNight, Robt.
Manning, Chas.
Marshal, Jas.
Marshal, Mathew
Marshon, Andrew
Martin, Wm.
Mashbourn, Elisha
Mason, Jno.
Mathews, Moses
Medlock, Geo.
Mershon, Enos
Miles, Wm.
Millegan, Jno.
Miller, Archabauld
Milligan, Jos.
Mills, David
Mills, Moses
Milner, Benj.
Moore, Moses
Moore, Richd.
Morgan, Isaac D.
Mott, Zepheneah
Murrell, Jno.
Murry, Wm.
Napier, Richd.
Newgent, Jno.
Newgent, Wm.
North, Rober
O'Neal, Wm.
Orr, Jno.
Oxford, Edwd.
Oxford, Janathan
Parker, Saml.
Parks, Jno.
Parmer, Edwd.
Patterson, Jno.
Penton, Jaber
Penton, Wm.
Perry, Micajah
Phinizy, Ferdinand
Piper, Jno.
Pittee, Benj.
Porter, Richd.
Porter, Wm.
Poss, Henry
Poss, Nicholass

Powel, Arthur
Prather, Jos.
Price, Danl.
Raley, Henry
Ray, Jno.
Ray, Zachh.
Renfroe, Nathl.
Revear, Wyatt
Revier, Henry L.
Revier, Richd.
Reynolds, Jos.
Richardson, Wm.
Riddle, Archibald
Robertson, Thos.
Roling, Jno.
Rucker, Fielder
Ruff, Chas.
Ruff, Jno.
Ruff, Stephen
Rushing, Jno.
Russell, Geo.
Russell, Jas. G.
Russell, Wm.
Ryan, Nathan
Scott, Jos.
Scott, Wm.
Scudder, Isaiah
Scudder, Natl.
Scudder, Wm.
Self, Stephen
Shannon, Patrick
Shearer, Jas.
Shurley, Edwd.
Silbey, Nathan
Silvey, Wm.
Silvey, Wm. Jr.
Simons, Wm.
Skinner, Phenix
Slaydon, Jno.
Sleighs, Wm.
Smallwood, Wm.
Smith, Ebenezer
Smith, Jas.
Smith, Peter
Smith, Roland
Smith, Wm.
Springfield, Aaron
Stallings, Jesse
Staples, Stephen
Stewenter, Jno.
Stokes, Robt.
Stokes, Young
Strange, Isham
Strothea, Francis

Stubblefield, Thos.
Stubblefield, Wm.
Suddeth, Elijah
Suddeth, Jno.
Sutton, Jno.
Sutton, Wm.
Sympson, Jas.
Symson, Jno.
Terrell, Richmond
Thomas, Jno. H.
Thomas, Massy
Thomas, Wm.
Thompson, Jas.
Thompson, Saml.
Thompson, Wm.
Thomson, Wm.
Thornton, Sol.
Tigert, Jos.
Todd, Jno.
Tolbott, Benj.
Tolbott, Thos.
Traner, Jas.
Tucker, Robt.
Tyson, Abraham
Upton, Geo.
Veneble, Abraham
Veneble, Chas.
Vinson, Jno.
Wade, Moses
Waggoner, Jas.
Waggoner, Wm.
Walker, Jno.
Walker, Saml.
Walker, Thos.
Wallis, Jno.
Waters, Bradford
Webb, Wm.
Webster, Abner
Webster, Jonathan
West, Andrew
West, Wm.
Whatley, Tisdel
Whatley, Wiley
Whatley, Withe
Whitker, Benj.
Whitlock, Heppe
Whitlock, Jno.
Whitten, Saml.
Wiley, Jno.
Wilkerson, Baley
Wilkerson, Jno.
Wilkerson, Saml.
Wilkinson, Hazlewood
Willard, Saml.

Williams, Arthur
Williams, Benj.
Williams, Bowery
Williams, Jas.
Williams, Joshua
Williams, Thos.
Williams, Wm.
Willingham, Jeremiah
Willis, Moses
Winfree, Ruben
Wolf, Andrew
Woods, Jas.
Wright, Jno.
Wright, Reuben
Wright, Stark
Wright, Wm.
Young, Patrick

Indian Depredations
1787

Barber, Geo.
Bridges, David
Bridges, Nathl.
Bridges, Thos.
Eberhart, Jacob
Elsbury, Benj.
Elsbury, Benj. Jr.
Elsbury, Jos.
Elsbury, Michael (est.)
Garner, Stephen
Griffith, Jno.
Hail, Luke
Holms, Robt.
Johnson, Henry
Johnson, Nathan
Jordon, Eliz.
Lucky, Jas.
McCartney, Jas.
McCartney, Jas. (est.)
McCartney, Jno.
McDowell, Thos.
Walls, Richd.

Nesbit, Jeremiah
Norris, Jonah
Patrick, Wm.
Simmons, Adam
Smith, Jas.
Sparks, Mathew
Sparks, Wm.
Spratting, Henry
Strather, Wm.
Stuart, Geo.
Trebel, Benj.
Woods, Josiah

Tax-defaulters: 1793

Barkley, Jno.
Brown, Jno.
Chandler, Jno.
Cooper, Thos.
Dill, Peter
Downs, Jonathan
Fiske, Jno.
Graves, Francis
Graves, Wm.
Ivey, Mrs. Winnie
Jones, Gabriel
Keith, Jno.
Kelley, Wm.
Mathews, Moses Jr.
Mayhorn, Chas.
Mills, Jno.
Penton, Wm.
Ray, Zach.
Rovell, Geo.
Russ, Jno.
Shaw, Robert
Sheaver, Jas.
Skinner, Phineas
Thomas, Jno. Hames
Thomas, Saml.
Walker, Jno.
Whitaker, Benj.
Whitlock, Hopps
Whitaker, Saml.

(?), Abraham 39
(?), Ben 40
(?), Fernandez 44
(?), Fleming 44
(?), Gandonch 45
(?), Harry 46
(?), Janet 47
(?), Jem 47
(?), John 47
(?), Oronoke 50
(?), Samuel 27
(?), Stephen 53
Abbet, Bennett 136
Abbit, Wm. 85
Abbot, Bennet 7
  Wm. 85
Abbott, Joel 58
  Jos. 164
  Wm. 84
Abendanon, David 39
Abercrombie, Chas. 108,
  127, 153, 160
  Robt. 115
Abercromby, Chas. 111,
  119
Abercrumbie, Chapman 174
Aberhart, Geo. 79
  Jacob 79
Abernathy, Chas. 132
Abernethie, J. 170
Able, Jno. 95, 99
Abraham, (?) 39
Abrahams, Abrah. 39
  Isaac 39
  Isaac Jacob 33
  Jos. 31, 33
  Levy 35, 39
Acee, L. (Dr.) 111
Achin, Jas. 115
Ackhard, Lewis 39
Acney, Wm. 158
Adams, Ann 35
  Betsey 111
  David 74, 76, 78, 87,
    88, 117, 119, 164
  Edmund 35, 39
  Elcy 7
  Elijah 39
  Elisha 39
  Eliz. 148
  Ephraim 1
  Jane 87
  Jane Stutz 35
  Jas. 39, 74, 108, 114,
    115, 117, 119, 127
  Jesse 7
  Jno. 7, 39, 108, 117
  John 119
  Jonathan 115, 117, 119
  Mary 114
  Nathan (Jr.) 39
  Nathl. 35, 39
  Pelithal 145
  Robt. 99
  Samuel 29

Adams (cont.)
  Thos. 99
  Wm. 111, 136
Adcock, Jas. 148
Addington, Henry 39,
  130, 134
Adear, Jacob 157
Aderhold, Conrad 83
Adinal, Jas. 39
Adkerson, Nathan 115
Adkins, Arthur 103
  Asa 164
  Shadrack 15
  Terry 39
Adkinson, Abner 119
  Jos. 1
Afssy, Jas. 119
  Thos. (Jr.) 119
  Thos. (Sr.) 119
Aiken, Jas. 25
  Tho. 20, 25, 85
  Wm. 85
Aikens, Arther 105
  Jno. 111
  Tho. 88
Ailey, Elijah 7
Ainsley, Benj. 39
Aires, Thos. 126
Airs, Thos. 157
Akin, Jas. 125
  Jno. 111
  Saml. 84, 164
Akins, Jas. 117, 119,
  127
  Jno. 119, 127
Alberry, Jno. 15
Albord, Jas. 111
Albritton, Geo. 13
  Jno. 1
Alday, Ann 1
Aldridge, Alsner 61
  Jas. 63
  Nicholas 58
  Rebbekah 58
  Reuben 61
  Saml. 58
  Wm. 61
Alet, Henry 10, 11
Alexander, Adam 105,
  131, 132, 133, 134,
  135, 136
  Adlay 89
  Asa 119
  Bethiah 111
  Chas. 39
  Edmund 164
  Elias 89
  Esau 114
  Ezekiel 164
  Faitha 114
  Geo. 87, 88
  Hugh 13
  Isaac 84, 89, 90, 99,
    174
  Jas. 39, 89, 110, 114,

Alexander (cont.)
  119
  Jno. 20, 24, 25
  Jno. B. 89
  Jno. Brown 90
  Jno. Lister 111
  Mary 111
  Nathl. 89, 110
  Saml. 111, 127
  Tabitha 111, 114
Alford, Jas. 114, 119
  Jno. 119
  Jul. 119
  Julean 111
  Julius 111
  Wm. 115, 119
Alger, Jas. 39, 151
Alice, Chas. 78
  Francis 78
Allan, Alexdr. 20
Allard, Lewis Nicholes
  39
  Mary 39
  Peter 39
Allbritton, Jno. 79
Allen, Andrew 58
  Benj. 81, 82, 88, 90,
    164
  Beverly 85
  Daniel 1
  Drury 84
  Geo. 39
  Gideon 142
  Isabella 7
  Jas. 64, 99
  Jeames 15
  Jno. 1, 7, 15
  Jos. 164
  Joshua 39
  Josiah 125
  Marget 111
  Nathl. 73, 78, 82, 83,
    90, 164
  Reuben 79, 83
  Robert H. 29
  Robt. 57, 64
  Saml. 109, 142
  Sherwood 152
  Tho. 14
  Thos. 10
  West 119
  Wm. 1, 15, 39, 78, 82,
    84, 85, 87, 88, 90,
    110, 173
Alleson, Wm. 117
Allison, Henry 142
  Robt. 119
  Wm. B. 39
Allston, Wm. 82
Allum, Edmond 158
  Jno. 158
Almand, Jas. 76, 78
  Jno. 79
Almond, J. L. 85
  J. P. 85

Almond (cont.)
Jas. 84
Alner, Jas. 39
Alsop, Geo. 39
Alston, Phillip 159
Wm. 74, 78
Alter, Mary 39
Peter 39
Altmon, Thos. 174
Alvera, Isaac 174
Ammons, Wm. 67
Anciaux, Eliza 39
Lydia (Mrs.) 39
Nicholas 39
Anclaux, Nicholas 1
Anderson, Aaron 174
Adam 39
Benj. 108, 119
Braza C. 109
Brazar 125
Brazier 119
Clement Wm. 39
Deb. 39
Douglas 39
Elijah 130
Elisha 15
Geo. 39, 151
Henry 39, 97
Jas. 21, 28, 39, 90
Jean 114
Jno 39
Jno. 19, 20, 31, 39,
90, 127, 137, 160
Jno. (Jr.) 114
Jno. (Sr.) 117
Jordan 169
Margt. 67
Martin 174
Mary 151
Robt. 94, 99
Susannah 40
Susanne 31
Thompson 7
Thos. 174
Wm. 90, 127, 174
Andrew, Benj. 57, 60
Jas. 60
Saml. 15
Andrews, Benj. 61, 133,
152
Jas. 117, 119
Jno. 117, 119
Jos. 137
Micajah 137
Sanders 133
Warren 174
Wm. 15
Anglin, David 174
Angling, Henry 169
Anthony, Jas. 174
Mark 174
Micajah 90, 173
Antoine, Andrew 40
Antonio, Emanuel 40
Jno. 40
Apiers, Alex. Jonhstone
134
Appleby, Wm. 74
Appling, J. 60
Jno. 57, 60, 151
Martha 58
Wm. 64
Archer, Jas. 140
Jos. 21, 28
T. 35
Archibald, Jos. 103
Ariano, Peter 40
Arinandus, Casper 40

Arinton, Henry 147
Arline, Jno. 7, 153, 160
Armer, Andrew 119
Jas. 164
Armor, Andrew 128
Jas. 58, 119
Jno. 117, 119, 129
Martha 117
Armour, (?) 127
Andrew 114
Eliz. 114
Jas. 127
Jno. 33, 40, 127
Armstead, Jno. 134
Armstrong, Alex 164
Alexdr. 153
Edwd. 158
Jas. 20, 22, 23, 173
Jas. (Col.) 90
Jas. Col. 90
Jesse 170
Jno. 73, 99, 106, 158,
159, 160
Jonathan 174
Sally 145
Thos. 125
Arnets, Jonathan 29
Arnett, Edwd. 174
Geo. 142
Saml. 174
Arnold, (?) 40
Aaron 1
Jas. 90, 174
Jno. 142, 174
Jonath. 89
Jonathan 78
Jos. 40
Simkins & 40
Tingley & 40
Wm. 78, 79, 174
Arres, Benj. 64
Arrington, Henry 152
Jno. 90
Arskins, Dorcas 104
Jas. 103, 104
Jno. 104, 105
Jno. (Jr.) 105
Jno. (Sr.) 103
Wm. 105
Arthur, Mathew 164
Matthew 98
Asbury, Jno. 40
Ash, Geo. 40
Matthias 35
Wm. 174
Ashbury, Jonathan 1
Reb. 151
Asher, Wm. 102
Asheson, Nathan 78
Ashfield, Dorothy 110
Frederic 111
Hannah 115
Ashley, Jas. 164
Lodewick 20
Ludowick 24
Nathan 22
Nathaniel 23
Nathl. 20, 24
Wm. 20, 23, 24, 79, 99
Ashmore, Jno. 133, 174
Peter 174
Wm. 174
Ashton, Saml. 40
Ashworth, Benj. 98
Asmus, Jno. 40
Aspay, Thos. 127
Asper, Michael 40
Aspy, Jno. 169

Asselin, Anthony 40
Athorn, Anthony 158
Athy, Zephaniah 64
Atkerson, Geo. 40
Jas. 106
Atkins, Nathan 114
Wiley 21
Wm. 106, 174
Atkinson, Andrew 31
Jas. 19, 104
Jeremiah 1, 10, 14
Jos. 1
Nathan 21, 26, 164
Valentine 61
Atsat, Jno. 40
Attaway, Jos. 15
Atwood, Isaac 142, 160
Audebert, Jno. 40
Audibert, Jno. Baptist
40
Auga, (?) (Madam) 40
Madam 40
Augur, Isaac 7
Austin, David 134
Davis 135
Henry 40
Jas. 40
Jno. 59
Jos. 135
Mary Ann 40
Richd. 151
Wm. 15
Autrey, Absalom 119
Alexdr. 117, 119
Jno. 114
Autry, Absalom 153
Alex 164
Avary, Jno. 142
Aven, Nancy 159
Avera, Arthur 174
Averitt, Albright 157
Archibald 157
Arthur 142
Avery, Frederick 40
Avren, Jno. 75
Avrit, Alexdr. 15
Awtrey, Jno. 127
Aycock, Richd. 90, 164
Wm. 74, 75, 85, 90
Ayers, Abrah. 64
Abrham 90
Baker (Jr.) 101
Baker (Sr.) 101
Benj. 64
Danl. 102
Jane 64
Aylet, Henry 14
Aylett, Archibald 157
Ayres, Abrham 90
Anna 97
Danl. 97, 98
Nancy 97
Thos. 142
Wm. 142
Baas, Rebecca 31
Saml. 31, 40
Babb, Will 173
Babcock, Wm. 11
Bache, N. 40
Bachellor, Cornelious
114
Jean 114
Bachelor, Cornelius 119
Bachler, Garton 40
Jno. 40
Backet, Jno. 40
Backford, Benj. 40
Backsted, Israel 59

Bacon, Agnes 148
Daniel 27
Danl. 23, 24, 28
Eliz. 131
Isaac 125
Jno. 131, 132, 133
Jno. (Jr.) 137
Jonathan 137
Jonathan (Sr.) 137
Josiah 131, 133, 135
Lyddall 145
Mary 145
Nathl. 132, 135, 137
Nicholas 153
Saml. 131, 137
Susannah 133
Badulet, (?) (Madam) 40
Madam 40
Baduly, Wm. 12, 15
Bagby, Geo. 114, 115,
117, 119
Baggs, Archibald 137
Jos. 153
Bagley, Israel 40
Bags, Jas. 174
Baileu, Abner 40
Bailey, Briton 142
Chris. 67
Dudley 40
Ezekiel 85
Green 174
Hezekiah 84, 87, 164
Jas. 61, 140
Jno. 26, 111, 119
Jos. 1, 11, 170
Lewis 159
Matthew 117
Moses 85
Ransford 40
Robt. 119
Simon 174
Thos. 115, 119
Wm. 90, 99
Bailie, Robt. C. 134
Baillee, Geo. (Jr.) 137
Robt. 137
Baillie, Geo. 40
Harriet 40
Robt. Carnaby 133
Bain, Jno. 58
Baird, Benj. 172
Jonathan 111, 125
Mickey 172
Baisden, Jas. 104, 107
Baker, Absalom 74
Absolom 76, 79
Ann 131
Artemas 131, 134, 135,
137
Benj. 81
Chas. 174
Comfort 81
Eliz. 137
Jesse 40
Jno. 73, 76, 85, 131,
134, 135, 137
Jno. (Jr.) 136
Jno. A. 85
Jno. Armstrong 78
Jno. B. 137
Jonathan 131
Jos. 40, 160
Joshua 153
Martha 133
Mary 76, 131, 137
Mary (Mrs.) 137
N. 131
Nathl. 134

Baker (cont.)
Rebecca 131
Saml. 79, 88, 99
Sarah 131
Steph. 134, 135
Stephen 131
Thos. 94, 131, 137
Whitmarsh 132, 135,
137
Wm. 98, 135, 137
Wm. (Sr.) 137
Wm. B. 134, 137
Wm. I. 135
Wm. J. 133, 137
Wm. R. 135
Balch, Eliz. 1
Balckstock, Jno. 132
Baldwin, A. 117
Abraham 149
Benj. 114
David 151
Ebenezer 40
Francis 164
M. 127
Marg. 117
Mordecai 111, 164
Robt. 119, 129
Saml. 119
Sarah 114
Thos. 119
Wm. 174
Baley, Francis 126
Thos. 127
Balkey, Ichabod 27
Ball, Ezek. 40
Isaac 164
Jno. 164
Richd. 117
Ballard, Benj. 164, 170
Chris. 153
Jno. 172, 174
Lovin 174
Nathan 174
Reuben 164
Wm. 174
Xpher 160
Ballenger, Jno. 78
Balthazer, Sarah 40
Bandy, Jno. 71
Banks, Elijah 94
Elisha Fowler 160
Gerard 64, 153
Gerrard 160
Jno. 84, 164
R. 173
Ralph 88
Richd. 164, 169
Wm. 74
Bankston, David 117
Jacob 108
Jno. 94
Laurence 153
Nancy 170
Peter 164
Thos. 119
Bankstone, Lawrence 160
Bannen, Ellinor 111
Jno. 111
Banton, Benj. 173
Baptist, Jean 40
Barber, (?) (Mrs.) 40
Geo. 98, 178
Jno. (Jr.) 71
Jno. (Sr.) 71
Jos. 153
Matthew 96
Penny 29
Robt. 135

Barber (cont.)
Will 96
Barbery, David 157
Barbree, Stancil 61
Barcley, David 20
Barden, Charlott 81
Gilbert 81
Wm. 40
Wm. (Jr.) 40
Barfield, Richd. 149
Bargeron, Elisha 1
Barker, Ephram 119
Jno. 119
Wm. 88
Barkley, Jno. 178
Barksdale, Jeffrey 150
Jos. 111
Barnaby, Rebecca 105
Wm. 105
Barnap, (?) 153
Barnard, Jas. 35
Jno. 40
Robt. 38, 40
Timothy 40, 151
Wm. 40
Barnay, Jno. 61
Barnes, (?) 40
(?) (Cpt.) 7
Benj. 119, 174
Geo. 147, 148, 150,
151
Isaac 14
Jas. 145, 147
Jemmina 145
Jesse 13, 15
Lewis 57
Saml. 110
Barnet, Abraham 110
Chas. 133
Jno. 94
Richd. 40
Timothy 40
Barnett, Abraham 119,
127
Benj. Johnson 76
Caroline 97
Claiborne 60
Elenor 147
Jesse 148, 149
Jno. 73, 88, 97, 99,
164
Jo. 79
Joel 64, 142, 149
Leonard 88
Lucy 76
Mary 111, 127, 173
Mial I. 164
Nathan 76, 88, 108,
115
Nathl. 64, 85, 145,
173
Nelson 85
Nyal 79
Patsey 76
Robt. 164
Saml. 119, 127
W. 84
Wm. 38, 78, 79, 85,
87, 142, 145, 148,
149, 173
Wm. (Sr.) 142
Barnette, Jesse 147
Barnhard, Geo. 108
Barnhart, Geo. 174
Philip 108
Barnheart, Geo. 119
Barns, Jesse 10
Barran, Saml. 108

Barren, Prudence 164
　　Thos. 79
Barret, & Co. 40
　　(?) 40
Barrett, Benj. 94
　　Wm. 94
Barron, Absalam 157
　　Jno. 94
　　Jos. 160
　　Wm. 12, 15, 145, 160,
　　　174
Barrons, Jno. 174
Barrot, Joel 94
Barrow, Jas. 14
　　Reuben 140
Barry, J. B. 40
　　Jas. 40
　　Jas. J. 40
　　Jos. 7
Bartan, Ruth 90
Bartholomew, Geo. 40
Bartlett, Jonathan 20,
　　24, 25
　　Robt. 164
Barton, Benj. 94
　　Jas. 21
　　Robt. 96, 164
　　Willoughby 140
　　Wm. B. 15
Basdale, Abner 119
Basket, Tho. 20
　　Thos. 19
Baskett, Rebeka 26
Bass, Abraham 14
　　Dewry 1
　　Esaw 154, 160
　　Jared 79
Bassett, Geo. 142
　　Richd. 157
Bassit, Abrah. 40
Batchelor, Cornls. 125
Bates, Francis 83
　　Tho. 21
Batey, David 126
Batharton, Wm. 61
Batier, Wm. J. 136
Batley, Jas. 58
Batson, Jos. 64
Batting, Jas. 103, 105,
　　106
Battle, Jesse 111
　　T. 119
　　Wm. 119
Bauchanneau, Nich 29
Baughman, Jno. 84
Baxter, Andrew 108, 109,
　　114, 117, 119
　　Jas. 117
　　Josiah 40
Bayless, Isham 64
Baylis, Isham 150
Baylor, Jno. 40
　　Matthew 40
Bayne, Jno. 61
Bazar, Caleb 119
　　Jno. 119
Beach, Adam 40
　　Nathl. 40
　　Thos. 40
Beacher, David 160
Beal, Eleanor (Mrs.) 38
　　Jas. 140
　　Jno. 150
　　Nathl. 15
　　Wm. 151
Beale, Jas. 140
　　Wm. 147
Beall, Archibald 150

Beall (cont.)
　　Daniel 90
　　Danl. 99
　　Hezekiah 140
　　Jas. E. 151
　　Jesse 67
　　Mitchell Z. 151
　　Thos. 149
　　Zebedee 58
　　Zepha 149
Bealle, Jas. 64
　　Jno. 64
　　Jonathan 63
Bealles, J. N. 63
　　Wm. P. 63
Bealy, Jas. 67
　　Wm. 13
Beamis, Ebenezer 21
Bean, Robt. 98, 99
Beard, Edmond 117
　　Edmund 119
　　Jno. 84
　　Jonathan 119
Bearden, Humphrey 127
　　Richd. 127
Bearfield, Richd. 174
　　Wm. 15
Beaseley, Richd. 164
Beaser, Wm. 119
Beasley, Jas. 25, 27
　　Jno. 1, 19, 21
　　Jos. 164
　　Richd. 164
　　Robt. C. 125
　　Thos. 1
　　Thos. (Jr.) 1
Beason, Peter 1
　　Robt. 173
Beattie, Eleanor 40
Beatty, John (Dr.) 29
Beaver, Martin 61
Beavers, Daniel 119
Beavin, Wm. 154
Beavoir, Jno. 129
Beazely, Jno. 28
Beazley, Sarah 20
　　Wm. 170
Beazly, Jas. 28
Bebe, Richd. 20
Bechtly, Geo. 67
Beck, Jno. 40, 64, 79
Beckcom, Allen 154, 160
　　Saml. 154
　　Sherod 154
　　Sherwood 160
　　Simon 154, 160
　　Sol. 154
Beckcu, Saml. 160
Beckcum, Sol. 160
Beckelow, Frederick 56
Beckett, Isaac 7
Beckham, Abner 1
　　Dempsey 59
　　Saml. 7
　　Sol. 148
　　Wm. 7
　　Young 59
Becroft, Saml. 33
Becu, Abrah. 40
Beddenback, Apolina 71
　　Christian 71
　　Matthew 71
　　Matthias 71
Beddingfield, Jos. 160
Bedell, A. 117
Bedford, Thos. 157
Bedingfield, Chas. 147
　　Jno. 147, 148

Bedingfield (cont.)
　　Jos. 154
　　Martha 147
　　Mary 147, 148
Bedsell, Godfrey 7
Becroft, Saml. 40
Beek, Jos. 157
Been, Robt. 94
Beesly, Jno. 26
Beeson, Jonathan 94
Beezly, Jos. 154
Beggs, Alexdr. 38
　　Thos. 40
Behn, Arthur 40
Belcher, Allen 14
　　Jas. 40, 134
　　McCain 1
　　Obediah 125
　　Philip 1
　　Phillip 40
　　Wm. 40
Belden, Wm. 7
Belen, Peter 24
Belin, Peter 20
Belingslea, Francis 60
Bell, (?) (Cpt.) 7
　　Allen 1
　　Andrew 164
　　Arthur 12
　　David 38, 40
　　Elisha 12
　　Eliz. 76
　　Francis 61
　　Green 15
　　Hannah 99
　　Hugh 159
　　J. L. 85
　　Jas. 79, 82, 99
　　Jesse 67, 72
　　Jos. 76
　　Nathl. 119
　　Richd. 151
　　Robt. 61, 137
　　Wm. 12, 15, 40, 59,
　　　138
Bellamy, Wm. 64, 147
Belsell, Jno. 35
Belvill, Robt. 71
Belville, Rebecca 71
Belvin, Wiley 21
　　Wiley I. 28
Belving, Willey J. 26
Ben, (?) 40
Benden, Jno. 95
Benedict, Isaac 64
Benedix, Isaac 33, 40
Benion, Jno. 160
　　Wm. 160
Bennet, Anne 64
　　Jno. (Cpt.) 160
Bennett, (?) 40
　　Ann 56
　　Anne 64
　　Arthur 154, 160
　　Benj. 89
　　Chas. 148
　　Eliz. 138
　　Grissel 111
　　Hugh 130, 131, 134
　　Jas. 21, 27, 28
　　Jno. 58
　　Jno. B. 140
　　Jno. Baker 147
　　Jos. 35
　　Lucy 111
　　Mathew 134
　　Matthew 130
　　Rebecca 131

Bennett (cont.)
  Reuben 133, 173
  Richd. 67, 72
  Stephen 111
  Wm. 67, 72, 138
Benningfield, Jos. 157
Bennion, Wm. (Sr.) 57
Bennis, Jno. 154
Benois, Lewis 40
Benson, Ben 40
  Jno. 154
  Martin 164
Bentley, Balaam 160
  Balam 154, 164
  Catherine 170
  Jane 170
  Jas. 170
  Jeremiah 174
  Jno. 170
  Lewis 170
  Susannah 170
  Wm. 154, 160, 170
Benton, E. 40
  Eliz. 7
  Mordecai 97, 98, 99
  Nathan 98
  Wm. 11
Berlingham, Saml. 21
Berneviz, Wm. 40
Berrien, Jno. 33
  Thos. 35
Berry, Anderson 174
  Francis Hubert 40
  Jelson 174
  Jos. 40
  Presley 174
Berryhill, Alex 140
  Alexdr. 142, 153
  Andrew 1, 160
  Saml. 140, 142
Bertrand, Lewis 40
Besinger, Peter 40
Bessett, Alexdr. 103
Best, Jno. 103, 106, 107
  Wm. 164, 170
Bethune, Jas. 40
Betsell, Jno. 1
Bettis, Jno. 151
Bettison, David 40
Beverly, Anthony 78, 85
Bevers, Jas. 125
Bevill, Paul 67
Beville, Paul 71
Bexley, Jno. 40
Bibb, Jas. 164
  Sally S. 75
  Thos. 117
  Wm. 73, 75
Bichon, Bernard 40
Bickerstaff, Jno. 90
  Johnson 96
Bickham, Abner (Cpt.) 6
  Jas. 11
Biddenback, Christian 69
  Mary 69
  Matthias 72
Biffett, Alexdr. 106
Bigbee, Francis 29
Bigham, Jas. 1
Bilbo, Jas. 71, 111
  Mathew 111
Bill, Avery 40
  Every 40
Billups, Wm. 119
Bingham, Jno. 20, 28
Binion, Wm. 174
Binn, Ann 142
Birch, Chas. 142

Bird, (?) (Cpt.) 129
  Abraham 67, 134
  Andrew 40
  Capt. 129
  Israel 67
  Jas. 129
  Jesse 1
  Michael 154
  Michel 160
  Philemon 164, 170
  Robt. 170
  Saml. 67, 130, 137
  Thompson 170
Birdsdale, Decker 40
Birky, Rudolph 40
Bishop, (?) (Madam) 40
  Edw. 117
  Elijah 20
  Jane 138
  Jas. 117, 149
  Joshua 120
  Madam 40
  Martha 67
  Peter 134, 138
  Phebe 150
  Seth 40
  Wm. 67, 72, 120
Bisset, Alexdr. 40
Bissett, Alexdr. 104, 105
Bithelheimer, Jno. 107
Bixley, Wm. 21
Blache, S. 148
Black, Benj. 164
  Henry 97, 99
  Jno. 154, 160, 170
  Robt. 89
  Saml. 90
  Steph. 106
  Wm. 1, 82, 97, 98, 102
Blackburn, Nathan 174
  Saml. 78, 85
Blacke, Jno. 85
  Sessums 164
Blackenrigg, Jean 67
Blackman, Wm. 15
Blackmar, Steph. 27, 28
Blackmon, Ann 71
  Wm. 71
Blackmone, Steph. 26
Blackshear, David 159, 160
Blackstock, Jno. 40, 130, 134, 135
  Jo-- 135
Blackstone, Jas. 145
  Jno. 145
  Winefred 145
  Winifred 140
Blackwell, Chas. 147
  Dunstan 99
  Geo. 63
  Jeremiah 85
  Jno. 87
  Jos. 84, 85, 164
Blair, Hugh 60, 64, 147
  Jno. 7, 129
Blake, Benj. 170
  Henry 170
  Jno. 159
  Mary 170
  Sessoms 169
  Wm. 74, 164
  Wm. (Jr.) 85
  Wm. (Sr.) 85
Blakey, Ch. 120
  Jno. 169
  Jos. 173

Blanc, Jno. 40
Blanchard, Benj. 160
  Judith 1
  Reuben 147
  Robt. 164
  Sarah 147
Bland, Mary 31, 33
Blankenship, Danl. 120
  Reuben 120
  Reubin 117
  Womack 79, 85
Blanks, Jas. 111
Blanton, Chas. 174
  Jno. 61, 67, 90
Blasingame, Harvey 71
Blasius, Frederic 40
Bledsoe, Benj. 64, 148
  Peachey 58
Bletaher, Benj. 63
Blitcher, Benj. 61
Blockman, Jas. 7
Blogg, Wm. 33, 40
Blont, Jas. 136
Bloodworth, Saml. 149
Blount, Hugh 40, 136
  Redding 24
  Steph. 40
Blunt, Jas. 154, 160
  Steph. 21
Board, Abraham 69, 73
Boardman, Hill 40
  Wms. 40
Boars, Joal 157
Boasman, Saml. 15
Boatright, David 15
  John 15
Bobb, Thos. 160
Bobo, Lewis 82, 90, 102
  Sampson 94, 98
Boggus, Jeremiah 164
Bohannon, Dunkin 169
  Jno. 116
Bold, Benj. 40
Boles, Wm. 125
Bolina, Jas. 25
Bolling, Jas. 107
Bollinger, Frederic 41
Bolls, Wm. 174
Bolton, Jno. 35, 41, 164, 174
  Robert 26, 133
  Robt. 20, 25, 33, 35, 41, 133
  Robt. (Jr.) 29, 33
Boman, Wm. 110
Bond, Chas. 94, 95
  Eliz. 78
  Jos. 79
  Nathan 76, 78
  Richd. 85, 89
  Venable 35
  Wm. 95
Bonds, Chas. 160
  Nathan 173
  Richd. 78, 87
Bonell, Anthony 67
  Danl. 67
  Jno. 67
Boneman, Jobe 61
Bonnell, Anthony 1
Bonner, Geo. 152
  Henry (Jr.) 164
  Richd. 140, 147
  Robt. 60, 151
  Thos. 120
  Zadok 120
Booker, Eideon 57
  Gideon 64

Booker (cont.)
Jno. 58, 60, 61, 145
Wm. 57
Wm. (Sr.) 75
Wm. F. 58, 108
Boon, Fred 12
Garrett 106
Boorom, (?) 41
Carpenter 41
Isaac 41
Booth, Abraham 169
Dred 7
Jno. 115, 127
Jno. (Jr.) 120
Wm. 1, 11
Zachrh. 117
Boothe, Jno. 7
Wm. 142
Boother, Andrew 174
Boozman, Mary 11
Saml. 11
Boram, David 116
Jas. 117
Border, Gilbert 85
Borel, Claud 23
Borland, Andrew 108,
117, 120, 154, 160
Boroum, Wm. 120
Bosman, Jacob 16
Jos. 16
Nathan 16
Saml (Sr.) 16
Saml. (Jr.) 16
Bostick, Littleberry 111
Nathan 147
Saml. 67
Wm. 140
Boston, Jas. 69
Bostwick, (?) 41
Heyman 41
Littleberry 164
Saml. 67
Boswell, Benj. 147
Bothwell, David (Rev.) 1
Bottomly, Michael 11
Boucher, Adrian 41
Boudin, Agnes 111
Wm. 111
Boudon, (?) 41
Bouquet, Pierre 41
Bourke, Jane 41
Thos. 133
Bourneman, Benj. W. 105
Bourquin, Benedict 38,
41
David 38
David F. 41
David Francis 35
Henry 41
Jane Judith 41
Jno. 41
Jno. L. 151
Boutinat, Derivaus 41
Bovis, Geo. 174
Bowdre, Edmond 117
Elisha 60
Richd. 117
Robt. 60, 61, 63
Bowen, Ann 41
Clifton 69
Horatio 172
Jas. 41
Jas. F. 35
Jno. 172
Joel 90
Jonathan 7
Jos. 90
Martha 67, 69

Bowen (cont.)
Mary 31
Mary D. 41
Mathew 131
Matthew 138
Oliver 41
Rachel 172
Saml. 35
Saml. F. 41
Saml. Flint 31
Wm. 172
Bowie, (?) 160
Jas. 90, 149
Reson 149
Bowin, Jas. 160
Joel 160
Bowling, Robt. 10, 11,
14
Simon 14
Wm. 13
Bowls, Salley 173
Wm. 173
Bowman, Jno. 41
Leonard 174
Bowram, Benj. 174
Bows, Thos. 125
Box, Eliz. 41
Jos. 102
Phillip 41
Richd. 35, 131, 138
Thos. R. 41
Wm. G. 41
Boxwood, Jas. 41
Boyd, Archibald 1
Chas. 41
David 64, 160
Eliz. 64
Jas. 1
Jno. 41, 59, 60, 64,
79, 88, 90, 117, 142
Nicodemus 59, 64
Saml. 1, 56
Susannah 41
Thos. 154
Boyed, Eliz. 145
Boyett, Eliz. 1
Boyington, Joshua (Jr.)
41
Boykin, Francis 1
Jesse 1, 12, 16
Jno. 20, 67, 69
Sol. 13, 16
Wm. 7
Boyzer, Wm. 127
Bozman, Luke 161
Brack, Benj. 10, 14, 16,
161
Eleazar 161
Eleazer 11
Eli 14
Eliz. 11
Rich. 16
Richd. 11
Bracken, Isaac 154, 161
Wm. 154, 161
Brad, Pat 142
Bradbury, Jas. 59
Braddock, Jno. 103, 104,
106, 107
Bradford, Jno. 135
Nathl. 164
Oseah 90
Thos. 120
Wm. 41, 79
Bradley, (?) (Lt.) 103
E. 117
Edwd. 120, 129
Joshua 64

Bradley (cont.)
Reehard 103
Richd. 105, 107, 120
Wm. 16
Bradshaw, Brice 1
Jas. 164
Bradwell, Thos. 133,
135, 137, 138
Brady, D. 85
Jas. 85, 174
Jno. 83
Saml. 58
Stancel 61
Thos. 41
Wm. 117
Bragdon, Meredith 99
Bragg, Elijah 16, 64,
142
Brailsford, Jno. H. 41
Jno. N. 35
Braksdale, Stith 173
Brandon, Jno. 7
Josiah 1
Branham, Jno. 96
Spencer 99
Brannon, Jas. 7
Thos. 1, 164
Wm. 1
Brantley, Benj. 147
Jeremiah 104, 106
Philip 64
Thos. 108, 111, 120,
161
Brantly, Jeremiah 107
Brasel, Jno. 82
Brasfield, Caleb 110
Lucey 111
Brassfield, Geo. 140
Braswell, Benj. 147
Kendred 161
Kindred 154
Robt. 161
Saml. 117, 161, 164
Wm. 159
Brawner, Basil 79
Bazel 83
Benj. 85
Henry 85
Jas. 87
Jesse 85
Jno. 79, 84, 85, 88
Wm. 85
Bray, Jno. 83
Thos. 67
Braydy, Jas. 1
Brazdal, Jno. 74
Mary 74
Brazeal, Frederick 73
Henry 1
Brazel, Frederick 83
Brazell, Jno. 67, 164
Robt. 67
Brazoal, Henry 159
Brazwell, Bird 164
Breedlove, Benj. 110
Mary 120
Bremer, Jno. 154
Brewer, Barrot 174
Benj. 99
Chas. 120
Edmund 79
Elisha 74
Geo. 90, 111, 120
Jas. 67
Jas. (Sr.) 67
Jno. 74, 120, 127
Wm. 90
Brewston, David 28

Brewton, Jas. 90
Briant, Benj. 158
Brickell, Jno. 31, 35, 41
Bridges, Ben 173
  Berry 96
  David 164, 178
  Haynes 96
  Henry 96
  J. 96
  Nathl. 164, 169, 178
  Thos. 178
  Wiseman 96
  Wm. 102
Briers, Lawrence 90
Briges, Walton 95
Briggs, Elkanah 28
  Isaac 90
  Jno. 161
Brinkley, Brittain 103
Brinson, Adam 1, 10, 14
  Fereby 1
  Jno. 1
  Moses 1
  Susannah 1
Brinton, Andrew 88
  Jno. 159, 161
  Wm. 161
Brisbane, Adam F. 41
Briscoe, Jno. 142
Britt, Chas. 97
  Ester 150
  Jno. 147, 150
  Jonathan 159
  Malachi 159
Britton, Jno. 41
  Steph (Jr.) 41
  Steph. 35, 41
Brogdon, Merideth 94
  Robt. 99
Broner, Rolling 89
Brooke, Thos. 33
Brooks, Francis 33, 41
  Jas. 161, 165
  Jean 164
  Jno. 90
  Job 174
  Joel 174
  Martha 170
  Peter 20
Broughs, Jas. 59
Broughton, Jno. 159
Brower, Jno. 41
Brown, (?) (Mrs.) 41
  Alex 165
  Alexdr. 99, 111
  Allen 170
  Amy 81
  Andrew 117
  Ann 31
  Bedford 165
  Benj. 1, 78, 81, 85, 88, 165
  Betty 173
  David 41, 78, 98, 99
  Edw. 59, 174
  Elisha 61
  Francis 79, 88
  Franklin 41
  Frederick 56, 60, 61, 64, 142
  Henry 7, 41, 161
  Hue 26
  Hugh 20, 23, 25, 28
  Isaac 157
  Jas. 7, 41, 74, 78, 85, 138, 145, 148, 150

Brown (cont.)
  Jeremiah 7
  Jno. 1, 20, 21, 78, 81, 85, 88, 90, 98, 151, 165, 174, 178
  Jos. 161, 175
  Langley 20
  Meredith 165
  Meroday 79
  Nancy 81
  Peter 82
  Richd. 41
  Robt. 21, 25, 26, 28
  Robt. (Jr.) 21
  Rolen 79
  Ruth 41
  Ruth (Mrs.) 41
  S. 145
  Saml. 16, 142
  Sarah 76
  Thos. 41, 76, 78, 173
  Wm. 16, 31, 33, 35, 41, 64, 76, 79, 82, 116, 120, 125, 126, 140, 165
  Wm. (Maj.) 41
Brownell, David 41
Brownen, Jesse 75
Brownhill, Thos. 41
Browning, Elis 7
  Isaac 127
  Jesse 127
  Jno. 115, 120, 127
  Jno. (Jr.) 111, 129
  Jno. (Sr.) 129
  Robt. 120
  Wm. 126
Brownson, Galen 130, 133, 134
  Gillon 136
  Nathan 67
  Reuben 56, 64
  Reubin 60
Broyce, Jno. C. 41
Bruce, Chas. 16
  Jas. 1, 105, 106
  Jno. 58
  Rebecca 103, 105
  Townley 117
Brucus, Wm. 106
Brummet, Jno. 1
Brummutt, Jno. 16
Brunie, Thos. 41
Brunor, Jno. 161
Brunson, Reuben 61
Bruster, Hugh 117
Bruton, Jas. 16
  Jno. 16, 161
Bryan, Andrew 41
  Augustine 79
  B. 120
  David 161, 165
  Edw. 95
  Elijah 95
  Fanny 41
  Geo. 11
  Jane 142
  Jas. 41
  Jno. 16, 95, 97, 98
  Jos. 19, 41, 150
  Langley 23
  Mathew 133
  Matthew 130
  Moses 10, 11
  Nancy 97
  Saml. 90
  Thos. 98, 145
  Wm. 33, 99

Bryan (cont.)
  Zach. 98
Bryant, Archibald 140
  Benj. 7
  Henry 11, 13, 14
  Jane 142
  Jas. 69, 73
  Jno. 1, 7, 90, 102, 140, 161
  Jno. B. 106
  Jno. C. 106
  Langley 20, 23, 24, 25, 26, 27, 28
  Mary 11, 20
  Moses 1
  Needham 1
  Simon 127
  Wm. 11, 90, 127
  Wm. (Sr.) 56
Brydie, David 41
Bryson, (?) (Widow) 41
  Widow 41
  Wm. 21
Buchanan, Jno. 79, 111
  Jos. 125
Buchenau, (?) (Widow) 41
  Widow 41
Buchhalter, Isaac 41
  Jesse 41
  Joshua 41
Buck, Jno. 41
Buckanan, Jas. 145
Buckels, Wm. 175
Buckhalter, Jno. Michael 1, 67
  Randolph 16
  Wm. 108
Buckhanan, Jos. 173
Buckhannan, Jno. 120
Buckhannon, Jno. 117
Buckle, Margareth 41
Buckley, Butler 13
  Ich. 26
  Jas. 13
  Richd. 13
Buckner, Ricy 175
Bucks, Jacob 117
Buffington, Jos. 151
Buford, Jno. 13, 14
  Jno. (Cpt.) 6
Bugg, Anselm 147
  Charlotte 150
  Edmd. 145
  Eliza 145
  Jacob 79, 81, 88
  Jeremiah 147
  Jno. 59, 159
  N. H. 99
  Nancy 81
  Nicholas 147
  Nicholas H. 150
  Nicholas Hobson 64
  Sherwood 57, 60, 64, 150
  Thos. 152
  Wm. 142, 147
Bulard, Jno. 94
Bulkley, Ichabod 21, 28
Bull, Absalom 29
  Jno. 41
  Serina 41
  Thomas 29
Bullard, Thos. 84
  Wily 161
Bullmen, Geo. 61
Bulloch, Jas. 41
  Mary 41
  Priscilla 41

Bulloch (cont.)
Richd. 140
Wm. B. 41
Bullock, Archibald 35
Burel 63
Burwell 142
Jas. 35
Nathl. 165
Richd. 142
Bunce, Wm. 41
Bunkley, Briatin 105
Britain 103, 104
Brittain 106, 107
Britton 103
Jesse 117
Mary 105
Buntery, Zach. 157
Bunwitz, Wm. 41
Burch, Chas. 140, 151, 153
Edwd. 140, 150
Garard 116
Jared 116, 120
Jos. 140
Martha 150
Richd. 117
Wm. 85
Burchill, Arthur 41
Burd, Phillip 175
Price 175
Shadrick 158
Burden, Humphrey 120
Richd. 172
Richd. Ash. 41
Burdet, Jas. 175
Burdett, Humphry 165
Burdin, Archibald 85
Burford, Amelia (Mrs.) 138
Daniel 129
Daniell 115
Danl. 120, 125
Emelia 130
Judith 115
Leonard 117, 120
Mary 111
Mitchel 120
Mitchell 111
Sol. 120, 127
Wm. 110, 115, 120, 125
Wm. (Jr.) 116
Burgamy, Wm. L. 158
Burge, Jno. 154, 161
Burger, Jacob 111
Burges, (?) 41
Elias 95
Josiah 95
Burgess, Elias 99
Jno. 133
Josias 98
Richd. 135
Burgholder, Rudolph 71
Burgois, Peter 41
Burgstiner, Danl. 71
Burk, Chas. 117, 165
Edmon 159
Edw. 59
Nimrod 158, 161
Thos. 74
Thos. (Sr.) 79
Burke, (?) (Mrs.) 41
Chas. 111
Edwd. 140
J. 35
Jno. 41
M. 133
Michael 147
Michael (Dr.) 41

Burke (cont.)
Rich 64
Robt. 79, 165
Thos. 1, 41, 165
Thos. (Jr.) 165
Burkes, Edwd. 142
Burket, Geo. 95
Burkett, Tho. 25
Burkit, Jos. 41
Burks, Edwd. 140
Burleson, Jesse 1
Burlong, Henry 175
Burn, Hugh 41
Burnet, Danl. 154, 161
Jno. 104, 165
Matthew 130
Sol. 161
Burnett, Anthony 41
Clayborn 60
Jno. 58, 61, 103, 105, 106, 107, 150
Jno. (Jr.) 104
Moses 103, 104, 107
Saml. 16
Sol. 7
Wm. 7, 142
Burnette, Crad. 145
Burney, Andrew 41
David 91, 154, 161
Hardy 111
Jas. 157, 161
Jemimah 111
Jno. 41, 111, 161, 170
Polly 111
Randal 161
Richd. 1, 161
Saml. 131
Shadrack 111
Simon 110, 170
Thos. 131
Burnley, Saml. 136
Burns, (?) 41
Andrew 91, 116
Andrew (Jr.) 91
Aquilla 97, 98
Eliz. 91
Felix 91
Jean 91
Jno. 91
Martha 91
Mary 69, 91
Robt. 91
Terrenu (?) 129
Tho. 16
Thos. 1
Burnsides, Jno. 1
Nathan 140
Wm. 41
Burnwell, Cradock 142
Burroughs, Bennett 59
J. 23
Jas. 60
Burrows, J. 35
Jno. 23, 26, 35
Robt. 7
Burson, Jos. 1
Burt, Fanny 150
Moody 150
Burton, Archer 74
Archibald 87
Jacob 76
Jno. A. 16
Nancy 76
Rachel 1
Richd. 145
Robt. 88
Tho. 85
Thos. 1, 74, 79, 87,

Burton (cont.)
88, 165
Walthall 16
Wm. Allen 2
Bush, Danl. 98, 99
Jeptha 89
Jno. 111, 120
Thos. 116, 117, 120
Bussey, Benj. 175
David 175
Thos. 169, 175
Busson, Jonathan 165
Butlar, Edmond 120
Butler, Benj. 33, 38, 41, 58
Edmond 117
Edmund (Sr.) 111
Jas. 76, 165
Jno. 29, 33, 41, 126
Jos. 31, 33, 38, 41
Mary 81
Meshack 31, 33, 38
Noble 147
Patrick 78, 99, 165
Salley 76
Shadrack 33
Shem 35
Wm. 33, 41
Zach. 165
Zachariah 81
Buttery, Zachary 161
Butts, Azariah 116
Karan 115
Byne, Edmund 10, 14
Wm. 2, 10, 16
Bynum, Jno. 60
Byron, Terrance 126
Cabbin, Jno. 99
Cable, Denbo 29
Cade, Drury 165
Cadmis, Abraham 41
Cahoon, Aquilla 2, 16
Jos. 157
Philip 13
Caig, & Co. 41
(?) 41
Cain, Benj. 20
Jas. 158
Jno. 99, 111, 116, 120
Jos. 41
Richd. 120
Rosannah 83
Ruth 83
Wm. 117, 159
Calder, Jas. 106
Caldwell, (?) 41
Alex 91
Alexdr. 97, 98
Geo. 138
Harry 79, 84
Henry 88, 91
Henry G. 16
Hy 16
Jas. 58, 59
Jno. 41, 59, 138
Ogelby & 41
Paul 59, 60, 64
Ruthy 97
Sarah 60
Will 111
Wm. 111, 120
Calhoon, Adam 13
Aquilla 14
Jas. 2
Calhoun, Jas. 98
Call, Jno. 142
Richd. 79, 99, 142
Wm. (Jr.) 99

Callaghan, Thos. 41
Callahan, Edwd. 173
　Wm. 41, 173
Callingham, Jno. 2
Calvert, Jas. 88
　Jno. 75, 84
　Jos. 74
Calwell, Paul 140
Cambridge, Jno. M. 99
Cameron, Ambrose 96
　Duncan 111
　Jas. 74, 85
　Thos. 74
　no. 74
Cammell, Robt. 169
Cammenn, Jno. 61
Camp, Andr. W. 111
　Edw. 99
　Saml. 161, 165
　Wm. 42
Campbell, (?) 127
　(?) (Widow) 42
　--es 127
　Aaron 99, 102
　Duncan 84, 91, 99
　Edwd. 145
　Jno. 19, 29, 35, 42,
　　91, 138
　McCartan 42, 152
　McCarton 145
　Peter 42
　Sarah 69, 145
　Thos. 67, 69
　Widow 42
　Wm. 130, 161
Cample, Wm. 125
Camron, Jas. 78
Canada, Jos. 165
Canady, Wm. 7
Canavan, Andrew 42
Candelr, Henry 147
Candler, Henry 56, 64,
　140
　Wm. 150
　Wm. (Jr.) 147
Candlish, Alexdr. 42
Cane, Jno. 108
Cannon, (?) (Widow) 7
　Caleb 2
　Jno. 7
　Jos. 103
　Russell 99
Cant, Jno. 42
Canter, Thos. 98
Cantey, Joshua 138
Cantor, Jacob (Jr.) 33
Capers, Gabriel 42
　Morgan 42
　Richd. 35
Caplen, Jas. 67
Capps, Jno. 126
Caregon, Wm. 125
Cargile, Clement 147
Cargmile, Jno. 165
Cargo, Saml. 99
Carleton, Thos. 127
　Thos. (Sr.) 129
Carlise, Robt. 125
　Wm. 159
Carlton, Jno. 42
　Thos. 109
　Wm. 120
Carmichael, Jno. 60, 64,
　109, 142
　Jos. 109, 111, 116,
　　120, 129, 130
　Mary 60, 64
Carmichall, Jos. 128

Carmill, Wm. 28
Carnal, Wm. 106
Carne, Wm. 61
Carnel, Thos. 43
Carnes, Peter 99
　Rich. 28
　Richd. 19, 22, 24
　Robt. 21, 106
　Tho. 64
　Thos. P. 145, 150,
　　151, 154, 161
　Thos. Peter 98
Carns, Peter 16
　Richd. 26
　T. P. 99
Carpenter, (?) 41, 42
　Baley 16
　Thos. 7
Carpter, Edwd. 157
Carr, Catherine 64
　Fanny 150
　Isham 154
　Mary 131
　Patrick 7
　Richd. 128
　Tho. 23, 28
　Thomas 99
　Thos. 56, 103, 117,
　　140, 142, 148, 150
Carragan, Edw. 31, 39
Carragin, Edwd. 157
Carraway, Jas. 35
Carregan, Wm. 120
Carrell, Mary 76
　Peter 76
Carrol, Jno. 61
　Wm. 61
Carroll, Jno. 2
　Wm. 60, 140, 142, 148
Carson, Adam 111, 120
　David 111
　Jean 111
　Jno. 29, 31, 35, 42,
　　109, 120, 140, 147
　Jos. 111, 157
　Marg. 111
　Rachel 147
　Thos. 111
Carswell, Alex. 140
　Edw. 42
　Edwd. 142
　Jno. 72
　Mathew 16
Carter, Alex 2
　Alexdr. 11, 13, 16
　Ann 97
　Chas. (Sr.) 7
　Elisha 151, 175
　Ezekiah 126
　Geo. 2
　Giles 140
　Hepworth 131, 132,
　　135, 136
　Isaac 67, 126
　Isaiah 10, 11, 13
　Jacob 169
　Jas. 74, 78, 79, 81,
　　131, 136
　Jno. 20, 25, 42, 95,
　　97, 161
　Jno. M. 79
　Jos. 132
　Josiah 91, 115, 165
　Kindred 64
　Lucy 81
　Martha 132
　Mary 97
　Matthew 67

Carter (cont.)
　Nancy 97
　Patrick 42
　Tho. (Jr.) 85
　Thos. 79, 85, 91, 97,
　　102, 110, 132
　Thos. (Sr.) 76, 82
　Wm. 82
Carthon, Usley 159
Cartledge, Edmond 64
　Jas. 64
　Martha 165
Cartlidge, Edmond 147
　Jas. 147
　Saml. 147
Cartnell, Wm. 21
Cartright, Peter 117,
　129
Cartwright, Hezk. 111
　Jno. 108, 129
　Peter 108, 120, 127,
　　130
Casey, Abraham 89, 95
　Jno. 85
　R. 84
　Wm. 111, 173
Cash, Howard 73
　Preshus 170
Cashan, Jas. 42
Cashen, Jas. 132, 133,
　134
Cashin, Jas. 133
Cask, Zack 96
Caskan, Jas. 24
Cason, Ransom 107
Cassells, Wm. 2, 165
Cassels, Elias 137, 138
　Rebecca 138
　Sarah 137
　Wm. Henry 134, 138
Cassity, Peter 20
Casson, Adam 129
　Jos. 129
Castle, Wm. 175
Castleberry, Henry 116,
　149
　Jeremiah 117
　Peter 165
　Thos. 175
Castlebery, Asa 175
Castlebury, Richd. 165
Castles, Jno. 61
Castmell, Wm. 26
　Wm. & Co. 26
Caswell, Jno. 67, 161
Catcham, Nancy 2
Catching, Benj. 165
　Jos. 161
Catchings, Benj. 154
　Jos. 154
　Meredith 165
　Seymour 165
Cates, Richd. W. 161
　Thos. 154, 161
　Wm. 16
Cathan, Jas. 25
Cathell, Jas. 111, 127
Catledge, Edwd. 149
Catler, Mary 133
Catlett, Geo. 152
　Jno. 147, 151
　Wm. 7
Cato, Starling 116, 117
　Stearling 108
　Sterling 120
Catoe, Sterling 128
Catonnet, Mary Alexis 33
Catter, Geo. 133

Cattonet, Peter 42
Caughran, Jos. 67
Caursey, Peter 99
Cavanah, Chas. 16
  David 16
Cave, Wm. 161
Cavenah, Chas. 2
  Nicholas 67
Cavgur, Jno. 175
Cawthon, Chas. 95
  Claborn 95
  Cleyborn 102
  Wm. 98, 99, 154, 161
Cawthorn, David 95
Cazey, Danl. 165
Ce--, Chas. 130
Cecil, Harriet 31
  Leonard 31, 33, 35,
    38, 39, 132, 133
  Mary 133
  Philip 133
Celsna, Jno. 111
  Mary 111
  Saml. 110
Cent, Jas. 16
Certain, Jas. 85
  Josiah 78
Cessna, Chas. 116, 120
  Jno. 115, 120
  Saml. 120
Chadirac, Mons. Trust 42
Chalmers, Geo. 157
Chambers, Jno. 7, 142
  Jonas 2
  Lettice 76
  Robt. 76, 79, 165
  Saml. 117
  Thos. 61
  Wm. 61, 142
Chambless, Littleton 175
Champagne, Eliz. 35
  Nicholas 35
Champaign, Nicholas 42
Champion, Henry 140, 142
  Jno. B. 35
Chance, Henry 161
  Isaac 154
  Philemon 2
  Sampson 161
  Simpson 154
  Vincent 154, 161
  Vinson 7
Chandler, Abednego 154
  Henry 56, 151
  Hezekiah 85
  Jno. 172, 178
  Jos. 82, 91
  Mordecai 154
  Mordecia 161
  Obednya 161
  Wm. 64, 151
Chaney, Moses 110
Chany, Emanuel 154
Chaplin, Jos. 157
Chapman, Israel 42
  Wm. 88
Chappell, Jno. (Sr.) 116
Charis, Jos. 2
Charon, Atmil 42
Chatham, Jane Seagrove
  26
Chattin, Jno. 64
Chaurin, Wm. 42
Chavenet, Policarpe 42
Chavis, Wm. 158
Cheney, Greenberry 127
Chesher, Jno. 133
Chesser, Benj. 89

Chesser (cont.)
  Tho. 89
  Wm. 89
Chew, Benj. 42
Childers, Richd. 158
Children, Jas. 84
Childs, Nathan 78
  Wm. 42
Chiles, Jno. 85
Chisholm, Angus 42
  Wm. 74
Chisler, Danl. 42
Chislom, Wm. 84
Chivers, Joel 157, 161
  Larkin 161
Chrisa, Elijah 84
Christie, Archibald 131
  Robt. 42
  Wm. 15
Christmas, Nathl. 108,
  161
  R. 99
  Robt. 115
Christopher, Jas. 120,
  147
  Spencer 24
  Spicer 24
  Wm. 79, 117
Church, Sylvanus 42
Churchill, N. H. 173
  Nathl. H. 91
Cimbro, Jno. 120
  Shadrick 120
  Wm. 111, 120
Clack, Wm. 165
Cladus, Geo. 88
Clancy, Jas. 134
Clankenship, Danl. 120
Clarendon, (?) (Mrs.) 42
Clark, (?) 42
  Agatha 79
  Ann Ross 35
  Arthur 2
  Barnes 99, 142
  Bolign 81
  Bolling 81
  Chris. 16, 76, 85, 88
  David 79, 85
  Edw. 82, 85
  Elijah 20
  Geo. 42
  Jacob 20
  Jas. 29, 33
  Jean 35
  Jno. 16, 91, 95, 170
  Jno. (Jr.) 94
  Jno. (Sr.) 91
  Johnston 75
  Jos. 21, 136
  Joshua 85
  Judith 79
  Lewis 158
  Mark 35
  Martha 81
  Mathew 132
  Nancy 170
  Robt. 117
  Saml. 85, 96
  Sampson 117
  Sarah 75
  Tandy 13
  Thos. 2
  Wm. 2, 35
  Zack 85
Clarke, Barnes 117
  Benj. 2
  Chris. 74
  Eliz. 99

Clarke (cont.)
  Geo. 97, 99
  Gilbert 64
  Henry 11
  Jacob 19, 25, 28
  Jas. 35, 42
  Jesse 60, 98
  Jno. 42, 91, 97, 102,
    165
  Jno. (Sr.) 91
  Jonathan 11, 35
  Jos. 42
  Lemuel 42
  Matthew 42
  Moses 97
  Tandy 15
  Tho. 16
  Wm. 16, 42, 60, 98
Clarkson, Jno. 79
  Wm. 42
Clashier, Jno. C. 7
Clay, Abia 152
  Abia-- 145
  Abraham 142
  Evans 42
  Jesse 165, 173
  Jos (Jr.) 35
  Jos. 29, 35, 42
  Nathan 117
  Pearee 158
  Perceble 165
  Ralph 42
  Royal 173
  Saml. 145
Clayton, Isaac 28
  Isac 26
  Jacob 26
  Jas. 129
  Jno. 154
  Philip 133, 147, 151
  Phillip 153
  Thos. 140
Cleary, Jno. R. 71
Cleckley, Jno. Web 33
Cleghorn, Jas. 79
  Jno. 79
  Lettice 165
Cleland, Jas. 42
  Mary 2
  Moses 42
  Wm. 42
Clem, Catherine 145
  David 145
  Henry 145
  Valentine 145
Clement, Stephen 172
Clements, Eliz. 115
  Henry 165
  Jesse 120
  Jno. 14
  Phillip 116
  Tyre 111, 115, 116,
    120, 129
  Wm. 10, 15
Clemm, Adam 81
  Jemmia 81
Clemons, Jesse 128
  Philip 128
Clendinnon, Mathew 120
Clerk, Arthur 142
  Jas. 16
  Lewis 161
Cleveland, Absalom 98
  Absolom 95
  Benj. 99
  Fanny 97
  Jacob 75, 85
  Jeremiah 75, 91, 95,

Cleveland (cont.)
  99
  Jno. 85, 94, 98, 102
  Jno. C. 99
  Larkin 94, 97, 99
  Neal 91
  Wiat 89, 98
  Wm. 91, 95, 99
  Wm. (Jr.) 95
Cliet, Jesse 61
Clifton, Jno. 67
Cline, Abram 42
  Jonathan 42
Cliot, Jonithan 61
Cloud, Eliz. 173
  Ezekiel 73, 165
  Jeremiah 173
  Jno. 99, 165, 173
  Noah 88
  Sarah 173
  Ziak 96
Clough, Geo. 20, 111,
  129, 161
Clower, Jno. 108
Club, Jas. 103
  Wm. 103, 105
Clubb, Eliz. 105, 106
  Geo. 103, 105, 107
  Jas. 103, 105, 107
  Selah 105
  Thos. 103, 106, 107
  Wm. 103, 104, 105,
  106, 107
Cluff, Geo. 129
Clunt, Jas. 158
Clyatt, Isaac 59
  Jas. 35, 42, 67
  Sarah 35
Clyatte, Jas. 29
  Sarah 29
Coale, Wm. 42
Coales, Wm. 29
Coan, Wm. 147
Coates, Harwell 16
  Jesse 13
Coats, Lasley 154
  Lesley 117
Cobb, Benj. 158
  Danl. 61
  Ezekiel 165
  Harriet 138
  Howell 57
  Japhet 138
  Jas. 103, 154
  Jepheth 134
  Jno. 58, 99, 161
  Liout 158
  Rachel 165
Cobbet, Eliz. 42
Cobbison, Ann 147
  Jno. 140, 147
Cobbs, Frederick 64
  Howell 99
  Jno. 64, 98, 99, 117,
  150
  Thos. 117
Cochran, (?) 42
  Abner 115, 120
  Jas. 31, 33
  Jno. 120, 129, 165,
  172
  Marah 172
  Nancy 115
  Pickens 120
  Reubin 128
  Saml. 172
  Wm. 73, 84, 111, 120,
  127

Cock, Caleb 15
  Zebulon 15, 161
Cockbun, Geo. 80
Cockburn, Archable 94
  Ezek. 106
  Geo. 80, 94, 98, 165
Cocke, Nathl. 20, 142,
  147, 150
  Richd. 152
  Whitman 170
  Zebulon 154
Cockerham, Jas. 154
Cockraham, David 147
Cockran, Jno. 117
  Wm. 117
Cocks, Henry 16
  Wm. 157, 165
Coddington, C. B. 132
  F. 35, 134
  Francis 33, 132, 136,
  138
Coe, Joshua 61
Coffee, Nathan 94, 98,
  99
  P. 120
  Peter 108, 111
Coffey, Mary 97
  Nathan 97
Coffield, Gresham 16
Cofield, Graham 13
Cohen, Jacob 29
  Judith 31
  Moses 31, 39
  Philip 29
  Philip Jacob 29
Coil, Jas. 75
  Jno. 84, 96
Coit, Jno. 42
Coker, Isaac 74, 75, 78,
  85
Colbert, Jas. 85
  Nicodemus 74, 99
  Rich. 87
  Susanna 76
  Thos. 80, 87
  Tukedmark 80
Coldmon, Curtis 158
Coldwell, Jane 58
Cole, Allice 134
  Jas. 134
  Jas. A. 103
  Jno. 42, 103, 104,
  106, 173
  Jno. (Jr.) 173
  Josiah 91
  Mark 134
  Thos. 150
  Wm. 91, 161, 175
Coleman, Anna 147
  Caleb 147
  Chas. 125
  Eden 91
  Francis 2
  Harry 42
  Harry (Jr.) 42
  Jacob 7
  Jas. 78, 87
  Jno. 7, 28, 76, 80,
  82, 83, 91
  Jonathan 154, 161
  Levin 42
  Moses 7
  Paul 64
  Peter 42, 107
  Reuben 145, 147
  Sarah 64
  Susannah 64, 151
  Thompson 99, 175

Coleman (cont.)
  Thos. 165
Colemon, Jno. 27
  Wm. 16
Colhoon, Aquilla 10
Colisseaux, Peter 42
Collage, Margaret 64
Collee, Micader 103
Collers, Mathew 74
Collert, Wm. 61
Colley, Anderson 42
  Jas. 165
Collier, Benj. 42
  Edw. 165
  Jno. 59, 91, 142
  Thos. 57
Collins, Catherine 131
  Cornelius 33, 138
  Jas. 99
  Jno. 58, 83, 87, 142,
  161
  Jonathan 63
  Jos. 7
  Levin 140
  Peter 165
  Saml. 2
  Stephen 142
  Willis 7
  Wm. 85, 161
  Zach. 85, 165
  Zachariah 73, 76, 83,
  88
Colson, Abraham 76, 81
  Abram 85
  Nancy 81
  Sanders 154, 161
  Wm. 71
Colter, Uriah 138
  Wm. 158
Colton, Richd. 91
Columbus, Lewis 42
Colvin, Thos. 61
Combs, Jas. 128, 175
  Jno. 173, 175
  Philip 165, 175
  Sterling 175
Comer, Anderson 111,
  115, 116, 120
  Chas. 16
  Jas. 108, 120
  Jno. (Jr.) 91
Comins, David 154
  Eleazer 154
Compstock, Jno. 42
Cone, Aaron 67, 72
  Jno. 59
  Middleton 59
  Saml. 59
  Wm. 59, 64, 67, 148,
  151, 153
Conklin, Henry 27
Conn, Geo. 147
Connell, Danl. 145
  Eliz. 150
  Jesse 120, 154
  Jno. 11
  Thos. 145
Connelly, Jno. Wm. 154
Conner, Chas. 7, 16
  Danl. 108, 117, 161
  Jeremiah 111
  Jno. 11
  Jos. 2
  Martha 11
  Simon 30, 35
  Wm. 140, 142
Connerway, Jeremiah 106
Connor, Bryan 42

Connor (cont.)
  Geo. 42
  Jno. 95
  McMillion M. 95
  Simon 32, 33, 42
Conway, Phillip 84
Conyers, Jno. 2
  Jno. (Jr.) 2
  Jno. (Sr.) 2
  Steph. 24
Cook, Benj. 67, 73, 85,
  88, 111
  Benj. (Jr.) 85
  Danl. J. 42
  Deborah 76
  Dudley 85
  Edoshus 80
  Endosine 85
  Fra 85
  Francis 73, 76, 80, 84
  G. 26
  Geo. 16, 24, 85
  Jas. 42, 76, 78, 80,
    87, 88
  Jno. 85
  Jos. 98, 111
  Joshua 16
  Josiah 85
  Lewis 72
  Reuben 85, 159
  Reubin 88
  Robt. 105
  Sarah 76
  Smith 84, 85
  Tho. 85
  Thos. 74, 75
  Wm. 42, 85, 89
Cooke, Jas. 67, 74, 88
  Jas. Watson 74, 88
  Reuben 74
Coolidge, (?) 42
Cooper, Cannon 16
  Elijah 111, 130
  Elisha 111
  Frederick 7
  Henry 175
  Jno. 105, 136, 138,
    161
  Jos. 69, 73, 108, 175
  Mary 138
  Richd. 138
  Saml. 60
  Thos. 108, 169, 175,
    178
Coosan, Peter 42
Cooxy, Wm. 161
Cope, Adam 42
  Chas. 42
  Jno. 72
  Rosannah 42
Copeland, (?) 7
  Jas. 16, 67, 105, 106,
    107
  Jno. 165
  Richd. 111
Coppat, Aime 42
Coppe, (?) (Madam) 42
  Madam 42
Coquilion, Francis B. 42
Corbert, Jas. 42
Corbet, Richd. 11
Cord, Danl. 44
Corethers, Robt. 78
Corker, David 24, 135
  David R. 138
  Edw. 104
  Edwd. 130
  Jas. 138

Corker (cont.)
  Jesse 137
  Nathan 138
  Steph. 104
  Stephen 138
Corley, Edmond 120
Cornelieson, Jno. Allen
  42
Cornelion, Geo. 28
Cornelison, Jno. 56, 142
Cornelius, Benj. 21, 24
Cornelous, Jno. 42
Cornelus, Geo 26
Cornett, Eli 60
Cornick, Jos. 35
Corry, Alexdr. 111
  Robt. 111, 125
Cosby, Chas. 85, 88
  D. 85
  Henry 88
  Hickerson 170, 175
  Jas. 74
  Jno. 88
  R. 82
  Richmond 85
  Robt. 76, 80, 85, 88
  S. 100
Cossey, Wm. 120
Costy, Jesse 7
Cothan, Thos. 91
Cothers, Wm. 78
Cothral, Josiah 175
Cothron, Jno. 84
Cothum, Eliz. 97
  Thos. 97
Cotter, Jno. 85
Coulter, Chas. 80, 82
  Francis 76
  Jesse 120, 128
  Richd (Jr.) 78
  Richd. 74, 81
  Sarah 76
  Seara 80
Couper, Jno. 134, 138
Couplen, Coulston 108
Course, (?) (Mrs.) 42
  Daniel 30
  Danl. 32, 35
  Eliz. 32
  Jno. 30, 35, 165
  Mary 32
  Saml. 63
  Wm. 32, 33, 152
Coursey, (?) (Cpt.) 7
  Wm. 10, 14
Courson, Wm. 21, 26
Courtenay, Jno. 42
Courter, Harmon 32
Courton, Richd. 149
Courvoisie, Francis 32,
  33, 35, 42
  Mary 32
Cousins, Chas. 63
  Jas. 59
  Wm. 64
Covington, Jno. 147, 175
  Jos. 147
Cowan, Edw. 42
Coward, Jas. 7
Cowart, Elias 111, 116
Cowden, Jas. 173
  Robt. 165
Cowdon, Robt. 76, 80
Cowen, Edw. 7
  Geo. 120
  Wm. 154, 165
Cowens, Eleazer 154
Cowin, Wm. 149

Cowles, Wm. 140, 153
Cowling, Slaughter 30,
  42
Cox, Calib 142
  Casper 42
  Henry 56, 154, 161
  Jas. 7
  Jasper 67
  Jesse 80, 117
  Jno. 154
  Josiah 161
  Martin 142
  Mary 97
  Spence 42
  Thos. 95, 97, 98, 102
  Wm. 42, 154, 159, 161
Coxe, Jno. 33
  Jonathan 35
Cozart, Elias 129
Crabb, Asa 142
Crabtree, Jas. 175
  Jno. 170
Craddox, Saml. 67
Crafford, Oliver 78
Craford, Jno. 27, 28
Craft, D. 42
Crain, Joel 98, 102
Cramer, Ann Catherine 69
  Christopher 69
Crance, Lewis 61
Crane, Joel 95
  Lewis 147
  Matthew 42
  Wm. 95
Cranford, Saml. 120
Crapps, Jno. 42
Crawdie, (?) 42
Crawford, A. 63
  Alexdr. 70
  Anderson 56, 57, 60,
    64, 142, 145, 150
  Arthur 74
  Chas. 57, 60, 64, 67,
    142, 151
  David 148
  Frances 145
  Francis 64
  Jno. 22, 25, 26, 59,
    61
  Joe 145
  Joel 148
  Mary (Mrs.) 70
  Mr. 63
  Nathan 145
  Nelson 60, 64
  Peter 57, 58, 91, 150
  Robt. 138, 142
  Sarah 170
  Strauder 2
  Wm. 42, 60
Creaff, Wm. 175
Credille, (?) 120
  Thos. 58, 111, 116
Cree, Moses 103, 104,
  106, 107
Creel, Thos. 111
Creemor, Wm. 64
Creighton, E. 42
  Edw. 42
Crenshaw, Maybourn 74
Creswell, David 73, 100
  Saml. 91
Crews, Isaac 22
  Jno. 7, 26
  Thos. 102
  Thos. (Cpt.) 94
Cribbs, Gilbert 120
  Thos. 115, 120

Criddle, Thos. 154
Criswell, David 149, 161
Crittendon, Thos. 140
Crittenton, Jno. 154
Crocker, Thos. 120
Crocket, Robt. 74
  Saml. 74
Croft, Jno. 136
Crook, Jonathan 140, 142
  Thos. 11
Crookshank, Patrick 42
Crookshanks, Chas. 35
  Patrick 30, 35
Croome, Elijah 161
Crosby, Geo. 154, 161
  Jno. 76, 80, 82
  Thos. 140
Crossley, Jno. 80
Crother, Jno. 157
Crouder, Robt. 88
Crow, Hannah 81
  Jas. 78, 82
  Jos. 85
Crowder, Jno. 88
Crowell, Ezra 42
Crowley, Pleney 140
Crozier, Alexdr. 16
  Jane 20
  Jno. 7, 16
Cruger, Nicholas 42
Crum, Harmon 70, 73
  Sol. 103, 104, 107
Crumb, Sol. 103
Cruse, Jno. 22
Crutchfield, Geo. 80
  Richd. 2
Cryer, Morgan 19
  Tho. 20, 23, 25, 26
  Thos. 19
  Wm. 20, 22, 24, 25,
    26, 28
Cryher, Morgan 26
Cuddy, Geo. 42
Cuins, Jacob 26
Culbertson, David 91,
  109
Culbreath, Jane 58
  Jas. 60, 142
  Jno. 64, 142
  Peter 58, 64, 151
  Thos. 142
Culbreth, Jane 60
  Peter 60
Cullen, David 88
Culpepper, Chas. 159
  Jno. 161, 170
  Malachiah 91
  Sampson 140, 154
  Wm. 140
Culver, Celethiel 126
  Joshua 126
  Nathl. 158
Culwell, Jno. 63
Cumble, Antony 158
Cumming, Jno. 33
  Lawrence 39
  Tho. 64
  Thos. 106, 147, 150
Cummings, (?) 42
  Eleazer 161
  Jno. 42
  Robt. 159
Cummins, Thos. 107
Cuncan, Jas. 44
  Wm. 117
Cunes, Jacob 42
Cuningham, Alexdr. 42
  Jos. 96

Cunningham, Ann 76
  Harry 42
  J. 80
  Jane 172
  Jno. 35, 76, 80, 84,
    87, 91, 100, 125
  Pat 172
  Wm. 165, 175
Cunnom, Chas. 137
Cunns, Jacob 28
Cup, Barbara 115
  Michael 91, 115
Cupp, Michael 120
Cureton, Boland 165
  Wm. 111
Curient, Nicholas 42
Curiton, Wm. (Jr.) 120
Currey, Larkin 84
Currie, Jno. 33, 35, 64
Curry, (?) 128
  --h 128
  Alexdr. 108, 120, 128
  Carey 2
  David 154, 161
  Jno. 43, 157
  L. W. 85
  Nicholas 16
  Robt. 117, 120
  Wm. 120, 126, 128
Cusack, Sarah 43
Cuthbert, Geo. 43
  Jas. 43
  Jas. (Dr.) 43
  Jos. 32, 35, 43
  Lewis 43
  Penelope (Mrs.) 43
Cuyler, Jeremiah 11, 70
  T. 35
  Telamon 13
Cuylers, H. 16
Cuzart, Elias 120, 128
D'Scheuber, I. H. 43
Dabbs, Jos. 91, 100
Dabney, Christian 7
  Wm. 16
Dacosta, Sarah 43
Dadd, Jesse 165
Dailey, Jno. 80
  Saml. 85
Daily, Jno. 151
Dale, Robt. 120, 128
  Saml. 126
Dallas, Angus 152
  Maria 152
  Wm. 23, 24
Dallis, Wm. 26
Dalton, Christian 112
Daly, Benj. 67, 71
Dameron, Jno. 154
  Saml. 43
Dameson, Jno. 161
Dampier, Stephen 104
Danale, Wm. 117
Danelly, Frances 142
  Jas. 64, 142
Daniel, Allen 78, 80
  Bengamin 158
  Chas. 120, 158
  Conner 159
  Edw. 108
  Elias (Jr.) 2
  Eustace 120
  Ezekiel 158, 159
  Hopkins 175
  Jas. 120
  Jno. 2, 43, 140, 161
  Nancy 76, 82
  Thos. 108, 120

Daniel (cont.)
  Wm. 64, 76, 78, 82,
    85, 91, 108, 120,
    165
Daniell, Benj. 154, 161
  Chas. 20, 91, 112, 129
  Edmund 117
  Estace 128
  Eustus 129
  Jas. 115
  Levi 117
  Mary 115
  Sarah 112
  Tho. 20
  Thos. 91, 112, 116,
    128, 129
  Wm. 91, 100, 112, 115,
    117, 128, 165
Daniells, Wm. 129
Danielly, Jno. 154
Danily, Andrew 175
Dannard, Jacob 154
Dansmore, Patrick 2
Danworth, Peter 135
Darby, Jno. 16
Darcey, Benj. 2
  Jno. 56
  Joel 2
  Jos. 56
Darcy, Jos. 11
Darden, Geo. 73, 88
  Jno. 76, 98
Dardins, Jno. 161
Daricott, Wm. 175
Darling, Eliz. 135
  Euphenie 135
Darnel, Henry 43
  Wm. 43
Darracott, Rebecca 170
Darsey, Benj. 14
  Jos. 64
Dasher, Benj. 67
  Christian 72
  Jno. M. 67, 72
  Jno. Martin 70, 71, 72
  Martin 70
Dassey, Jas. 136
Daugherty, Niel 64
  Patrick 64
Daughtrey, Chris. 95
Davenport, Jno. 2, 16
  Joel 7
  Richd. 165
Daves, Patsy 172
  Thos. 129
David, Anne 11
  Jno. 80
  Wiley 100
  Wm. 11
Davidson, Jas. 63
  Jno. 2
  Robt. 151
  Wm. 43, 151
Davies, Benj. 43
  Edw. 35
  Eliz. 43
  Francis 16
  Jno. 16, 43
  Jno. M. 43
  Jos. 43
  Richd. 43
  Sarah 43
  Thos. 43
  Willis 14
  Wm. 7, 43
  Wm. Jno. 43
  Wm. John 20
Davis, Abiatha 140

Davis (cont.)
  Abiathar 142, 147
  Absalom 115, 165
  Absolom 74, 83
  Ann 71
  Augustin 165
  Benj. 2, 10, 11, 16,
    76, 149
  Blandford 63
  Blanford 61
  Clementine 56, 60
  Clementius 142
  David 14, 70, 73
  Foster 64
  Francis 43
  Gehazi 2
  Geo. 20
  Gideon 83
  Isaac 85
  Jas. 2, 67, 109, 149
  Jno. 2, 11, 13, 64,
    67, 70, 140, 142,
    165
  Jno. (Jr.) 165
  Jos. 64, 70
  Joseth 61
  Joshua 175
  Kehaze 56
  Larkin 84
  Lewis 74
  Mary 2
  Miles 14
  Moses 88, 175
  Nancy 115
  Peter 43
  Rody 78
  Saml. 170
  Suckey 76
  Susannah 148
  Theophilus 147
  Tho. 7, 63
  Thos. 125, 161
  Vachel 61
  W-- 10
  Wiley 80, 83
  Wm. 30, 43, 67, 70,
    74, 88, 100, 173
  Wm. Hackney 76
Dawson, Britton 147, 152
  David 140
  Eliz. 11
  Geo. 112, 117
  Jas. 108, 161
  Jno. 11, 43, 96
  Lemuel Gulliver 24
  Martin 165
  Richd. 30, 43
  Richmond 91, 154
  Thos. 43
  Wm. 22, 26, 28
Day, Ambrose 91
  Jno. 61
  Jos. 32, 33, 38
  Jos. (Maj.) 39
  Richd. 7
  Stephen 64
  Stephen (Jr.) 63
De La Villabucker,
    Nicholas Francis
    Magon 33
DeChapedelaine, Hyacinth
    43
DeChesse', Aubert Jas.
    43
DeChessee, (?) 43
DeCosta, Abraham 32
DeGlaubick, Baron 39
DeJernett, R. 173

DeLamotta, Emanuel 33
DeLyon, Abraham 35
  Isaac 32, 33
  Reina 32
DeMiklasruveitz, Felix
    132
DePriest, Jno. 86
Deadwiler, Chris. 88
Deadwyler, Jos. 86
Deale, Peter 175
Dean, Chas. 165
  Jacob 64
  Jas. 7
  Jno. 117, 142
  Jos. 32
  Luke 2
  Seth 2
  Steph. 32, 43
Deane, Jos. 43
Dearizeaux, Stephen 154
Dearmond, Ann 152
Deas, David 43
  DeWitt 154
  Jas. 154
Deason, Jno. 161
  Rachael 154
Debosk, Peter (Cpt.) 161
Dechenaus, Thos. 43
Dedgings, Jere 173
Deem, Jno. 140
Dees, Duett 161
Delacaze, Jos. 43
Delacrois, Jean Francois
    43
Delaney, Lewis 61
Delany, Thos. 39
Delarocque, Jane 43
Delaroque, Jno. 32, 33
Delarue, D. 43
Delavaver, Frances 33
Delavel, Jos. 43
Delbose, Jno. 43
Delegal, David 132
  Philip 43
Delegall, David 138
  David (Sr.) 38
Deleion, David 43
Delk, David 30
  Jos. 158, 161
Dell, Dorothy 71
  Phillip 71, 165
Deloach, Hardy 67
Deloache, Hardy (Sr.) 67
Delveoque, Jno. 43
Delyon, (?) (Mrs.) 43
  Abrah. 43
  Abraham 43
Dement, Absalom 43
Demere, Mary 30, 33
  Mary (Mrs.) 43
  Mary Eliz. 30
  Raymond 30, 32, 33,
    39, 43, 104, 105,
    106, 107, 133
  Raymond (Jr.) 103, 104
  Raymond (Sr.) 103, 104
Demey, Jno. 94
  Josiah 94
Demsey, Jno. 100
Denison, Gideon 130
Denman, Jas. 170
Denmark, Stephen 67, 72
  Wm. 67
Denmon, Jas. 95
Dennard, Shadrack 158
  Wm. 157, 159
Dennis, Abram 16
  Jno. 16, 159, 161

Dennis (cont.)
  Nicholas Jos. 43
  Richd. 43
Dennison, Gideon 132,
    133, 134
Densler, Catherine
    Barbary 30
  Henry 30, 43
  Michael 30, 35, 38, 43
  Philip 43
Dent, Geo. 63
  Peter 120
Denton, Wm. 142
Depart, Eliz. 151
Depee, Wm. 175
Deprest, Jas. 94
Depriest, Jno. 76, 78,
    80, 87, 100
  Randolph 89
Derdains, Jno. 161
Deschmettaux, (?)
    (Madam) 43
  Madam 43
Deusht, Geo. 112
Devant, Eliz. 43
  Thos. 43
Deveaux, Ann 30, 43
  Jno. Bermers 30
  Peter 32, 35, 43
  Wm. 30, 35, 43
  Wm. Fairchild 30
Devereaux, Saml. N. 126
Deville, Jno. 43
Devin, Alexdr. 112
  Eliz. 112
  Jos. 112
  Lucy 112
Devine, Jas. 107
Dews, Jno. 43
Dial, Saml. 43
Diamond, Jno. 91, 112
  Wm. 91
Dick, Jno. 43
  Robt. 148, 151, 165
Dickens, Jno. 165
Dickerson, Wimbowin 120
Dickey, Patrick 2
Dickinson, Jere. 135
  Jeremiah 43
  Jno. D. 43
Dickison, Joel 120
Dicks, Alexdr. 35
  Andrew 36
  Jno. 7
Dickson, Arthur Bridge
    78
  David 117
  Jno. 2, 7, 34, 130,
    133
  Jos. 7
  Michael 67, 71
  Michel 154
  Reuben 158, 161
  Reubin 157
  Robt. 67, 70, 71, 120
Die, Thos. 157
Diedrick, Nicholas 43
Dikes, Geo. 68, 145
  Georges (Sr.) 145
  Jesse 145
  Levi 145
  Martha 145
  Mary 145
  Noah 145
  Rebecca 145
  Unity 145
Dill, Peter 178
  Phillip 68

Dillard, Nicholas 154
Tho. 15
Thos. 2, 10
Dillingham, Simeon 24,
25, 26, 28
Simon 22
Dillon, Ann Mary 43
Edmond 34
Edmund 30
Jno. 43
Robt. 43
Dilworth, Jas. 24
Jno. 23, 26, 28, 103
Dimond, Jno. 170, 175
Dinney, Robt. 7
Dismuke, Reuben 120
Dismukes, Wm. 165
Divine, Jas. 58, 106
Jno. 43
Dix, Andrew 130
Tandy 175
Dixon, Ann 145
Caroline McD. 145
David 120
Henry 145
J. L. 117
Jas. 43
Jno. 58
Jno. Lydell 145
Maria Felishia 145
Michel 161
Robt. 145, 147, 154
Sarah Parks 145
Thos. 161
Tillman 145
Wm. 43, 120
Dixton, Robt. 16
Doane, Nehamiah 25
Nemiah 20
Dobb, Jno. 117
Dobbins, Jane 109
Wm. 109, 120
Dobbs, Elias 89
Jno. 89
Jos. 91, 94
Josiah 89
Lodday 95
Loddy 100
Silas 84, 89
Doddere, Saml. 43
Doddson, Isaac 112, 120
Joshua 120
Dodreel, Noe 120
Dodril, Noel 126
Dodson, Jno. 43
Wm. 43
Doggett, Geo. 96
Doggitt, Will 96
Doherty, Jas. 26
Dollaghan, Thos. 43
Dollar, Jno. 136, 138
Jno. (Jr.) 135
Jno. (Sr.) 135
Dolly, London 43
Quash 43
Domini, Frederick 161
Donaldson, Wm. 43
Donelson, Jane 2
Jean 2
Robt. 2
Dongar, Philip 157
Doniphan, Gerard 43
Donnaly, Jno. 161
Donnelly, Francis 161
Jas. 140
Donny, Wm. 105
Donworth, Mary 134, 138
Patrick 138

Donworth (cont.)
Peter 136, 138
Doolen, Daniel 100
Danl. 91
Jno. 91
Dooly, Geo. 76
Doorman, Hugh 43
Doors, Jas. 43
Dopson, Jos. R. 43
Dorrel, Saml. 28
Samuel 26
Tho. 26
Thos. 43
Dorsett, Eleanor 58
Jno. 58, 64
Jno. (Sr.) 60
Dorsey, (?) (Col.) 39
Larkin 64
Leakin 150
Seakin 64
Thos. 36
Thos. E. 36
Doss, Crisler 175
Jno. 140
Joel 100
Stephen 165
Dougharty, Margareth 43
Warren (Mrs.) 43
Dougherty, Alex. 151
Chas. 125
Jno. 63, 151
Jno. (Sr.) 151
Jos. 68
Neill 151
Niel 63
Patrick 151
Doughety, Neal 58
Doughtery, Jacob 70, 73
Doughton, Wm. 96
Doughty, Jos. 76, 165
Simon 43
Douglas, Alexdr. 7
Andrew 25, 28
Edw. 2
Edwd. 154
Eliz. 7
Jno. 64
Nancy 2
Robt. 2
Tho. 16
Wm. 10, 15, 16
Wright 7
Douglass, Edwd. 161
Jas. 70, 71
Douther, Wm. 58
Dowder, Richd. 161
Dowdey, Richd. 154
Dowdle, Jas. 112, 120
Dowdy, Richd. 149
Dowell, Peter 43
Thos. 43
Dowies, Hugh 39
Dowl, Tho. 30
Downey, Huze 7
Downs, Ambrose 59, 91,
97
Geo. 142
Henry 175
Jeremiah 43
Jno. 64
Jonathan 175, 178
Richd. 59
Sabra 97
Dowse, Gideon 131, 136,
138
Doyle, Dennis 43
Francis 36, 43
Dozier, Jas. 65

Dozier (cont.)
Jno. 165
Drake, Tho. 16
Wm. 159
Drane, Walker 140
Walter 57, 147
Walton 60
Wm. 65
Draper, Jno. 153
Draughon, Biol 7
Drawdy, Danl. (Jr.) 7
Dreed, Wm. 14
Drennen, Danl. 140
Dresler, Chas. 34
Drew, Josiah 161
Wm. 15
Driggers, Jno. 68
Drisdale, Alexdr. 138
Drouillard, Andrew 43
Drummond, Walter 142
DuBignon, Poulain 107
DuBoys, Francis 20
DuCord, Bouyer 43
Dubbin, Wm. 130
Dubose, Isaac 2, 14
Duck, Jeremiah 149
Ducla, Jno. Baptist 43
Maria Louise 43
Dudlee, Wm. 78
Dudley, Edw. 103
Jas. 74, 86, 87
Jno. 74, 105
Wm. 82, 86, 88
Duff, Jas. 26
Duger, Hamson 43
Dugless, Andrew 20
Duke, Buckner 175
Green 44
Jno. 20, 24
Taylor 175
Dukes, Buckner 165
Danl. 7
Henry 161
Jno. 72
Susannah 2
Dumoussay, Frances Marie
Louis 34
Marie Loys 33
Dumoussy, Francis 44
Dun, Thos. 158
Dunagain, Joshua 94
Duncan, Andrew 2
David 132, 136, 138
Henry 76, 78
Jas. 44
Joanna 76
Mark 76
Mary 76
Matthew 58, 150, 151
Wm. 117
Dunham, Chas. 138
Jas. 138
Mary 138
Dunkon, Henry 91
Dunlap, Jos. 36, 44
Dunmphin, Jas. 7
Dunn, Alexdr. 115
Benj. 61
Geo. 30
Jno. 7, 13, 80, 109,
112, 128, 135, 159
Jos. 61, 116
Nehemiah 65, 142
Simon 117
Tabitha 115
Tho. 7
Waters 58
Wm. 14, 165

Dunneven, Jas. 44
Dunwody, Jas. 136
Dunwoody, Jas. 138
  Robt. 68
Dupies, Wm. 68
Dupoys, Jos. 170
Durcis, Marie Magdalene
  44
Durden, Elisha 61, 142
  Jesse 44
  Josiah 61
Durgan, Wm. (Sr.) 11
Durham, Matthew 2
  Nathan 100
Durkee, Nathl. 24, 63,
  91
  Wm. 63
Durkie, Nathl. 91
Durousseaux, Peter 44
Durr, Geo. 34, 44
Durrah, Jno. 44
Durrance, Francis 68
Durrence, Wm. 68, 72
Dushe, Peter 26
Duty, Littleton 175
  Richd. 175
Dye, Hopkins 2
  Ralph 14
Dyer, Elijah 2
Dykes, Jesse 70
  Levi 70
Dysart, Charity 150
  Cornelius 150
  Jno. 165
Eades, Jno. 61
  Tho. 63
Eads, Jesse 165
  Jno. 56, 165
  Mary 98
  Sol. 100
Eady, Jno. 165
Ealy, Wm. 173
Eammis, Jonathan 161
Earls, Will 120
Early, Betsy 100
  Jacob 100
  Jeffery 98
  Jeffry 165
  Jno. 98
Earnest, Geo. 154
Easley, Benj. 96
  Chloe 112
  D. W. 112
  Danl. 91, 125
  Thos. 112
Easleys, Ben (Cpt.) 96
Easly, Jno. 96
  R. 91
Eason, Jno. 22, 25, 28,
  106
  Robt. 22
  Wm. 22, 27, 28
East, Jos. 98, 165
Easter, Augustus 16
  Elisha 2
  Ephraim 2
  Jas. 75, 88
  Jno. 80
  Rich 88
  Robt. 74
  Sarah 75
  Wm. 80
Eastis, Elisha 2
Easton, Chas. 74, 88
  Edw. 44
  Jno. 88
  Reubin 88
  Richd. 84

Easton (cont.)
  Sally 88
Eastus, Augustus 16
Eastwood, Elijah 2
  Elisha 7
  Israel 2
Eavenson, Eli 86
Eaverhurt, Jacob 80
Eberhart, David 78
  Jacob 178
Echols, Benj. 91, 97,
  98, 100
  Betse 100
  Sabra 97
Ector, Hugh 165
Edds, Joel 95
Edmonds, Jas. 7, 91
  Jno. 165, 175
Edmondson, Jos. 63
  Richd. 120
Edmonson, Humphry 173
  Jno. 165
Eds, Isaac 94
Edwards, Catherine 142
  Jno. 103, 107, 175
  Jos. 95, 100, 102
  Reuben 165, 173
  Reubin 129
  Susannah 76, 82
  Wm. 10, 14, 15, 76,
  82, 175
  Wm. (Cpt.) 7
Egan, Wm. 142
Ege, Jacob 150
Ehrhard, David 44
  Jacob 44
Eidson, Jno. 175
Eiland, Absalom 154
  Jno. 117
Eimbeck, Ann (Mrs.) 44
Eirick, Catherine 36
  Cumba 44
  Jno. 44
Ekels, Joel 158
Ekridge, Eliz. 1
  Ezekiel 1
Elam, Daniel 57
  Danl. 57, 91, 145, 151
  Wm. 151
Elands, Absalom 154
Elbert, Eliz. 30, 39
  Saml. 30, 142
Elder, Joshua 100
Elese, Robt. 91
Elfe, Thos. 38
Eliott, Archabel 125
  Robt. 125
  Wm. 125
Elkins, Jonas 44
Ellace, Walter 108
Ellerbee, (?) 44
  Edw. 44
Ellerson, Jas. 91
Ellery, Isham 8
Ellet, Drury 16
  Wm. 16
Ellington, Stephen 75,
  80
Elliot, Henry 16
  Wm. 28, 78
Elliott, Alex. 26
  Alexdr. 28
  Amos 13, 133, 135
  Andrew 75
  Benj. 170, 175
  Jas. 75
  Jno. 136, 137, 138,
  142

Elliott (cont.)
  Jno. (Jr.) 138
  R. (Mrs.) 138
  Renchie 137
  Rich. 28
  Richd. 22, 26
  Richd. M. J. 24
  Saml. 8
  Sarah 77
  Steph. 44
  Thos. 132, 135, 138,
  175
  Wm. 2, 10, 15, 26, 27,
  44, 77, 83, 91, 100,
  142, 173
Ellis, --ese 120
  Chas. 80, 172
  Edw. 44
  Ephram 158
  Henry 44
  Jas. 159
  Jno. 172
  Jos. 172
  Joshua 120
  Robt. 82
  Sol. 57
  Thos. 44
  Walter 116, 120
  Wm. 44
  Zachariah 44
Ellison, David 98
  Robt. 2, 15
Ellot, Andrew 86
Ells, Jno. 80
Elon, Ann 36
  Elisha 34, 36, 44
Elrod, Hannah 165
  Jas. 165
Elsberry, Benj. 170
  Benj. (Jr.) 170
  Jeremiah 165
  Jos. 165
Elsbury, Benj. 178
  Benj. (Jr.) 178
  Jos. 178
  Michael 178
Ely, Wm. 172
Elzy, Michael 72
Emanuel, Amos 2
  Asa 16, 30, 34, 71
  Asa (Col.) 12
  David 2, 12, 160
  Jno. 13
  Jno. (Cpt.) 7
  Levi 12, 16
Embree, Jno. 170
Embrey, Wm. 165
Embry, Jesse 2
  Jno. 100
  Jonathan 91
  Jos. 170
  Nancy 100
  Wm. 170
Emmerson, Robt. 149
Emmett, Jas. 65, 91
English, Benj. 44
  Corneluis 161
  Henry 117, 125, 173
  Jno. 158
  Menas 174
  Thos. 44, 154
Ennis, Andrew 147
  Andrews 148
Enoe, Geo. 44
Eppinger, Barbarah 30
  Geo. 44
  Jas. 44
  Jno. 30, 44

Eppinger (cont.)
Jno. (Jr.) 44
Matthew 44
Epsie, Jas. 147
Wm. 147
Ernest, Jno. Balthazer
34
Ernst, Christina 44
Ervin, David 165
Eskridges, Hetor R. 161
Espey, Jas. 125, 154
Jos. 125
Thos. 112, 125
Espy, Thos. 100
Estes, Asa 98
Jno. 100
Richd. 100
Ethemton, Wm. 56
Eton, Jno. 26
Eubank, (?) (Maj.) 151
Daniel 2
Geo. 16
Major 151
Richd. 165
Stephen 19
Eubanks, Danl. 8
Richd. 96, 104, 142
Stephen 107
Stephens 104
Thos. 8
Eupperson, Saml. 96
Evand, David 44
Evans, (?) (Maj.) 73
Benj. 116
Daniel 2
Daniel (Col.) 6
Danl. 14, 16, 44, 140,
142, 165
Danl. (Cpt.) 7
David 154
E. 63
Eliz. 63
Harwood 91
Henry 63, 91, 142
Jno. 16, 59, 142, 149
Jos. 56
Lucy Williamson 151
Major 73
Martha 30
Mordecai 16, 151
Richd. 151
Robt. 161
Saml. 44
Sarah 44, 150
Stephen 147, 150, 151
Susannah 63
Wm. 65, 112
Wm. M. 44
Evarts, Fredrk. 44
Evens, Geo. 77
Everage, Marmaduke 68
Everett, Jno. 68, 72
Everingham, Hannah 147
Jno. 147
Everitt, Jno. 68, 130
Evins, Nathan 88
Wm. 20
Ewen, Wm. 44
Ewing, Jos. 22
Mary 32
Wm. 32, 34, 44
Wm. A. D. 82
Exley, Jno. 44
Fabain, Jno. 107
Fabian, Jno. 105
Jonathan 138
Fabin, Jno. 106
Fablan, Jno. 105

Fagan, Geo. 161
Faham, Jacob 44
Fahm, Frederick 36
Fredrk. 44
Fail, Arthur 140
Jepthey 157
Thos. 154
Failey, Thos. 56
Faily, Thos. 142
Fain, Chas. 73
Peter 175
Wm. 125
Fair, Saml. 2
Fairchild, Abraham 16
Fairchilds, Abihud (?)
97
Falkner, Wm. 84
Faming, Chevalier Noel
36
Fannin, Benj. 86
Jno. Hubberd 82
Laughlin 86, 88
Fanning, Jno. 91
Saml. 13
Fanshaw, Elijah 20
Farer, Parent 80
Faries, Geo. 36, 44
Farish, Robt. 145
Farley, Jno. 44
Saml. 132
Farmer, Abner 126
Benj. 142
David 2
Geo. 15, 16
Saml. 16
Thos. 157
Wm. 2, 91, 142
Farnall, Tho. 14
Farniel, Danl. 8
Farr, Peter 158
Wm. 107
Farrar, Eliz. 133
Field 132
Fields 147
Farrer, Absalom 65
Farrow, Britton 78
Jesse 2
Jno. 32, 36, 78
Micajah 78
Needham 78
Perin 77
Rosetta 36
Sally 78
Wilie 78
Fauche, Jonas 161
Faulconer, Jacob 154
Faulkner, Chas. 44
Faver, Jacob 175
Favors, Wm. 161
Fawner, Benj. 120
Fean, Jno. 14
Fears, Absolom 142, 151
Featherstone, Howell 154
Fee, Jno. 56, 140
Fell, Eliz. 32
Frederick Shick 34
Isaac 32, 34, 44
Fellsday, Thos. 175
Felnniken, Jas. 110
Felps, David 165
Felt, Eliz. 34
Isaac 34
Felts, Jno. 172
Fendin, Susannah 32
Fenley, Archibald 26
Fenn, Jno. 2, 13, 16, 36
Jno. (Cpt.) 7
Travis 2

Fenn (cont.)
Wm. 13
Fennell, Jno. 172
Fenny, Wm. 15, 16
Zach. 16
Fenshaw, Eliza 27
Fenwick, Jno. 145
Fergus, Jno. 84, 100,
165
Ferguson, John 82
Jos. 140, 142
Ferm, Zachariah 8
Fernandez, (?) 44
David 23, 24
Rachel 23
Fernando, David 19
Ferr, Ignatius 56
Ferrel, Byrd 112
Hubbard 120
Ferrell, Enoch 8
Jno. 74
Martin 74
Ferrie, Jno. 20
Few, Ann 58
Benj. 65, 151
Ignatius 56, 57, 140,
147, 151, 161, 165
Wm. 58, 150
Wm. (Jr.) 57, 58, 91
Fhilaire, Jacinthe 26
Fidler, Jas. 120
Jno. 121
Field, Jas. 154
Fielder, Jas. 128, 129
Jno. 128, 129
Fields, Jas. 161
Files, Steph. 44, 135,
136
Stephen 132
Finch, Andrew 28
Ichabod 22, 28
Wm. 165
Findley, Eliz. 112
Geo. 116, 121
Jacob 109
Jas. 121
Jno. 121, 128
Norris 121
Thos. 112, 165
Findly, Harris 129
Jno. 125, 129
Jos. 125
Leven 129
Robt. 125
Uz 129
Wm. 129
Finley, Chas. 128
David 2
Jas. 20, 24, 25, 116
Robt. 126
Finney, Alexdr. 121, 128
Benj. 65
Dury 61
Jas. 91, 117, 121
Jno. 2, 8, 117, 121
Robt. 121
Wm. 2
Finni, Benj. 61
Fish, Elisha B. 44
Jno. 175
Fisher, David 44
Hendrick 44
Henry 44
Robt. 44
Wm. 108
Fiske, Jno. 178
Fitch, Andrew 27
Fitzgerald, (?) (Mrs.) 8

Fitzgerald (cont.)
 Edw. 44
 Mary 2
Fitzpatrick, Benj. 129
 Dyer 116
 Jno. 44
 Mary 138
 Tabitha 115
 Wm. 108, 112, 115,
  116, 127, 128
Fitzsimmons, E. L. W.
 109
Flanigan, Saml. 127
Flanigin, Wm. 78
Flannakin, Saml. 161
Fleetin, Richd. 2
Fleetwood, Jno. 61
Fleming, (?) 44
 Geo. 102
 Jas. 57
 Jno. 20, 22, 23, 24,
  25
 Moses 73, 88
 Robt. 2, 83, 84, 98
 Wm. 10, 12, 15, 96
Flemming, David 150
 Elijah 91
 J. 27
 Jno. 2, 165
 Wm. 91
Flenniken, Jas. 121
Fletcher, Jno. 68
 Wm. 165, 170
Flewellin, Alex 91
Flimming, Jno. 91
Flin, Jeremi 16
 Wm. 16
Flinn, Jno. 44, 61
 Michel 61
Flint, Tarpley 165
 Tho. 44
Floman, Jno. 89
Floro, Peter 100
Flourman, Robt. 108
Flourney, Robt. 130
Flournoy, Jacob 175
 R. 100, 133
 Robt. 65, 100, 108,
  116, 117, 140, 142,
  161, 165
 Thos. 108, 161
Floyd, Chas. 8
 Eady 2
 Jos. 16
 Richd. 44, 80
 Saml. 175
Fluker, Baldwin 158
 David 158
 Jno. 65
Flyming, (?) (Mrs.) 44
 Mary 44
Flynn, Jas. 133, 138
Folds, Geo. 140
 Geo. (Jr.) 61
 Richd. 61
Folis, Thos. 61
Fontain, Mary 147
 Peter 147
Footman, Richd. S. 44
Forbes, Atkins 83
Ford, Chas. 44
 Danl. 44
 David 44, 59
 Isaac 84, 86
 Jno. 2, 10, 15, 16,
  60, 157
 Tho. 16
 Willis 61

Ford (cont.)
 Wm. 60, 65, 158
Foreman, Wm. 8
Forester, Alexdr. 133
Forkner, Wm. 86
Forrester, Steph. 12
Forson, Beal 86
 Wm. 86
Forster, Jno. 57
 Jos. 32, 38
Forsyth, Benj. 2, 44,
 142
 Fanny 145
 Jno. 145
 Robt. 2, 142, 145,
  150, 161
 Robt. Moriah 145
Forsythe, Mary 30
Fort, Arthur 117, 165
 Drury 19, 20, 23, 25,
  26, 28
 Jane 24
 Martha 20
 Owen 161
 Rhoda 117
Forth, Henry 2
 Sarah 2
 Thos. 8
Fortson, Benj. 74
 Thos. 78
Fortune, Wm. 56
Foster, (?) (Cpt.) 59
 Arthur 112, 121, 125,
  126
 Eliz. 150
 G. W. 129
 Geo. 132, 133, 134,
  135, 138
 Hardy 63
 Jno. 16, 57, 59, 60,
  65, 131, 140, 142,
  147, 150
 Jonathan 63
 Pattey 170
 Richd. 20
 Tho. 86
Fouche, Jonas 126
Fouer, Geo. 127
Foule, Alexdr. 142
Foulk, Saml. 44
Fountain, Jas. 100
Fourrer, Chas. 44
Fowler, David 117
 Hammond 26
 Hammond & 26
 Hillery 175
 J. M. 26
 Jno. 28, 44, 89
 Jno. M. 22, 23
 John M. 26
 Robt. 44
 Saml. 44
 Sarah 44
 Simmons 117
 Thos. 44
 Zepheniah 175
Fox, Benj. 32
 Benj. (Jr.) 34
 David 44
 Eliz. 44
 Jas. 147, 153
 Jno. 34, 44
 Josiah 44
 Martha 36, 44
 Mary 44
 Richd. 44
 Sarah 147
 Wm. 34, 44

Foy, Jno. 70, 73
Foyer, Zachariah Lewis
 10
Foyil, Eliz. 2
 Jno. 2
Frand, Steph. 44
Franklin, Abner 94, 98,
 100, 102
 Abnon 95
 David 73, 83
 Geo. 142, 160, 161
 Philimon 154
 Tho. 14
 Wm. 142, 159, 165
Frannks, Isaac 44
Fraser, (?) (Dr.) 44
 Dr. 44
 Dyer 70
 Eliz. 70
 Robt. 44
Frasher, Andrew 157
Frazer, Alexdr. 149
 Andrew 115, 116
 Jno. 115, 117, 121
 Simon 133, 138
Frazier, Andrew 100
 Jno. 100
 Moses 175
 Simon 136
 Stephen 19
Freeman, Diana 23, 24
 Holman 100, 173
 Jacob 2
 Jas. 77, 82, 86, 91,
  100, 125
 Jenny 75
 Jno. 2, 100, 108, 173
 Jno. (Jr.) 2
 Jno. (Sr.) 2
 Joshua 44
 Noah 2
 Saml. 170
 Steph. 24, 26, 28
 Stephen 23
 W. 151
 Wm. 2, 143, 145
French, Robt. 2, 16
 Steph. 44
Friend, Thos. 175
Frish, Chas. 36
Fry, Jno. Newton 44
 Mary 44
Fryar, Feilding 100
 Jno. 2, 14
 Zach. Lewis 100
Fryer, Hayden 58
 Jno. 44
 Zachariah L. 10
 Zachariah Lewis 15
Fueller, Jacob 44
Fulcher, Jas. 140, 151
Fulford, Jas. 44
Fulgham, Jno. 2
 Matthew 74, 82, 166
 Stephen 74, 82, 166
Fuller, Abner 62
 Elijah 128
 Isaac 100, 140, 143,
  149
 Jno. 62, 65, 140, 149,
  166
 Joshua 56, 65, 143,
  149
 Ryal 62
Fulton, David 166
 Jno. 2, 16, 19
 Saml. 98, 138
 Saml. (Jr.) 154

Fuqua, Moses 62
  Prater 154
  Prator 62
Furey, Jno. 140, 145
Furgus, Jno. 74, 80
Furlow, Jas. 121
  Jno. 121, 128
  Wm. 121, 128
Fusils, Thos. 154
Fussell, Thos. 12
  Wm. 2, 14, 15
  Wm. (Cpt.) 7
Gaar, Abraham 75
  Adam (Sr.) 75
  Benj. 75
  Lewis 75
  Michael 75
Gabard, Thos. 2
Gable, Abraham 30, 36
  Jno. 44
Gadsden, Philip G. 146
Gaffney, Jas. 44
Gainer, Jno. 8
Gainery, Bartholomew 136
Gaines, Danl. 105
  Francis 73
  Gerome 100
Gainor, Wm. 161
Gains, Jesse 44
Gairdner, Jas. 44
Gaither, Brice 121
Gaits, Saml. 2
Galache, Ann 34
  Ann Eliz. 30
  Eliz. Ann 36
  Jas. 30, 34, 39, 44
Galacher, Js. 45
Galbreath, Wm. 121
Gale, Wm. (Dr.) 30
  Wm. W. 133
Gallman, Harmon 160
Gallup, Prentiss 23
Galphin, Thos. 45, 143
Galt, Gabriel 150
Galtney, Jno. 65
Galton, Joel 125
Gamage, Wm. 166
Gamble, Jno. 98
  Wm. 135
Gambol, Saml. 98
Gammage, Thos. 91
  Wm. 166
Gan, Jas. 121
  Nathl. 121
Gandonch, (?) 45
Ganer, Wm. 154
Gann, Jno. 126
  Saml. 112, 126
  Wm. 126
Ganner, Geo. 94
Gantt, Benj. 84
Gar, Adam 86
Garbet, Geo. 45
Gardener, Jno. 161
  Jno. F. 100
Gardiner, Isaac 45
  Jno. 45, 154
Gardner, Alexdr. 59, 60
  Ashel 147
  Asshel 62
  Danl. 45
  Elisha 45
  Hezekiah 109
  Jas. 2, 148, 151
  Jason 147
  Jno. 45, 147
  Jno. T. 91
  Lewis 57, 63, 143,

Gardner (cont.)
  147, 151
  Mary 63
  Rudolph 8
  Saml. 91
  Sarah 63, 147
  Simeon 16
  Thos. 45, 151
  Wm. 45, 56, 68, 143,
  147
Garey, Saml. 105
Garley, Abraham 175
Garmeny, Wm. 158
Garner, Jas. 146
  Richd. 158
  Saml. 112
  Stephen 178
  Urias 158
Garnet, Eli 150
Garnett, Eli 65
  Ely 149
  Jas. 59
  Jno. 59, 65, 151
  Thos. 71
Garnette, Jno. 149
  Zachariah 63
Garr, Adam 88
  Lewis 88
  Michael 88
Garren, Moses 91
Garret, Henry 174
  Jas. 110
Garrett, Catharine 150
  Elijah 8
  Jas. 121
  Jno. 19, 68, 150
  Mourning 112
Garrison, Shadrack 96
Garrott, Jacob 175
  Jno. 166
  Robt. 175
Gartnell, Jno. 62
Gartrel, Jno. 147
Gartrell, Francis 91
Garvin, David 26
  Robt. 2
Gary, Saml. 103, 107
Gascoigne, Richd. 23,
  24, 26
Gascongee, Rich. 27
Gascongne, Rich. 28
Gaston, Isaac 121
  Mathew 112, 121
  Matthew 129
Gates, Benj. 98, 102
  Chas. 2
  Jas. 96, 98
  Josiah 96
  Saml. 3
  Valentine 8
  Wm. 95, 98
Gatewood, Henry 86
  Jno. 86
  Larkin 80, 86
  Richd. 75, 78
Gathright, Miles 108,
  166
Gatland, Shadrack 112
Gatrell, Jos. 175
Gatril, Francis 175
Gatter, (?) 62
Gaugh, Wm. 91
Gaultier, Genevieve 45
Gavin, Jas. 15
Gay, Abraham 45
  Allen 115
  Jas. 3
  Jno. 3

Gay (cont.)
  Josiah 157
  Mathias 12
  Theodore 45
  Wm. 3
Gayet, Bertrant 45
Gaylord, Giles 148
Gayrie, Saml. 106
Gazer, Jno. 112
Gearlin, Jas. 108
  Wm. 108
Geary, Saml. 104
Geer, Jno. 116
Geerman, Christian 19,
  23, 24
Geiger, Abraham 68, 72
  Cornelius 72
  Etheldred 72
  Felix 68, 72
  Jno. 68, 72
Gentry, Elijah 170
Geoghegan, Ignatius 30,
  32, 36
Geoghigan, Ignatius 34
George, Bailey 125
  Jas. 175
  Jno. 121
  Traves 121, 125
  W. 117
  Wm. 84, 88, 109, 121,
  125, 126, 127, 129
  Wm. (Jr.) 121
Gerdine, Henry 45
Gerecken, Wm. 45
Germain, Michael 36, 39,
  45
German, Christopher 28
  Jno. 28
Germany, Herd 151
  Jas. 59, 60, 63
  Jno. 65
  Jos. 151
  Saml. 150
  Wm. 65
Geroud, Danl. 45
  Lewis 45
Gest, Adam 166
Gevinn, Jas. 3
Ghomas, Massa 93
Gibbons, Ann 32, 36, 45
  Barach 45
  Barack 34
  Fitz 70, 73
  Hannah 45
  Jno. 36, 45
  Jno. B. 45
  Jos. 32, 45
  Sarah 30
  Sarah (Mrs.) 39
  Tho. 16
  Thos. 32, 34, 36, 38,
  45
  Wm. 34, 45
  Wm. (Jr.) 3, 32, 45
  Wm. (Sr.) 34
Gibbs, Eliz. 36
  Gerod 84
  Miles 125
  Philip 166
Gibosn, Danl. 34
Gibson, Adam 154
  Daniel 30
  Danl. 45
  Humphrey 112, 126
  Jas. 95, 100
  Jno. 60, 140, 175
  Judah 172
  Robt. 30

Gibson (cont.)
  Sarah 30, 45
  Sarah (Mrs.) 45
  Sylvanus 172
  Walter 172
  Wm. 26
Gidden, Richd. 154
Gideon, Francis 91, 166
Gieger, Felix 68
Gignilliat, Jas. 136
Gilbart, Michael 116
Gilbert, Benj. 108, 110,
  112, 117, 121
  Benj. (Jr.) 115, 121
  Benj. (Sr.) 121
  Betsey 112
  Chas. 95, 97, 98, 100,
    102
  Hannah 97
  Jno. 30, 132
  Marten 121
  Martin 112
  Mary 45
  Michael 115, 117, 121,
    127
  Milly 115
  Nancy 112
  Robt. 112
  Sally 112, 115
  Saml. 166
  Sarah 97
  Thos. 91, 94, 100
  Wm. 45, 112
Gilder, Philip 28
Gilen, Jas. 100
Giles, Ebenezer 45
  Jas. 100
  Jno. 75
  Thos. 166
  Wm. 45
Gilispey, Alex. 166
Gilkey, Robt. 3
Gill, Bettey 112
  Days 140
  Ezekiel 112
  Jas. 68
  Jno. 75, 82, 83, 86,
    121
  Judea 112
  Robt. 68
Gillam, Ezekiel 112
  Wm. 170
Gillaspie, Alexdr. 121
Gillaspy, David 100
Gillelan, Jacob 84
Gilleylen, Agness 77
  Jacob 77, 78
Gilliam, Richd. 91
  Wm. 91
Gills, Jos. 72
Gillson, Dannis 14
Gillylen, Jacob 80
Gilman, Harmon 161
Gilmer, Jno. 172
  Peter 45
  Thos. 83, 173
Gilmore, Humphrey 166
  Jno. 117
  Saml. 166
Gilphin, Wm. 147
Gilpin, Ignatius 62,
  143, 148, 152
Gilstrap, Jno. 16
Gindrat, Henry 68, 70
  Jno. 45
Gines, Edw. 45
Ginn, Jesse 73
Girardeau, Jas. 131, 134

Girardeau (cont.)
  Jno. B. 135
  Richd. 131, 136, 137
  Wm. 134
Girdine, Lewis 146
Gireadeau, Jas. 138
Gireaudeau, Wm. 138
Givens, Jno. 45
Glascock, Eliz. 146
  Thos. 100, 140, 143,
    146, 151, 153, 162
  Wm. 146, 150, 152, 153
Glass, Jno. 30, 45
  Wm. 121
  Zachariah 112
  Zachrh. 121
Glasscock, Tho. 65
Glen, Duke 110
  Jas. 30, 45
  Jno. 30, 45
  Jos. 36
Glenn, Ann 112, 121
  David 112, 154, 158,
    162
  Duke 128
  Jno. 112, 158
  Robt. 158
  Wm. 94, 112, 121, 158
Glisson, Abraham 3
  Frederick 14
Gloster, Robt. 143
Glover, Beal 86
  Benj. 78
  Darling 8
  Jas. 86
  Jesse 59
  Jno. 77
  Jno. G. 45, 48
Gnann, Andrew 68
  Jacob 71
Gobert, Benj. 45
  Jos. 45
Godbe, Cary 3
  Wm. 3
Godbee, Saml. 3
Godfrey, Jno. 27, 28
Godichaw, Jacques 45
Godwin, Catherine 45
  Richd. 36
Goff, Barnett 131
  Charity 104
  Chas. Barnett 135
Goffe, Jane 30
Goin, Elisha 80
Golden, Matthew 160
Golding, Palmer 130
  Richd. 166
Goldsbey, Peter 166
  Richd. 166
Goldsmith, Jno. 68, 72
Goldwire, Benj. 36
  Jno. 70
  Jno. (Jr.) 70
  Jno. (Sr.) 70
Golsby, Richd. 170
Goodall, Pleasant 3
Goodbread, Philip 22,
  27, 28
  Phillip 23, 26
Goodbred, Philip 20
Goode, Edw. 100
  Edwd. 80, 162
  Jno. 16, 38, 103, 104,
    105, 106, 107
  Wm. 78, 82
Goodin, Jonathan 172
  Wilkinson 172
Goodlet, Jas. 96

Goodman, David 68
  Theodoric 3
Goodson, Josiah 136
Goodwin, Jno. 97
  Jno. (Jr.) 98
  Peter 57
  Wyche 172
  Zachariah 8
Goodwyn, Jas. 3
  Theo. 16
  Theodrick 3
Goolsby, Aaron 96
  Isaiah 98
  Wm. 148
Goram, Jno. 20
Gorbett, Geo. 3
Gordon, Alex 73, 166
  Alexr. 112
  Ambrose 45, 140, 153
  Catharine 82
  Catherine 32
  Jno. 13, 45, 60
  Moses 175
  Thos. 96
  Will 96
  Wm. 36, 82
Gore, Jacob 60, 62
  Jno. 143
  Rachel 60
Goredeaux, Peter 138
Goreham, Jno. 91
Gorham, J. 80, 100
  Jenny 80, 91
  Jinny 97
  Jno. 91, 97, 98, 100
  Sanford 91
  Wm. 91
Gorman, Jno. 26, 84
  Wm. 3, 26
Gosley, Jno. 175
Goss, Benj. 77, 86, 166
  Chas. 80, 86
  Eliz. 77
  Wm. 16
Gotear, Josiah 45
Gotier, Josiah 36
Gough, Jesse 95, 102
  Jno. 130
  Roger S. 130
  Thos. 95
  Wm. 95, 98, 100
  Wm. W. 129
Gouldin, Peter 136
Goulding, Ann 132
  Ann (Mrs.) 138
  Jno. 132, 134, 138
  Marg. 132
  Palmer 132, 133, 134,
    138
  Peter 132, 138
  Peter Jno. 138
  Thos. 131, 132, 137,
    138
Goupy, Jno. Baptist 45
Grabershine, Jno. 72
Grace, Thos. 115, 116
Grady, Jno. 96
Gragg, Jas. 22, 88
Graham, Elias 45
  Jas. 103, 108, 130,
    134, 137
  Jno. 3, 91, 121
  Richd. 143
  Saml. 158
  Thos. 166
  Wm. 78
Grall, Thos. 112
Grant, Alex'r. 45

Grant (cont.)
 Andrew 16, 103, 104,
  106, 107
 Harry 45
 Jas. 106, 107
 Jno. 16, 130
 Jos. 3
 Nasan (Mrs.) 45
 Percival Ward (Mrs.)
  45
 Peter 68, 136
 Sarah 105
 Thos. 154, 175
 Wm. 16, 103, 104, 105,
  107
Grantham, David 59
 Jno. 162
 Wm. 162
Graves, Francis 175, 178
 Geo. 91, 147, 151
 Humphrey 56, 91, 108,
  143
 Jno. 105, 131, 132,
  133, 135, 136, 138,
  175
 Jno. W. 104, 106, 107
 Jonas 175
 Joshua 91, 143
 Perry 91, 140
 Rebec. 133
 Rebecca 132
 Richd. 175
 Robt. 140, 152
 Thos. 132, 143, 147,
  150, 175
 Thos. (Jr.) 91
 Thos. (Sr.) 91
 Wm. 65, 91, 117, 132,
  166, 175, 178
Gray, (?) (Cpt.) 7
 Ann 172
 Anne 20
 Basel 14
 Basil 11, 13, 14
 Bazil 16
 Chloe 45
 Christian 146
 Danl. 175
 Flower 172
 Geo. 108, 172
 Hezekiah 75, 86
 J. 11, 16
 Jane 45
 Jas. 11, 20, 25, 28,
  109, 166, 172
 Jas. (Jr.) 107
 Jas. (Sr.) 106, 107
 Jno. 19, 20, 22, 25,
  26, 27, 28, 172, 175
 Jno. T. 45
 Jos. 3, 166, 172
 Jurdina 45
 Lewis 26
 Mathias 3, 11, 16
 Robt. 143
 Tho. 65
 Thos. 109, 117
 Zachariah 3
Graybill, Henry 117, 121
 Mary 115
Grayhill, Henry 112
Grayson, Jno. 34
Greef, Joshua 149
Green, Amos 65, 140, 166
 Ann 138
 Benj. 3, 11, 14, 16,
  135, 162
 Burket 86

Green (cont.)
 Burton 75
 Ephram 175
 Isaac 147
 Jas. 22, 121, 162, 175
 Jesse 83
 Jno. 3, 8, 45, 70, 149
 Mary 132, 138
 Mathew 15
 Mathew (Jr.) 16
 McKean 8
 Michael 36
 Moses 140
 Peleg 162
 Sollivent 8
 Sutton 96
 Thos. 138, 154
 Uriah 132, 138
 Willeway 70
 William (Cpt.) 7
 Wm. 3, 8, 14, 117,
  149, 174
 Wm. (Jr.) 117
Greene, (?) (Gen.) 45
 Catherine 30
 Danl. Jno. 45
 General 45
 Geo. W. 39
 Henry (Jr.) 166
 Isaac 143
 Jas. 154, 166
 Wm. 45, 117
Greenhow, Jas. 45, 70,
  72
Greenstreet, Jas. 80,
  89, 166
Greenwood, Fleming 83
 Jno. 78, 86, 88
 Wm. (Jr.) 45
Greer, Aaron 166
 Aquila 112
 Aquilla 110, 121
 Asel 116, 121
 Eliz. 112
 Gilbert 65
 Grace 32
 Jas. 112, 126
 Jean 115
 Jno. 45, 115, 117
 Josiah 162
 Mary 45
 Moses 166
 Robert 32
 Robt. 34, 38, 45, 56,
  117
 Sarah 115
 Thos. (Jr.) 60
 Thos. (Sr.) 60
 Vinson 112
 Wm. 108, 112, 115,
  117, 121, 127
 Yel 112
Gregg, Henry 83
 Tho. 88
 Thos. 77, 100
Gregory, Ethelred 45
Greir, Jno. 121
 Robt. 121
 Wm. 121
Grenage, Joshua 65, 148
Gresham, Archibald 117
 Davis 112, 117, 127,
  128
 Edwd. 173
 Ferdinand 121
 Harris 128
 J. 80
 Jas. 173

Gresham (cont.)
 Javis 121
 L. B. 112
 Thos. 91, 173
Grey, Geo. 175
 Matthias 11
 Zachariah 14
Greyham, Jas. 162
 Jno. 16
 Tho. 16
Gribben, (?) (Cpt.) 45
 Capt. 45
 Patrick 45
Grice, Richd. 159
 Thos. 115
Grier, Robt. 38
 Thos. 147
 Uriah 112
Grierson, Jas. 152
Griffen, Leonard 162
Griffey, Jno. 166
Griffin, (?) (Maj.) 154
 A. 63
 Abel 59, 63
 Allen 45
 Andrew 109
 Asa 59
 Edmond 125
 Farnafol 154
 Jas. 8
 Jeremiah 58
 Jinney 109
 Jones 157
 Lenn 154
 Lewis 59
 Majer 162
 Major 154
 Matthew 45
 Nancy 109
 Peggy 110
 Polly 110
 Rowland 59
 Sally 171
 Thos. 59, 110
Griffith, Edw. 36, 45
 Edwd. 133
 Jno. 91, 166, 178
 Robt. 88, 166
Grigg, Thos. 100
Griggs, Jane 36, 45
 Jno. 121
Grimes, Francis 8
 Jno. 91, 166, 173
 Jno. (Jr.) 173
 Lucy 173
 Mildred 76, 88
 Sterling 173
 Thos. 121
 Thos. Wingfield 173
 Wm. 73, 76, 78, 84, 88
 Wm. Garland 173
Grimmet, Robt. 110
Grimmett, Robt. 129
Grinage, J. 60
 Joshua 140, 143, 151
Grinatt, Robt. 126
Griner, Jacob 3
 Sol. 45
Grinnell, Jno. 87
Grisham, Benj. 175
 Geo. 175
 Jno. 175
 Thos. 175
Gritman, Jno. 121
Groathouse, Jacob 140
Grommet, Jno. 45
Groover, Jno. 68
Gross, Mund. 130

Grove, Jno. 20
  Wm. 16
Grover, David 68
  Jno. 68
  Mary 68
  Stephen 83
Gruas, David 96
Grubar, Jacob 3
  Solomon 3
Grubbs, Benj. 60, 140,
  143
  Francis 65
  Isaac 143
  Jno. 3, 8
  Joab 62
Gruber, Sol. 68
Gruver, David 72
  Sol. 72
Guard, Jas. 45
Guenin, Mons. 45
Guerard, Ann 32, 34
  Godin 32
  Robt. G. 45
  Wm. 45
Guess, David 96
Guest, Moses 102
Gugel, Chris. 45
  Christian 45
  Danl. 45
  David 45
  Joshua 45
Guilder, Philip 26, 27
Guillam, Richd. 100
  Susanna 100
  Wm. 100
Guillet, Michael 45
Guillett, Wm. 26
Guinn, Eliz. 138
  Richd. 138
Guinovily, David Saml.
  45
Guise, Jno. 166
  Nicholas 166
  Philip 166
·Gullet, Andrew 94
Gunby, Wm. 58, 62
Gunn, Chris. 45
  Jas. 38, 45
Gunnell, Jos. 166
Gunnells, Jos. 91
Gunnels, Jno. 96
Gunnolds, Jos. 102
Gurdain, Thos. 95
Gurthie, Robt. 83
Gutrey, Jno. 143
Guttery, Betsy 77
  Robt. 77, 82
Guy, Geo. W. 45
  Wm. 78, 91
Gwin, Jas. 17
Habersham, Alexdr. 45
  Hester 32
  Jas. 32, 45
  Jas. (Jr.) 45
  Jno. 30, 36, 45
  Jos. 36, 45
  Joseph 28
Hackett, (?) 28
Hackle, Wm. 12
Hackneys, Henry 45
Hadden, Wm. 3
Haddin, Wm. (Jr.) 3
Hadding, Wm. 3
Haddock, Zach. 28
Hadduck, Zach. 26
Haden, Allen 160
Hadley, Benj. 3
  Geo. 20

Hadley (cont.)
  Thos. 8
  Wm. 3
Hadon, Wm. 162
Hagan, Ann 112
  Edw. 112
  Jas. 110
Hagans, Edwd. 160
  Jas. 158
Hagen, Jno. 68
Hagerty, Sarah 108
Hagwood, Jno. 106
Haigs, Geo. 45
Hail, Luke 178
Hailey, Wm. 78
Hainer, Nicholas (Jr.)
  30
Haines, Moses 75
  Stephen (Sr.) 75
Hairege, Jno. J. 175
Hairon, Hugh 82
Hairrass, Peter 175
Haist, Geo. 34, 45
  Harriet 45
Haisten, Juhue 17
Halcom, Henry 100
  Thos. 100
Hale, Jesse 166
  Jno. 17, 30
  Joshua 166
Haley, Mary 77
  Wm. 77
Halhill, Luther 17
Hall, Benj. 13
  Bolling 146
  Bradley 68, 157
  Danl. 46
  David 158
  Eliza Ann 36
  Geo. 116, 121, 125,
    166
  Harvey 46
  Henry 121
  Hugh 110, 121, 128
  Jas. 34, 109, 110, 125
  Jas. H. 105, 106
  Jas. M. 104
  Jno. 13, 26, 34, 36,
    38, 91
  Lyman 12, 13, 32
  Mary 8, 32
  Mary (Mrs.) 12
  Saml. 125
  Talmadge 22, 23
  Talmage 20, 25, 28
  Thos. 112
  Willis 46
  Wm. 83, 86, 125, 157
Hallenworth, Stephen 162
Halley, Wm. 78
Halliday, Wm. 121
Hallinger, Titus 153
Halviston, Jaccob 104
Halwell, Luther 3
Ham, Ambrose 86
  Jno. 84
Hambilton, Wm. 121
Hamblen, Richd. 121
Hambleton, Edwd. 157
  Francis 75
  Isiah 83
  Rachel 98
Hamblin, Elhannah 46
Hambrick, Jos. 110, 112
  Marg. 112
  Robt. 112
  Susannah 112
  Thos. 110, 112, 121

Hambricks, Benj. 166
Hamill, Sol. 160
Hamilton, Andrew 175
  Ann 46
  Archibald 91
  Arthur 46
  Concord 60
  David 8
  Edw. 26
  Geo. 166, 175
  Jas. 57, 65, 140, 143,
    152
  Jno. 30, 32, 34, 46
  R. C. 132
  Richd. 152
  Robt. 175
  Tho. 65
  Thos. 46, 57, 60, 153
Hamlin, Richd. 112, 154
Hammett, Jno. 3
  W. M. 100
  Wm. 117, 154
Hammitt, Wm. 100
Hammock, Jno. 166, 175
  Jos. 117
  Robt. 175
  Saml. 175
  Wm. 3, 175
  Wm. (Sr.) 171
Hammon, Jacob 88
Hammond, Abner 19, 22,
  23, 28
  Ann 23
  Anthony 121
  Catherine 36
  Course (Mrs.) 46
  Elnathan 46
  Jas. 26
  Joshua 46
  Martin 112
  Nathl. 46
  Richd. 46
  Saml. 46, 140
Hammonds, Anthony 112
  Jno. 166
Hammons, Abraham 166,
  175
Hamphill, Jas. 46
Hampshire, H. 60
Hampton, (?) 157
  Benj. 166
  Edwd. 160
  Jno. 22, 26, 28, 91,
    159
  Jos. 17
  Lerraney 3
  Mr. 157
  Wm. 157, 159
Hamson, Sarah 46
Hanbury, Jno. 8
Hancock, Douglas 8, 15
  Isham 95
  Thos. 82
Hand, Henry 62
  Jno. 62
Handbern, Jno. 3
Handley, Geo. 150, 153
  Jas. 154
  Jesse 3
Handly, Geo. 152
Handon, Sevan 95
Haner, Nicholas 46
Haney, Geo. 91, 95, 100
  Thos. 75, 92
Hanley, Geo. 20
Hanna, Jas. 78, 80
  Jno. 173
  Mary 173

Hannah, Jas. 74
 Jno. 166
 Mary 115
 Thos. 3, 115
 Wm. 3
Hanner, Eliz. 30
 Nicholas 30, 39
 Thos. 159
Hansard, Wm. 80, 82
Hansford, Wm. 86, 87
Hanson, Tho. 63
 Thos. 59, 60
Haralson, Bradley 125
 Jonathan 121, 125
Harben, Thos. 166
Harber, Esaias 166
Harbin, Thos. 80, 82
 Wm. 80
Harbor, Talmon 89
Harbour, Catharine 77
 Esaias 77, 78
 Isaiah 98
 Talmon 78, 80
 Thos. 80
Hardee, Jno. 22, 26
Harden, Edw. 30
 Jno. 96
 Mark 95
 Voll 157
 Wm. 30, 94, 102
Hardin, Mark 94, 100
 Wm. 15
Harding, Steph. R. 46
 Wm. 46, 152
Hardman, Wm. 166
Hardwick, Geo. 46, 117
 Wm. 8, 17, 117
Hardy, Isaac 166
 J. 131
 Jno. 133, 135, 136,
  138
 Jno. Francis 100
 Jos. T. 133, 138
 Mary 133
 Mary (Mrs.) 138
 Thos. 46
Hardzman, Thos. 68
Hare, Jno. 70, 73
Hargrove, Emanuel 152
 Emnl. 175
 Howell 3
 Josiah 162
Hargroves, (?) (Dr.) 8
 Jno. 65
Harkens, Jno. 171
Harling, Ezekiel 166
Harmar, Christ. 78
Harn, Jno. 46
 Saml. 30
 Wm. 30
Harns, Bucker 92
Harold, Kerson 8
Harper, Charter 86
 Edmond 166
 Geo. 118
 J. P. 86
 Jno. P. 83, 88
 Jno. Peterson 78
 Lenard 104
 Leonard 107
 Robt. 121, 166
 Robt. (Jr.) 118
 Saml. 166
 Thos. 46
 Wm. 46, 102
Harragall, Sarah 140
Harral, Geo. 46
Harrel, Abraham 26

Harrel (cont.)
 Bailey 159
 Moses 133
Harrell, Abner 22
 Edwd. 154
 Elisha 8
 Mary 3
Harrill, Geo. 3
Harrington, Cunnil 95
 Jno. 92, 100, 102, 166
 Mary 3
 Sarah 97
 Thos. 97
Harris, Anne 173
 Augustin 129
 Baker 112, 118, 121
 Buckner 20, 92, 97,
  98, 100, 173
 Cath. 46
 Chas. 36, 46, 126, 132
 Chris. 84
 D. 17
 David 62, 65
 Edwin 19
 Elisha 121
 Eliz. 104
 Francis H. 46
 Geo. 118, 121, 129,
  154, 166
 Giles 148
 Jane 112
 Jas. 143, 153, 157,
  159, 160
 Jeremiah 112
 Jesse 162
 Jno. 68
 Jno. Geo. 46
 Joshua 110, 121, 129
 Lewellyn 104
 Lewis 104, 146
 Marg. 105
 Mary 30, 112
 Mathew 121
 Mordica 30
 Nancy 173
 Nathan 57, 62, 65,
  140, 143, 151
 Patrick Cunningham 110
 Robt. 19, 23, 26, 28,
  175
 S. B. 112
 Saml. 103, 104, 106,
  110, 121
 Saml. B. 126
 Sampson 22, 92, 129
 Sarah 46
 Tho. 20, 22, 25, 28
 Thos. 36, 108, 110,
  112, 118, 121, 129
 Walton 22, 116, 127,
  129
 Watson 121
 Wm. 30, 36, 46, 104,
  105, 106, 107, 109,
  118, 121, 129, 160
 Wm. (Jr.) 104, 105,
  106
 Wm. (Sr.) 105, 106
 Wm. Thos. 136
 Zach 22
Harrison, Benj. 62, 92,
  98, 147, 162
 Catherine 32
 Clem King 58
 David 112, 121
 Davis 108, 128
 Edwd. 121, 154
 Gad. W. 58

Harrison (cont.)
 Geo. 121
 Gideon 110, 118
 Gilbert 133, 135
 Gilbery 105
 Jas. 104, 105, 106,
  107
 Jno. 46, 105, 126, 153
 Mary 46, 56, 143, 147
 Reuben 140
 Rich 65
 Richd. 148
 Thos. 46, 100
 Thos. (Sr.) 100
 Wm. 110
Harriss, Elisha 126
Harry, (?) 46
Hart, Abraham 106
 Benj. 88, 106
 Benj. (Sr.) 107
 Esther 146
 Geo. 17
 Henry 22, 26
 Jno. 96
 Robt. 162
 Saml. 128, 158, 159,
  162
 Thos. 106
 Wm. 3, 12, 17
Hartfield, Asa 46
Harthorn, Eliz. 3
Harton, Thos. 166
Hartridge, Jno. E. 46
Hartsfield, Geo. 162
 Godfrey 166
 Jas. 166
 Jno. 3
 Richd. 166
Hartstein, Joachim 46
Hartzog, Henry 106
Harvard, Jno. 8
Harvey, Arnold 46
 Blasingame (Cpt.) 7
 Blass (Jr.) 17
 Blass (Sr.) 17
 Blassingame 3, 154
 Blassingame (Jr.) 14
 Emanuel 68
 Evan 121
 Jas. 12, 14, 108, 112,
  116, 118, 121
 Jas. (Cpt.) 7
 Jno. 160
 Michael 112, 121
 Robt. 17, 46
 Tho. 17
 Thos. 110, 112, 121,
  160
 Wm. 121, 157
Harvie, Richd. 171
 Wm. 76, 88
Harvil, Jas. 62
Harvill, Jas. 126, 141
Harville, Jos. 56
Harvy, Evan 112
 Richd. 76
Hasinack, (?) 46
Haslip, Terobabel 3
Hastings, Arch. 135
 Archibald 131
 Robt. 65
Hatcher, Henry 154
 Jno. 17, 22, 27, 28,
  57, 58, 62, 70, 73,
  143, 149
 Josiah 173, 174
 Priscilla 143
 Wm. 75, 76, 78, 80, 87

Hathaway, Jno. 46
Hathcock, Jno. 86
Hathorn, Robt. 86
  Thos. 158
Haughleiter, Jno. 72
Haughton, Jno. 104
Haupt, Jno. 46
Havens, Philetus 46
  Wm. 46
Haverd, Geo. 175
Haviel, Sol. 159
Hawkins, A. 152
  Benj. 92
  Ezek. 112
  Francis 154, 166
  Jas. 65
  Mathew 121
  R. D. 17
  Saml. 116, 121, 154
  Susannah 112
Haworth, Edmond 153
Hawthon, Thos. 155
Hawthorn, Jos. 46, 68
  Nathl. 46, 68
  Nathl. (Jr.) 46
  Robt. 12
  Stephen 138
  Thos. 166
  Wm. 166
Hawthorne, Jno. 75
  Jno. (Sr.) 84
  Nathaniel 138
Hay, And. 146
  Andrew 58, 60
  Gilbert 92
  Hugh 92
  Jas. 92
  Jno. Booker 121
  N. 63
  Wm. 92, 97, 98, 100,
    121, 166
Hayes, Andrew 57
  Patrick 128, 146, 148
  Wm. 121
Hayhart, Jacob 46
Hayman, Henry 3
  Henry (Sr.) 8, 17
  Jas. 8
  Staunton 155
  Stephen 3
  Stouton 3
Haynes, Anthony 65, 143
  Delia 112
  Geo. 118
  Henry 118
  Isaac 118
  Moses 75, 80, 88
  Phelps 174
  Sarah 80
  Sary 112
  Thos. 57, 58, 60, 108,
    141, 143
Haynie, Bridger 82
  Bridgor 80
Hayns, Stephen 89
  Tho. 17
Hays, Adam 121, 130
  Andrew 58
  Henry 92
  Hugh 115, 121
  Patrick 121, 130
  Robt. 118
  Wm. 100, 151
Haythorne, Martha 112
Head, Benj. 75, 77
  Eliz. Janet 76
  Jas. 80
  Richd. 100

Head (cont.)
  Thos. 78
  Wm. 100
Heard, Abraham 128
  Barnett 65
  Eliz. 115, 173
  Geo. 129
  Jas. 112
  Jesse 166
  Jno. 86, 110
  Jos. 118, 126
  Stephen 80, 88, 126,
    166, 173
  Stephen (Jr.) 129
  Thos. 115, 116, 121,
    128, 166
  Wm. 118, 121, 126, 129
Hearill, Reubin 59
Hearing, Moses 128
Hearn, Hen. 94
  Philip 36
  Wm. 158
Hearndon, Jos. 175
  Lewis 175
Heart, Saml. 121
  Wm. 8
Hearton, Thos. 155
Heat, Jas. 76
Heath, Abraham 166
  Mark 118
  Rich. 17
  Richd. 3
Heathcote, Wm. 46
Heatley, Jas. 80
Heaton, Robt. 162
Heavy, Dennis 46
Hebbard, E. 23
  Elihu 22, 24
Hedgepath, Josiah 8
Hefcoat, Wm. 8
Heineman, Jno. 46
Heisler, Geo. 46, 68
  Jno. 46
Helena, Beal 30
Helms, Jno. 98
Helton, Abraham 166
Helvestin, Jacob 103
  Jas. 103
Helveston, Jacob 104,
    105, 107
  Jas. 104, 105
  Jeremiah 107
  Jno. 107
  Sarah 105
Hemphill, Robt. 157
  Saml. 17, 112, 129,
    143
  Wm. 155, 162
Henan, Wm. 94
Henbrick, Thos. 128
Henck, Henry 46
Henderson, (?) (Widow)
    46
  Geo. 86
  Jas. 46
  Jno. 3, 75, 83, 88, 96
  Jones 96
  Jos. 75, 88, 128
  Michael 3
  Robt. 8, 100
  Robt. L. 95
  Zach. 121
Hendley, Derby 175
  Geo. 39
Hendrake, Anderson 175
  Thos. 175
  Wm. 175
Hendrick, Chas. 86

Hendrick (cont.)
  Eliz. 77
  Jesse 86
  Whitehead 84, 86
Hendricks, Hillary 83
  Jno. 107
  Sarah 83
  Wm. 104
Hendry, Chas. 17
  Geo. 8, 17
  Geo. (Sr.) 17
  Jacob 17
  Jas. 17
Hening, Geo. 97
Henlay, Ann 46
Henley, Geo. 46
  Jno. 76
Henly, Philip 176
Hennan, Wm. 98
Henning, Geo. 92, 98
Henry, Benson 80
  Hugh 138
  Jno. 3
  Jos. 112, 118
  Lyon 12, 17, 46
Hensler, Jno. 36
Henson, Caleb 176
Hepkins, Saml. 96
Herb, Frederic 46
  Frederick 36, 39
  Fredk. (Jr.) 30
  Jno. 34, 36, 46
  Ursula 46
Herbach, (?) (Widow) 46
  Henry 46
  Jacob 46
  Michael 46
  Susannah 46
Herback, (?) (Widow) 46
  Casper 46
Herndon, Jos. 159, 160
  Lewis 160
  Reuben 121
  Reubin 118
Heron, Jas. 46
Heros, Jno. 36
  Lucy 36
Herrin, Ann Madelin 146
  Betsy 146
  Nancy 146
Herring, Jas. 162
  Wm. 3, 155
Herrington, Jno. 98, 102
  Richd. 3
Hersley, Tarlton 3
Herson, Herman 30, 36,
    46
  Herman (Mrs.) 39
Hester, Allen 17
  Jas. 17
Hewbanks, Daniel (Jr.) 8
Hewett, Wm. 92
Hewitt, Jno. 129
  Wm. 129
Hext, Eliza 130
  Jno. 132
  Marid 130
Heyton, Wm. 68
Hibbard, Elihu 23
Hickenbotom, Burer 146
· Hickerson, Larkin 86
Hickman, Furney 46
  Theophilus 155
  Wm. 162
Hickmon, Jos. 159
Hickom, Jos. 176
Hicks, Anchelm B. 46
  Ansell 146

Hicks (cont.)
  Edmond 146
  Edmond B. 166
  Edwd. 143
  Mary 146
  Nathl. 146
  Saml. 8, 118
Hickson, Jno. 3, 141
  Thos. 8
Higdon, Chas. 162
  Robt. 8
Higginbotham, Benj. 74,
  76, 86, 87, 88
  Burris 24, 143
  Burroughs 65
  Caleb 86, 88
  Eliz 76
  Frances 77
  Francis 86
  Jacob 74, 83, 86, 147
  Jno. 86
  Jos. 77, 86
  Saml. 80, 86, 88
  San'd. 86
  W. 80
  Wm. 74, 78, 84, 86, 88
Higgins, Ichabod 34, 46
  Jos. 121
Higginsbotham, Saml. 74
Higgs, Abraham 159, 160
  Jno. 159
High, Jno. 3
Highland, Nicholas 162
Highsmith, Thos. 166
Hightower, Charnel 86
  Jno. 77
  Richd. 152
  Sarah 77
  Thos. 83
  Wm. 74, 86, 87, 88, 92
Hilbert, Conrad 36, 46
Hilburn, Holiman 3
Hill, (?) 8
  Abraham (Jr.) 171
  Abraham (Sr.) 170
  Christian 171
  Ebenezer 132
  Edw. 3
  Edwd. 149
  Geo. 112, 121, 155
  Gillon 8
  Henry 171
  Jacobs 74
  Jas. 92
  Jesse 95
  Jno. 82, 118, 121,
    128, 149, 166, 170
  Jool 141
  Jos. 46
  Joshua 149, 155
  Mary 3, 171
  Matthew 46
  Moses 77, 82, 84, 166
  Mountain 171
  Myles 171
  Noah 171
  Richd. 46
  Robt. 108, 116, 121
  Saml. 46
  Stark 3
  Theophilus 166, 171
  Thos. 46, 118, 141,
    162, 166, 171
  Wm. 108, 112, 121
  Wylie 171
Hillard, Majer 162
Hillary, Chris. 104,
  106, 107

Hillary (cont.)
  Geo. 46
Hillery, Chris. 104,
  105, 106
  Hendrick 77
  Thos. 80
Hilley, Thos. 83
Hillhouse, David 92
Hilliard, (?) (Maj.) 8
  Henry 8
  Jesse 68
  Major 8
  Silas 8
Hills, Marg. 148
  Nathan 153
Hillseamore, Richd. 8
Hillyer, Jas. 56
Hilton, Abraham 166
  Jas. 166
Hilyard, Jesse 73
Hilyards, Jesse 70
Hinds, David 17
  Wm. 17
Hines, David (Sr.) 70
  Jas. 68, 70, 155, 166
  Robt. 59
  Sarah 3
  Wm. 3
Hinson, Chas. 8
  Clayborn 131, 136, 138
  Philip 8
  Sarah 131, 138
  Wm. 17, 155
Hinton, Allen 147
  Caleb 160
  Clayborn 138
  Hardy 88
  Harvey 92
  Micajah 60, 166
  Wm. 60
Hirshman, Jno. 46
  Susannah 46
Hitchcock, Rebecca 131
  Wm. 170
Hitche, Thos. 170
Hitcherson, Jas. 65
Hitower, Charnel 17
Hoag, Jas. 115
Hobbs, Jno. 34, 46, 143
  Joel 92
  Robt. 126
Hobby, Sally 153
  Wm. 13, 152
  Wm. J. 80, 147
Hobkirk, Wm. 36, 46
Hodge, (?) 46
  Alex. 80
  Archibald 170
  Jacob 166
  Jno. 83, 87
  Wm. 76, 82, 88, 109
Hodgens, Jno. 65, 147
Hodges, Elias 68
  Francis 3
  Jeames 17
  Jno. 68, 105, 106
  Jos. 3
  Joshua 3
  Wm. 68, 121
Hodgins, Jno. 143
Hodgkins, Jno. 46
Hodo, Peter 166
Hoffmire, Peter 135
Hofman, Martha 46
Hogan, Absalom 68
  Danl. 20
  Edw. 118
  Eliz. 172

Hogan (cont.)
  Griffin 172
  Jno. 68, 106
  Mary 172
  Thos. 143
  Wm. 17
Hogar, Isham 121
Hogen, Griffin 159
Hogg, Eunice 36, 46
  Jacob 162
  Jas. 3, 108, 121, 149
  Jno. 88, 112, 126, 149
  Martha 112
  Mary 112
  Saml. 112, 121, 126
  Thos. 34, 46
  Wm. 110, 121, 143
Hoggans, Edw. 112
Holbrook, Jesse 80
Holcom, Henry 95
  Jno. 94
  Jos. 94
  Moses 94
  Sherard 94
  Thos. 94
Holden, Jonathan 135
Holder, Wm. 62
Holderness, Jas. 162
  Wm. 176
Holdness, Jas. 155
Holiday, Ambrose 143
Holladay, Jos. 3
  Thos. 149
Hollaman, Ann 68
Holland, Henry 109
  Jno. 46, 65
  Sewel 160
Holleman, Ann 71
  Nancy 71
Hollerman, Hartman 8
Holley, Thos. 162
Holliday, Ambrose 65
  Ares 176
  Elisabeth 112
  Jos. 3
  Owen 176
  Wm. 65, 110, 166, 176
Holliman, David 149, 166
  Mark 149
  Richd. 149
Hollinger, Wm. 3
Hollingshead, Jno. 166
Hollingsworth, Jacob 100
  Jos. 143
  Stephen 8, 155
  Valentine 68
  Vear 68
  Zebulon 8
Hollinshed, Saml. 82
Hollon, Suel 158
Hollongsworth, Saml. 94
Holloway, Barnes 112
  Jeremiah 8
  Jno. 70, 73
Hollstead, Wm. 133
Holly, Jno. 8
  Jonathan 3, 8, 155,
    162
  Thos. 88
Holman, (?) 46
  Thos. 36
Holmes, Jas. 26, 28
  Jas. M. 19
  Jno. 46, 125, 171, 172
  Lathrop 131
  Richd. 112, 121
  Robert 34
  Robt. 125

Holms, Benj. 176
　Robt. 178
Holt, Harmon 125
　Wm. 65
Holton, Francis (Sr.) 8
　Saml. 17, 155, 162
Holtzendorf, Jno. L. 46
Holzenback, Jno. 143
Holzendorf, Wm. 46
Homer, Joshua 84
Homes, Benj. 166
　Joshua 89
Hood, Benj. 141
　Jno. 46, 121, 173
　Nathl. 155, 162
　Wm. 8
Hoof, Benj. 135
　Saml. 116, 129
Hoofe, Wm. 58
Hooks, Wm. 15, 155, 162
Hooper, Absalom 155
　Jesse 92
　Jno. 92, 95
　Obadiah 95
　Obediah 94
　Thos. 170
Hopkins, C. B. 28
　Elisha B. 103, 104
　Jason 46
　Jno. 20
　Lambert 121
　Lambeth 129, 166
　Wm. 121, 155
Hopson, Briggs 162
Horkins, Thos. 109
Horn, Ferrybe 63
　Henry 3
　Jacob 155
　Jesse 63
　Joab 162
　Wm. 63
Hornby, Francis 60
　Phillip 39
Horne, Absolom 176
　Jesse 58
　Moses 3
　Persilla 58
Hornsby, Chas. 46
　Weldon 118
Horsburgh, Jno. 46
Horsley, Tarleton 155
Horton, Hugh 128
　Jas. 126
　Moses 71
　Proser 176
Hoskins, Ceaser 46
　David 46
　Mariam 155
Houghston, Henry 122
Houghton, Alexdr. 126
　Hugh 122
　Joe 126
　Joshua 98, 110, 112,
　　122, 127
　Joshua (Jr.) 122
　Josiah 122, 126
　Saml. 46
　Sarah 112
　Thos. 112, 116, 118,
　　122, 127, 129
　Wm. 112, 122, 126, 127
House, Jas. 96, 166
　Jesse 3
　Jos. 162
　Quilton 84
Housley, Nerred 108
Houston, Jno. 100
　Thos. 136

Houston (cont.)
　Wm. 92
Houstoun, Ann (Lady) 46
　Doll 46
　Geo. 34
　Geo. (Sir) 46
　Hannah 46
　Henry 155
　Jas. 46
　Jno. 34, 46
　Lady Ann 46
　Lucy 46
　Patrick (Sir) 46
　Robt. 47
　Sir Geo. 46
　Sir Patrick 46
Houstown, Jas. 30
Hover, Conrad 47
How, Robt. 19
Howard, Benj. 47, 84,
　　89, 149
　Daniel 68
　Geo. 92
　Hermon 92
　Jas. 62
　Jos. 116, 122, 176
　Julius 82, 88, 92, 100
　Martha 60
　Nehemiah 80, 92
　Rhesa 57, 60, 65, 147
　Saml. 3, 60
　Tho. 14, 63
　Thos. 143
　Whilliam 26
　Wm. 22, 28
Howe, (?) 47
Howel, Gabriel 158
Howell, Abel 86
　Caleb 68, 71, 72
　Danl. 68, 71, 72
　Deannel 17
　Henry 3, 126
　Jno. 3, 47, 103, 143,
　　150, 153, 166
　Jos. 162
　Lewis 3
　Miller 135
　Theophilus 8
　Wm. 8, 17
Howington, Wm. 83
Howley, Sarah 132
Howlin, Peyton 112
Howsley, W. 122
Hoxy, Asa 47
Hubbard, Benj. 77, 92,
　　166
　Catron 77
　Elihu 26, 28
　Jno. 20, 47, 74, 77,
　　86
　Richd. 80
　Richmond 86
　Sally 77
Hubert, Mathew 155, 162
　Matthew 152
Huck, Wm. 112
Huckabey, Phillip 176
Huckeby, Jno. 162
Huddleson, Robt. 84
Huddleston, Jno. 170
　Jos. 86
　Robt. 78, 86
Hudgens, Josiah 176
　Wm. 176
Hudler, Jno. 8
Hudnall, Ezekiel 65
Hudson, (?) 86
　Burrel 95

Hudson (cont.)
　Chas. 82, 88
　Chris (Sr.) 70
　Chris. 80, 138
　Chris. (Jr.) 70
　Cutbird 77, 100
　Cuthberd 75
　Cuthbert 92
　David 88
　Eliz. 77
　Hall 17
　Hines 125
　Isaac 71, 131, 138,
　　155
　Jas. 19, 23, 26, 28
　Jno. (Sr.) 88
　Joachim 92
　Jos. 100
　Martha 12
　Nat. 86
　Nathl. 72
　Robt. 71
　Wm. 12, 80, 162
Hudspeth, Chas. 3
　Robt. 159
Huett, Wm. 176
Huff, J. L. 86
　Saml. 122, 162
　Wm. 62, 63
Huffman, Jacob 68
Hughbanks, Richd. 84
Hughes, Frederick 20, 25
　Jas. 155
　Jno. 133
　Nicholas 122
　Wm. 47, 62, 65, 143
Hughet, Sol. 94
Hughs, Jas. 162
　Simon 176
　Wm. 141
Hughy, Peter 100
Huguenet, Louis 47
Huguenin, David 47
Hull, Jno. 26
　Sarah 3
Hulling, Jas. 173
Human, Alex. 77
　Bazzie 78
　Bazzle 76
　Isabel 76
Hume, Jno. 8
Humphres, Geo. 95
　Shadrack 95
Humphrey, Jos. 92
Humphreys, Spencer 138
Humphries, Jos. 94, 97,
　　100
　Rebekah 97
Hunlook, (?) 47
Hunt, Fitz M. 58
　Fitz Maurice 143
　Fitzmorris 57, 62
　Geo. 146
　Henry 65, 86
　Jas. 78, 89, 95, 100,
　　102
　Jno. 95, 155
　Nathl. 100
　Philip 22
　Phillip 26
　R. 80, 84
　Richards 86
　Richardson 74, 77, 78,
　　80, 83, 88, 173
　Ruth 146
　Thos. 135, 143
Hunter, D. 152
　Dalzeel 65

Hunter (cont.)
  Dalziel 92, 143, 150, 152
  Edwd. 112
  Eleanor 152
  Ellinor 151
  Ephriam 47
  Evan T. 92
  I. W. 28
  J. P. 146
  Jane 56
  Jesse 130
  Jno. 8
  Jno. W. 19, 23
  Miles 68, 130
  Phil 126
  Phillip 122, 128
  Phillip 112, 116, 127, 130
  Saml. 80, 82, 83, 88, 97
  Sarah 97
  Sol. 135
  Wm. 47, 160
Hunts, Fitz Maurice 141, 155
Huntzinger, Michael 39
Hurd, Jno. 176
  Jno. (Jr.) 176
Hurley, Henry 170
Hurst, (?) (Maj.) 3
  Wm. 3
Hurt, Joel 174
Husso, Robt. 36
Huston, Wm. 106, 107
Hutcheson, (?) (Mrs.) 8
Hutchings, Chas. 77, 80
Hutchins, Jno. 88
Hutchinson, Jas. 162, 166
  Jos. 56
  Wm. 113
Hutson, C. 86
Hydrick, Geo. 3
Hylar, Jas. 143
Hyler, Jas. 56
Idler, Jacob 47
Ihley, Philip 47
  Saml. 47
Ilands, Jno. 149
Ingerfall, Jno. 39
Ingersoll, Jno. 47
Inglis, Wm. 47
Ingram, David 3
  Jas. 36, 147, 151
  Jno. K. 47
  Mary (Mrs.) 153
  Rich. 17
  Richd. 3, 155
Inloe, Mary 172
Inman, Jesse 17
  Joshua 32
Inmon, Danl. 17
Innes, Andrew 146, 151
  Danl. 47
Irby, Henry 143
  Jos. 141, 143
Irins, Geo. 86
Irvin, Jno. 149
Irvine, Chas. 131
  Jno. 36, 132, 133, 136, 138
  Tho. 26
  Wm. 30
Irwin, Alexdr. 157
  Eliz. 3
  Hugh 158
  Jared 162

Irwin (cont.)
  Robt. 3
  Wm. 157
Irwins, (?) (Cpt.) 157
Isaacs, Elijah 98
  Elisha 97
  Saml. 98, 100
Isbell, Pendleton 98
Ishaw, Edw. 83
Islands, Abner 138
Iting, Frederic 47
Iverson, Rebecca 134
  Robt. 11, 12, 131, 134, 135, 137
  Saml. 8, 17
Ivey, Robt. 68
  Winnie (Mrs.) 178
Jack, Archib. 47
  Kitty 150
  Saml. 143, 146, 150, 151
  Wm. H. 146
Jackson, A. 36
  Abrah. 30
  Abraham 3, 8, 12, 32, 36, 155
  Absalom 19, 22, 23, 24, 100, 155, 162
  Absalom & Co. 19
  Amasa 147, 150, 151
  Ann (Mrs.) 153
  Ann Agnes 32
  Ann Eliza 36
  Benj. 65, 95, 166
  Chas. 162
  David 113, 160, 162
  Ebenezer 34, 36, 47
  Edw. 110
  Henry 118, 122
  Isaac 65, 113, 118, 122, 158
  J. 143
  Jacob 47
  Jas. 23, 32, 34, 47, 118, 130, 159
  Jno. 110, 138, 152, 176
  Jos. 71, 108, 113, 118, 162, 166
  Lucy 115
  Mary 113
  Mary E. 32
  Montague 47
  Moses 176
  Peter 108, 115, 122
  Pharbea 24
  Randolph 122
  Reuben 143
  Reubin 122
  Robt. 19, 80, 92, 100, 155, 157, 162, 166
  Robt. D. (Dr.) 47
  Roger 47
  Stephen 158
  Susannah 20
  Tho. 65
  Thos. 122
  Tobe 158
  Walter 19, 92, 155, 162
  Wm. 95, 104, 122
Jacobs, Mordica 176
Jains, Wm. 171
Jameison, Jno. 19
Jamerson, Wm. C. 92
  Wm. C. & Co. 92
James, Abner 172
  Chas. 32

James (cont.)
  E. 47
  Jackson 95
  James 3
  Jas. 131, 134, 138
  Jno. 143
  Wm. 8
Jameson, Jno. 19, 23, 24, 26, 27, 28, 143
  Ralph 24
Jamieson, David 8
  Jno. 19, 23, 24, 26
  Ralph 23
Jamison, Jno. 47
  Ralph 22
  Wm. 162
Janet, (?) 47
Janiken, Needham 113
Janson, Jno. 138
  Wm. 138
Jard, Cornelius 176
Jarratt, Howell 92
Jarrell, Jas. 108
Jarrett, Howell 173
Jarrot, Howel 176
Jarvis, F. 63
  Floyd 63
Jaudon, Thos. D. 47
Jeffers, Jno. 3
Jeffreys, Jas. 8
  Jno. 17
Jeffries, Ann 138
  Jas. 132, 136, 138
  Nancy 131, 132
Jem, (?) 47
Jenkins, Arthur 147
  Benj. 63, 118, 141, 143
  E. B. 63
  Edmund B. 56
  Edw. B. 58
  Elijah 122
  Francis 155, 162
  Geo. 104
  Jas. 122
  Jesse 126
  Jno. 22, 122
  Lewis 116
  Lewis (Sr.) 122
  Little B. 126
  Mary 47
  P. 63
  Phillip 8
  Priscilla 63
  Richd. 21, 25
  Ruth 3
  Starling 17
  Sterling 166
  Susannah 47
  Zachariah 162
Jennings, David 96
  Jonathan 92
  Moody 170
  Patrick 21
  Priscilla 166
  Sarah 155
  Wm. 65, 92, 151
Jernegan, Neden 176
Jernigan, Elias 70, 73
  Hardy 118, 143
  Henry 116
  Moses 70, 73
  Needham 115, 122
  Needham (Jr.) 118
Jervais, Anson Ward (Mrs.) 47
Jiles, Thos. 155
Jinkins, Edmund B. 57

Jinkins (cont.)
  Philip 28
  Wm. 158
Jinnings, Johnathan 96
Joe, Spanish 27
John, (?) 47
  Arley 17
Johns, Eliz. 58
  Jno. 58
  Robt. 60
Johnson, Abraham 60
  Abram 147
  Adkerson 176
  Alexdr. 47, 65, 143,
    160
  Andrew 75, 77, 80, 84,
    166
  Benj. 22, 155, 157,
    162
  Cobb 166
  Danl. 68, 162
  David 162
  Donald 89
  Edmond 74, 80
  Geo. 17
  Henry 178
  Isaiah 171
  Isham 47
  Jas. 3, 47, 92
  Jas. (Jr.) 3, 36, 162
  Jas. (Sr.) 155
  Jesse 12, 47, 118
  Jno. 17, 84, 103, 137,
    149, 155, 162, 170
  Jno. H. 77
  Jno. Hutchins 78
  Jos. 171
  Margt. 21
  Micajah 3
  Nancy 77
  Nathan 178
  Nicholas 172
  Peter 89
  Richd. 172
  Saml. 141
  Sarah 171
  Stephen 3, 11, 15
  Thos. 113, 170
  Upton 171
  Usual 47
  Walter 19, 171
  Wilson 155
  Wm. 20, 21, 25, 26,
    27, 83, 92, 113,
    118, 162, 166, 170,
    172
Johnston, Abel 157
  Abrah. 57
  Abraham 146, 147
  Agnes 115
  Alexdr. 47, 176
  Andrew 30, 47
  Andrew W. 47
  Benj. 28
  Danl. 47
  David 34, 36, 47, 68
  Elijah 176
  Elisha 82
  Eliz. 47
  Jacob 176
  Jas. 17, 47
  Jas. (Jr.) 36, 47
  Jno. 47, 88, 104, 113,
    116
  Jno. H. 75, 82
  Jos. 70, 73
  Joshua 171
  Leroy 122

Johnston (cont.)
  Malcolm 118
  Matthew 47
  Nelson 95
  Nicholas 47
  Robertson 47
  Steph. 17
  Stephen 11
  Thos. 47, 115, 122
  Wilson 159
  Wm. 8, 23, 24, 28, 56,
    68, 147, 148, 160,
    176
Johnstone, Alexdr. 60
  Danl. 26
Joice, Henry 68
Joiner, Benj. 143
  Isarel 3
  Jno. 8, 47
Joins, Edmond 162
Jolly, Jno. 17
  Michael 176
Jones, Abraham 80, 146
  Abram 148
  Adam 57, 60, 147, 176
  Allen 86
  Ambrose 92, 152
  Anne (Mrs.) 39
  Basil 65
  Batt 3, 15, 17
  Batte 11
  Benj. 8, 36, 176
  Betty 113
  Cartna 82
  Chas. 47
  David 8
  Drury 68, 70, 71
  Edw. 47, 100, 106, 166
  Edwd. 172
  Eliz. 3, 77, 115
  Francis 17, 68
  Frederrick 17
  Gabriel 176, 178
  Geo. 30, 32, 34, 36,
    47
  H. 63
  Harrison 62
  Henry 141, 143, 150,
    166
  Henry (Jr.) 151
  Henry B. 47
  Henry C. 47
  Hezekiah 65
  Hugh 110, 122, 128,
    153, 170
  Inigo 47
  Isaac 77, 82
  Jacob 110, 128
  Janes 83
  Jas. 17, 38, 59, 71,
    84, 104, 130, 143,
    151
  Jemmimah 150
  Jesse 76, 80, 162
  Jez. 146
  Jno. 3, 8, 12, 17, 20,
    26, 28, 59, 65, 70,
    73, 77, 80, 95, 104,
    138, 152, 162
  Joel 59
  Jonathan 158
  Jos. 95, 106
  Keziah 150
  Lew 152
  Lewellen 148
  Malachia 92
  Mark 141, 143
  Mary 36, 138

Jones (cont.)
  Mary Gibbons 36
  Mathew 68
  Milachi 94
  N. 122
  N. W. 36
  Nathan 82, 110, 115,
    116
  Nimrod 62
  Noble 23, 47
  Noble W. 30, 34, 38,
    47
  Obadiah 47
  Peter 102
  Philip 14
  Phillip 162
  Rachel 113
  Reuben 122
  Reubin 116
  Richd. 60, 100
  Robt. 84, 89, 141,
    149, 150, 152
  Russell 98
  Saml. 58
  Sarah 113
  Seaborn 30, 143, 146,
    150
  Tho. 17, 65
  Thos. 11, 56, 58, 59,
    62, 86, 92, 96, 141,
    143
  Thos. S. 60
  W. 30
  Wm. 3, 47, 62, 92,
    100, 102, 110, 122,
    128, 133, 143, 146,
    150, 166
Jordan, Charity 3
  Demcy 118
  Elijah 8
  Fleming 92
  Henry 8
  Jacob 166
  Jas. 22, 36
  Jno. 3, 84, 92
  Josiah 166, 171
  Palsy 171
  River 84
  Robt. 47
  Sol. 166
  Sterling 15
  Thos. 8
  Wm. 32, 155
Jordon, Baxton 17
  Eliz. 178
  Matthew 17
Joseph, Jno. 47
Josey, Henry 166
Jossey, Henry 173
  Mary 173
Jourdan, Danl. 122
  Jno. 80
Journingan, Jas. 68
Jowedin, Sterling 4
Joyce, Alexdr. 100
  Henry 68, 70, 72
Joyner, Jos. 137
Judah, (?) (Mrs.) 47
Judson, Jos. 24, 26, 28
Julin, Benj. 176
Jurdine, Jno. 138
  Leonard 134, 137
  Leonard (II) 134
  Macy 138
  Wm. 136
Justice, Aaron 14
  Demsey 122
  Jno. 122

Kaehler, Jno. 47
Kagle, Roger 65
Kail, Jno. 143
Kain, David 47
  Richd. 83, 167
Kane, (?) (Mrs.) 47
Kanedy, Chas. 125
Kapper, Jacob 47
Karr, H. 118
  Henry 122
  Peter 36, 39
  Walter 83
Kaupt, Jno. 34
Keal, Jno. 47
  Martha 47
Kean, Susan (Mrs.) 47
Keane, Benj. 25
Keanor, Wm. 143
Kearnes, Thos. 146
Keath, Saml. (Jr.) 155
Keating, Edw. 92
  Richd. 47
Keaton, Jno. 155
  Kadish 107
Kee, Jas. 122
Keebler, Joshua 36
Keegan, Allen 21, 24
Keen, Gilbert 167
  Massey 167
Keeth, Jno. 176
Keggan, Allen 26, 28
Kegler, Jno. 72
Keith, Alexdr. 30
  Jno. 178
Kelcey, Noah 150, 151
Kell, Jno. 135
Kellebrew, Lawrence 4
Keller, Geo. 47
Kelley, Jno. 122
  Morriss 59
  Peter 122
  Wm. 178
Kellogg, Enoch 21
  Jos. 47
Kellough, David 167
  Issac 167
Kelly, Barnard 167
  Jas. 167
  Jno. 62, 141, 143,
    155, 162, 167, 176
  Lloyd 162
  Morris 65
  Thos. 100
  Wm. 8, 162, 176
Kelpherson, Jno. 143
Kelsall, Amelia 132,
    135, 138
  Ann 47
  Jno. 47
  Roger 133
Kemp, Benj. 159
  Danl. 4
  Jno. 130, 136
  Jonathan 11, 15
  Jos. 159
  Reuben 159
  Stephen 159
  Wm. 155, 159, 162
Kendall, David 162
  Henry 60
  Jeremiah 162
  Wm. 162
Kendrick, Burrell 155
  Jno. 58, 62, 159
  Thos. 62
Kenedy, Henry 47
Kengrey, Danl. 4
Kennedy, Chas. 82

Kennedy (cont.)
  Eliz. 77
  Fields 110
  Jno. 141, 143, 152
  Rich. 28
  Richd. 27
  Robt. 77
  Wm. 109, 127
Kennelly, Joshua 126
Kennerly, Thos. 92
Kennon, Wm. 57
Kent, Jno. 4
Ker, Wm. 47
Kerr, Alle 171
  David 171
  Eliz. 30
  Henry 127
  Jno. 113
  Peter 30
Kersey, Elijah 8
Kershaw, Isaac 36
Kertin, (?) (Mrs.) 8
Ketler, Geo. 47
Kettle, Mary 162
Kettler, Mary 36
Kettles, Jno. L. 47
Key, Jno. M. 88
  Sandy C. 17
  Tandy C. 4
  Wm. Bibb 78
Keyes, Jno. 88
Keys, Jno. 75
Kezay, Richd. 4
Kidd, J. 86
  Jas. 167
  Webb 76, 86
  Wm. 75
Kieffer, Barbara 47
  David 34, 47
  Frederic 47
  Henry 47
Kilbee, C. 13
  Chas. 14
  Christopher 4
  Christopher (Cpt.) 7
Kilbey, Jno. 113
Kilgore, Jno. 88, 115,
    167
  Peter 167
  Robt. 176
Killbee, Christy 17
Killey, Thos. 95
Killingsworth, M. 63
Killough, Allen 96
Kilpatrick, Thos. 4
Kimbrel, Chas. 4
Kimbrough, Jno. 113, 162
Kinder, Eliz. 47
Kindill, Henry 62
Kindrick, Barrie 162
  Jonas 162
  Nathl. 155
  Nathl. O. 152
Kiner, Jno. 158
  Nathl. 158
King, Alexdr. 113, 122
  Curtis 110
  Edw. 92
  Edw. Edmond 92
  Eliz. 113
  Ezekiel 86
  Henry 70
  J. P. Thomas 28
  Jas. 113
  Jno. 20, 21, 22, 23,
    26, 28, 59, 80, 84,
    89, 92, 109, 118,
    122, 167

King (cont.)
  Jonathan 63
  Jos. 75, 110
  Lombard 86
  Nancy 110
  Parks 155
  Roswell 103, 107
  Saml. 17, 63
  Sarah 23, 131
  Tho. 23, 26, 28
  Thos. 20, 22, 24, 83,
    122, 131, 136
  Wm. 21, 22, 25, 26,
    27, 28, 47, 68, 70,
    72
Kingsley, Saml. 47
Kinkade, Hugh 75
Kinman, Jas. 167
Kinna, Danl. 96
Kinney, Joshua 122
Kinsey, Valentine 47
Kirby, Wm. 47, 68
Kirk, Jas. 34, 36, 47
  Thos. 47
Kirkland, Christiana 138
  Saml. 17
  Wm. 132, 138
Kirkpatrick, Jas. 100
  Thos. 96
Kirkwood, Hugh 176
  Nathan 176
Kitchen, Benj. 155
Kitchens, Benj. 160, 162
Kittle, Wm. 12
Kitts, Jno. 4
Klenett, (?) 47
Knap, Charely 113
  Justice 110
Knight, Jno. 8
  Nehemiah 141, 143
  Robt. 8
  Thos. Jones 72
  Zach. 134
  Zachrh. 130
Knoles, Jas. 113
Knotts, Nathl. 17
Knowles, Edmund 116
Knox, Jno. 167
  Saml. 92
Kogler, Jno. 68, 72
Kolb, Peter 17
Kollock, Lemuel 47
Kraft, David 47
Krafz, Jno. Conrad 47
Kraus, Saml. 70
Krieger, Jno. 47
Krutz, Conrod 36
L'homaca, Antoinette 48
  Eliz. 48
  Lacques 48
  Reine Francois 48
Lachner, Frederic 48
Lacy, Jane 59
  Jno. 59
Ladson, Jane 131
Lafearse, Isaac 157
Lafferty, Jno. 98
Laffitte, (?) (Mrs.) 48
  Peter S. 36
  Peter Saml. 48
  Pierre Thos. 48
Lafitte, Peter S. 30
Lagarde, Peter 48
Lain, Jno. 102
Laine, Etheldred 4
Laird, Absalom 70, 73
  Jno. 110
  Margery 113

Lam, Sol. 17
Lamar, Basil 141, 143,
  146, 167
  Catherine 146
  Frances 115
  Jas. 126, 152
  Jno. 110, 113, 115,
    122, 146, 147
  Jno. (Sr.) 65
  Luke 155
  Saml. 11
  Sarah 143, 173
  Thos. 110, 118
  Z. 80
  Zach. 173
  Zachariah 92, 147, 167
Lamare, Thos. 122
Lamas, Jas. 58
Lamb, Abraham 8
  Abraham (Jr.) 8
  Abram 17
  Barnaby 17
  Bethal 8
  Charlotte Cryer 24
  Geo. 48
  Jesse 155, 162
  Jno. 83
  Jno. (Sr.) 88
  Robt. 113
  Sol. 8
  Tho. 21, 24, 25
  Thos. 8
  Wm. 34, 36, 48
Lambe, Tho. 28
Lambert, Andrew 4
  David 150
  Jas. 4, 13, 15
  Jno. 13, 106
  Wm. 106
Lambeth, Jas. 48
Lambkin, Saml. 92
Lambright, Jno. 131,
  136, 137
  Jno. J. 138
  Marg. 131, 138
Lamkin, Jas. 59
  Jeremiah 65
  Jno. 58
  Winifret 59
Lamkins, Saml. 155
Lampkin, Jas. 148
  Jeremiah 143, 148
  Jno. 148
Lanair, Clement 68
Lancaster, Jos. 4
  Levi 115, 122
  Thos. 118
  Wm. 108, 118, 122, 162
Land, Henry 155
  Isaac 8
Lander, Jas. 148
Landers, Abraham 115
  Jacob 115
Lane, Alex. (Jr.) 68
  Alexdr. 72
  Bryant 72
  Chas. 100, 167
  Etheldred 4
  Jas. 170, 176
  Jno. 72, 94, 98, 100
  Jonathan 96
  Mary (Mrs.) 70
  Thos. 68, 70, 71
Lanear, Saml. 15
Lang, Isaac 26
  Jno. 122, 128
  Jno. Peter 48
  Peter 48

Lang (cont.)
  Sarah 26
Lange, Ann Marie
  Gertrude 32
  Ann Mary Gertrude 48
  Jno. Peter 32, 39
  Wm. Henry 34, 48
Langford, Jas. 155
  Sarah 97
  Wyatt 97, 102
  Wyett 98
Langley, Benj. 48
  Eliz. 48
  Jno. 48
  Nathl. 48
  Saml. 36
Langlois, Jacques 48
  Jas. 48
Langstaff, Jas. 26
Langston, David 62, 148
  Jno. 59
  Saml. 59, 62, 148
Lanier, Ann Mary 68
  Benj. 72
  Clement 70, 72
  Jno. 68, 72
  Lem. 17
  Lewis 22, 127
  Saml. 11
  Wm. 113
Lankester, Wm. 76
Lankeston, Jese 122
Lankford, Edmond 136
  Jno. 135, 167
  Wiet 95
Lansum, Jas. 128
  Richd. 128
Lanton, Tho. 65
Lantorn, Tho. 65
Larcey, Wm. 4
Lard, Jno. 128
Larice, Wm. 4
Larmarre, Jacques Lucien
  48
Laroche, Isaac 48
Larrie, Jno. 148
Lartieque, Gerard 48
Larvin, Jno. 149
Lary, Jeremiah 4
Laseter, Lemuel 17
Lasiter, Lemuel 14
Lassater, Jno. 4
  Saml. 4
Lasseter, Hansil 155
  Jno. 13, 14, 15
  Jno. (Cpt.) 7
  John 12
  Jos. 11
  Saml. 11, 15
Lastinger, David 72
  Hannah 68
  Jno. 68
Lauderdale, Jno. 167
Laughlin, Tho. 65
  Wm. 65
Lavender, Benj. 48
  Wm. 48
Laville, Mons'. 48
Lavinder, Benj. 48
Law, Geo. 131
  Jos. (Jr.) 138
  Jos. (Sr.) 132
  Mary Esther 133
  Thos. E. 138
Lawed, Sarah 122
Lawler, Jno. 22
Lawrence, Abm. 122
  Abraham 116

Lawrence (cont.)
  Henry 48
  J. T. 36, 48
  Jas. T. 48
  Jno. 170
  Richd. M. 48
  Saml. 48
  Wm. 100
  Zachariah 167
Lawson, Eliz. 131
  Francis 118, 122
  H. 17
  Hugh 4, 14, 159
  Jno. 48, 57, 58, 62,
    130, 131, 162
  Jno. (Jr.) 131, 132,
    135, 136
  Jno. (Sr.) 131, 135,
    136
  Roger 17
  Will (Jr.) 122
  Will (Sr.) 122
  Wm. 115
  Wm. C. 131
Lawton, Jos. 48
  Jos. J. 48
  Robt. 34
LeConte, Jno. 136
  Wm. 34
LeFils, Bernard 48
LeGrand, Jesse 102
Lea, Wm. 167
Leach, (?) (Mrs.) 48
  Eliz. 48
Leak, Jas. 127
  Jno. 129
Leake, Jean 105
  Richd. 38, 103, 104,
    105, 106, 133, 134,
    138
Leamonts, Jos. 122
Leanes, Jacob 59
Leapham, Aaron 155, 162
Leapour, Jas. 74
Lear, Jonathan 75
Lears, Jno. 48
Leath, Jno. 141
Leatherlin, Wm. 141
Leaughton, (?) 122
Leavenworth, Eli 36
Leaver, G. 36
  Gabriel 30, 32, 39
  Mary 48
Leaves, Eliz. 32
  Gabriel 32
  Jno. 32
  Mary 32
Leavin, Jno. 113
Leavit, Jos. 48
Lebey, Andrew 30
Lecase, Behie 47
Ledbetter, Drury 76
  Isaac 158, 162, 176
  Jno. 167, 176
Ledson, Thos. 118
Lee, Ambrose 60
  Giles 167
  Hugh 26, 27, 28
  Jane C. 138
  Jas. 167
  Jessee 176
  Joshua 98
  Mason 107
  Sol. 36, 39
  Timothy 65
  Wm. 4, 100, 141, 143,
    151, 152
Leech, Henry B. 100

Leech (cont.)
Wm. 95
Lefever, Abraham 4
  Jas. 4
Lefils, Bernard 39
Leftridge, Jno. 167
Leftwich, Jno. 173
Legett, Jno. 92
Legget, Abrah. 135
Leghorn, Wm. 157
Legrand, Jesse 95
Lehalf, Marris 48
Lehre, J. 30
Leigh, Anselm 153
  Benj. 152
  Edmund 153
  Walter 65
Leimburger, Apolinia 71
Leion, David 34, 36, 48
  Hannah 48
Leith, Jno. 59, 148
Lemar, Jesse 176
Lenair, Clement 68
  Jno. 68
  Lemuel 68
Leonard, Benj. 122
  Elijah 143
  Henry 138
  Saml. (Dr.) 138
  Wm. 143
Leqous, (?) 48
Leroy, Francis 48
Lesley, Jas. 107
Lesly, Jas. 133
Lester, Ezekiel 4, 15
  Jas. 4
  Jno. 4
  Wm. 4
Lett, Jno. T. 48
Levecque, Pierre Louis
  48
Levens, Jas. 176
Leverett, Absolom 176
  Henry 176
  Robt. 172
  Thos. 170, 176
Levett, Francis 30, 48
Levily, Jesse 160
Levin, David 133
Levingston, Robt. 115
  Saml. 116
Lewden, Wm. 30, 32, 34,
  36, 48
Lewis, (?) (Mrs.) 48
  Abraham 4
  Abraham (Jr.) 4
  Christiana 36
  Elazer 4
  Elijah 131
  Freeman 92, 103
  Geo. 17
  Jacob 11, 12, 13, 17,
  160
  Jas. 17
  Jno. 4
  Joel 12, 17, 160
  Jos. 133
  Nancy 4
  Nathl. 48
  Philip 80
  R. W. 17
  Robt. 22
  Robt. B. 28
  Steph. 48
  Tho. 17
  Tho. (Jr.) 17
  Thos. 12, 14, 160
  Winslow 48

Lewis (cont.)
Wm. 48, 68, 102
Lightfoot, Jno. 155, 162
Lillibridge, Hampton 48
  Jno. 48
Lilly, Ens. 158
Limbert, Jno. W. 107
  Jno. Wm. 105, 106
  Wm. 48
Limeburger, Apolina
  (Mrs.) 70
  Christian Ireal 70
Linch, Jno. 158
Lindsay, Jno. 155
Lindsey, Benj. 34, 36
  Benj. (Rev.) 32
  Chas. 48
  Eliz. 4
  Jacob 100
  Jas. 26
  Jas. M. 22
  Jno. 97, 100, 167
  Mary 32, 97
  Moses 143
  Reuben 86
Lindsy, Jacob 125
Liner, Henry 98
Lines, Dorcas 131, 138
  Saml. 131, 133
Lingo, Moses 155, 162
  Patrick 155
Linn, Anne 59, 65
  Chas. 59, 65
  Geo. 59
  Jane 65
  Jno. 100
  Wm. 65, 167
Linsey, Dennis 62
  Reubin 84
  Wm. 62
Linton, Jno. 155
  Wm. T. 167
Linville, Wm. 143
Lipham, Aaron 173
  Frederick 92, 167
  Moses 176
Lipsey, Ricketson 152
Lister, Jno. 113
Litch, Wm. 88
Little, Absalom 84
  Archibald 4
  Frederick 4
  Isabell 77
  Jas. 92
  Jas. (Sr.) 77
  Jas. H. 94, 100
  Wm. 11, 14
  Wm. (Cpt.) 7
  Wm. (Jr.) 17
  Wm. (Sr.) 155
Littleton, Wm. 122, 167
Lively, Jno. 96
  Matthew 4
Liverman, B. 63
  Livia 153
Livingston, Aaron 113,
  118
  Robt. 122, 129
Lloyd, Ben 36
  Benj. 34, 36, 48
  Chas. 113, 127
  Ed. 32
  Edw. 38, 48
  Jno. 110, 113, 127
  Josiah 48
  Mary 48
  Patience (Mrs.) 12
  Rebecca 48

Lloyd (cont.)
Thos. 12, 48
Locke, Jesse 4
Lockerman, Persiana 32
Lockett, David 113
Lockhart, Isaac 4
  Jno. 170
  Jos. 8
  Richd 118
  Richd. 92, 122, 167
  Saml. 12
Lockon, Peter 32
Lodge, Francis 4, 15
Loffitte, Peter S. 36
Loftie, Daniel 60
Loftin, Jno. 15
Lofton, Ezekiel 141
  Marg. 155
  Van 155
Logan, Saml. 17
London, Jno. 68, 70
Long, Evans 92, 176
  Frederic 48
  Frederick 36
  Geo. 8
  Henry 122
  Jas. 8
  Jno. 48
  Jos. 74, 83
  Matthew 48
  Nicholas 83, 133, 155,
  162, 167
  Nicholas (Jr.) 155
  Nimrod 74, 92
Longan, Saml. 17
Longdon, Saml. 157
Longstreet, Danl. 92,
  143, 152
  David 143, 148
  Saml. 162
  Wm. 21, 148, 153
Longworth, Jas. 48
  Jos. 48
Loper, Joshua 68
Lord, Geo. 48
  Laudwick 162
  Richd. 113
  Wm. 4, 15, 113, 122
Lott, Abraham 17
  Arthur 17
  Jas. 17
  Jno. 17, 68, 162
  Jno. (Jr.) 17, 72, 155
  Jno. (Sr.) 72
  Mark 17, 155, 162
  Nathan 17, 68, 159
  Reuben 17
  Reubin 11, 14
  Reubin (Cpt.) 7
  Wm. 8, 17
Lousol, Peter 48
Love, David 113, 118,
  122, 129
  David (Col.) 109
  Jno. 36
  John (Dr.) 48
  Wm. 167
Lovelady, Jane 77
  Thos. 77, 86, 88
Loveless, Wm. 143
Lovell, Jas. 65
Loveman, Robt. 80
Lovett, Tho. F. 68
Lovin, Adam 176
Low, Ann 146
  Aquila 4
  Danel 126
  Danl. 113, 122, 141

Low (cont.)
E. 17
Frances 159
Geo. 146
Isaac 62, 65
Isaac (Jr.) 146
Isaac (Sr.) 146
Jane 135
Jas. 126
Mary (Mrs.) 139
Phillip (Maj.) 139
Ralph 126
Thos. 126
Wm. 146
Lowe, Beverly 148
Danl. 143
David 116
E. 13
Edmund 11
Geo. 153
Henry 13
Isaac 65
Lowery, (?) (Jdg.) 172
Ja. (Jr.) 83
Jno. 82, 113
Judge 172
Mashack 83
Lowrey, Elisha 86
J. L. 86
Jas. 86
Jno. 86
Robt. 8
Lowrman, Jas. 71
Jno. 71
Jno. (Jr.) 71
Mary 71
Lowry, Ben 174
Benj. 109, 127
Edmond 82
Henry 167
Jas. 74
Jno. 4, 110, 113
Mary 110, 127
Simeon 155
Wm. 74
Lowther, Chas. 48
Edw. 68
Jno. 48
Lowtrip, Abagail 65
Loyalless, Jas. 170, 171
Sarah 171
Loyd, Chas. 126
Danl. 167
Jas. 122
Thos. 65
Loyed, Jno. 126
Wm. 126
Loyer, Abrian 48
Lucas, Jno. 36
Moses 162
Lucena, Jas. 48
Lucas 48
Lucenburg, Tabias 20
Lucke, Moses 158
Luckey, Alex. 92
David 92
Jno. 113
Thos. 118
Wm. 92
Luckie, Hez. 80
Jane 82
Jno. 82, 98
Lucky, Jas. 178
Wm. 167
Lucous, Wm. 149
Lumpkin, Geo. 74
Lumsden, Jerh. 113
Luncy, Nathl. 70

Luncy (cont.)
Theophilus 71
Lunday, Nathl. 68
Theophilus 71
Lundy, Francis 71
Geo. 71
Jane 71
Mary Esther 71
Lungino, Bartholomew 4
Lunsden, Jesse 122
Lunsford, Enoch 176
Lutzenburg, Tobias 25
Lyle, Rhoda 167
Robt. 48
Lyles, Matthew 21, 25
Lyman, Elihu 17, 36,
110, 127, 167
Lynch, Dennis 126
Jno. 155
Lyner, Chris. 92
Christee 96
Lynes, Benj. 34
Moses 32
Lynn 135
Lynn, (?) (Dr.) 135
Dr. 135
Lynum, Wm. 158
Lyon, Grace 48
Henry 48
Jas. 8
Jno. 48, 107
Jos. 70
Richd. 158
Lyons, Danl. 22, 26
Maberry, Joel 60
Mabrey, Joel 58
Mabry, Parham 48
MacMillian, Jon 76
Mace, Wm. 9
Machin, Jos. 48
Machogin, Jno. 48
MackAllen, Wm. 118
Mackay, Jas. 4
Thos. 155
Mackey, Gallant 96
Jas. 17
Jno. 75
Mackie, Jno. 92, 101
Saml. 80, 92
Thos. 80
Mackinstosh, Wm. 106
Mackleroy, Reuben 167
Wm. 167
Maclean, Jos. 34
Sophia Sarah 34
Macleod, D. 30
Jno. 39
Macon, H. 152
Macray, Jno. 49
Madden, Peter 49
Maddock, Jos. 143
Maddocks, Jos. 141
Maddox, Clayborn 113
Jacob 109, 110, 113
Jno. 60, 143, 149
Jos. 62, 65, 122
Sally 113
W. 122
Wm. 65
Maddux, Alexdr. 122
Leaven 126
Saml. 126
Wm. 60, 118, 126
Zach. 122
Madison, Jas. 101
Madkin, Jas. 80
Madock, Wm. 113
Madox, Wm. 162

Magahee, Jno. 62
Magee, Hugh 148, 149,
151
Luis 149
Routon 62
Wm. 167
Magehee, Wm. 59
Magiapan, Antonio 49
Magruder, Ninian Offutt
143
Ninian offcutt 65
Saml. 148
Mahan, Patrick 65
Maher, Matthias 148
Main, Wm. 49
Mainer, Jno. 116, 122
Mains, Robt 101
Robt. 49
Saml. 62
Maires, Tho. 63
Malet, Gidson 68
Mall, Margareth 49
Mallard, Lazarus 133,
136, 139
Mallory, Francis 49
Maloan, Martin 143
Malone, Peter 58
Malpas, Jas. 25
Malsap, Jeremiah 68
Mandline, Francis 89
Maner, Wm. 133
Manifee, Geo. 96
Richd. 96
Mann, Jas. 21
Jno. P. 131, 139
Jno. Preston 132
Luke 32, 34
Luke (Jr.) 34
Milley 167
Newby 4
Nuby 4
Thos. 34
Mannen, Wm. 71
Manners, David 49
Manning, Chas. 176
Wm. 49
Manor, Henry 103, 107
Manson, Dennison 105
Duncan 104, 106
Jesse 17
Jno. 4
Marbury, Ann 152
Horatia 92
Horatio 4, 58, 150
Horatis 58
Joel 60
Leonard 21, 32, 101,
106, 141, 149, 150
Wm. 101
March, Geo. 20, 23, 27,
28
Marck, Geo. 26
Marcon, Jas. 167
Marcus, Jno. 68, 101,
118, 122
Mare, Wm. 9
Marie, Jos. 49
Marien, Renault 49
Mark, Eli 143
Saint 70, 73
Markham, Arthur 143
Marks, Jas. 101, 167
Jno. 172
Jno. Haistens 172
Lucy 172
Polly Garland 172
Marran, Margt. 71
Marreer, Jno. 26

Marress, Edw. 62
Marritt, (?) (Mrs.) 49
Marsh, Gilbert 90
Marshal, Jas. 176
  Mathew 176
Marshall, (?) (Dr.) 56
  Albert 153
  Danl. 57, 59, 60
  Jno. 4, 22, 56, 65
  Jos. 59
  Levi 58, 60
  Levy 56
  Manham 15
  Matthew 4, 11, 14
  Moses 58
  Sol. 63, 141, 143, 162
Marshon, Andrew 176
Martain, Elijah 94
  Merritt 95
Martin, Barkley 78
  Claborn 84
  Clem 9
  Clement 70, 139
  David 78, 86
  Eliz. 110
  Eliza 77
  Geo. 72
  Godfrey 122, 128
  Jacob 4
  Jas. 17, 68, 74, 84
  Jno. 4, 49, 68, 84,
    86, 160
  Jos. 98, 118, 155
  Joshua 174
  Martin 4, 14, 68
  Murdoch 49
  Murdock 9, 80
  Oliver 159
  Peter 49, 109
  Robt. 77, 167
  Thos. 89, 162
  Wm. 11, 14, 15, 39,
    70, 92, 122, 155,
    176
Marton, Jas. 158
Mashbourn, Elisha 176
Mason, Jno. 4, 22, 28,
  95, 174, 176
  Thos. 49
  Wm. 174
Massey, (?) (Widow) 9
  Jas. 21
  Jos. 139
Mathe, Jas. 135
Mather, Jas. 133
Mathers, Daniel 28
  Danl. 22, 26
  Francis 49
  Peggy 32
  Wm. 32
  Wm. H. 49
Mathes, Francis 134
Mathews, Benj. 14
  Francis 139
  Geo. 98, 101
  Jas. 98, 101
  Jno. 139
  Jos. 62
  Mary 143
  Moses 176
  Moses (Jr.) 178
  Wm. 62
Mathis, Benj. 13
  Meshick 141
Matkin, Daniel 80
  Jas. 78
Matthew, Jane 4
Matthews, Benj. 14

Matthews (cont.)
  Danl. (Jr.) 92
  Geo. 172
  Henry 49
  Jas. 4, 95, 167, 171
  Jenny 60
  Jeremiah 167
  Jesse 148
  Jno. 68, 80, 172
  Mary 60
  Meshack 56, 61, 143
  Mesheck 148
  Moses 167
  Ralph 167
  Wm. 9, 49
Matthias, Eliz. 65
Matthis, Jno. 116
  Josiah 9
Matthiss, Jesse 62
Maxey, Jonah 37
Maxwell, Audley 136, 139
  David 58, 61, 63, 143
  Eliz. 133, 139
  Jas. 83, 110, 131,
    136, 139
  Jno. 49, 80, 131
  Mary 131
  Robt. 155
  Sally 39
  Thos. 74, 83, 133, 135
  Walter 30, 37
  Wm. 37, 38, 133
May, Balam 167
  Jas. 155, 167
  Jos. 143
  Mark 4
  Thos. 11
Maybank, Andrew 135,
  136, 139
  Andrew (Jr.) 131
Maybe, Mattethias 95
Mayer, Aug. 30
  Augustus 30, 34
  Serenus 49
Mayers, Jacob 74
Mayhall, Wm. 62
Mayhorn, Chas. 178
Maynor, Henry 107
Mayo, Mark 162
Mazo, Jno. 107
  Wm. 104
McAlhattan, Abraham 113
McAlhenan, Jno. 83
McAllister, Jno. 110
  Matthew 36, 48
  Richd. 34, 36, 48
McAlpin, Robt. 113, 122,
  127, 129
  Sol. 75
McAlplin, Sol. 89
McAnally, Jno. 4
McBee, Jas. 92
McBride, Jno. 68
McBurnett, Daniel 167
McCabe, Jas. 48
McCagney, Batey 159
McCall, David 68
  Eliza Henrietta 39
  Geo. 70, 72
  Jesse 68
  Jno. 48, 68, 72
  Jos. 8
  Sarah 70
  Sherod 68
  T. 100
  Tho. 21
  Thos. 20, 38, 48, 68,
    70, 115, 118, 162

McCall (cont.)
  Thos. (Jr.) 68
  Wm. 68
McCallum, Jos. 17
McCann, James 102
  Jas. 98
McCannon, Jas. 92, 167
McCarcal, Jas. 155
McCardel, Henry 65
McCarrel, Jno. 4
McCarrol, Jno. 14
McCarroll, Jno. 14
McCartney, Jas. 178
  Jno. 178
McCarty, Danl. 65
  Jno. 65, 148
McCaskill, Donald 48
McCaule, Eliza (Mrs.) 48
  Francis 38
McCavy, (?) (Cpt.) 158
McCenley, Jos. 141
McCeymore, Emily 162
McClain, Thos. 24
McClair, Lewis 92
McClamy, Mark 4
McClane, Susanah 27
  Susannah 27
  Tho. 22
  Thos. 174
McClary, Robt. 75
McClean, Tho. 27, 28
McCleery, Jno. 28
McClellan, Wm. 122
McClelland, Francina 113
  Wm. 108
McClendon, Amos 171
  Bethaney 171
  Dennis 171
  Isaac 122, 171
  Jacob (Sr.) 170
  Jemima 171
  Joel 108, 155
  Laney 171
  Lewis 162
  Martha 171
  Nancy 171
  Penelope 171
  Saml. 171, 172
  Thos. 167
  Travis 167, 171
  Wilson 155
McClennan, Jno. (Jr.)
  133
McCleskey, Jas. 80
McCloud, Robt. 62
McClure, Jos. 25
McCluskey, David 82
  Jas. 88
  Mary 82
McClusky, David 87
  Jas. 75, 86, 87, 167
McColeal, Jas. 60
McCollack, Jno. 48
McCollum, Jas. 167
McComb, Andrew 130
McCombs, Andrew 113, 122
McConel, Jince 113
McConkey, Andw. 4
McConky, Ann 32
  Henry 71
  Jas. 32, 34, 36, 48
McConnell, Manuel 75
  Wm. 100
McCorcle, Jas. 162
McCord, Jno. 62
McCorkle, Jas. 176
  Jno. 176
  Robt. 65

McCormack, (?) (Mrs.)
  104
Jno. 128
Jos. 103
Saml. 8
McCormick, Jas. 167
Jos. 65, 167
Michael 14
McCoumb, Jas. 27
McCown, Jas. 167
McCoy, Danl. 167
Henry 122
Jesse 8
Jno. 63, 122
Wm. 8, 70, 73, 136
McCrary, Matthew 176
Moses 22
McCrea, Gustavus 130
Jno. 130, 131
McCredie, Andrew 23, 34,
  38, 48, 148
Mary 48
Sarah 39
McCree, Wm. 100, 167
McCullars, Bryant 162
McCullen, Bryant 4, 155
McCuller, Brittain 167
Bryant (Cpt.) 7
McCullers, B. 17
Britain 4
Brittain 167
Bryant 11, 14, 15, 155
Chas. 17
Jno. 8
McCullock, Jno. 32
McCullough, Alex. 122
Jacob 141, 143
Jas. 137
Jos. 141
Marg. 131
Mary 137
Saml. 141
Wm. 122, 137
McCune, Wm. 78
McCurdy, David 75
Hugh 48
Jas. 76
Jno. 75
McCurrda, Jno. 84
McCutchen, Jos. 125
Wm. 76
McCutchin, Jas. 92
Jos. 122, 167
McDade, Chas. 4, 141
McDaniel, Britan 17
Jno. 89
Wm. 143
McDonal, Hugh 21
McDonald, Absolom 143
Alex 4
Alexdr. 70
Andrew 62
Chas. 92
Donald 80, 83, 89
Helen 77
Henry 146
Henry M. 151
Hugh 77, 80, 83, 87,
  92, 100
Jas. 62, 77, 78, 82
Jno. 63, 70, 78, 141,
  143
Jno. M. 65
Jno. W. 83
Josiah 126
Mary 141
Norman 131
Patrick 167

McDonald (cont.)
Robert. 106
Ronald 139
Sarah 82
Thos. 160
Wm. 56, 106
McDonaldson, Jos. 48
McDonough, (?) 146
McDougal, Alex 92
McDougla, Jno. 95
McDougle, Alexdr. 84
McDowel, Wm. 146
McDowell, Robt. 122
Tho. 86
Thos. 155, 162, 167,
  178
Wm. 155
McDuffee, Jno. 62, 141
McDuffie, Jno. 143
McDugle, Daniel 89
Jno. 89
McEavert, Andrew 80
McElhanen, Jno. 83
McEver, Andrew 80
McFadzen, Jno. 48
McFall, Geo. 92, 167
McFarland, Jas. 58, 65,
  152
Wm. 152
McFarlane, Jno. 32
McFarlen, Jno. 30, 32
Peter 176
McFarlin, Edwd. 148
Jno. 32
Wm. 176
McFee, (?) 104
McGahey, Jas. 122
Jno. 122
McGar, Owen 143
McGardy, Edw. 89
McGarey, Edw. 92
McGarrey, Edw. 92
McGarry, Edw. 80
McGarver, Danl. 48
McGary, Edw. 92
McGee, Henry 8
Hugh 65
Patrick 122
Shadrack 4, 162
Wm. 143
McGehee, Micajah 167
Saml. 4, 155
Shadrack 68
McGehu, Wm. 11
McGillies, Benedict 28
McGillis, R. 23
Randolph 23, 27
McGinty, Jno. 171
McGirth, Danl. 21
Mary 21
McGlomry, Elijah 126
McGomery, Jno. 14
McGough, Wm. 108
McGowan, David 155
Robt. 92, 97, 100, 155
McGowen, Jas. 8
McGruder, Jno. 4
Offett 141
McGuire, Jas. 126
Thompson 78
McInsey, Jesse 63
McIntosh, Augus 139
Barbara 38
Donald 105, 152
Geo 48
Geo. 48, 139
Georgiana 139
Hampden 49

McIntosh (cont.)
Henry 49
Jas. 49
Jno. 32, 36, 106, 133
Jno. (Jr.) 105, 106
Joshua 17
Lachlan 32, 38, 133,
  139
Lachlin 49
Lachlon 105
Leah 36
Lochlin 92
Locklin 130
Sarah Simons 104
Wm. 23, 104, 139
Wm. (Jr.) 103, 130,
  136, 139, 152
McIver, Alexdr. 32, 135,
  136
Jno. 34
McKain, Alexdr. 49
McKay, Henry 167
Jno. 8, 86
McKeane, Robt. 49
McKee, Jno. 86
Thos. 84
Wm. 86
McKeen, Jno. 130, 132
McKegney, Jas. 4
McKengney, Jas. 4
McKenney, Wm. 176
McKennie, Jno. 153
McKensie, Jno. 159
McKenzie, Aaron 4
Jno. 80
Jno. (Cpt.) 7
Wm. 75, 78
McKie, Henry 171
Sarah 171
McKineah, Jno. 149
McKinley, Jos. 56, 143
McKinne, Garret 153
McKinney, Jno. 176
Littleberry 173
McKinnon, Jno. 49
McKinny, Lemuel 113
McKinsee, Jno. 4
McKinsey, Jno. 68, 83
Wm. 90, 129
McKinty, Pat. 72
Patrick 36, 71
McKinzie, Patrick 49
McKiver, Jno. 86
McKnight, Mary Ann 49,
  132
McKonkey, Jas. 4
McKoy, (?) 113
McLachlan, Mary 36
McLain, Cath. 49
McLallas, Danl. 36
McLane, Danl. 150, 155,
  162
Jas. 100
Wm. 174
McLaughlin, Isaac 36
McLean, Andrew 49, 136
Andrew Cowper 36
Catherine 36
Danl. 153
Jno. 170
Josiah 34
Mary 36
Wm. 36
McLemore, Matthew 141
McLendon, Mark 160
Thos. 160
McLeod, Anthony 34
Donald 34, 49

McLeod (cont.)
Jas. 104, 106, 107, 136
Jno. 32, 36, 134
Murdock 107
Norman 49
Roderick 49
Wm. 49
McLeroy, Jno. 167
McMahan, Jno. 4
McMahon, Jno. 49
McManes, Jas. 143
Jno. 146
McManus, Jno. 151
McMath, Jos. 171
McMichael, David 122
Jno. 122
McMichall, Ezekiel 128
Jno. 128
McMichell, Jno. 122
Wm. 122
McMikle, Jno. 129
McMillan, Abraham 8
Alexdr. 100
Jas. 65, 176
Mathers 155
Matthew 9
McMillian, Alexdr. 27
McMillion, Alexdr. 28
Matthew 162
McMillon, Matthew 162
McMinn, Jno. 65
McMorel, Wm. 15
McMullen, Jas. 4, 157
McMullin, Jas. 12, 125
Sarah 12
McMurphy, D. 17
Danl. 65, 143, 150
Susannah 150
McMurray, David 118
Wm. 155
McMurry, Fredrick 176
Wm. 162
McNair, Danl. 141
Gilbert 62, 141, 143
Jno. 62
McNatt, Clary 4
Jesse 9
McNeal, Malcolm 60
Michael 60
Mikel 149
Turquil 62
McNeel, Jno. 76
McNeely, Danl. 155
Patrick 9
McNeil, Danl. 17
J. 59
Jas. 57, 58, 65, 118, 143, 152
Michael 65
McNeill, Michael 148
McNeily, Danl. 49
McNiely, Danl. 4
McNier, Saml. 59
McNiever, Danl. 152
McNight, Robt. 176
McNorrill, Wm. 4
McQueen, Alexdr. 9, 36, 49
Ann 49
Betty 49
Jno. 32, 36, 38, 103
McRight, Matthew 83
McSwine, Jno. 62
Patrick 143
McTaser, Jno. 146
McWhann, Wm. 139
McWhirr, Mary 133

McWhirr (cont.)
Wm. 133
McWilliams, Jno. 155
MeWeir, Alegany 92
Thompson 92
Mead, Stith 152
Wm. 141
Meador, Jno. 122, 126
Joel 129
Jonas 129
Meadors, Jonas 126
Meadowns, Jno. 122
Meadows, Isaac 77, 78
Mary 77
Meagree, Davis 122
Meals, Jno. 146
Joshua 146
Means, Robt. 87
Wm. 74, 86, 87
Mears, Jno. 17
Saml. 20
Measles, Charlton 26
Charlton (Jr.) (Sen.) 26
Joshua 26
Sen. Charlton (Jr.) 26
Mecune, Wm. 82
Meddow, Jno. 155
Medleck, Jas. 167
Medlock, Geo. 176
Medors, Enoch 151
Jno. 151
Micajah 151
Richd. 150
Thos. 151
Medzgar, David 4
Meeck, Edw. 49
Josiah 49
Meed, Jane 61
Meers, Richd. 49
Sam 26
Saml. 23, 28, 32
Megredy, Robt. 76
Silas 76
Meigs, Jonathan 49
Mell, Jas. 135
Thos. 131
Melone, Peter 92
Meloy, Barney 4
Melson, Saml. 59
Melton, Jeremiah 4
Mr. 49
Nath. (Sr.) 4
Peter 9
Robt. 127, 130
Teagle 158
Wm. 110, 116, 118, 122, 127, 129
Melver, Andrew 86
Melvin, Andrew 86
Geo. 134
Martha 49, 134
Menefee, Geo. 83
Mercer, Mary 4
Peter 162
Silas 108
Thos. 9
Meredeth, Jas. 88
Meredith, Jas. 76
Sarah 76
Merit, (?) 86
Meriwether, Frances 171
Frans. 172
Nicholas 58, 65, 152
Tho. 65
Tho. (Jr.) 65
Thos. 92, 172, 173
Meroney, Philip 109

Merony, Jas. 167
Merrell, Jno. 167
Merret, Wm. 122
Merreties, Jas. 34
Merrett, Benj. 80
Merrian, Anthony 9
Merrillis, Jas. 49
Merritt, Benj. 77
Mary 77
Merriwether, David 126
Jas. 21
Mershon, Enos 176
Messer, Thos. 155
Metcalf, Isaac 122
Mezell, Luke 68
Wm. 68
Michael, Wm. 68, 122
Michel, Jno. 90
Michter, Jno. 72
Micken, Peter 28
Mickler, Danl. 21, 25
Jacob 27, 28
Mary 27
Peter 26
Middlebrooks, Micajah 126
Middleton, David 49
Eliz. 77, 115
Holland 116, 122
Holland (Sr.) 122
Hugh 12
Robt. 20, 65, 77, 78, 80, 82, 97, 101, 108, 115, 118, 122, 162, 167
Robt. (Sr.) 122
Saml. 12, 148
Wm. 49
Mikell, Barnett 68
Jas. 68
Jno. 68, 72
Thos. 157
Miles, Jno. 155, 163
Stephen 72
Wm. 49, 65, 176
Milker, Jno. 70, 73
Millar, Jacob 59
Jonathan 162
Millbanks, Wm. 65
Milledge, Jno. 30, 32, 37, 49
Philip 49
Phillip 32
Millegan, Jno. 176
Wm. 62
Millen, Anna Catherine 34
Catherine 34
Geo. 34, 49
Godlieb 49
Godlip 34
Jno. 34, 49, 106, 135
Mary Ann 34
Sarah 34
Steph. 32
Millens, Jno. 94
Miller, Agnes 110
Alexdr. 110, 128, 155
Andrew 49
Archabauld 176
Danl. 25, 28, 49, 152
David 49, 150
Eley 26
Elisha 135, 155
Ellenor 122
Ezekiel 149
Francis 49
Geo. 39

Miller (cont.)
J. A. 128
Jacob 30, 49, 86
Jno. 49, 75, 88, 104,
 105, 106, 107, 109,
 116, 122
Jno. Adams 116
Jno. Allen 116
Jno. Phillip 39
Jonathan 155, 167
Jos. 32, 37, 38, 49,
 134, 155
Joshua 103, 105, 107
Lewis 157
Margaret Young 49
Mary 32, 105, 150
Michael 49
Morris 34, 49
Moses 12
Nathl. 12, 61
Nicholas 32, 49
Peter 37, 49, 80
Philip 4
Phillip 49
Phineas 49
Richd. 49
Sarah (Mrs.) 12
Susannah 32
Thos. 49
Willis 101
Wm. 17, 167
Millican, Hugh 143
Jno. 86
Milligan, Ann 167
Hugh 141, 143
Jno. 49
Jos. 176
Millikin, Thos. 49
Millins, Edmond 113
Millir, Jacob 173
Mills, Alex 167
Alice 167
Archibald 4
David 176
Eliz. 37, 69
Geo. 113
Jane 37
Jeannett 23
Jno. 178
Mary (Mrs.) 70
Moses 176
Sarah 30, 32
Thos. 30, 32, 39, 49
Wm. 20, 23, 27, 37,
 49, 70
Wm. (Jr.) 28
Wm. (Sr.) 23, 28
Milner, Benj. 172, 176
Jno. 172
Pitt 172
Salley 172
Willis 172
Wm. 173
Milroy, Avington 89
Milton, Augustus Ceasar
 153
Jno. 92, 141, 146,
 150, 153
Thos. S. 49
Mimms, Wm. 167
Mims, Jno. 157, 167
Jno. (Jr.) 159, 160
Jno. (Sr.) 159
Judith 12
Mincey, Abraham 69
Mincy, Philip 4
Mingledorf, Annete 32
Geo. 32

Minis, Abegail 32
Abigail 49
Abraham 37, 49
Esther 37
Francis 37
Isaac 37
Leah 34, 49
Philip 37
Phillip 49
Phillipa 37
Minor, Wm. 146
Wm. (Jr.) 146
Minzey, Shadrack 49
Mirat, Abraham 84
Mirault, Pierre 49
Mirrilies, Jas. 30
Mitchel, Abner 27
Wm. 113
Mitchell, Abner 20, 22,
 106
Alexdr. 49
D. B. 37
Danl. 122
David 118
David B. 37
David Brydie 34, 37,
 49
Floodde 4
Jno. 118, 123
Jno. (Jr.) 130
Mary 65
Richard 118
Robt. 49
Stephen 130
Thos. 9, 34, 49, 118,
 123
Wm. 61, 151
Mixeen, Jesse 70
Mixon, Jess 69
Mizell, Jno. 72
Luke 71
Moats, Jno. 27
Mathew 27
Wm. 27
Mobler, Elisha 123
Stephen 123
Mobley, Allen 84
Mock, Andrew 141, 143
Jos. 69, 141, 143
Moffat, Danl. 25
Moffatt, Danl. 23
Moffet, Danl. 21
Moffett, Danl. 20
Mogin, Saml. 86
Molton, Jos. 98
Moncrief, Caleb 65
Mary 65
Monford, Jas. 49
Monger, Sampson 155
Mongin, Jno. D. 49
Monk, Aninan 63
Jno. 58, 62
Silas 63, 167
Monroe, Wm. 4
Montaigut, D. 37
David 37, 38, 49, 132
Montford, Henry 30
Robt. 38
Montfort, Jas. 130
Mary 153
R. 37
Robt. 32, 34, 49
Robt. (Cpt.) 39
Saml. B. R. 39
Montgomary, David 172
Montgomerh, Jno. 90
Montgomery, Bartlet 49
Eliz. 172

Montgomery (cont.)
Jas. 172
Jno. 9, 92
Jno. H. 141
Matthew 172
Robt. 172
Saml. 9, 89, 90
Montmollin, I. S. 49
Moody, Benj. 130
Burt 150
Mon, Jacob 110
Jos. 174
Robt. 80
Saml. 4
Wm. 89
Mooney, Briant 125
Chris. 90
Jno. 144
Moor, Arthur 17
Jas. 22, 49, 126
Obadiah 62
Wm. 174
More, Aaron 30
Abednego 167, 171
Anass 171
Ann 34, 49
Arthur 163
Benj. 171
Burges 49, 135
Catherine 30
David 123
Ebednego 173
Eliz. 105, 106, 167,
 171
Frederick 110
Henry 13, 17, 144
J. 60
Jacob 123, 127
Jas. 9, 20, 21, 25,
 27, 28, 56, 103,
 104, 105, 106, 107,
 116, 123, 141, 144
Jeramiah 123
Jeremiah 109
Jesse 171
Jno. 4, 11, 14, 15,
 17, 49, 57, 69, 70,
 71, 89, 101, 130,
 167, 171
Jos. 74, 80, 110, 127,
 170
Joshua 113, 116
Lewis 9, 86
Martin 144
Mary 171
Mordecai 56, 65, 144
Moses 176
Reubin 9
Rich. 65
Richd. 92, 163, 170,
 176
Risdon 113
Saml. 4, 9, 69, 74
Sararener 171
Susannah 49
T. Saml. 17
Tho. 65
Thos. 58, 141, 144,
 163
Willis 4
Wm. 9, 34, 37, 38, 49,
 50, 70, 78, 115,
 123, 163, 171
Wm. (Jr.) 9, 50
Wm. (Sr.) 9
Morce, Saml. 21
Mordecai, Saml. 50
Morecock, Wm. 50

214

Morel, Ann 32
  Benj. 50
  Henrietta 32
  Henry 133
  Jno. 32, 37, 50
  Peter 134
  Peter Henry 30, 32,
    34, 37, 50
Moreland, Francis 110
  Jno 4
  Jno. 18, 109, 110
  Robt. 109
  Wm. 14
Morell, Michael 4
Morgain, Danl. 95
  Garland 158
Morgan, Ann 50
  Betsy 97
  Danl. 92, 97, 98, 101
  Deborah 97
  Griffin 123
  Isaac D. 176
  Jas. 155
  Jeremiah 167
  Jno. 97, 98, 113
  Jno. F. 103
  Jno. T. 104
  Jos. 50
  Joshua 167
  Mary 144
  Morgan 4
  Richd. 34
  Steph. 18
  Wm. 30, 69
Morrell, I. 92
  Matthew 4
Morris, Isaac 75
  Jas. 75, 92
  Jno. 66, 80, 89, 141,
    148, 167
  Rees 66
  Rhesa 148
  Sally 75
  Sherod 75
  Thos. 135, 139, 167
  Wm. 86
Morrison, (?) 86
  Agnes 4
  Francis 148
  J. H. 86
  Jas. 76, 148
  Jno. 4, 14, 130
  Thos. 148
Morriss, Jno. 59
Morrow, Ewing 113
  Jno. 110, 116, 123
  Jos. 113, 118, 123
  Marg. 110
  Robt. 172
Morse, Danl. Paisley 50
  Jno. Julian 78
  Saml. 77
  Wm. 89
Morssie, Cashford 158
Mortimer, (?) (Mrs.) 50
Morton, Joel 96
  Jos. 59, 66
  Joshua 123
  Mary Ann 59
  Saml. 66
Moseley, Alexdr. 110
  Benj. 61
  Henry 86
  Jane 61
  Robt. 78, 86
  Wm. 144
Mosely, Benj. 149
  David 97, 98

Mosely (cont.)
  Henry 83
  Lewis 86
  Lucas 88
  Wm. 172
Moseman, Jas. 50
Moses, Bryan 15
  Jno. 18
  Philip 66
  Robt. 167
Moss, Alex 141
  Geo. (Dr.) 50
  Jno 70
  Jno. 73
  Wm. 75, 80, 83, 101
Mosse, Geo. 132
Mossman, Eliz. 152
  Jas. 37, 50
Motley, Jno. 50
Mott, Jean 146
  Nathan 144
  Sarah 146
  Uriah 146
  Zephamiah 146
  Zephaniah 50, 141
  Zepheneah 176
Motta, Emanuel 50
  Saunders 50
Motte, Jos. 155
  Nathan 155
Motts, Matthew 32
  Wm. 163
Motz, Matthew 50
Moubray, Wm. 20, 22, 27
Moubrey, Wm. 23
Moudray, Wm. 20
Moulfort, Robt. 20, 69
Mounger, H. 101
  Henry 80, 167
  Sampson 118
Mouson, Jean 80
Mowat, Danl. 50
Mowbray, Wm. 28
Mowbrey, Wm. 28
Mowet, Geo. 9
Moxham, Jno. 50
Moxly, Sarah 141
Moxtix, Wm. 50
Muckinfas, Jos. 50
Muckleroy, Avington 89
Muhlberque, Nicholas
  Victor 21
Muire, Eliz. 34
  Sarah 32
Muling, Henry 92
Mulkey, Jno. 167
  Philip 15
Mullady, Robt. 50
Mullen, Jas. 66
  Jno. 92
Mulligan, Isaac 167
  Jas. 92
  Moses 92
Mullin, Eliz. 97
  Jno. 95, 97
  Jno. (Sr.) 102
Mullins, Clem 123
  Jno. 98, 101
  Jno. (Sr.) 98
  Melone 123
Mulpar, Thos. 135
Mulryne, Jas. 131
Munden, Jno. 107
Munn, Chas. 50
Munns, Chas. 50
Munro, Eliz. 132
  Harry 139
  Saml. 23

Munro (cont.)
  Simon 139, 152
Munson, Robt. 130
Murchant, Isaac 163
  Jno. 163
Murdoch, Robt. F. 50
Murdock, Patrick 89
Murphee, Demsey 4
  Mills 4
Murphey, Humphrey 50
  Jno. 50
  Wm. 50
Murphie, Matrick 22
Murphree, Wright 37, 139
Murphrey, Morris 18
Murphry, Mills 18
Murphy, Bartholomew 163
  Edwd. 141, 144
  Jas. 174
  M. 15
  Miles 14
  Mills 11
  Thos. 135
  Willis 4
Murrah, Jno. 90
Murray, Chas. 50
  David (Jr.) 151
  Jas. 118
  Lucia 34
  Lucy 50
  Thos. 98, 167
Murrell, Jno. 176
Murrilies, Jas. 32
Murrino, Ann 34
Murry, Wm. 176
Muss, Jas. 129
Muter, Jas. 50
Myers, Danl. 135
  David 50
  Geo. 50
  Henry 135
  Jas. 30, 37, 50
  Jno. 50, 131
  Jno. (Jr.) 135
  Jno. (Sr.) 135
  Michael 27
  Thos. 50
  Wm. 135
Myhoney, Dennis 132
Myrick, Jno. 92
Myrover, Henry 104
  Jno. 107
Nail, Elisha 4, 155, 163
  Jos. 89, 90
  Julian 77
  Mary 77
Naile, Jno. 98
Nailer, Jas. 80
Nailon, Dixon 96
Nale, Jno. 95
Nall, Martin 163
Nalls, Richd. 178
Napier, Jas. 144
  Richd. 66, 176
  Tho. 66, 86, 89
  Thos. 58, 75, 118,
    141, 144, 152
Napper, Absolom 144
  Tho. 86
Nash, Jno. 62
Naylor, Arista 153
  Dickson 102
  Geo. 66
Neal, Robt. 83
  Thos. 130, 163, 167
Neale, Jno. 97
  Joanna 97
Nealey, Jno. 155

Neblack, Wm. 21
Needlinger, Jno. G. 69
Neel, Antony 158
  Thos. 167
Neelson, Christian 4
Neely, Jno. 4
  Richd. 21
Neewel, Saml. 50
Neidlinger, Hannah 71
  Jno. G. 71, 72
Neil, Jno. 135
  Jos. 89
  Wm. 14
Neilson, Jas. 28
  Saml. 87, 92, 167
Neily, Jas. 4
  Mary 4
  Thos. 5
Neley, Rich. 18
Nellams, Nial 113
Nelly, Jno. 163
Nelms, Jno. 118, 131
  Jno. (Jr.) 160
Nelons, Jno. (Sr.) 160
Nelson, (?) (Maj.) 78
  Chas. 62
  Christian 14
  David 167
  Geo. 50
  Jas. 21, 22, 25, 27,
    50, 62, 173
  Major 78
  Malcolm 70
  Martha 82
  Matthew 83
  Robt. 56
  Saml. 82, 83, 89, 92
  Tho. 18
  Thos 5
  Thos. 96
  Wm. 18, 155, 163
Nephew, Jas. 136
Nesbit, Jeremiah 178
  Jno. 123
Nesler, Adam 50
Netherclift, Alex. 50
  Ann 50
  Dolly 50
  J. 30
  Mary 50
  T. 30
  T. (Jr.) 30
  Thos. 32, 50
  Thos. Gordon 34
Nevill, Jno. 30
Nevills, Jacob 50
Newberry, Jas. 98
  Levi 62
  Thos. 144
Newbury, Tho. 62
Newdigate, Penelope 50
Newel, Rebecca 50
Newell, Cunningham 50
  Jas. 113
  Rebecca 32
  Thos. 32, 37
Newgent, Jno. 176
  Wm. 176
Newill, Jno. 69
Newman, Danl. 136
  Jno. 75, 83
  Saml. 134
  Thos. 5, 62, 144
  Wm. 9
Newmon, Wm. 18
Newnham, Jno. 155
Newsom, Frederick 157
  Jno. 157

Newsom (cont.)
  Sol. 61
Newton, Jas. 110
  Jesse 146
  Levi 109
  Levy 115
  Moses 163
  Philip 50
  Richd. 109, 118
Neye, Thos. 50
Neyle, Sampson 50
  Wm. 50
Niall, Haris 158
Niblack, Wm. 23, 25, 27,
  29
Nicholas, Williams 98
Nicholls, Geo. W. 50
Nichols, Shadrack 9
  Wm. 167
Nicholson, Alexdr. 107
  Benj. 155
  Jno. 5, 9
Nickler, Phillip 50
Nicolson, Jno. Paul 50
Niel, Jno. M. 95
Night, Nehemiah 155
Nightengale, Jno. C. 50
Niland, Jno. 158
Niles, Ephriam 50
Nipper, Jas. 167
Nisbet, Jas. 109
Nisbett, Jas. (Dr.) 110
Nixon, (?) 50
  Chas. 9
  Jno. 30
  Robt. 59, 153
  Wm. (Rev.) 50
Noble, Wm. 118
Nobles, Landers 5
Noel, Jno. Y. 50, 148
Nokels, Lavin 62
Nolan, Dennis 70, 73
Noles, Edmond 123
  Richd. 126
Nolin, Lucey 113
Norden, Lyon 50
Norgan, Jas. 155
Norman, Jno. 137, 139
  Rebecca (Mrs.) 139
  Reeecca 137
  Wm. 132
Norment, Wm. 50
Norrington, David 98
Norris, Geo. 9
  Jonah 178
  Josiah 167
  Tho. 21, 22, 23, 24,
    25, 27, 29
  Thos. 20
  Thos. Lamb 9
  Wm. 23, 24, 74, 83
North, Jno. 66, 141
  Rober 176
Northrop, Willis 50
Norton, Jonathan 37
  Jos. 30, 50
  Thos. 50, 170
Norvil, Geo. 50
Norwood, Geo. 12
  Sarah 146
Nottage, Thos. 50
Nounlamd, Jno. 18
Nowlan, Geo. 70
Nowland, Jno. 18
Nowlin, Bryan Waid 113
  David 113
  Dennis 50
  Jas. 113

Nowlin (cont.)
  Mary 113
  Peyton 113, 123
Nowtan, Geo. 69
Nugeon, Edmond 167
Numan, Jno. 90, 157
  Wm. 5, 155
Nunes, Moses 30
Nunez, Aaron 37
  Sue 50
Nungazer, Geo. 30, 50
  Henry 30, 50
  Mary Appolonia 30
Nunn, Jas. 158
  Wm. 62
Nunnelee, Eliz. 79
  Jas. F. 80
  Jas. Franklin 77
  Keziah 77
  Walter 80, 84, 89
  Wm. Womack 77
Nunnelle, Jas. F. 89
Nusom, Frederick 158
Nutt, Jno. 163
O'Bryan, Henrietta 37
  Jno. 107
  Wm. 71
O'Cannon, Jos. 104, 107
O'Donner, Wm. 18
O'Kelly, Larance 27
  Larence 23
  Lawrence 22, 24, 29
O'Neal, Axiom 109
  Edmond 123
  Edw. 60, 61
  Ferdinand 23, 105,
    136, 139
  Frederick 132
  Ruth 110
  Wm. 176
O'Neil, Wm. 72
O'Steen, Obediah 107
O'Sullivan, Derby 21, 25
O'duhigg, Francis 50
ONeal, Axion 123
  Jno. 149
Oakman, Mary (Mrs.) 39,
  70
  Wm. 34, 37, 39, 50
Oaldom, Jno. 95
Oar, Wm. 5
Oates, J. P. 18
  Jeremiah 157
  Jno. 30
  Jno. Peter 50
  Peter 37
Oatt, Barbara 30
Obannon, Elijah 158
Obar, with Winslow 50
Obryan, David 69
Obryant, Jno. 103
Obvey, Henry 69
Oceannon, Jos. 107
Odam, Isaac 5
  Malachi 18
  Whitmell 18
Odingsells, Chas 32
  Chas. 34, 50
Odom, Archibald 9, 63
  Eliz. 12
  Issac 13
  Jacob 81, 86
  Jas. 9
  Jno. 70, 73
  Joshua 12
  Sybert 9
Odum, Isual 163
Offcutt, Ezekiel 66

Offing, Jno. 113
Offut, Ezekiel 22
Offutt, Ezekiel 150
  Jemima 150
  Jesse 58
  Lettice 56, 144
  Nathaniel 144
  Sampson 61
Ogan, Jno. 107
Ogden, Betty 12
  Edw. 13
  Isaac 107
  Saml. 12
  Wm. 13, 18
Ogdon, Sol. 130
Ogelby, (?) 41
Ogelvee, Jas. 12
Ogg, Geo. 101, 144
Ogies, (?) (Madam) 50
  Madam 50
Oglethorpe, James Edward
  (Gen.) 29
Ogletree, Jno. 92
  Thos. 167
  Wm. 171
Oglivie, Alexdr. 50
Olfin, J. 113
Olive, Anthony 167
  Jno. 66
Oliver, Caleb 75
  Chas. 9
  Damiscus 167
  Dionysius 77
  Dionysius (Jr.) 81
  Dionysius (Sr.) 79
  Frances 27, 77
  Francis 22, 29
  Jas. 5, 50, 79, 92
  Jno. 56, 77, 79, 81,
    84, 89, 118
  Jno. (Jr.) 81
  Mary Ann 77
  Peter 79, 167
  Saml. 66
  Thos. 9, 81, 116
  Wm. 9, 20, 22, 24, 29,
    81, 82, 86, 118
Olney, Henry 50
Oneal, Ferdinand 103,
  130
Orear, Benj. 27, 29
Oronoke, (?) 50
Orr, Abraham 50
  Daniel 84
  Jas. 113, 123
  Jno. 176
  W. 123
Orriak, Jas. 123
Orrick, Ann 32, 34
  Anna 34
  Jno. 34, 39
  Jno. Hall 34
Osborn, Robt. 5
  Saml. 167
Osborne, Henry 21, 22,
  23, 24, 25, 152
  Robt. 5, 13
Osgood, Jno. 136, 137
  Josiah 103, 130, 136
  Josiah (Sr.) 139
  Rebecca 131, 137
Osmond, Lewis 50
Osteen, Obadiah 136
  Thos. 134
  Wm. 136
Ostend, Obediah 103
Ostry, Febeau 50
Oswald, Ann 133, 137,

Oswald (cont.)
  139
  Jos. 134
  Robt. 130, 133
  Thos. 137, 139
  Thos. H. 132, 139
Oswell, Thos. 136
Otes, Jeremiah 159
Ounsell, Danl. 18
Ousley, Newday 123
  Welding 123
  Wm. H. 118
Outlaw, Edw. 18
  Edwd. 156, 163
  Ludowick 12
Overby, Peter 66
Overstreet, Jas. 50
Owen, Elijah 90
  Geo. 126
  Spencer 62
  Thos. 110
  Thos. (Dr.) 113
  Wm. 98, 101
Owens, Benj. 144
  Elijah 79, 83
  Ephraim 144, 152
  Hannah (Mrs.) 39
  Jno. 72, 81
  Owen 34
  Owne 50
  Tho. 18
Oxford, Edwd. 176
  Jonathan 176
Oxshire, Geo. 98
Oxsin, Geo. 95
Pace, Agnes 77
  Barnabas 77, 86, 89,
    98, 168
  Doldzil 58
  Dreadzil 59
  Dredzill 66
  Jas. 5
  Mary 148
  Thos. 144
  Wm. 56, 144, 148
Page, Jos. 50
Paine, Wm. 135
Painter, Jno. 5
Pair, Zach. 157
Paisley, Jno. 50
Pall, Jas. 158
Palls, Jas. 156
Palmer, Edwd. 168, 170
  Geo. 18
  Jno. 21, 89, 104
  Martin 104, 105, 106,
    107
  Mary 30, 50
  Nathl. 27, 29
  Saml. J. 9
  Sol. 99
  Thos. 30, 37, 50
Palmour, Jno. 168
Pamour, Jos. 109
Pannill, J. 101, 152
Papot, Peter 37
Paramon, Wm. 18
Pardue, Morris 153
Parett, Elijah 152
Parham, Peter 56
Paris, Jno. 27, 29
  Peter 61
Park, Ezekiel 113, 127
  Ezekiel Even 21
  Jas. 84, 113
  Robt. 84, 113
  Saml. 113
Parker, (?) 9

Parker (cont.)
  Aaron 163, 168
  Abel 158
  Amos 5
  Ann 50
  Benj. 123
  Danl. 113, 123, 163,
    168
  Ebenezer 50
  Eliz. 128
  Gabriel 5, 9, 69
  Jacob 5, 110, 113
  Jane 113
  Jas. 9
  Jno. 29, 152
  Jonathan 5
  Js. 123
  Mary 113
  Moses 110, 123, 128
  Moses (Jr.) 128
  Moses (Sr.) 129
  R. 123
  R. (Jr.) 123
  Richd. 109
  Saml. 5, 11, 176
  Stephen 110, 113
  Thos. 37
  Timothy 50
  Williams 163
  Wm. 5, 21, 25, 50, 113
Parkerson, Jacob 129
Parks, Ezekiel 118
  Jas. 92
  Jno. 90, 176
  Laban 148
  Mary 148
Parler, Ann 50
Parmely, Saml. 96
Parmer, Edwd. 176
  Jonathan 99
Parr, Benj. 101
  Jno. 118
Parramore, Matthew 12
  Thos. 107
  Wm. 11, 15
Parrimore, Wm. 5, 14
Parris, Francis 5, 18
  Jno. 27
Parrish, Peter 66
Parrot, Nathl. 136
Parrott, (?) (Cpt.) 158
  Benj. 159
  Benj. (Sr.) 160
Parseille, Chas. 50
Parsley, Sarah 144
Parsons, Hillary 107
  Hillery 105, 106
  Jos. 9
  Sam. 123
  Thos. 50
  Wm. 14
Part, Jno. 113
Partain, Jno. 168
  Robt. 156
  Wm. 168
Partin, Josiah 101
  Norris 118
Paschall, Wm. 168
Patrick, David 109
  Jas. 123, 128, 129
  Jno. 123, 128
  Jos. 113
  Joshua 123
  Paul 101
  Rene 118, 130
  Rheny F. 127
  Robt. 116, 123, 126,
    130

Patrick (cont.)
  Wm. 115, 123, 168, 178
Patten, Jas. 125
  Saml. 88
  Wm. 173
Patterick, Wm. 101
Pattern, Saml. 96
Patterson, (?) (Widow)
  50
  Archibald 69
  Chas. 50
  David 141
  Francis 9
  Henry 50
  Jas. 168
  Jno. 32, 79, 81, 141,
    168, 176
  Jno. (Jr.) 34
  Mary T. 50
  Robt. 5, 12
  Teathover 34
  Wm. 50, 79, 170
Patton, Arthur 101, 125
  Jas. 74, 89
  Saml. 101
  Wm. 82, 87, 89, 92
Paul, Jas. 163
Paulett, Jesse 18
  Jno. 18
Paulidge, Geo. 50
Paulk, Micajah 148
Pauls, Casper 39
Paxton, Jas. 84
  Robt. 86
Payn, Saml. 95
Payne, Archelus 136
  Jno. 94, 95, 97, 99,
    101, 103, 107
  Jno. (Jr.) 102
  Jno. (Sr.) 102
  Jos. 102
  Ledford 113
  Mary 105, 106
  Moses 101
  Nancy 97
  Nathl. 101
  Poindexter 99
  Poyndexter 97
  Rewbin 95
  Saml. 148
  Saml. (Sr.) 144
  Scott 66
  Thos. 92, 99
  Thos. (Sr.) 168
  Walter 150
  Wm. 66, 95, 102, 104,
    106, 107
  Wm. (Sr.) 105
  Yamkey (?) 97
Peacock, Jas. 139
  Jno. 104, 137, 139
  Michael 32
  Wm. 139
  Wm. (Jr.) 105, 136,
    139
  Wm. (Sr.) 135, 136
  Wm. B. 139
Peaddick, Saloma 31
Peak, H. 123
  Jno. 144, 149
Peal, Wm. 104
Pear, Ann (Mrs.) 50
Pearce, Geo. 113
  Jas. 144
  Jno. 5, 103
  Stephen 70
  Thos. 144
Pearcy, Blake 56

Pearpoint, Larkin 76
Pearre, Jas. 153
  Jno. 57, 61, 148, 149
  Nathl. 151
Pearrie, Jas. 56
Pearson, Jas. 107
  Jones 168
Pechin, Peter 39
Peck, Henry 113
Pedero, Thos. 50
  Wm. 51
Peebles, Ephriam 18
  Henry 168
Peek, Henry 118
  Jno. C. 77
Peel, Wm. 5
Peeples, Burwell 109,
    113
  David 110, 113
  Eliz. 113
  Francis 113
  Nathan 110, 113
Peliott, Jno. 61
Pelley, Jno. 129
Pelot, Francis 51
Pemberton, Allen 51
Penace, Hugh 94
Pendleton, D. 37
  Danl. 51
  Gid D. 37
  Gideon 37
  Nathl. 24, 32, 37, 51
  Sol 23
  Sol. 51
  Susan 30
Penman, E. 51
  Edw. 37, 51
  Jno. 31, 33
  Robina 31
Penn, Thos. 79, 86, 87,
    172
Pennington, Abel 168
  Jacob 92, 94, 102
Penrose, Jno. 51
Penson, Enoch 157
Penton, Jaber 176
  Wm. 176, 178
Peoples, Burwell 109
  Ephriam 18
Pepper, (?) 51
Peres, Jno. 157
Perfel, Jno. 85
Perison, Jno. 156
Perkins, Abington 168
  Adam 156
  Archibald 113
  Jesse 168
  Jno. 160, 168
  Joshua 66
  Lewis 130
  Wm. 9
Perrett, Wm. 156
Perry, (?) (Dr.) 107
  Doctor 107
  Eli 62
  Isaac 5, 11, 13, 15,
    18, 163
  Jas. 150
  Micajah 176
  Nathl. 146
  Thos. 61, 81
Perryman, David 57
  Jas. 69
  Richd. 144
Perrymon, Tho. 18
Peter, Pierre 51
Petergrow, Geo. 96
Peters, Edmond 110

Peters (cont.)
  Richmond 115
Peterson, Jno. 71
Petit, Benj. 170
  Jane 171
Pettigrew, Geo. 77, 168
  Jno. 84
Pharies, Wm. 62
Pharr, Saml. 168
Phelan, Thos. 57
Phelps, Jas. 37
Philips, Demey 149
  Hilley 149
Phillios, Jos. 113
Phillip, Geo. 109
  Jno. 51
  Joel 168
  Jos. 116
  Levi 168
  Saml. 93
  Wm. 5, 109
Phillips, Chas. 51
  Danl. 24
  Geo. 115, 126
  Hillery 118
  Ichabod 62
  Isaac 115, 123
  Jas. 66
  Jno. 93, 156, 163
  Jos. 93, 109, 123,
    128, 129
  Josiah 127
  Lenyard 173
  Lochariah 156
  Mark 170
  Royall Budd 69
  Saml. 101, 156
  Sarah 128
  Stephen 144
  Sylvanus 127
  Wilda 62
  Wm. 107, 113, 115,
    118, 123, 127
  Zachrh. 118, 128
  Zechemiah 123
Philpot, Warren 102
Philpott, Martha 97
  Norman 95
  Warren 97, 99, 101
Phinizy, Ferdinand 176
Phinnizg, Ferdinand 101
Phips, Caleb 83
  Lewis 85
Pickens, Gabriel 168
  Jno. 118
  Joshua 83
Pickeron, Darcus 5
Pickhard, Henry 123
  Thos. 113
Pickings, Wm. 82
Pierce, (?) 62
  Ann 51
  Jno. 113, 123
  Joshua (Sr.) 69
  Levy 51
  Lewis 174
  Randall 9
  Somerset 51
  Stephen 69
  Thos. 9
Pierse, Wm. 9
Piggot, Jno. 130, 134
Pigot, Jno. 51, 136
Pigott, Jno. 137
Pilchar, Edw. 104
Pilcher, Stephen 105,
    107
Piles, Ebe (?) 104

Piles (cont.)
Jno. 103, 104, 106,
108
Pindar, Wm. 51
Wm. (Jr.) 51
Pindath, Wm. 144
Pinder, Wm. 31
Pinion, Ann 82
Thos. 82
Pinkerd, Jno. 126
Pinkerton, Jno. 159
Pinkston, Danl. 156
Jno. 156
Pinnel, Thos. 79
Pinnion, Jas. 5
Pinson, Valentine 51
Vinnie 144
Winny 151
Pior, Robt. 5
Piper, Jno. 176
Pitcher, Reuben 27
Reubin 22
Pitchford, Wm. 74
Pitman, Jesse 158
Phillip 157
Pitt, Thos. 37, 51
Pittee, Benj. 176
Pitteren, Mary 9
Plains, Jas. 51
Planter, Jno. 51
Pleym, Andrew 33
Plowden, Wm. 51, 132,
133, 134
Plowright, Robt. 51
Plumer, Ezra 31, 51
Mary 31
Plummer, Jos. 132, 137
Plunner, Jos. 69
Poage, Jno. 152
Poague, Marg. 97
Robt. 97
Poe, Wm. 146
Polack, Abraham 39
Cushman 33, 34
Polhill, Thos. 70
Polk, Andrew 113, 123
Chas. 123
Micajah 144
Pollard, J. 18
Jno. 75, 77, 83
Polly 77
Richd. 81
W. 18
Wm. 18, 163, 168
Wm. (Sr.) 9
Pollet, Jesse 157
Pollock, Allen 153
Isaac 12
Robt. (Sr.) 18
Polock, Isaac 31, 33
Rachel 33
Pomeroy, Jas. 135
Ponder, Amos 168
Ponsheire, Jno. 133
Mary 133
Pontheere, Jno. 139
Mary 139
Pool, B. 152
Baxter 93, 148
Middleton 123
Saml. 62, 63, 141
Wm. 85, 141
Poole, Saml. 144
Pooler, Ann 33
Jno. 33
Pope, Burrell 125, 168
Henry 75, 171
Jesse 123

Pope (cont.)
Jno. 101, 168, 173
Leroy 81, 83, 93
Saml. 116
Sarah 171
W. 81
Willis 168
Porcher, Paul 51
Port, Jas. 31, 51
Wm. 51
Porter, Ab-- 123
B. 118
Benj. 66, 77, 79, 93
Chas. 66, 141
Jas. 69
Jno. 107
Nathl. 115, 116, 128,
170
Oliver 113, 115, 116,
118, 128
Richd. 176
Robt. 72, 113
Saml. 102
Tho. 21
Thos. 93, 141, 144,
152
Wm. 69, 70, 71, 72,
176
Wm. (Jr.) 70
Porterfield, David 86
Wm. 51
Posey, Thos. 79
Wm. 51
Poss, Henry 176
Nicholass 176
Possner, Jos. 34
Post, Jno. 85
Postell, Billy 51
Jos. 51
Poston, Jno. 146
Pothree, Francis 156
Potter, Hughes 18
Jno. 70, 73
Sol. 83
Potts, Henry 127
Moses 170
Poullin, Ann Stutz 37
Jno. 37, 58
Pound, Newman 123
Powel, Arthur 177
Stephan 158
Powell, (?) 62
Abraham 105, 107
Alexdr. 9, 107
Anthony 93
Benj. 5
Cader 5
Eliz. 131
Geo. 5, 37, 163
Jas. 9, 107, 108, 131,
136, 139
Jno. 146, 150
Jos. 9
Josiah 131, 135, 136,
139
K. H. 139
Lecretary 57
Luis 149
Marg. 150
Moses 118
Rachel 57
Richd. 97
Stephen 5, 163
Wm. 156
Powers, Eliz. 82
Frances 82
Jno. 69
Tim 22

Powers (cont.)
Timothy 28, 29
Wm. 51, 159
Poynter, Argulus 150
Mary 150
Poythers, Francis 113
Poythes, Th. 123
Poythress, Geo. 13
Prater, Sarah 141
Prather, Edw. 66
Jos. 177
Pray, Clarisa 39
Jno. 37, 38
Job 31, 38
Wm. 158
Prescott, Ebenezer 37
Eliz. Stutz 37
Jos. 51
Willis 5
Prevost, (?) (Madam) 51
Madam 51
Wm. 51
Prewet, Jno. 123
Prewett, Jacob 82
Prewit, Jacob 86
Wm. 86
Prewitt, Levi 57
Price, Cabor 156
Cader 156, 163
Danl. 177
Edw. 5, 135
Edwd. 134
Howell 51
Jas. 9
Job 5
Jos. 109, 123, 125,
127
Meredith 115
Merideth 123
Peter 51
Rees 144
Richd. 9
Rosanna 127
Sarah 134
Thos. 125
Wm. 12, 137, 156
Prichard, Jas. 51, 113
Robt. 51
Prickhard, Thos. 123
Pridgen, Luke 69
Mark 69
Prier, Jane 61
Phillip 61
Priest, Jos. 168
Primrose, Edw. 51, 141
Prince, Silvenes 158
Prioleiu, Jno. 37
Prior, Hadon 144
Jno. 174
Jos. 84
Obediah 174
Pritchard, Richd. 106,
108
Pritchett, Chas. 123
Rodom 9
Proctor, Jordan 144
Thos. 5
Pruet, Jno. 128
Michael 128
Saml. 128
Pruitt, Elisha 171
Jacob 74
Pryce, Chas. 51
Pryor, Anna 12
Haden 149
Phillip 61
Pugh, David 37
David Guilford 51

Pugh (cont.)
  Francis 18
  Jesse 171
  Theophilus 163
  Whitson 5
  Willoughby 33, 34, 51
  Wm. 18
Pullen, Thos. 156, 163
Pulliam, Jno. 168
  Jos. 101
  Robt. 93, 168
Pullian, Robt. 74
Pulliom, Robt. 89
Pullom, Benj. 95
Puria, Peter 51
Purkins, Jno. 158
Purnell, (?) 51
Pursley, Jno. 144
  Wm. 144
Purtelar, David 123
Purvis, Geo. 106, 108
  Jas. 69
Putnam, Benj. 51, 135
  Henry 33, 38, 51, 135
Pyke, Wm. 37
Quails, Jno. 157
Quarteman, Wm. 130
Quarterman, Jno. 139
  Jos. 132, 134, 136,
    137
  Rebecca 131, 137
  Sarah 131, 137
  Thos. 131, 136, 139
  Wm. 131, 137, 139
Quere, Wm. 168
Quillen, Chas. 101
Quillian, Wm. 102
Quilling, Jno. 139
Rabeilliard, Jno.
  Francis 51
Rabourn, Jell 94
  Jno. 94
Rabun, Jno. 116, 118
  Mathew 123
  Matthew 109, 118
Rachel, Miles 156, 163
Radford, Reuben 168
Radiques, Chas. 51
Radsford, Absalom 62
  Miles 62
Rae, Ann 148, 150
  Jas. 144, 148, 150
  Patrick 51
Ragan, Jno. 109, 118
  Mark 168
Ragland, Benj. 76, 82,
    168
  Evan 75, 79, 81, 84,
    87, 89
Rahn, Jonathan 69, 70,
    72, 73
  Jos. 51, 72
  Matthew 72
Raiford, Morris 156, 160
Railey, Wm. 168
Raines, Thos. 109
Rains, Ignatus 168
  Thos. 116
Raley, Henry 177
  Sarah 163
Ralston, Geo. 51
  Jas. 168
Rambo, (?) (Madam) 51
  Madam 51
  T. 63
Ramsay, Jno. 96
Ramsey, Hannah 59
  Isaac 144

Ramsey (cont.)
  Jas. 59, 66
  Jno. 60, 148, 149, 152
  Randall 66, 144
  Randol 149
  Randolph 61, 66, 148
  Wm. 128, 149
Randle, Thos. 93
Randolph, Eliza (Mrs.)
    61
  Geo. 21
  Isaac 20, 93, 163
  J. F. 22, 27
  Jno. F. 23, 29, 51
  Mary 152
  Richd. 39
  Robt. 58, 61, 66
  Steph. 51
Raney, Jno. 163
  Jos. 158, 160
  Wm. 158
Rankin, (?) (Mrs.) 51
Ransan, Jno. 125
Ransom, Henry 123
Ransone, Henry 21
Rasbury, Eliz. 172
  Jas. 172
  Phillip 172
  Wm. 172
Rasco, Jas. 51
Raser, Isaac 59
Raskee, Jas. 158
Ratchford, Jos. 109
Ratcliff, Benj. 156
  Jos. 156
Ratliff, Eliz. 69
  Saml. 18
  Wm. 168
Rausaw, Wm. 156
Ravot, Abraham 70, 71
  Mary 71
Rawles, Jas. 14
Rawlings, Benj. 27
Rawls, Cotton 69
  Jas. (Jr.) 13
  Jno. 18
  Jno. (Cpt.) 72
Ray, Andrew 174
  David 128, 174
  Jas. 163
  Jno. 33, 62, 95, 118,
    123, 126, 174, 177
  Jno. Burris 34
  Jos. 57
  Nancy 59
  Sarah 33, 118
  Wm. 33, 71, 115, 125
  Zach. 178
  Zachh. 177
Rayford, Mauris 163
Raylah, Jno. 95
Rayle, Thos. 115
Rayley, Sarah 156
Read, Geo. P. 51
  Jacob 51
  Jas. 95
  Jas. B. 51
  Wm. 51
Readick, Michael 33
Readin, Saml. 95
Ready, Jas. 77, 89, 168
  Wm. 21, 24
Rean, Tanstall 123
Reardon, Yelverton 146
Reaves, Geo. 5
  Jeremiah 172
  Jos. 156, 163
Red, Jas. 5

Redd, Saml. 15
Reddick, Abraham 109,
    115, 118, 123
  Casper 51
  Catherine 51
  Hannah 115
  Jacob 51
  Nicholas 5
  Salome 51
  Shadrick 9
  Wm. 29
  Wm. R. 20, 23
Redding, Jno. 102
Reddock, Jas. 27
  Wm. 123
  Wm. R. 20
Reddy, Mary 23
  Wm. 23, 25, 27, 29
Redlick, Wm. 146
Redman, Benj. 59
Reece, Jacob 18
Reed, Achilles 51
  Alexdr. 116, 118, 125
  Andrew 118
  Charity 51
  Collin 77, 79
  Geo. 118
  Hugh 125
  Isaiah 125
  Jacob 51
  Jas. 66
  Robt. 85
  Saml. 94
  Saml. (Sr.) 116
Rees, Ben 58
  Benj. 58, 62, 66
  David 33, 131, 136,
    139
  Eliz. 33, 131
  Hardy 144
  Jno. 9
  Joel 69, 109
  Sally 118
Reese, Enoch (Jr.) 51
Reeve, Spencer 144
Reeves, Benj. 9
  Geo. 9
  Jno. 66
  Jos. 5
  Malachi 173
  Sarah 144
Reid, Alexdr. 113, 123
  Andrew 110, 123
  Eliz. 113
  Geo. 113, 127
  Jno. 51, 123
  Jonadab 113
  R. 123
  Robt. 113
  Saml. 123
  Saml. (Jr.) 123
  Thos. 123
  Yonadal 123
  Z. 123
Reigne, Peter 51
Reiley, Jos. 156
  Wm. 101
Reisser, Dorothy 33
  Nathl. 33
Remshard, Danl. 51
Renfro, Wm. 163
Renfroe, Nathl. 177
Renolds, Robt. 57
Renshaw, Christina 51
  Wm. 51
Rentfrow, Wm. 156
Rents, Jno. 31
Rentz, Agnes 38

Rentz (cont.)
Jno. 38, 51
Renzes, Jno. 51
Repon, Bernard 51
Rester, Frederick 69, 72
Revear, Wyatt 177
Reveir, Wiat 101
Revella, Peter 51
Revier, Henry J. 177
Richd. 177
Reyley, Jas. 74
Jno. 85
Jos. 156
Reynolds, Absalom 156
Benj. 172
Jno. N. 31
Jos. 172, 177
Richd. 172
Sarah Ann 172
Thos. 172
Rhae, Jno. 69
Rhemy, Wm. 15
Rhodes, Benj. 51
Jno. 51, 141, 149
Thos. 51
Rice, Edw. 95, 97
Jesse 146
Jno. 115, 123, 168
Leonard 77, 79, 86
Sarah 77
Sary 77
Thos. 51
Rich, Jno. 59, 62, 151
Peter 51
Richards, Barbara 33, 51
Catharine 153
Geo. 116
Jno. 31, 51
Jno. Hart 9, 33, 51
Martha 33
Wm. 128, 168, 174
Richardsin, Jos. 118
Richardson, (?) (Mrs.)
51
Amos 90
Burrell 51
Burrill 5
Danl. 113, 123, 141,
152
Geo. 31
Isam 168
Jno. 141, 168, 173
Jos. 66, 168
Margt. 31
Morgan 171
Obadiah 123
Obd. 113
Obediah 118, 126
Walker 20, 77, 81, 89
Wm. 9, 51, 177
Richee, Wm. 123
Richeron, Marmaduke 63
Richey, (?) 128
Jno. 20
Ricketson, Benj. 59, 66
Marmaduke 144, 146
Riddle, Archibald 177
Ridley, (?) 9
Ried, Alexdr. 128
Riggs, Bethuil 97
Right, Mical 129
Wm. 113
Riley, Jno. 51
Wm. 160
Rine, Wm. 15
Ring, Ann Margaret 31,
51
Chris. 31, 51

Rion, Nathan 110
Ritchie, Tho. 18
Ritter, Geo. 51
Matthew 51
Michael 51
Peter 51
Ritton, Michael 31
Rivers, Danl. 168
Jos. 15
Rives, Jos. 34
Rix, Johanan 9
Roan, Tudsdale 156
Tunstall 116
Robarts, Jno. 132
Wm. 134
Robartson, Jno. 83
Robbarts, Sallah 113
Roberson, Jas. 157, 172
Jno. 163
Robert, Peter 51
Roberts, (?) (Cpt.) 7
Abram 5
Alvan 156
Elias 71
Eliz. 12
Ezekiel B. 51
Gray 11, 15
Henrietta 51
Jabez. 51
Jas. 12, 51
Jeptha 9
Jno. 5, 11, 14, 93,
141, 168
Jos. 34, 38, 51
Joshua 123, 156
Nathan 59
Peter 51, 52
Richd. 159
Richeyson 52
Thos. 5, 141
Wm. 18
Robertson, Allen 59
Andrew 125
Bailey 9
Benj. 96
Christian 130
David 57, 93, 159, 163
Edw. 9
Edwd. 163
Geo. 52
Jas. 37, 52, 159
Jno. 9, 31, 52, 93,
170
Jno. (Sr.) 156
Jos. 163
Mark 144
Oliver 25
Saml. 159, 168
Thos. 52, 170, 174,
177
Wm. 125, 156
Robeson, David (Jr.) 148
David (Sr.) 148
Robinet, Ezekiel 109
Jno. 168
Robinett, Ezek. 123
Ezekiel 118
Jno. 114, 116, 118,
123
Robinette, Ezekl. 114
Robinson, Alden 18
D. 18
David 93
Edwd. 156
Israel 156, 163
Jas. 5
Jno. 5, 52, 134, 153,
163

Robinson (cont.)
Lark 14
Oliver 21
Peter 37
Philip 18
Robt. 163
Thos. 52
Wm. 5, 52
Robirds, Thos. 109
Robison, Jas. 158
Jno. 101
Jonathan 72
Saml. 158
Rochell, Miles 156
Roden, Zadoc 149
Rodgers, Ben 96
Dimpsey 96
Thos. 82
Roe, Hezekiah 163
Isaac 152
Jas. 156
Rogars, Robt. 5
Rogers, Benj. 81
Berry 116
Britain 123
Burrel 158
Dread 156
Jas. 81, 123
Jno. 9, 74, 75, 77,
81, 83, 93, 114,
116, 123
Jos. 9, 69
Josiah 118
M. 123
Mary 79
Matthew 52
Michael 116, 118
Moses 52
Nancy 75
Peleg 9
Richd. 9
Thos. 9, 79, 81
Unity 81
Wm. 31, 82, 123, 153,
168
Rogerson, Richd. 52
Rolberger, Joanna 70
Roles, Wm. 52
Rolfes, Frederick 132
Roling, Jno. 177
Rollin, Thos. 163
Rollison, Jno. 69
Roma, Francis 52
Romisa, Dirick 152
Ronaldson, Robt. 11, 15
Ronvel, Jno. 90
Roquemore, Jas. 168
Rorial, Steph. 18
Rose, Henry 74, 75, 93
Roseborough, Eliz. 66
Geo. 66
Rosel, Jona. 81
Roser, Isaac 59
Ross, Adam 123
Ann 37, 59
Cudjo 52
David 31
Donald 31, 33, 37
Drury 83, 84
Edw. 59
Francis 116
Geo. 118
Hugh 31, 52
Hugh (Jr.) 37
Hugh (Sr.) 37
Jane 31, 37
Jas. 59, 60, 152, 168
Jesse 86

Ross (cont.)
  Jno. 52, 75, 77, 90, 125
  Jno. A. G. 31
  Jno. Graham 37
  Marget 77
  Moses 156, 160, 163
  Nathl. 114
  Robt. 52, 89
  Sarah 31, 37
  Susannah (Mrs.) 52
  Wm. 37
Rottenbury, Richd. 107
Rotton, Jno. 57
Rouce, Bartlett 159
Roughton, Jno. 18
Roundtree, Wm. 156, 163
Rountree, Wm. 52
Rousey, Jno. 87
Rousru, Wm. 125
Rousseau, Jno. 144
Rousy, Edmund 87
Routon, Jno. 101
Rovell, Geo. 178
Row, Hezekiah 156
Rowel, Jesse 83
Rowell, Edwd. 146, 148, 151
  Henry 52
  Jno. 9, 152
  Robt. 18
Rowells, Edwd. 144
Rowland, Jas. 144
Rowns, Jno. 119
Rowton, Jno. 156
Rowzy, Jno. 79
Royal, Saml. 5, 69
  Wm. 11
Royall, Wm. 15, 18
Royston, R. C. 118
  Richd. C. 118
Rucker, Fielder 177
  Geo. 79
  Jno. 87
  Jos. 75, 89
  Presly 129
Rudolph, Michael 28, 29, 134
  Tho. 29
  Thos. 27
Rudulph, Michael 135, 136
  Tho. 22
  Thos. 22, 135
Ruff, Chas. 177
  Jno. 177
  Stephen 177
  Susannah 168
Ruffin, Jno. 12
Runnell, Thos. 118
Runnells, Chas. 62
  Geo. 168
  Hannan 156
  Herman 156
Runnels, Hermon 163
  Jno. 62
  Reuben 62
Rupert, Jno. 69
Rush, Burrows 52
  Jeptha 85
  Jesse 101
Rushen, Jno. 70
Rushin, Wm. 70
Rushing, Jno. 177
  Wm. 69, 72
Russ, Jno. 178
  Wm. 85
Russel, David 128

Russell, Ailsey Martin 101
  Andrew 62
  Ann 31
  Christian 74
  Geo. 177
  Hugh 144
  J. M. 101
  Jacob 52
  Jane 31, 33, 39
  Jas. 13, 18
  Jas. G. 177
  Jeremiah (Sr.) 160
  Jos. M. 93
  Jos. R. 89
  Nathan 89
  Robt. 174
  S. 31
  Sol. 9, 18
  Thos. 81, 168
  Thos. C. 83, 173
  Wm. 31, 177
Ruston, Jno. B. 168
Rutherford, Claborn 93
  Jas. 37
  Jno. 160
  Thos. B. 159
Rutledge, Edwd. (Sr.) 146
  Geo. 168
  Jas. 116
Ryal, Jno. 83
Ryall, Arthur 69
  Winn 18
Ryals, Wm. 11
Ryan, Chas. 69
  Eliz. 114
  Jos. 69, 101, 156, 163
  Nathan 174, 177
  Phillip (Jr.) 52
  Richd. 114, 123
Ryelye, Jas. 79
Ryle, Jno. 90
Ryley, Jos. 168
  Tho. 22
Sables, Wm. 52
Sackett, Simon 5, 9
Sade, Edw. 116
  Peyton 116
  Thos. 116
Sadler, Wm. Allen 15
Safesbury, Thos. 160
Saffold, Jno. 159
  Wm. 159
Sailors, Eliz. 173
Sainerie, Francis 52
Salfner, Mathew 31
  Matthew 52
Salisbury, Wm. (Sr.) 9
Sallens, Peter 134, 139
  Peter (Sr.) 139
Sallet, Robt. 134
Sallett, Robt. 131, 136
Sallins, Robt. 139
Sallis, Jno. 156
Sallisbury, Jos. 156
Salter, Jas. 156, 163
  Jno. 9, 14
  Simon 149
Saltus, Saml. 131, 134
Saltzberger, (?) 67
Salyer, Benj. 144
Sample, Nathl. 5
  Saml. 9
Sampler, Chas. 62
  Jesse 62
  Thos. 144
Samples, Saml. 5

Sampson, Howell 156
  Jas. 129
  Jno. 118
Samson, Patsey 114
Samuel, Edmund 57
Sanderlin, Robt. 163
Sanders, Abraham 66, 128
  Chris 110
  Ephraim 148
  Jacob 128
  Jesee 66
  Jesse 58, 118, 151
  Joel 66
  Joshua 99, 152
  Lewis 63
  Mark 123
  Roger Parker 139
  Yancey 58
Sandford, Joshua 136
Sandidge, Clabourn 81
  David 52
  Jno. 93
Sandiford, Audley 133
  Jas. 134
Sands, Ray 52
Sanford, Jesse 123
  Robt. 123
  Saml. 156
Sansom, Francis 110
  Jackie 110
  Jas. 109, 110, 123
  Jno. 110
  Nancy 110
  Pattey 110
  Polly 110
  Richd. 123
  Thos. 110
  Wm. 110, 114
Sapp, Benj. 11, 15
  Caleb 5, 9
  Darling 5
  Dill 12, 14
  Dill (Cpt.) 7
  Elijah 11, 15
  Jas. 5
  Shadrock 5
  Wm. 11, 12, 101
Sargent, Jno. 136
  Saml. G. 52
Sarsit, Wm. 158
Sartain, Jas. 163
Sartam, Jas. 18
Sartin, Jas. 157
Sasser, Britton 9
  Stephen 5
  Thos 5
  Wm. 5
Satterwhite, Danl. 141
  David 144
  Francis 75, 81, 88, 89, 168, 172
  Frank 87
  Jno. 87
Saucy, Gabriel 52
  Joachim 52
Saunders, Jno. 52
  Mary 52
  Ricd. 74
  Robt. 168
  Roger P. 130
Savage, Elia 94
  Geo. 52
  Loveless 66, 144, 152
  Wm. 97
Savidge, Amey 148
  Jas. 62
  Loveless 146
  Osel 62

Savidge (cont.)
 Robt. 148
Sawyer, Jno. Martin 134
Saxon, Saml. 133
Saxton, Nathl. 135
Sayler, Chris. 81
Saylors, Eliz. 82
Scales, Jno. 79
 Thos. 75, 79, 82
Scallions, Andrew 25
Scarborough, Aaron 5,
 163
 Arthur 5
 Miles 156, 163
 Moses 5, 163
 Saml. 5
Scarbrough, David 159
Scarlet, Jas. 123, 128
Scart, Jno. 104
Scavesley, Thos. 144
Schermerhorn, Cornelius
 52
 Peter 52
Scheuber, J. H. 37
 Justice H. 69
 Justus H. 31, 35, 37,
 52
Schley, Michael 9
 Richd. 9
Schmerber, Jas. 52
Schmid, Christina D. 139
 Mary Screven 139
 Philip Jacob 139
Schmidt, Christina
 Dorothy 131
 E. Henry 139
 Egidius Henry 131
 Geo. Henry 139
 Philip Jacob 133
Schubert, Frederick 15
Schueber, J. H. 37
 Justus H. 37
Schweighofer, Thos. 52
Schweighoffer, Abell 72
 Thos. 69
Schweinitz, Jans
 Christian 52
Scot, Philip 52
 Swidney 123
 Wm. 123
Scott, (?) 52
 Alexdr. 69
 Eliz. 18
 Gavin 52
 Geo. 52
 Hugh 31, 37, 52
 Jas. 79, 96, 171
 Jno. 66
 Jos. 177
 Nancy 77
 Phillip 9, 52
 Robt. 69
 Saml. 148
 Theodore 127
 Tho. B. 87
 Thos. 77, 87
 Thos. B. 76, 81, 84,
 88, 101
 Wm. 5, 96, 127, 177
Scranton, Jas. 52
 Jno. G. 52
Screven, Chas. O. 52
 Jno. (Jr.) 52
 Jno. (Sr.) 52
Scrimminger, Chas. 35
Scrimsger, Chas. 52
Scrivner, Thos. 168
Scroggins, Geo. 96

Scruggs, Gross 11, 15
 Jas. 66
 Richd (Jr.) 71
 Wm. 18
Scudden, Wm. 168
Scudder, Isaiah 177
 Natl. 177
 Wm. 177
Scull, Danl. 52
Scurlock, Jas. 171
 Josh. 128
 Joshua 114
Seagrove, Ann 23, 33
 Jas. 20, 21, 23, 24,
 25, 29, 33
 Robt. 22, 23, 24, 25,
 27, 29, 37
Seal, Anthony (Sr.) 101
Seale, Wm. 163
Seals, Tho. 90
 Thos. 74
Seaman, Gideon 52
Sear, Saml. M. 18
Sears, Willard 52
Searson, Jno. R. 52
Seaver, Jno. 9
Seawright, Jas. 123
Seay, Wm. 57
Seckinger, Jonathan 72
Seegar, Geo. 11, 15, 18
Segar, Claude 52
 Jos. 52
 Lewis 52
 Prosper 52
Self, Ezekiel 69
 Stephen 177
Selfridge, Robt. 101,
 168
Sell, Jonathan 144
Sellers, Saml. 69
Selman, Thos. 83
Seloy, Benj. 9
Selph, Jesse 12
Sempel, Nathl. 18
Semple, Alexdr. 21, 25,
 26
Senior, Mary 131
Sessions, Jos. 156, 163
Sevarr, Jno. 5
Sewell, Joshua 87, 168
 M. 87
 Saml. 79
 Wm. 74, 87
Sexon, Davis 93
Seymour, Gurdon J. 52
 Richd. 33, 35, 37
Shackleford, Edmond 77,
 79, 81
 Edmund 87
 Henry 79, 87
 J. W. 63
 Jas. 101
 Jno. 58, 59, 74, 87,
 123, 152
 Mordecai 59, 63
 Wm. 81
Shad, Catherine 31
 Sol. 31, 35, 52
 Solomon 38
Shaeffer, Balthaser 37
Shaffer, Balthasar 52
 Balthaser 31
 Henry 9
 Jno. 69
 Wm. 52
Shandley, Thos. 52
Shanke, Elijah 95
Shannon, Patrick 177

Sharard, Simon 18
Shareman, Robt. 93
Shares, Simon 168
Sharp, Cade 12
 Earl 18
 Jacob 18
 Jas. B. 31, 93
 Jno. 5, 9, 18
 Jno. (Jr.) 18
 Joshua 18, 70, 73
 Mary 5
 Michael 18
 Paschal 12
 Robt. 96
 Saml. 20, 21, 123
 Timothy 18
 Wiley 156
Sharpe, Jno. 14
 Jos. Lewis 66
Shaw, Danl. 74
 Geo. 52
 Jas. 35, 52
 Jno. 52
 Jno. R. 52
 Jonathan 38, 135, 136
 Jos. 127, 129
 Mary 101
 Mathew 123
 Robert 178
 Robt. 60, 63, 144
 Saml. 114, 123
 Wm. 5, 52, 126, 163
Shearer, Alex. 148
 Jas. 177
Shearman, Zohett 52
Sheaver, Jas. 178
Sheffield, Austin 9, 69,
 72
 Jno. 5, 160
 Mark 5
 Robt. 156
 Wm. 156, 160
 Zach. 168
Sheftall, Abr. 52
 Benj. 38, 39
 Benj. (Jr.) 37
 Esther 52
 Frances (Mrs.) 52
 Levi 31, 52
 Mordecai 31, 33, 37,
 38, 52
 Moses 31, 37, 52, 152
 Perla 52
 Sarah 52
 Sheftall 52
Sheilds, Thos. 93
Shelby, Jno. 101, 156
 Moses 114, 116, 118
 Sarah 115
 Wm. 114, 115, 116,
 118, 123
Shelley, Absolom 96
 Amous 96
 Rubin 96
Shelly, Phillip 93
Shelman, I. 156
 J. 18
 Jno. 9, 156, 163
 Michael 163
Shelmon, Jno. 14
Shelton, Henry 168
Shepard, Francis 134
 Jno. 159
 Mary 133
 Thos. 131, 134, 137
Sheperd, Peter 84
Shepherd, David 159
 Jas. 81

Shepherd (cont.)
  Mary 139
  Wm. 66, 139
Sheppard, Andrew 9
  Jno. 9, 160
  Labon 9
  Mary 139
  Peter 75
  Thos. 156
  Wm. 72, 139, 156
Shepperd, Mourning 69
Sheppherd, Peter 168
Sheridan, Owen 52
Sherman, Ann 75
  Danl. 52
  Isaac 21
  Jared 52
  Jno. 21, 26
Sherod, Simon 5
Sherril, Geo. 96
Sherrill, --d 128
  Geo. 99
  Saml. 99
Sherwood, (?) 9
  Charity 146
  Mary 146
  Moses 146
  Wm. 146
Shewmaker, Jesse 95
  Lindsey 79
Shfield, To. 123
Shick, Frederic 38
  Frederick 35, 37, 52
  Geo. 52
  Jno. 31, 37
  Jno. (Jr.) 52
  Jno. (Sr.) 52
  Jos. 52
  Peter 52
Shield, Robt. 156
Shields, Jno. 81
  Marg. 151
  Patrick 125
  Thos. 93, 125
  Wm. 61, 66, 125, 144,
    156
Shiers, Wm. 85, 90
Shiffield, Wm. 69
Ship, Benj. 123
  Richd. 116, 123
Shipley, Robt. 93, 99,
    156
Shirley, Martin 5
  Wm. 141
Shite, Saml. 6
Shoars, Wm. 70, 73
Shoemake, Jos. 12
  Josiah 150
Shoemaker, Josiah 144
  Lindsey 84
Shores, Richd. 9
Short, Edw. 61
  Tho. 66
  Thos. 61
Shorter, Rachel 70
Showers, Jno. 57
Showes, Jno. 144
Shows, Danl. 62
  Jno. 62
Shropshere, Abner 21
Shropshire, Jno. 174
Shuffield, Geo. 126
Shuffle, Wm. 156
Shuman, Henry 130
Shurley, Edwd. 177
  Wm. 149
Sibley, Isaac 70, 73
Sidwell, David 57

Sigmon, Jno. 75
Signon, Jno. 81
Sikes, Danl. 18, 156,
    159
  Elesabeth 159
  Wm. 144
Silbey, Nathan 177
Sill, Jno. 61
Silmon, Ely 96
Silvey, Wm. 177
  Wm. (Jr.) 177
Simkins, (?) 40
  Arnold 52
Simmery, Wm. 21
Simmons, Adam 178
  Caleb 9
  Chas. 9, 148, 152, 153
  J. M. 152
  Jas. 85
  Jesse 85, 96
  Jno. 9, 52, 124, 157
  Joshua 110
  Richd. 107, 174
  Willis 5
Simms, Jas. 57, 58
Simon, Andrew 21
Simons, A. 63
  Jas. 99
  Malbery 149
  Moses 52
  Saul 52
  Wm. 177
Simonton, Adam 114, 116,
    127
  Adams 124
  Danl. 118
  Thophelis 125
  Thos. 118
Simpkins, Chas. 156
Simpson, Eliz. 52
  Green 52
  Jas. 52
  Jno. 31, 37, 39, 52
  Wm. 21, 25, 27
Sims, (?) 52
  Abner 63
  Benj. 66
  Frederick 173
  Jas. 57, 60, 63, 141,
    157
  Jenning 168
  Joel 168
  Man 62
  Mann 144
  Robt. 168
  Wm. 57, 141, 144, 150
Simson, Jas. 168
Sinclair, Jos. 99, 102
  Robt. 52
Singletary, Danl. 27
Singleton, Robt. 93
Sinkins, Arnold 52
Sipham, Abram 124
Sitton, Reubin 85
Skelly, Saml. 52
Skelton, Jacob 90
  Jno. 81, 90
  Robt. 81, 82, 93
  Sol. 90
Sketo, Jno. 52
Skinner, (?) (Cpt.) 7
  Archer 81, 168
  Henry 59
  Jesse (Jr.) 9
  Jesse (Sr.) 9
  Jonas 9
  Jonathan 64
  Nathan 9

Skinner (cont.)
  Nathaniel 9
  Nicholas 5, 11, 13,
    15, 18
  Phenix 177
  Phineas 178
  Wm. 5, 9, 11, 15, 18
Skrine, Jno. D. 24
  Mary 24
  Susannah 24
  Tho. 22
  Thomas 24
Slade, Jos. 146
  Nicholas 168
Slaten, Saml. 62
Slater, Jno. 66
  Wm. 5
Slatter, Sol. 93
  Wm. 93
Slaughter, (?) 124
  Ezekiel 111, 114
  Jno. 111, 114
  Lucy 114
  Reuben 114
  Saml. 114, 118, 124
Slaydon, Jno. 177
Sled, Jos. 93
  Joshua 81, 93, 156,
    168
Sledd, Joshua 97
  Winifred 97
Sleet, Jas. 53
Sleighs, Wm. 177
Sloan, Jno. 69
  Wm. 101
Smalley, Michael 66
Smallwood, Benj. 134,
    139
  Francis 139
  Isaac 136, 139
  Wm. 177
Smart, Eliz. 53
  Thos. 174
Smedly, Thos. 126
Smellers, Jos. 93
Smelt, Dennis 146
Smith, (?) 53
  --lius 128
  Abraham 168
  Agnes 114
  Archer 85
  Archib. 53
  Archibald 109
  Archibald (Jr.) 124
  Archibald (Sr.) 124
  Benj. 14, 18, 53, 93,
    168
  Burnard 168
  Burrill 168
  Chas. 53, 136
  Cornelius 115
  Danoel 53
  David 53, 125
  Ebeneezer 62
  Ebenezer 59, 66, 168,
    177
  Edwd. 148
  Eliz. 53, 79, 82
  Ezekiel 22, 29, 66
  Frances 144
  Francis 57, 62
  Frederic 53
  Frederick 9, 18
  Gabrel 90
  Gabriel 168
  Gay 168
  Geo. 53, 118, 163
  Gilbert 114

Smith (cont.)
  Godheip 72
  Godhielf 69
  Gottlieb 72
  Henry 96
  Isam 5
  Israel 157
  Jacob 57
  Jas. 9, 37, 53, 57,
    62, 69, 71, 108,
    124, 125, 133, 139,
    168, 177, 178
  Jasper 76
  Jeremiah 135
  Jesse 96
  Jno. 5, 31, 35, 53,
    59, 62, 66, 75, 79,
    93, 97, 99, 101,
    109, 124, 125, 126,
    148, 157, 163, 168,
    170, 173
  Jno. C. 53
  Jno. E. 148
  Jos. 5, 9, 37, 111,
    114
  L. 64
  Leonard 141
  Levy 135
  Mary 35, 99, 114
  Mary Ann Eliz. 133
  Nat. 87
  Nathl. 81, 89, 168
  Nathl. A. 168
  Peter 119, 171, 177
  Peyton 124, 127
  Peyton (Jr.) 129
  Ralph 90, 93
  Rebeckah 76
  Rebekah 59
  Robt 119
  Robt. 114, 116, 124,
    159, 168
  Roland 177
  Saml. 5, 21, 22, 23,
    29, 109, 124, 125,
    160
  Samuel 24, 25
  Samuell 27
  Sarah 134
  Sherod 170
  Sol. 53
  Steph. 53
  T. 134, 144
  Thos (Jr.) 53
  Thos. 9, 13, 31, 53,
    93, 141, 144, 148,
    160
  Val. 87
  Valentine 74, 79
  Wm. 5, 53, 59, 66, 77,
    83, 96, 101, 114,
    124, 141, 157, 163,
    168, 173, 177
  Wm. (Jr.) 96
Smithers, Betty 53
Smitton, Wm. 25
Smyth, Thos. 93
  Thos. (Jr.) 93
Snares, Anthony 29
Snebly, E. 152
Sneed, Catherine 5
  Chas. 163, 168
  Dudley 18
  Robt. 9
  Wm. 95
Snell, Chris. 18, 156,
    163
  Jacob 15

Snell (cont.)
  Saml. 18
Snider, Andrew 53
  B. 64
  Barnett 64
  Jacob 53, 64
  Jno. 59
  Philip 53
Snow, Edmind 99
Snyder, Jno. 69
Socks, Saml. 53
Sody, Jane Delarrocque
    53
  Mary 53
Soloman, Frances 172
Solomon, Baker 31
  Ellis 172
Somerall, Stafford 136
Somerford, Richd. 104
Somersall, Stafford 135
Sommers, Wm. 53
Sorell, Geo. 168
Sorrah, Jno. 66
Sorrell, Jno. 168
Sorrells, Jno. 144
Sorril, Green 174
  Jno. 174
Soslder, Scantling 159
Southerland, Jno. 57
Spain, Jno. 93
Spairs, Jno. 74
Spalding, Henry 57
  Isham 22, 25, 29
  Jas. 38, 103, 104,
    105, 106, 132, 133,
    139
  Marg. 106
  Margery 105
  Thos. 103, 105
Spaldon, Ishem 21
Spann, Francis 156
  Geo. 163
  Jas. 153
Sparkes, Jenk 96
  Jeremiah 96
Sparks, Elijah 99
  Jas. 95
  Jere 102
  Josiah 156
  Mathew 178
  Matthew 173
  Matthew (Jr.) 93
  Thos. 102
  Wm. 93, 178
Spears, Alexdr. J. 37
  Jno. 87
  Saml. 75
  Sol. 157
  Wm. 87, 124
Speight, Jno. 18
  Moses (Jr.) 18
Speirs, Polly 53
Spekes, Thos. 156
Spell, Celah 5
  Geo. 10
Spence, Jno. 18, 71
  Moses 5, 18
  Robt. 10
  Tharp 18
  Tho. 18
Spencer, Ann 35
  Eliz. 31
  Geo. B. 53
  Geo. Basil 31, 33
  Jabez. 53
  Jno. 5, 71
  Jno. Butler 10
  Jos. 53

Spencer (cont.)
  Jos. W. 53
  Jos. Wm. 31
  Mary 35
  Mildred 150
  Mildred (Mrs.) 153
  Peter 61
  Saml. 132, 134, 137,
    139
  Sarah 134
  Wm. 72, 93, 131, 139,
    149, 150, 151
  Wm. H. 31
  Wm. Henry 35, 53
  Wm. Jos. 35
Spider, E. 64
Spiers, Alex. J. 33
  Alex. Jonhstone 134
Spight, Jos. 10
  Moses 10
Spikes, Jonas 10
  Josiah 111, 124
  Mary 114
  Matthew 160
  Nathan 168
  Tho. 18
Spillers, Danl. 124
Spives, Geo. 5
Spivey, Francis 5
  Jas. 5, 10
  Jethro B. 18
  Joshua 159
Spooner, Zoar 10
Spowser, Priscilla 168
Spradling, Joshua 109,
    124
  Zachrh. 128
Spratlin, Jas. 97, 171
  Winifred 97
Spratt, Hugh 109
Spratting, Henry 178
Springfield, Aaron 177
Spruce, Wm. 93
Spurlock, Allen 96, 159
  Eliz. 149
  Jas. 83
  Jno. 5, 149
  Robt. 149
  Saml. 72
  Wm. 153
Squires, David 53
St. Hebert, Theresa 52
St. Marc, Latoison 52
Stacey, Wm. 134
Stacker, Henry Bedon 21
Stacy, Jas. 134, 139
  Jno. 134, 136, 137
  Mary 132
  Wm. 139
Stafford, Edw. 53
  Joshua 5, 130, 137
  Robt. 20, 21, 24, 26,
    28, 29
  Tho. 21, 26, 29
  Thos. 20, 22, 24
  Thos. P. 134
Staley, Jas. 139
  Jno. 139
  Jno. (Sr.) 139
Stallings, Bethia (Mrs.)
    153
  Ezekiel 37, 59, 141
  Jas. 18, 33, 35, 37,
    152, 153
  Jesse 5, 177
  Jno. 5
Stamp, Jno. 114
Stamper, Howell 156

Stamps, Thos. 124
Standford, David 62
  Robt. 141
  Thos. 62
Standifer, Jesse 127
  Scotton 126
  Skelton 127
Standley, Jas. 61
  Jno. 53
Standly, Shade 158
Stanford, Elijah 144
  Jonathan 59, 141
  Nelle 59
  Rich. 15
  Robt. 62, 144
  Stephens 5
Stanley, Jno. 24
  Michael 53
  Sam 163
  Thos. 116, 124
Stannaland, Jno. 5
Stanol, Jno. 10
Stanson, Wm. 10
Stapler, Jno. 144
Staples, Jno. 74, 75, 79
  Stephen 177
  Tho. 66
Starkey, Eliz. 114
Starky, Aquilla 174
  Jno. 174
Starnes, Ebeneezer 156
  Ebenezer 168
Starr, Henry 168
  Jno. 93
  Wm. 53
Stataly, Francis 18
Stateham, Robt. 53
Statham, Chas. 146, 160
  Jno. 79, 89, 168
  Love 76
Statom, Jas. 87
  Jno. (Sr.) 87
Stead, Wm. 93
Steadman, Wm. 53
Steagall, Eliz. 82
  Richd. 82
Steal, Culbreath 168
Stearman, Henry 153
Stebbins, Clement 53
  Edw. 53
  Rebecca 53
Steed, Philip 144
  Phillip 141
Steedman, Thos. 124
Steel, Hugh 15
  Jos. 53
  Sampson 58, 62
  Thos. 24
Steele, Geo. 53
  S. 61
Stegle, Nicholas 14
Stelphen, Benj. 163
Stenchcomb, Absolom 79
Stephen, (?) 53
  Alex 81
  Alexdr. 131
  Richd. 21
  Thos. 172
Stephens, Benj. (Sr.) 5
  Chas. 10
  Gabriel 10
  Jno. 10
  Jos. 93
  Margt. (Mrs.) 39
  Martha 37
  Nancy 82
  Reb. 150
  Richd. 22

Stephens (cont.)
  Stephen 83
  W. 37
  Wm. 35, 37, 38, 53
  Wm. Jos. 150
Stephenson, Hannah 110
  Jno. 10, 109
  Thos. 110
  Wm. 110
Steptoe, Jno. 5, 15
  Thos. 5
Sterling, Frances 27
  Jno. 5
Steuart, Josiah 134
Steurman, Henry 152
Steven, Wm. 104
Stevens, Jno. 130, 144
  Mathew 114
  Rich. 29
  Richd. 21, 25
  Saml. 131, 139
  Sarah 132
  Thos. 132, 136, 139
  Wm. 104, 106, 132, 139
Stevenson, E. 101
  Thos. 124
Steward, Wm. 53
Stewart, (?) (Col.) 133
  Alex 69
  Allen 53, 127
  Ann 57
  Ann (Mrs.) 37
  Archibald 10
  Chas. 124, 163
  Col. 133
  Danl. 133, 136, 137,
    139
  Gravener 168
  Grissell 33
  Henry 114, 124
  Isaac 93
  Jas. 66, 119, 124, 168
  Jas. M. 139
  Jno. 10, 37, 66, 96,
    107, 119, 131, 134,
    141
  Josiah 139
  Martha 170
  Peter 53
  Robt. 96
  Susannah 137
  Thos. 109, 168
  Wm. 18, 53, 66, 96,
    124
Stewenter, Jno. 177
Stewert, Ann 144
Stibblefield, Theodrick
  173
Stidham, Adam 18
Stiles, Benj. 31
  Jno. 146
  Jos. 146
  Richd. M. 53
  S. 71
  Saml. 53
  Wm. 85
Stillwell, Ann 114
  Wm. L. 29
Stinchcomb, Absalom 87
  Absolom 83
  Alex. 79
Stiner, Christian 70
  David 70
  Margt. (Mrs.) 70
Stinson, Nathan 156, 163
Stirk, Jos. 37
  Saml. 33, 35, 53, 134
Stith, Jno. 58, 62, 144

Stith (cont.)
  Paton R. 93
  Peyton K. 22
  Peyton Randolph 144
  Will 101
  Wm. 93, 144, 148, 149,
    152
  Wm. (Jr.) 57
Stiver, Michael 22
Stocks, Isaac 109, 116,
  124, 127, 128, 129,
  168
  Isaacs 119
Stodgill, Joel 75
  Martitia 75
Stoeo, Wm. 5
Stogner, Jno. 136
Stokes, Archibald 53
  Geo. 124
  Hartwell 119, 144
  Jas. 53
  Jno. 93, 159, 163
  Montford 87
  Robt. 177
  Saml. 114, 156
  Sarah 76
  Tabitha 114
  Wm. 76, 93
  Young 177
Stomas, Sarah 116
Stone, (?) (Mrs.) 53
  Ann 132
  David 10
  Henry 103
  Henry D. 132
  Henry Dassex 35
  Henry Dessex 133
  Jno. 57
  Matthew 109
  Micajah 168
  Ransom 53
  Richd. 53
  Susannah (Mrs.) 39
  Thos. 133, 139
  Uriah 85, 97
  Wm. 5, 124
Stonecyffer, Jno. 93
Stoner, Francis 33
  Peter 33
Stonesipher, Jno. H. 96
Stoneycffer, Jno. (Cpt.)
  95
Stoneycyffer, Ann 97
  Jno. 97, 101
  Nancy 97
Stoneycypher, Jno. 94,
  99, 102
Storie, Jane 35
  Jas. 33
  Jno. 12, 31, 33, 53
  Margaret 12
  Margt. 33
Story, Prudence 66
  Richd. 144
  Robt. 66
  Thos. 53
Stouff, Isidore 53
Stoy, Henry W. 18
Stradley, Nimrod 5
Strahacker, Rudolph 33
Strange, Isham 177
  Owen 53
Strather, Wm. 178
Strawder, Francis 5
  Wm. 10
Strawhon, Neal 22
Street, Jane 33
  Jno. 33, 53

Streetman, Garrett 77
  Martin 10
  Mary 77
  Sarah 5
Stregles, Nich. 14
Strength, Jno. 57
Strickland, Jos. (Jr.)
  101
  Jos. (Sr.) 101
  Sol. 101, 168
Stricklin, Henry 87
  Jacob 85
Stringer, Danl. 5
  Francis 10
  Geo. 94
  Jas. 168
  Jno. 5, 109
  Noah 14
  Noah (Cpt.) 7
  Wm. 5
Stringfellow, Enoch 119,
  124
Stripling, Francis 93,
  168
Stroball, Abrah. 53
Stroder, Ezbell 168
Strohacker, Eliz. 53
Strong, Elijah 99
  Wm. 84, 89, 93, 99
Stropper, Will 174
Strothea, Francis 177
Strother, Jno. 97
Stroud, Isham 75
  Jno. 124, 129
  Jno. (Jr.) 129
  Sherod 125
Struthers, Wm. 53
Stuard, Jno. 94
Stuart, (?) 128
  Alexdr. 71
  Ann 53
  Clements 115
  Geo. 178
  Jas. 71
  Jas. M. 139
Stubblefield, Margaret
  59
  Peter 59, 61, 168
  Seth 168, 170
  Thos. 177
  Will 96
  Wm. 74, 169, 177
Stubbs, Eliz. 81
  Jas. 6
  Jno. (Jr.) 66
  Jos. 57
  Peter 75
Stubs, Peter 87
Stuerman, Henry 53
Sturdivant, Jno. 124
Sturges, Andrew 61
  Robt. 169
Sturgess, Danl. 93
Sturgis, Andrew 163
  Jno. 62
  Thos. 58
Sturivant, (?) 53
  Nathl. 53
  S. 53
Stutts, Allen 53
Stutz, Jos. 37, 53
  Michael 53
Styers, Michael 23, 29
Suarez, Antoine 24
Suaris, Anthony 22
  Antoine 24
Suarvis, Anthony 20
Suddeth, Elijah 177

Suddeth (cont.)
  Jno. 177
Suder, Jno. 53, 62
  Peter 53
  Peter (Jr.) 53
Sudthard, Jno. 66
Sulivant, Wm. 62
Sullavant, Danl. 105
Sullevant, Danl. 105,
  139
Sullivan, Danl. 33, 35,
  37
  Florence 152, 153
  Jno. 141
  Owen 57, 144
  Wm. 12, 57, 141, 144
Sumerlain, Jacob 96
Sumerland, Wm. 104
Summerall, C. 70
  Jesse 70
Summerlin, Henry 93, 169
  Lazarus 96
Sumner, Ann 134
  Cynthia 134
  Edwd. 132
  Eliz. 134, 139
  Job 132
  Jos. 6
  Mary Osgood 134
  Richd. 10
  Thos. 137, 139
Sumsder, Elijah 124
Sunner, Saml. 6
Sunter, Stephen 126
Sutherland, Alex. 148
  Eliz. 150
  Jno. 37, 144, 150
Sutten, Ralph 101
Suttle, Isaac 81
  Margret 82
  Wm. 82
Suttles, Isaac 77, 79,
  87
  Wm. 87
Sutton, Abraham 107
  Alsay 75
  Jas. 87
  Jeams 79
  Jeremiah 156
  Jno. 177
  Reuben 81
  Wm. 75, 177
Swain, Jas. 146
  Stephen 156
  Wm. 108
Swan, Jno. 59
  Mathew 132
Swanson, Andrew 125
  Nathan 174
  Wm. 114, 124
Swarbreck, Edw. 53
Swares, Antirine 27
Swearingen, Josiah 157
Sweeny, Barnard Wm. 6
Swella, Saml. 163
Sweney, Henry 21
  Jno. 119
Swepson, Jno. 119, 124
Swieghoffer, Abel 69
Swift, Jno. 96
  Wm. 96, 99, 102
Swilley, Jno. 157
  Saml. 157
Swiney, Henry 20
Swinney, Jno. 109, 119,
  124
Swint, Jno. 144
Swringe, Peter 96

Sykes, Margarett 6
  Wm. 53
Sympson, Jas. 177
Symson, Jno. 177
Taas, Chas. 124
Taber, Jno. 157, 169
Tabley, Key 10
Tabor, Jno. 141, 144
Tacker, Wm. 6
Taff, Wm. 174
Taggert, Jno. 10
Tait, Jas. 74, 75, 77,
  79, 81, 82, 84, 87,
  89, 101, 119
  Rebecca 77
  Wm. 81
  Wm. H. 81
  Zimry 79
Talbot, Edwd. 135
  Jno. 81, 116
  Mathew 101
  Matthew 152
  Patsy 93
  Thos. 93, 169
Talbott, Jno. 74
  Mathew 97
  Thos. 97, 99
Taliaferro, Ben 81
  Jno. Boutwell 99
Tallas, Jno. 6
Talley, Henry 152
  Wm. 27
Talliaferro, Benj. 169
Tallis, Willoughby 6
Tally, Jno. 24
  Mary 24
  Wm. 24
  Wm. (Jr.) 24
Talor, Chapman 18
Talpley, Jno. 15
Tanecel, Saml. 18
Tankersley, Jno. 60, 61,
  124, 152
Tankersly, Jno. 57, 58
Tanner, Asa 69
  Jno. 27, 114, 125,
  169, 170
  Jos. 6, 96
  Noah 163
  Thos. 10
Tannyhill, Jno. 156
Tapley, Aaron 144
  Arven 57
  Jno. 6, 11, 18, 163
  Joel 61, 141, 144
  Mary 61
  New 6, 61
  Wm. 10
Tapperly, Mary 114
Taque, (?) (Dr.) 53
  Doctor 53
Tarver, Benj. 6, 13, 114
  Bird 11, 15
  Jno. 169
  Thos. 10
  Wm. 66
Tarvin, Geo. 66
Tash, Jno. 53
Tate, Arthur 87
  Jas. 79, 81
  Jeremiah 21, 22, 25,
  29
  Robt. 152
  Wm. 76, 77, 89
  Wm. H. 87
  Zimre 75
Tatem, Abner 93
Tates, Jerimiah 27

Tatnall, Josiah 38, 134
  Josiah (Jr.) 146
Tatom, Jno. 169
Tattnall, Josiah 33, 38,
  53
  Josiah (Jr.) 35, 37
Tatum, Abel 169
  Apps 174
  Epps 172
  Howel 174
  Howell 172
  Jno. 169
  Nancy 172
  Nathan 124
  Peter 172, 174
  Polly 172
  Rebeccah 172
  Sally 172
  Seth 124
  Thos. 172
Taunt, Wm. 157
Tauser, Jno. 53
Taylor, Aaron 6, 10
  Abraham 53
  Ann 6, 59
  Benj. 85
  Caleb 6
  Champman 6
  Charlotte P. 53
  Chas. 66
  Edmond 6
  Edmund 101, 169
  Eliz. 53
  Geo. 53
  Grant 93, 101
  Henry 57, 144
  J. G. 31
  Jas. 39, 114, 116,
    124, 160
  Jeremiah 96
  Jno. 22, 27, 29, 38,
    53, 66
  Joannah 119
  Jordan 10
  Jos. 93
  Jos. G. 109
  Joshua 10, 156, 163
  Josiah 69
  Nathl. 132
  Right 158
  Robt. 21, 22, 25, 93
  Robt. (Sr.) 27
  Robt. H. 81
  Rowland 101
  Shadrack 160
  Susanna A. 139
  Susannah 132
  Ward 6
  Wm. 6, 20, 22, 24, 26,
    27, 29, 53, 61, 70,
    73, 135, 163
  Wright 119, 156
Tears, Jos. 125
Teas, Chas. 124
Tease, Chas. 114
  Wm. 125
Teasley, Fanny 77
  Jno. 89
  Silas 77, 169
Teaver, Jacob 169
Tebeau, Jno. 53
Telfair, Edw. 53
  Edwd. 146, 150
Temple, Jas. 53, 144
Templeton, Jno. 89, 93
  Thos. 57
  Wm. 144
Tennill, Thos. 69

Tennille, Benj. 163
  Frances 163
Terendate, Danl. 93
Terondet, Danl. 171
Terrell, David 93
  Jno. 81
  Jos. 93, 94, 102
  Richmond 177
  Will 171
  Wm. 101
Terrien, (?) (Mrs.) 53
Terril, Jos. 94
  Moses 94
Terrill, Hezekiah 99
  Jas. 101
  Jos. 79
  Pierce 136
Terry, Champness 18
  Champness (Cpt.) 7
  David 103, 104, 108
  Jno. 172
  Jos. 87
  Stephen 107
  Tho. 18
  Thos. 62
Tetard, Benj. 21, 53
Thacker, (?) 124
Tharp, Eleazer 152
  Wiley 163
Thatcher, Daniel (Rev.)
  114
  Danl. 116
Theis, Jacob 53
  Jacob (Jr.) 53
Thetford, Wm. 93
Thies, Peter 31, 33
Thiner, Michael 163
Thomas, Allen 20, 21,
    22, 25, 27, 29
  Benj. 93, 169
  Camm 66
  Eliz. 12
  Etheldred 169
  Ezekiel 90, 101
  Feaby 146
  Gideon 6, 10, 18, 156,
    163
  Gills 93
  Gilshot 10
  Jas. 125, 163
  Jesse 95, 97, 99
  Jno. 119, 169
  Jno. (Jr.) 119
  Jno. (Sr.) 119, 124
  Jno. H. 177
  Jno. Hames 178
  Joel 75, 87
  Jos. 53, 66
  Josiah 119
  Lucy 21
  Massa 93
  Massy 177
  Peter 6, 66
  Phillip 11
  Robt. 119, 124, 152
  Saml. 169, 170, 178
  Theophilus 119
  Turby Phillip 12
  Wm. 18, 22, 58, 66,
    75, 84, 89, 90, 93,
    119, 159, 177
Thomason, Geo. 85
Thompkins, Eliz. 163
Thompson, Abraham 93
  Agnes 114
  Alexdr. 89
  Archibald 170
  Benj. 119, 163

Thompson (cont.)
  Benj. (Jr.) 109
  Catharine 148, 150
  Clare 97
  Claud 35
  Claude 35
  Claus 97
  Drewry 81
  Drury 89
  Elihu 6, 13, 14, 18
  Geo. 114
  Gideon 157
  Isham 22, 77, 82, 89
  Jas. 53, 54, 116, 124,
    127, 177
  Jas. (Sr.) 10
  Jesse 75, 115
  Jno. 53, 81, 111, 124
  Jno. F. 89
  Jno. Farley 76, 77
  Jos. 114, 124, 125
  Laban 6, 14
  Oliver 75
  Peter 81, 93
  Reuben 27
  Robt (Sr.) 76
  Robt. 75, 77, 109, 114
  Sally 77
  Saml. 177
  Saml. M. 76
  Sarah 53, 77, 82
  Tabetty 54
  Wells 76, 101
  Wm. 6, 35, 38, 77, 81,
    84, 87, 101, 141,
    148, 149, 150, 177
  Wm. (Jr.) 81
  Wm. (Sr.) 75, 76
  Zach. 109
  Zachariah 116
  Zachrh 119
  Zachrh. 128
Thomson, Benj. 124
  Claud 69
  Cloud 131
  Jas. 124
  Jno. 72
  Wm. 177
Thorn, David 71
  Merrimon 58
  Merryman 61
  Wm. 71
Thorne, Merryman 101
Thornhill, Leonard 82
  Mary 82
Thornton, (?) 10
  Danl. 87
  Dread 169, 173
  Elam 54, 156, 163
  Herod 169
  Jno. 69, 70, 73
  Noel 169
  Reuben 81, 87
  Rober 109
  Rodgers 124
  Roger 114
  Saml. 10, 114, 172
  Sarah 171
  Sol. 169, 177
  Stephen 93
  Thos. 83
  Thos. H. 169
  Wm. 169
Thorp, Chas. 134
  Jno. 136
  Wiley 10
Thorpe, Geo. 33
Thrasher, Benj. 97

Thrasher (cont.)
Eliz. 97
Geo. 156
Jos. C. 114
Robt. 93, 96, 97, 101
Sarah 97
Threadcraft, Geo. 33, 71
Throop, Geo. 33, 54
Thrower, Levi 10, 71
Wm. 69
Thurman, David 169
Jno. 169
Thurmond, Phillip 84
Thweat, Jas. 109, 124
Tice, Mary 54
Tichenor, Isaac 54
Tieagan, Allen 26
Ties, Jacob 31
Tigert, Jos. 177
Tighlman, Aaron 146
Tigner, Phillip 116,
119, 124
Tillery, Henry 96
Tilley, Cunningham C.
141
Jno. 10
Tillingast, Danl. (Jr.)
132
Tillinghast, Danl. 134,
139
Stukely 54
Tillman, Gideon 70, 73
Wm. 6, 12
Tillmon, L. B. 18
Littleberry 156
Stephen 156
Stephenson 156
Wm. 18
Tilman, Francis 6
Gideon 69
Littleberry 163
Wm. 6
Tilmon, Littleberry 15
Timmerman, Godfrey 66
Timmons, Catherine 31
Jno. 31
Richd. 132, 136, 139
Timrod, Susannah 54
Tims, Benj. 27
Tho. 27
Tinch, Wm. 169
Tindal, Jas. 18
Jno. 18
Tindall, Booker 58, 144
Jno. 141, 144
Wm. 144, 149
Tindel, Wm. 66
Tindell, Booker 66
Jno. 144
Wm. (Sr.) 66
Tindil, Booker 62
Pleasant 62
Wm. (Jr.) 62
Tindill, Betty Ann 146
Jno. 57, 63, 141
Tindol, Jno. 149
Tingley, (?) 40
Otis 54
Tinnall, Jno. 144
Tinsley, David 144, 148,
150
Jas. 63, 64, 66, 141,
144
Mary 146
Tiot, Chas. 54
Tippen, Jos. 54
Tippens, Philip 136
Tippin, Benj. 54

Tippin (cont.)
Jos. 54
Tippinn, Phillip 6
Tippins, Phillip 6, 12
Tipton, Thos. 6
Tisker, Allening 29
Tison, Aaron 119
Isaac 10
Toan, Geo. 125
Tobler, U. 37
Ulric 37
Ulrich 31, 54
Todd, Eliz. 6
Jno. 54, 169, 177
Wm. 57, 144
Todhunter, Evin 96
Tolar, Lewis 158
Tolbert, Jno. 119
Saml. 87
Thos. 119
Tolbott, Benj. 177
Nathl. 144
Thos. 177
Tolds, Geo. 64
Toler, Demsey 169
Tolland, Jno. 29
Tollett, Jno. 83
Tomason, Turner 66
Tombs, Gabriel 128
Wm. 128
Tomkins, Chris. 12
Tomlin, Jno. 11, 12
Redden 10
Tomlinson, Aaron 163
Ann 6
David 156, 169
Jno. 11, 15
Tommerlin, Betty 6
Tommey, Mary 10
Tompkins, Christopher 6
Eliz. 163
Jno. 104, 105, 157
Wm. 104
Tompson, Saml. 169
Tomson, Jas. 126
Jno. 126, 158
Robt. 126
Tondee, Chas. 33, 35, 54
Peter 33
Tonnell, Fred'k. 18
Tonny, Mary 6
Tony, Littleberry 101
Toombs, Robt. 119
W. 109
Wm. 129
Torrence, Jno. 169
Tottman, Benj. 90
Touceston, Chris. 103
Touchston, Chris. 104,
108
Richd. 104, 108
Touchstone, David 144
Touchton, Christopher
106
Danl. 25
Toussaint, Jean Baptiste
54
Toutchston, Danl. 103
Towena, Jno. 148
Towers, Asaph 54
Jno. 37
Robt. 106
Robt. (Jr.) 37
Towns, Jno. 93, 101,
119, 144
Townsen, Saml. 124
Townsend, Ruth 146
Thos. 148

Townshend, (?) 54
Thos. 54
Trailer, Wm. 93, 169
Trammel, Elijah 10
Thos. 124
Trammell, Wm. 102
Traner, Jas. 177
Tranfield, Mary 54
Sarah 54
Trant, Jno. 6
Trapnell, Archibald 148,
159
Travis, Asa 146
Jno. 58, 63
Simeon 69
Thos. 57
Wm. 57, 141
Trawick, Joel 107
Richd. 107
Tray, Mary 156
Trayler, Thos. 119
Traywick, Francis 169
Treadwell, Jno. 18
Trebel, Benj. 178
Tredwell, Jno. 14
Trefeten, Benj. 54
Treman, Stephen 22
Trent, Henry 169
Trentham, Absolom 77
David 99
Treutlen, Christian 69
Treutlin, Frederick 54
Trevor, Jno. 54
Trewitt, Riley 93
Tribble, (?) (Mrs.) 54
Trice, Jas. 119, 156
Jno. 128
Triebner, Chris.
Frederick 71
Trimble, Jno. 81
Katharin 77
Moses 77, 93
Trinquart, Lewis 54
Triplet, Francis 18
Triplett, Frances 12
Rachel 12
Tripp, Jno. 116
Trippe, Henry 111, 124
Jno. 114
Sarah 114
Troup, Cath. 134
Geo. 132
Troupe, Geo. 54
Truchet, Chas. 54
Truetlin, Chris. 71
Jno. A. 71
Tucker, Andrew 107, 108
Ann 54
Geo. 169, 170
Henry C. 10
Hezekiah 10, 107
Isaac 10
Jas. 54
Robt. 177
Sarah 6
Thos. 10, 105, 107,
108
Willoughby 107
Tudor, Jno. 66, 141
Tuft, Sinnickson 39
Soonickson 33
Syniston 31
Tuggle, Wm. 102
Tuiss, Tho. 64
Tulley, Moses 169
Tullis, Moses 169
Tully, Wm. 15
Tuly, Wm. 70, 73

Tunno, Adam 35
Tunro, A. 54
  Wm. 54
Tureman, Eliz. 77
  Geo. 77
  Martin 79
Turk, Jno. 74
  Theodicius 119
  Theodosus 124
Turle, Edw. 15
Turman, Geo. 89
  Jos. 87
  Leonard 87
  Martha 81
  Martin 82, 89
  Robt. 89
  Tho. 89
Turmerson, Turner 149
Turnbull, Andrew 54
  Mary (Mrs.) 54
  Nicholl 54
Turner, (?) 54
  J. H. 37
  Jas. (Jr.) 114, 124
  Jas. (Sr.) 124
  Jesse 124
  Jno. 37, 54, 94, 99,
    101
  Joshua 124
  Lewis 35, 54
  Richd. 54
  Saml. 124
  Shadrack 169
  Thos. 81
  Venerius 6
  Will 124
Tushet, Chas. 135
Tusing, Paul 69
Tuttle, Isaac 76
  Jas. 79
  Jas. (Jr.) 77, 79, 89,
    169
  Jas. (Sr.) 75, 77, 82,
    169
  Jos. 87
  Nicholas 77, 81
Tweedle, Jno. 74, 78, 81
  Sarah 78
Twiggs, Jno. 144, 148
Tyler, Henry 172
  Wm. 119
Tylor, Wm. 22
Tyner, Caleb 25
  Jno. 21, 25
  Richd. 89
Tyson, Abraham 171, 177
Ulmer, Phillip 33, 54
  Wm. 54
Umphrees, Wm. 10
Underwood, Benj. 156,
  163
  Jno. 136
  Jos. 89
  Josiah 160
  Thos. 160
  Wm. 54, 63
Unselt, Barbara 54
Upshaw, Jno. 74, 169
Upton, Benj. 163
  Geo. 66, 144, 177
  Jas. 146
  Philip 66
  Sarah 66
Urquhart, Wm. 152
Usher, Jno. 54
  Richd. 54
Ussery, Abner 10
Vainyard, Jno. 87

Vales, Saml. 90
Valleau, Ann 37
Valley, Geo. 108, 131
Vallotton, Benj. 54
  David 54
  Jeremiah 54
  Jeremiah O. 54
  Moses 54
  Paul J. 54
Van, Edw. 63
  Jos. 94
Van Dyke, Peter 134
Van Hook, Saml. 84
VanHeddeghem, (?) (Mrs.)
  153
VanYeverson, M. 37
Vance, Davis 6
  Patrick 98
  Sarah 98
Vanderlocht, Wm. 39
Vandyke, Ann 139
  Peter 135, 139
Vanhook, Aron 82
Vann, Edw. 58
  Geo. 94
  Jesse 144
  Jno. 159
  Lovey 54
  Martha 81
  Wm. 54
Vanse, Patrick 102
Vanzant, Geo. 21
  Steph. 21
Varner, Geo. 6
Varniel, Wm. 94
Varum, Isum 63
Vasdimon, Will 96
Vassells, Jas. 157
Vasteen, Jeremiah 54
Vaughan, Alex 57
Vaughn, Alexdr. 144
  Ephraim 11, 15, 111
  Ephriam 127
  Evans 144
  Jane 146
  Jas. 146
  Jno. 108, 146
  Jno. Daniel 23
  Joshua 63
  Robt. 146
  Wm. 146
Vaughter, Whorton 6
Veasey, Jas. 111
Veazey, Eliz. 114
  Ezekiel 114, 124
  Jas. 124
  Jesse 114, 124
  Jno. 114
  Wm. 114, 128
  Zebulon 114
Veazy, Ezekiel 109, 116
  Jas. 119
  Wm. 172
Vedheidingem, Jno. Peter
  149
Venable, Abraham 177
  Chas. 177
Venables, Wm. 54
Vencent, Geo. 27
Verdery, Peter 54
Vergnin, Chas. 54
Verner, Geo. 6
Vernon, Isaac 66
  Nathl. 141, 144
Verriere, Paul 54
Vessells, Jas. 160
Vessey, Wm. 174
Vial, Lawrence 35

Vickers, Benj. 156
  Drury 159
  Jno. 6, 15, 156
  Joshua 159
  Robt. 156
  Saml. 54
  Thos. 163
Vickery, Wm. 169
Vincent, Jas. 20, 21,
  24, 27
  Jas. S. 29
  Steph. 27
Vineyard, David 79, 87
  Isham 81
  Ishmael 169
  Jas. 89, 169
  Jno. 89
Vining, Cader 18
  Jesse 18
  Jno. 15
  Shadrack 6
Vinson, David 63, 66
  Jesse 81, 82
  Jno. 177
  Liab 90
  M. 64
Vint, Wm. 97
Vivan, Thacker 156
Vivion, Thacker 163
Vodan, Bradock 75
Voden, Bradock 81
Voicle, Louis 152
Vollotton, David Moses
  31
  Francis 31
Waddel, Wm. 124
Waddell, Alexdr. 97
  Jno. 110
Wade, Benj. 12
  David 114
  Edw. 111, 114, 124
  Eliz. 12
  Hezekiah 18
  J. 152
  Jas. 170
  Jno. 13, 15, 33, 144
  Mary 114
  Moses 177
  Nehemiah 12, 13
  Peyton 114, 124
  Saml. 6, 18
  Thos. 109, 114, 124,
    127
Wadsworth, Jas. 156, 163
  Jas. (Jr.) 156
Wafford, Benj. 94
Waggamon, Jno. Michael
  111
Waggner, Jas. 169
Waggoner, Jas. 177
  Thos. 144
  Wm. 177
Waggonnar, Michael 128
Wagnon, Jno. 95
  Jno. P. 101
  Jno. Peter 33, 150,
    151
  Rebecca 24, 150
  Thos. 148
Wagoner, Geo. 57
  Henry 57
  Jno. 145
Waid, Chas. 152
Wakefield, Chas. 97
Walch, Edmund 54
Waldburger, Bartholomew
  37
  C. (Mrs.) 54

Waldburger (cont.)
J. 37
Jacob 37
Jno. B. 54
Walden, Henry 14
Waldhaeur, Jno. 71
Waldhoeur, Jacob C. 33
Waldhouer, Jacob C. 54
Walding, Saml. 6
Waldon, Jno. 69
Walker, (?) 54
  Andrew 82
  Ansiel 137
  Archelaus 83
  Archibald 87
  Barbara 160
  Chas. 95, 99, 134
  David 18, 60, 66, 141,
    145, 146
  Elijah 95
  Elisha 59, 64, 107,
    108, 156
  Eliz. 78
  Enoch 18
  Geo. 12, 81, 101, 152,
    153, 160
  H. Graves 83
  Henry 169
  Isaac 11, 18
  Isham 137
  J. 81, 84
  Jacob 95
  Jas. 78, 79, 124, 163
  Jere 79
  Jeremiah 76, 79, 89,
    156
  Jesse 99
  Jno. 6, 11, 111, 141,
    177, 178
  Jno. (Jr.) 124
  Jno. (Sr.) 124
  Joel 6, 107, 108, 132,
    133, 137, 139, 160
  Landers 6
  Little B. 137
  M. 81
  Mary 137
  Mel 124
  Milly 76, 81
  Moses 169
  Nathl. 129
  Phillip 93, 101
  Randal 95
  Richd. 137
  Robt. 145
  Saml. 177
  Sanders 6, 169, 171
  Sarah 169
  Silvanus 114, 124, 156
  Syl. 129
  Tandy 107, 108
  Tho. 15
  Thos. 156, 163, 177
  Thos. (Jr.) 12
  Wm. 13, 54, 63, 107,
    108, 114, 119, 160,
    169
  Wyatt 101
Wall, Ann 61
  Benj. 33, 35, 37, 54
  Billy 54
  David 141, 145
  Francis 109, 124, 156
  Henry 95, 158
  J. 101
  Jno. 54, 115, 124
  Jos. 158
  Mary 115

Wall (cont.)
  Micajah 127, 129
  Richd. 37, 54
  Saml. 54
  Wm. 158
Wallace, Channal 156
  Jas. 35, 54, 169
  Jno. 37, 54, 84, 119,
    163
  Wm. 31, 54, 146, 148,
    150, 151, 159, 170
Wallas, Absalom 13
Wallecon, Danl. 148
Waller, Benj. 12
  Elisha 126
  Jas. 126
  Mary 12
  Saml. 12, 54, 124
  Steph. 126
  Wm. 10
Wallis, Absalom 6
  Carnill 93
  Chas. 156
  Jno. 177
  Micajah 93
Walraven, Jno. 83
Walter, Thos. 158
Walters, Clement 96, 99
  Jno. 95, 98, 102
  Jos. 125
  Mary 98
  Moses 95
  Peter 95, 99, 102
  Robt. 95, 101
  Saml. (Cpt.) 94
  Wm. 54
Walthall, Edw. 78, 89
  Garrard 75
  Jas. 89
  Nancy 78
Walthour, Andrew 136,
  139
Walton, Asa 27
  Blanche 146
  Geo. 81, 150
  Jess 93
  Jesse 101
  Jno. 57, 58, 61, 141
  Jno. C. 153
  Mary 98
  Newell 169
  Robt. 11, 145, 146
  Simon 93
  Thos. 101
  W. 101
  Walker 93, 96, 99
  Wm. 57, 61, 66, 74,
    75, 141, 145, 150,
    169
Wamack, Wm. 124
Wambersie, Emaniel 153
  Emanuel 54, 150, 151
Wambles, (?) (Cpt.) 7
Wamock, Jno. 163
Ward, Albritton 107
  Allen 64
  Bryan 98
  Bryant 98
  Chas. 145, 153
  Elias 10
  Elijah 6, 149
  Eliz. 6
  Francis 6, 18
  Jno. 96, 160
  Jno. Peter 54
  Moses 156, 163
  Richd. 54, 124, 125
  Riley 54

Ward (cont.)
  Saml. 96, 98, 101, 160
  Saul 66
  Sol. 64
  Tho. 64, 66
  Thos. 63
  Wm. 39
Wardlaw, Wm. 116
Ware, Edw. 87
  Henry 81
  Jas. 110, 169
  Jno. 101
  Robt. 66
  Wm. 87
Warerton, Thos. 109
Warlick, (?) 159
  Valentine 6
Warmack, Mary 6
Warnal, Wm. 137
Warnick, Jno. 124
Warnock, Hansell 119
  Jesse 6
  Jno. 114, 125, 129
  Mary 6
  Matthew 109, 111
  Robt. 19, 114, 127,
    129
  Wm. 129
Warrant, Abraham 128
Warren, A. 64
  Carless 6
  Carlos 10
  Chas. 95
  Elias 37, 131, 134,
    137
  Gabriel 10
  Jesse 137
  Jno. 131, 137
  Jos. 131
  Joshua 25
  Lot 169
  Richd. 6
  Saml. 137
  Thos. 99, 124
  Valentine 95
Warthen, Richd. 163
Wasden, Thos. 6
Washam, Joshua 12
Washburn, Jos. 29
Washington, David M. 54
  Wm. 109, 124
Waterman, Eleazer 28, 29
Waters, Bradford 177
  Jas. 66, 128, 141, 145
  Jno. 38, 54, 93
  Jos. 124
  Matthew 85
  Peter 54
  Saml. 54
  Tamar 33
  Thos. 103, 108
  Wm. 54
Watkins, Benj. 169
  Jno. 6, 19, 101, 114,
    129, 151, 169
  Robt. 66, 79, 101,
    145, 153
  Saml. 75
  Tho. 66
  Thos. 146, 151, 153
  Wm. 78, 83
  Wm. (Jr.) 151
  Wm. (Sr.) 150
Watley, Owen 149
  Sherod 149
  Walton 149
  Willis (Jr.) 149
  Willis (Sr.) 149

Watlington, Eliz. 54
  Jno. N. 31
Wats, Jacob 159
Watson, Benj. 63, 102,
    129, 163
  Caroline (Mrs.) 12
  David 156, 158, 163
  Douglas 119, 127
  Elisha 158
  Jas. 54, 128, 129,
    135, 136
  Jas. T. 54
  Jno. 66, 145, 169
  Joshua 6, 15
  Lewis 63
  Nathl. 145
  Nelly 6
  Robt. 127
  Tho. 63, 66
  Thos. 146
  Willis 14, 19
  Willis (Cpt.) 7
Watt, Alex. 31
  Alexdr. 33, 35, 38, 54
  Chas. 132
  Jesse 163
  Wm. 38, 125
Watters, Moses 102
Watts, Benj. 114, 124
  Chas. 127
  Edw. 12, 19, 90, 141
  Edwd. 152
  Geo. 89, 90
  Jacob 156, 163
  Jno. 160, 163
  Jos. 12, 130, 131,
    150, 151
  Presly 127
  Robt. 54
  Saml. 126
  Thos. 111, 114, 119,
    130
Wattson, Jno. 78
Wauls, Wm. 157
Way, Ann 132, 139
  Hannah 137, 139
  Jno. 132, 137, 139
  Jos. 131, 136
  Jos. (Jr.) 137, 139
  Jos. (Sr.) 136, 139
  Mary 139
  Moses 137, 139
  Parmenas 133
  Sarah 137
  Thos. 136
  Wm. 132, 137, 139
  Wm. (Jr.) 139
Wayne, Eliz. 54
  Richd. (Jr.) 54
  Wm. 19
Weakley, Eliz. 150
  Lewis 150
Weakly, Lewis 151
Weatherby, Geo. 93
Weathers, Edw. 6, 19
  Eliz. 12
  Geo. 6, 12
Weaver, Stephen 141
Webb, Austin 79, 89
  Chas. 87
  Claban 79
  Claborn 79
  Claiborn 101
  Henry 70
  Jeremiah 145
  Jesse 101
  Jno. 21, 54
  Pleasant 87, 99

Webb (cont.)
  Thos. 81, 169
  Wm. 71, 74, 177
Webley, Benj. 54
Webster, Abner 169, 177
  Archa 169
  Frances 146
  Honner 146
  Jacob 66
  Jno. 74, 93, 101
  Jonathan 79, 177
  Saml. 20, 22, 24
Weed, Henry 136
  Jacob 21, 22, 24, 25
  Jno. N. 136
Weekes, Wm. 124
Weeks, Jno. 116, 124,
    135
Weimingham, Jas. 11
Weitman, Danl. 71
Welborne, David 21
Welch, Benj. 114
  Jacob 6
  Jas. 12, 19
  Jno. 10
  Jos. 10
  Nicholas 157
Welcher, Jos. 38
Welen, Jno. 10
Wellmott, Wm. 90
Wells, Absalom 12
  Andrew. Elton 71
  Henry 69, 70
  Jacob 70, 73
  Jno. 6
  Jno. (Jr.) 10
  Julius 6
  Mary (Mrs.) 139
  Mary Jane 12
  Saml. 145
  Stephen 10
Wellson, Saml. 19
Welsch, Andrew 54
  Jas. 11
Welscher, Jos. 31, 35,
    38, 54
Welsh, Jno. 6
Welton, Jas. 160
Were, Jas. 6
Wesley, Lemmons 157
West, A. (Dr.) 114
  Andrew 177
  Eli 81
  Elias 115
  Ellis 119, 126
  Jas. 60
  Martin 146
  Sion 156
  Wm. 109, 111, 126,
    137, 177
Westbrook, Jno. 89, 169
  Stephen 74, 75, 79,
    101
Wester, Jno. 174
Westley, Lemon 156
Weston, Jno. 126
  Job 54
Weterson, Jno. 97
Wetherby, Stephen 169
Wetherspoon, Jas. 131
Wever, Jno. (Sr.) 75
Weyrich, Jno. 54
Whaley, Danl. 114
  Eli 114
  Hannah 114
  Jno. 124
  Wm. 111
Whalis, Isham 169

Whaly, Nathl. 116
Whatley, Archibald 174
  Curby 172
  Danl. 109
  Jesse 156
  Jno. 115, 149
  Kirby 174
  Michael 169, 173
  Richd. 149, 169
  Tisdel 177
  Walton 174
  Wiley 177
  Willis 174
  Withe 177
Whealer, Jos. 98
Whealler, Wm. 99
Whealy, Eliz. 114
Wheat, Jno. 169
Wheaty, Wm. 111
Wheeler, Ambrose 6
  Emperor 169
  Isaac 11, 21, 24, 25
  Isham 124
  Jno. 107
  Jos. 99
  Richd. 107
  Wm. 90, 169
Wheelon, Amos 160
Wheelright, Jos 169
Whiddon, Lott 10
Whiggens, Wm. 164
Whigham, Agnes 6
  Alex. 6
  Jno. 6
  Wm. 10
Whitaker, Amos 19
  Benj. 14, 178
  Benj. (Cpt.) 7
  Hudson 11, 14, 15, 19
  Hudson (Cpt.) 7
  Jacob 19
  Joshua 63
  Saml. 63, 145, 178
Whitcomb, N. 64
  Notley 66
Whitcumbe, Nolley 59
White, (?) 54
  Abe 96
  Benedick 102
  Benedict 64, 94
  Chas. 135
  Danl. 87, 89
  Edw. 10, 54
  Eusebius 55
  G-- 114
  Jas. 12, 19, 31, 38,
    119
  Jepthah 96
  Jesse 74, 87
  Jno. 19, 31, 76, 78,
    79, 93, 99, 114,
    124, 126, 128
  Jno. Y. 55
  Jno. Younger 31
  Jos. 63, 109, 116,
    124, 127, 129
  Luke 87
  Milley 78
  Nicholas 145
  Pollie 153
  Rachel 12
  Reuben 76
  Reubin 115, 116
  Richd. 93
  Richd. F. 58
  Richd. P. 58
  Robt. 63
  Saml. 14

White (cont.)
Saml. (Cpt.) 7
Thos. 58, 135
Wm. 63, 96
Wm. B. 10
Whiteacon, Saml. 141
Whiteaire, Thos. 98
Whitecum, Holley 64
Whitefield, Adam 55
Benj. 119
Eliz. 55
J. 31, 38
Jas. 38, 39, 55
Martha 38
Richd. 55
Saml. 55
Whiteford, Saml. 55
Whitehall, Lewis 6
Whitehard, Sarah 55
Whitehead, Amos 6, 11,
15, 19, 157
Jacob 19
Jane 157, 164
Jno. 131, 133, 139
Rezin 158
Thos. 157, 164
Whitehurst, Jno. 124
Whiteside, (?) 55
Jas. 174
Whitfield, Lewis 11
Whiting, Jno. A. 152
Whitker, Benj. 177
Whitley, Jno. 6, 55
Thos. 149
Whitlock, Heppe 177
Hopps 178
Jno. 177
Whitmire, Thos. 101
Whitney, Eli 55
Jas. R. 93
Jno. M. 83, 93, 99
Lott 70, 73
Whitsill, Geo. 93
Whitten, Robt. 141, 150
Saml. 177
Whittendal, Jno. Thos.
38
Mary 38
Whittendell, Jno. 55
Whittington, C. 141
Cornelius 145, 148,
169
Wm. 141, 145, 148
Whitton, Auston 115
Whitworth, Jno. 93
Whyche, Geo. 55
Jno. 55
Whyte, O. 81
Wicker, Bol. 158
Jula 158
Robt. 157, 164
Wm. 157
Wiggens, Lewis 124
M. 124
Wiggians, Jesse 19
Wiggins, Edmund 31
Frederick 69
Jos. 69
Lewis 116, 119, 129
Mary 31, 33, 38
Wm. 164
Wilborn, Curtis 164
Joshua 109
Wilborne, Aephzeleat 171
Elijah 109
Isaac 171
Johnston 171
Nancy 171

Wilborne (cont.)
Shapely 171
Wm. 170
Wilbourn, Curtis 157
Thos. 169
Wm. 93
Wilbourne, Abner 171
Wilkes 171
Wilburn, Wm. 102
Wilby, Benj. 38
Wilcher, Benj. 169
Wilcox, Moses 87
Wilder, Dread 169
Eliz. 169
Malichi 149
Sarah 69
Wildred, Jos. Dred 87
Wiley, Alexdr. 111
Jas. 94
Jno. 177
Peter 93
Wm. 124
Wilford, Lewis 159
Wilkerson, Baley 177
Jno. 177
Saml. 177
Wilkes, Jas. 66
Wilkey, Jno. 10
Jonathan 10
Wilkins, Ann 55
Camillus 55
Clement 99, 169
Element 74
Eliz. 78
Jno. 87, 89
Jonathan 145
Obadiah 55
Saml. 55
Tho. 89
Thos. 78, 82, 141
Wm. 63, 64, 69, 145
Wilkinson, Hazlewood 177
Jas. 132, 134
Jno. 109, 124
Jno. B. 55
Jos. 55
Reuben 164
Reubin 160
Wm. 93
Wilks, Benj. 126
Willard, Saml. 177
Willcox, Jno. 146
Willen, Wm. 89
William, Danl. 89
Wilson 21
Williams, Abner 21, 22,
24, 25
Abraham 27
Anna 114
Archibald 174
Arthur 11, 12, 178
Benj. 61, 178
Bowery 178
Chas. 11, 13, 164
Chris. 169
Curtis 119
Daniel 66
Danl. 171
Drury 173
Edw. 59
Edwd. 124, 128
Eliz. 24, 55
Fanny 10
Farr 108
Gernier 35
Hannah 24
Henry 55, 149
Jaret 76

Williams (cont.)
Jas. 6, 55, 93, 145,
178
Jno. 6, 55, 58, 64,
93, 101, 124, 129,
145
Jno. (Col.) 153
Jonathan 64, 109
Jos. 76, 87, 93, 173
Joshua 93, 178
Lewis 10, 72
Lud 148
Martin 102
Mat. J. 75, 81
N. 13
Noah 6, 14
Patrick 10
Richd. 107
Robt. 70, 71, 73
Rosannah 55
Saml. 35, 69
Steph. 55
Steph. S. 55
Stephen 31, 139
Sugar (?) 174
Tho. 87
Thos. 178
Thos. F. 55
Willis 70, 73
Wilson 22, 24, 25, 27,
29
Wm. 23, 82, 90, 93,
104, 106, 157, 178
Wm. C. 93
Williamson, Acquilla 6
Andrew 27
Aquilla 70, 73
Arthur 11, 15
Bird 171
Chas. 93
Elijah 99
Eliz. 171
Henry 55
Jas. 93, 170
Jefferson 171
Jno. 10, 38, 169
Jno. G. 38, 55
Macajah (Jr.) 171
Micajah 93, 98
Micajah (Jr.) 94
Micajah (Sr.) 170
Patsy 171
Peter 94, 98, 101,
119, 171
Robt. 6, 94, 101, 102
Sally 98
W. 81, 146
Zorobabl 124
Williman, Chris. 99
Willingham, Jeremiah 178
Jno. 145
Jno. (Jr.) 66
Ollie 66
Tho. 66
Thos. 111
Wm. 61, 145
Willington, Eleanor 12
Thos. 12
Willis, Britton 101
Francis 152
Moses 178
Willoby, Wm. 63
Wills, Jno. 88
Willshire, Jeremiah 145
Wm. 145
Willson, Arkeclair 97
Hugh 19
Jas. 124

Willson (cont.)
Jno. 124
Perry 119
Willy, Jas. 55
Thos. 76
Wilmoth, Ezekiel 83
Nancy 83
Thos. 82
Wm. 83, 85
Wilmouth, Stephen 74
Wilscher, Jos. 31
Wilsher, Jurdin 149
Wilshire, Ann 171
Benj. 170
Eliz. 171
Mary 171
Sarah 171
Wm. 171
Wilson, (?) 55
Agnes 6
Alexdr. 55
Benj. 55, 94
David 38
Delphia 55
Eliz. 139
Geo. 31
Goodwin 55
Jas. 35, 55, 69, 72,
87, 131, 133, 137,
139, 170
Jason 74, 81
Jesse 70
Jno. 55, 101, 109,
116, 119, 128, 148,
149, 151, 169
Jos. 94, 169
Mary 6, 132
Mildred 101
Milley 94
Party 61
Pearre 61
Perry 57, 60, 63, 94,
148
Peter 58
Robert Wm. 139
Robt. 114, 119, 158
Wm. 55, 109, 124, 128,
133
Wimberly, Zacharia 6
Wimbish, Saml. 78
Wimpson, Wm. 29
Windingham, Jno. 145
Windslette, Saml. 124
Winekoff, Ann 35
Matthew 33
Winfree, Jess 141
Ruben 178
Winfrey, Jess 141
Jesse 64, 145
Wingate, Jesse 21
Wingfield, Ann 171
Garland 171
Jno. 82, 87, 119, 169,
170, 171
Mary 82
Thos. 171
Wingom, Philip 81
Winket, Saml. 6
Winkfield, J. 60
Winn, Banister 31
Bannister 55
Jno. 114, 137, 139
Jos. 131, 136, 137
Martha 137
Martha (Mrs.) 139
Peter 132, 133, 134,
136, 137, 139
Peter (Sr.) 11

Winn (cont.)
Thos. 55
Wm. 14
Winne, Jno. 157
Winney, Josiah 10
Winningham, Jas. 12, 15
Thos. 145
Winslett, Saml. 128
Winslow, Elisha 55
Winston, Jno. 170
Winter, Frederick 142
Nelly 101
Richd. 55
Wise, Jos. 169
Sheridy 157
Wm. 69
Wiseman, Jos. 55
Wisenbaker, Jacob 72
Wisleay, Sol. 19
Witherspoon, Jas. 131,
132
Wm. 94
Wm.Cone 151
Woard, Benj. 149
Woffard, Nathl. 101
Wofford, Jas. 94
Wm. 99
Woldridge, Wm. 79
Wolf, Andrew 178
Geo. 69
Jno. 69
Wolridge, Wm. 89
Womack, Allen 71
Frederick 71
Jesse 19
Jno. 31
Wm. 71, 124
Womble, (?) (Widow) 10
Allen 11, 15
Drury 19
Woocock, Thos. 126
Wood, (?) 63
Abraham 157, 159, 164
Ann 152
Aristarchus 128
Aristarcus 124
Benj. 157
Cath. 55
Catherine 132
David 157, 164
Dempsey 157
Eliz. 133, 137
Etheldred 109
Ethelred 115
Francis (Dr.) 134
Geo. 81
Henry 133, 134, 136,
139
Isaac 135, 148
Jacob 31, 38, 139
Jane 109
Jas. 20, 55, 115, 125,
128, 132, 133, 137,
139, 159, 169
Jonathan 64
Jos. 132
Joshua 19
Josiah 94
Mary (Mrs.) 115
Mathew 27
Matthew 20, 24
Middleton 87
Saml. 87
Sol. 157, 160, 164
Thos. 139
Wm. 6, 157
Woodall, Chas. 170
Jacob 111

Woodall (cont.)
Jno. 114
Jos. 114
Woodard, Warwick 164
Woodbridge, Geo. 55
Robt. 55
Thos. M. 132
Thos. R. 55
Woodbridhe, Robt. 55
Woodham, Edwd. 114
Woodhouse, Geo. 31, 38,
55
Robt. 33, 38, 69
Woodland, Eliz. 24
Geo. 21, 25
Jas (Jr.) 21
Jas. 21, 22, 24, 25,
27, 28
Jas. (Jr.) 27
Jas. (Sr.) 25, 29
Jno. (Jr.) 29
Susannah 21
Woodroof, Wilson 152
Woodruff, Geo. 55
Jos. 131, 132
Wilson 145
Woods, Aristarcus 127
Austarcus 109
Hannah 110, 127
Jacob 134
Jas. 110, 127, 178
Jno. 6, 55
Josiah 94, 178
M. 81
Margaret 55
Middleton 74, 79, 83,
94, 169
Nathl. 152
Richd. 169
Saml. 94
Thos. 69
Willis 19
Wm. 19, 83, 94
Woodward, Wm. 55, 132,
135, 136
Woolf, Jacob 55
Woolhopter, Phillip 55
Wooten, Jas. 125
Jeremiah 169
Thos. 169
Wooters, Phillip 131
Wooton, Thos. 101
Wootson, Eliz. 115
Jas. 115
Wootten, Thos. 119, 173
Word, Saul 63
Woreat, Jno. 21
Wormack, Wm. 128
Wornock, Jas. 19
Wornouch, Jno. 19
Worsham, Mary 114
R. 81
Richd. 114, 173
Wrae, Wm. 131
Wray, Jno. 151
Phillip 76
Wright, (?) 27
A. 61
Abednego 142, 145
Abednigo 57
Albert 59, 61
Asabel 55
Barbara 55
Bednego 149
Chas. 152
David 6
Dyonisius 66
Edw. 35, 55

Wright (cont.)
  Eve 24
  H. 150
  Habakkuk 145
  Habakuh 27
  Habbakkak 24
  Habk. 22
  Habukkuk 24
  Henry 21, 22, 23, 25,
    27, 29
  Isaiah 61, 63, 66, 145
  J. 60
  Jas. 22, 25, 27, 29,
    142, 145
  Jas. N. 27
  Jas. Nickles 24
  Jno. 14, 20, 55, 66,
    72, 95, 142, 178
  Johnson 57
  Josiah 61
  Mary 103
  Mary (Mrs.) 23
  Nancy 101
  Obadiah 99, 102
  Obediah 94
  Rebecca 33
  Reuben 178
  Richd. 169
  Robt. 119
  Saml. 33, 38, 103,
    104, 105, 106, 108,
    145
  Sarah 55
  Stark 178
  Tho. 21, 22, 26, 27,
    29
  Thos. 24, 149
  Wm. 10, 22, 23, 24,
    25, 28, 29, 38, 55,
    169, 178
Wyatt, Jno. 173
  Peyton 94
Wych, Geo. 87
Wyche, Geo. 83, 145,
    148, 149
  Jno. 11
  Peter 79, 83, 87, 101
  Tho. 19
  Thos. 12
Wyld, Cleavers D. 55
  Jno. 55
Wyler, U. 19
Wyley, Jas. 99
Wylley, Thos. 70
Wylly, Edw. 10
  Jas. 55
  Mary (Mrs.) 55
  Richd. 38, 55
  Thos. 55, 69, 72
  Wm. 55
Wynn, (?) (Cpt.) 7
  Jno. 10
  Lucy 171
  Mary 171
  Obediah 171
  Peter (Sr.) 11
  Rhodea 171
  Thos. 170, 171
Wynne, Jones 10
  Peter 13, 19
  Wm. 13, 19
Wyter, D. 81
Yarborough, Jas. 125
  Littleton 142
  Tho. 15
Yarbrough, Jas. 146
  Littleton 64, 146
  Martha 146

Yarbrough (cont.)
  Thos. 12, 13
  Wm. 146
Yeasley, Jno. 74
Yeaton, Jno. 10
Yonge, Christiana 35, 55
  Geo. 145
  Thos. 134
York, Jas. 169
  Jno. 169
Yorke, Saml. 38
Young, Alex. 20, 27
  Alexdr. 21, 24, 25, 29
  Betsy 171
  Chas. 31, 145
  Daniel 129
  Danl. 94
  David 63, 142
  Edw. 10
  Edwd. 157
  Eliz. 55
  Fanney 171
  Geo. 57, 152
  Geo. (Jr.) 170
  Isaac 38, 55
  Jacob 6
  Jas. 6, 10, 19
  Jas. B. 55
  Jas. Box 38
  Jas. Box (Dr.) 31
  Jno. 10, 20, 21, 27,
    29, 94, 127, 129,
    171
  Jos. 116, 125
  Lucy 171
  Margaret 49, 55
  Martha (Mrs.) 153
  Moses 107
  Patrick 178
  Pearson 6
  Phillip 55
  Robt. 94, 97
  Sherwood 171
  Sophia 31, 38, 55
  Thos. 38, 55, 171
  Wm (Sr.) 6
  Wm. 19, 170
Youngblood, Abraham 66
  Isaac 149
  Jacob 63
  Joshua 63
  Peter 142, 145, 152
Yvonnet, Gabriel 55
Zachary, Bartholomew 109
  Burton 63
  Wm. 63
Zachry, Betty 146
  Jas. 146
  Jno. 145, 147
  Mary 147
  Peter 64, 145
Zackry, Peter 147
  Wm. 147
Zane, Jno. 55
Zeigler, Emanuel 69
  Geo. 69
Zettrover, Ernest 72
Zettrower, Jno. Geo. 71
Zimmerman, Godfrey 147,
    149, 151
Zittarover, Jno. G. 69
Zittler, Danl. 69
Zubly, Ann 33
  Jno. 33
  Jno. J. (Rev.) 31
  Jno. Joachim 35